Constantine

Blackwell Ancient Lives

At a time when much scholarly writing on the ancient world is abstract and analytical, this series presents engaging, accessible accounts of the most influential figures of antiquity. It re-peoples the ancient landscape; and while never losing sight of the vast gulf that separates antiquity from our own world, it seeks to communicate the delight of reading historical narratives to discover "what happened next."

Published

Cleopatra and Egypt
Sally-Ann Ashton

Alexander the Great in his World
Carol G. Thomas

Nero
Jürgen Malitz

Tiberius
Robin Seager

King Hammurabi of Babylon
Marc Van De Mieroop

Pompey the Great
Robin Seager

The Age of Augustus, second edition
Werner Eck

Hannibal
Serge Lancel

Constantine: Dynasty, Religion and Power in the Later Roman Empire
Timothy Barnes

Constantine

Dynasty, Religion and Power in the Later Roman Empire

Timothy Barnes

WILEY-BLACKWELL

A John Wiley & Sons, Ltd., Publication

This edition first published 2011
© 2011 Timothy Barnes

Blackwell Publishing was acquired by John Wiley & Sons in February 2007.
Blackwell's publishing program has been merged with Wiley's global Scientific,
Technical, and Medical business to form Wiley-Blackwell.

Registered Office
John Wiley & Sons Ltd, The Atrium, Southern Gate, Chichester, West Sussex, PO19 8SQ,
United Kingdom

Editorial Offices
350 Main Street, Malden, MA 02148-5020, USA
9600 Garsington Road, Oxford, OX4 2DQ, UK
The Atrium, Southern Gate, Chichester, West Sussex, PO19 8SQ, UK

For details of our global editorial offices, for customer services, and for information about how to
apply for permission to reuse the copyright material in this book please see our website at
www.wiley.com/wiley-blackwell.

The right of Timothy Barnes to be identified as the author of this work has been asserted in
accordance with the UK Copyright, Designs and Patents Act 1988.

Library of Congress Cataloging-in-Publication Data

Barnes, Timothy David.
    Constantine : dynasty, religion, and power in the later Roman Empire / Timothy Barnes.
       p.   cm. – (Blackwell ancient lives)
    Includes bibliographical references and index.
    ISBN 978-1-4051-1727-2 (hbk. : alk. paper)
1. Constantine I, Emperor of Rome, d. 337.   2. Constantine I, Emperor of Rome, d. 337–Political
and social views.   3. Constantine I, Emperor of Rome, d. 337–Religion.   4. Emperors–Rome–
Biography.   5. Rome–Kings and rulers–Biography.   6. Rome–History–Constantine I, the Great,
306-337.   7. Royal houses–Rome–History.   8. Christianity and politics–Rome–History.
9. Church history–Primitive and early church, ca. 30-600.   10. Power (Social sciences)–
Rome–History.   I. Title.
    DG315.B36 2011
    937'.08092–dc22
    [B]
                                                        2010047212

A catalogue record for this book is available from the British Library.

Set in 10/12pt Bembo by SPi Publisher Services, Pondicherry, India
Printed in Malaysia by Ho Printing (M) Sdn Bhd

1   2011

τοῦ δὴ συγγραφέως ἔργον ἕν, ὡς ἐπράχθη εἰπεῖν

The sole task of the historian is to say how it happened
Lucian, *On how history should be written* 39

CONTENTS

ILLUSTRATIONS

PREFACE

In the 'few bibliographical notes' (amounting in fact to more than seventy pages) which Norman Baynes added to the published version of the paper on Constantine which he delivered before the British Academy on 12 March 1930 as the Raleigh Lecture on History for 1929, he severely castigated Eduard Schwartz for his second thoughts on Constantine. Baynes contrasted Schwartz's article in the first volume of *Meister der Politik*, edited by Erich Marcks and Karl Alexander von Müller (Stuttgart & Berlin, 1922: 171–223) with his earlier book *Kaiser Constantin und die christliche Kirche* (Leipzig, 1913). In the later essay, Baynes complained, Schwartz not only 'carries to yet further lengths the views expressed in the book,' but 'this harsher restatement reads as a gage of challenge flung down before the critics.' The present book bears a similar relationship to my *Constantine and Eusebius*, though its distance in time from a book published in 1981 is much closer to the interval between the two editions of Jacob Burckhardt's classic *Die Zeit Constantin's des Grossen*, which was first published in his native Switzerland in 1853 and issued in a revised edition in Germany twenty-seven years later (Leipzig, 1880). There is, however, a fundamental scholarly difference between my second thoughts and those of both Burckhardt and Schwartz, neither of whom was able to use significant new evidence that had come to light in the intervening period. Since 1981 there have been advances in our understanding of Constantine and the age in which he lived on many fronts, and an unexpected and startling increment in our evidence.

In December 2008 a young Canadian scholar working in the Beinecke Rare Book and Manuscript Library at Yale University contacted me out of the blue and asked if I would look at the draft of a monograph on the Late Greek epigrammatist Palladas. Until then, since I had read Palladas' anti-Christian poems before I ever began to think seriously about Constantine, I had accepted the prevailing view of enlightened Anglo-Saxon scholarship that the anti-Christian epigrams of Palladas preserved in the Greek Anthology were written decades after the death of Constantine, during the reign of the emperor Theodosius (379–395). But as soon as I read what Kevin Wilkinson had sent me and tested his arguments, I saw that he had proved beyond any serious possibility of doubt that Palladas was in fact writing during the reign of Constantine – a redating very relevant to my interpretation of Constantine's religious policies. Kevin's chronological arguments appeared in the *Journal of Roman Studies* in November 2009, and he has most generously allowed me to read and use in advance of their publication both two more articles on Palladas and his edition of and commentary on P.CtYBR 4000. I have thus been able to reflect upon Kevin's discoveries before their entry into the public domain, so that he is in a very real sense the 'onlie begetter' of this book.

My researches into the Constantinian period have been assisted over the last three decades by so many others who have shared information with me or engaged with me in constructive discussion of matters of interpretation that it seems invidious to single out a few by name. But I must make three specific acknowledgments. Since 1990, when I first met him, I have received very considerable help from Simon Corcoran, whose expertise in analyzing legal texts far surpasses my own. During the actual composition of the book, which began in earnest in October 2009, I learned much from Paul Stephenson's recently published study of Constantine, which proposes some important, original and (to my mind) convincing ideas on central problems of interpretation. My final text owes much to my wife Janet, who read a full draft of the completed work and has improved both the logic and phrasing of many passages.

The errors and misjudgments that remain are my own, as are all translations from Greek and Latin except where I have explicitly attributed them to an earlier translator. I have of course usually consulted existing English versions when preparing mine, but I believe that, except where I make a specific acknowledgment, I have so modified and adapted earlier translations as to have earned the right to call what I have produced my own. I must also apologize for the frequent repetitions which may sometimes seem otiose or inelegant: they are there because I have often deemed it necessary to repeat the same facts in several different contexts.

Timothy Barnes
Edinburgh, 21 August 2010

The passage from Lucian which I have used as an epigraph will probably be more familiar to most readers in the reformulation which Leopold Ranke gave it in the programmatic preface to his first published work. Rejecting the notion that the function of a historian might be to pass judgment on the past or to provide guidance for the future, the young Ranke declared of his own work that 'er will bloß sagen, wie es eigentlich gewesen' (Geschichten der romanischen und germanischen Völker von 1494 bis 1535 [Leipzig & Berlin, 1824], v), where the German *sagen* is a straight translation of Lucian's εἰπεῖν. Fifty years later, in a second edition of his first book, the mature Ranke changed the wording to 'er will bloß zeigen, wie es eigentlich gewesen' (Sämmtliche Werke 33 [Leipzig, 1874], vii) – where the change of verb from 'say' to 'show' considerably diminishes the similarity of his formulation to that of Lucian.

ABBREVIATIONS

AE	*L'année épigraphique*
Anth. Pal. / *Plan.*	*Anthologia Palatina* / *Planudea*
Barrington Atlas	*Barrington Atlas of the Greek and Roman World*, ed. R. J. A. Talbert (Princeton & Oxford, 2000)
BEFAR	*Bibliothèque des Écoles françaises d'Athènes et de Rome*
BHG	*Bibliotheca hagiographica graeca*, 3rd edition. *Subsidia Hagiographica* 8a (Brussels, 1967)
CCSL	*Corpus Christianorum, Series Latina* (Turnhout, 1954–)
Chr. Min. 1, 2	T. Mommsen, *Chronica Minora Saec. IV.V.VI.VII* 1, 2. *Monumenta Germaniae Historica*, Auctores Antiquissimi 9, 11 (Berlin, 1892; 1894)
CIL	*Corpus Inscriptionum Latinarum* (Berlin, 1863–)
CLRE	*Consuls of the Later Roman Empire*, ed. R. S. Bagnall, Alan Cameron, S. Schwartz & K. A. Worp (Atlanta, 1987)
CPG	M. Geerard, *Clavis Patrum Graecorum* 1–5 (Turnhout, 1974–1987); M. Geerard & J. Noret, *Supplementum* (Turnhout, 1998); J. Noret, *Clavis Patrum Graecorum 3A: Addenda volumini III* (Turnhout, 2003)
CPL	E. Dekkers & E. Gaar, Clavis Patrum Latinorum, 3rd edition (Steenbrugge, 1995)
CSEL	*Corpus Scriptorum Ecclesiasticorum Latinorum* (Vienna, 1866–)
CJ	*Codex Justinianus*
CTh, CTh[Barnes], *CTh*[Seeck]	*Codex Theodosianus*: *CTh* without superscript indicates that I accept the transmitted date, *CTh*[Barnes] or *CTh*[Seeck] that the date stated is the date as emended in Barnes 1982 or Seeck 1919
Dokument(e)	*Athanasius Werke* 3.1.3. *Dokumente zur Geschichte des arianischen Streites*, ed. H. C. Brennecke, U. Heil, A. von Stockhausen & A. Wintjes (Berlin & New York, 2007)

EOMIA	C. H. Turner and others, *Ecclesiae Occidentalis Monumenta Iuris Antiquissima* (Oxford, 1899–1939)
FGrH	F. Jacoby, *Die Fragmente der griechischen Historiker* (Berlin & Leiden, 1923–)
FIRA	S. Riccobono (& others), *Fontes Iuris Romani Anteiustinianei*, 2nd edition (Bologna, 1940–1943)
GCS	*Die Griechischen Christlichen Scriftsteller der ersten (drei) Jahrhunderte* (Leipzig, 1897–1918; Berlin, 1954–)
ICUR	J. B. Rossi and others, *Inscriptiones Christianae Urbis Romae* (Rome, then Vatican City, 1861–1992)
IG	*Inscriptiones Graecae* (Berlin, 1878–)
ILCV	H. Diehl, *Inscriptiones Latinae Christianae Veteres* (Berlin, 1925–1931; 2nd edition with supplementary volume ed. J. Moreau & H.-I. Marrou, Berlin, 1961–1967)
ILS	H. Dessau, *Inscriptiones Latinae Selectae* (Berlin, 1892–1916)
Lampe	G. W. H. Lampe, *A Patristic Greek Lexicon* (Oxford, 1968)
LP	*Liber Pontificalis*
LSJ⁹	H. Liddell, R. Scott & H. Stuart Jones, *A Greek-English Lexicon*, 9th edition with a supplement (Oxford, 1968)
OLD	*Oxford Latin Dictionary*, ed. P. W. G. Glare (Oxford, 1968–1982)
PG	Migne, *Patrologia Graeca* (Paris, 1857–1894)
PL	Migne, *Patrologia Latina* (Paris, 1844–1974)
PLRE 1	A. H. M. Jones, J. Martindale & J. Morris, *The Prosopography of the Later Roman Empire 1: A.D. 260–395* (Cambridge, 1971)
PLRE 2	J. Martindale, *The Prosopography of the Later Roman Empire 2: A.D. 395–527* (Cambridge, 1980)
RE	*Paulys Real-Encyclopädie der classischen Altertumswissenschaft*, ed. G. Wissowa and others (Stuttgart, 1893–1980)
RIC 6	C. H. V. Sutherland, *The Roman Imperial Coinage 6: Diocletian to Maximinus A.D. 294–313* (London, 1967)
RIC 7	P. Bruun, *The Roman Imperial Coinage 7: Constantine and Licinius A.D. 312/3–337* (London, 1966)
RIC 8	J. P. C. Kent, *The Roman Imperial Coinage 8: The Family of Constantine I A.D. 337–364* (London, 1981)
SEG	*Supplementum Epigraphicum Graecum* (Amsterdam, 1923–)
Urkunde(n)	H.-G. Opitz, *Urkunden zur Geschichte des arianischen Streites. Athanasius Werke* 3.1.1-2 (Berlin & Leipzig, 1934–1941)

1

INTRODUCTION

In the preface to his novel about Helena, the mother of Constantine, Evelyn Waugh proclaimed that 'the Age of Constantine is strangely obscure' and that 'most of the dates and hard facts, confidently given in the encyclopedias, soften and dissolve on examination.' Similarly, Michael Grant began the preface to his book on Constantine by observing that 'the problem of finding out about Constantine is an acute one', then quoted these words of Evelyn Waugh before characterizing his own work as 'another endeavor to walk over the same treacherous quicksands' (Grant 1998: xi). In their assessment of the ancient evidence for Constantine, which Grant pronounced 'wholly inadequate' (Grant 1998: 13), both Waugh and Grant showed far superior judgement to professional historians of the Later Roman Empire who have recently written about the emperor and his place in history.

One such historian goes so far as to make the palpably false claim that 'Constantine is one of the best documented of the Roman emperors, and a political narrative of his life and reign is straightforward enough' (Van Dam 2007: 15), while another asserts that, if Constantine remains a problematical figure, it is not 'because the events of his reign are obscured by a lack of relevant material' (Lenski 2006b: 2). But the last period of Constantine's reign from the surrender of the defeated Licinius on 19 September 324 to his own death on 22 May 337 is a truly dark period, in which the course of events is often obscure, except for the emperor's movements, which can be reconstructed in detail (Barnes 1982: 76–80), and certain aspects of ecclesiastical politics, for which many original documents are preserved (Barnes 1981: 208–244; 1993a: 1–33). For the last third of Constantine's reign, therefore, it is simply impossible to construct any sort of detailed military or political narrative. Nevertheless, it is possible to write a coherent and connected political and military narrative of the first third of Constantine's reign (Chapters 4 and 5). Moreover, even if we know far less about Constantine than we do about other periods of Roman history such as the last decades of the Roman Republic, we can understand the basic outlines of his life and career before he became emperor, his political and military achievements as emperor, and his religious policies and attitudes – provided that we allow ourselves to be guided by the ancient evidence and do not seek to impose our own antecedent assumptions on its interpretation.

OFFICIAL LIES AND THE 'CONSTANTINIAN QUESTION'

Constantine himself is in no small way responsible for creating many of the uncertainties about his religious convictions and religious policies which have been the subject of scholarly controversy since the sixteenth century. He was a highly skilful politician who, like all others of his breed, appreciated the necessity of using deceit in achieving his aims, and he had no compunction about eliminating those who obstructed his dynastic plans (Chapter 5). Moreover, he consistently employed propaganda in order to perpetrate deliberate falsehoods about both himself and important political and dynastic matters. Constantine's subjects perforce accepted official falsehoods and reiterated them in public – and many no doubt genuinely believed them, as so often happens even in our modern world. Gross falsehoods put out by what may aptly be described as Constantine's propaganda machine for contemporary consumption have also deceived many recent historians of Constantine and the Later Roman Empire – even those who prided themselves most on their critical acumen.

The prime (and most important) example of modern willingness to acquiesce in Constantine's misrepresentation of basic facts without proper critical scrutiny is what ought to be the uncontroversial matter of his date of birth. Without exception, ancient authors who offer a figure state that Constantine was in his early sixties when he died: according to Eusebius, for example, Constantine began to reign at the age when Alexander the Great died, lived twice as long as Alexander lived and twice as long as he himself reigned (*VC* 1.8, 4.53).[1] The explicit ancient evidence, therefore, unanimously and unambiguously places Constantine's birth in the early 270s (Barnes 1982: 39–40), and the indirect evidence indicates that he was in fact born on 27 February 273 (Chapter 2). Otto Seeck, however, rejected this early date and contended that 288 was almost certainly ('ziemlich sicher') the year of Constantine's birth (1895: 407; 1922: 435–436), adducing five specific items of evidence, namely (i) the mosaic in the palace of Aquileia invoked in the Gallic panegyric of 307 (*Pan. Lat.* 7[6].6.2i5); (ii) Eusebius' report that he saw Constantine accompanying Diocletian in 301 or 302 when he was an adolescent (*VC* 1.19, cf. Chapter 3); (iii) Constantine's own statement that he was a mere boy in 303 (Eusebius, *VC* 2.51); and retrospective statements that the emperor was young when he came to power in 306, especially those of (iv) Nazarius in 321 (*Pan. Lat.* 4[10].16.4: *adhuc aevi immaturus sed iam maturus imperio*) and (v) Firmicus Maternus in 337 (*Mathesis* 1.10.16). But the mosaic at Aquileia (i) probably depicted

Constantine as a young man in 293, which is perfectly compatible with his being twenty at the time (Chapter 3), while Nazarius (iv), Firmicus Maternus (v) and Eusebius (ii) are merely repeating Constantine's own deliberate misrepresentation for political reasons of how old he was in 303 and 306. In other words, it cannot be denied that contemporary writers presented Constantine in the last two decades of his life as being younger than he really was. Why? It is naive and simple-minded in the extreme to argue that 'his precise age was apparently unknown,' then to deduce from what Eusebius says that Constantine was 'about thirteen or fourteen' in 296 or 297 (Jones in Jones & Skeat 1954: 196–197, slavishly repeated by Winkelmann 1962b: 203). That is not only to date the occasion when Eusebius saw Constantine at the side of Diocletian five years too early (Chapter 3), but to allow undue credence to an official untruth. Constantine himself deliberately lied about his age for political reasons.

Writing to 'the provincials of the East' shortly after his defeat of Licinius in 324, Constantine subtly combined two lies about his situation when Diocletian consulted the oracles of Apollo immediately before launching the 'Great Persecution.' He claimed that 'I heard <about it> as a mere youth[2] at the time' (VC 2.51.1: ἠκροώμην τότε κομιδῆ παῖς ἔτι ὑπάρχων). That is doubly false: in the winter of 302–303 Constantine was a mature adult at the court of Diocletian waiting for promotion into the imperial college (Chapter 3). Constantine undoubtedly knew how old he was. His claim that he was a mere boy or youth in 303 is not a simple and straightforward statement of fact from an impartial witness. He was in Nicomedia when the 'Great Persecution' started in that city, as he told a different audience at Easter 325 (Chapter 6 at nn. 13–15) and he stayed silent in order not to compromise his position as a crown prince or damage his prospects of being co-opted into the imperial college. More than twenty years later and over a decade after his very public conversion to Christianity, Constantine reminded his new subjects in the East that in 303 his father had protected the Christians of his territories at a time when his three imperial colleagues were not only savage persecutors intent exclusively on their own advantage, but also mentally deranged (VC 2.29). Political animal as he was, the Constantine of 324 avoided the embarrassing question of why he had failed to protest when his Christian friends were being hauled off to execution for their religious beliefs (Vogt 1943a: 194). He simply claimed that, so far from being a grown man of thirty with a prominent position at court in 303, he was in fact in 303 'still just a boy.' For what could a mere boy have done to stop the persecution?

Historians who wrote about Constantine in the nineteenth century or most of the twentieth found it hard to believe that Constantine lied about his age and hence either allowed themselves to be taken in like Seeck or, like Jones, invented an excuse to palliate the misrepresentation. I write as one whose political awareness began in October 1956 with the invasion of Egypt by British, French and Israeli troops acting in concert at the same time as Russian tanks attacked Hungarian civilians on the streets of Budapest. Hence I have long been familiar with official stories designed to deceive. Indeed in 2003 I watched both the American Secretary of State and the British Prime Minister on television as they misled the Security Council of the United Nations and the House of Commons in Westminster about the necessity of invading a small country which they falsely claimed to possess 'weapons of mass destruction' ready to be deployed.

When I began to write about Constantine in the early 1970s, I immediately became aware that propaganda had played a role in shaping the surviving evidence for his reign (Barnes 1973: 41–43, cf. 1981: 37, 45, 47, 68, 268–269), but I underestimated quite how great that role really was until I read and reflected on Charles Pietri's analysis of what the four documents which Eusebius quotes in the second book of his *Life of Constantine* (*VC* 2.24–42, 46, 48–60, 64–72) reveal about imperial propaganda and the emperor's theology, self-presentation and self-promotion in and after 324 (1983: 73–90). It will be apposite, therefore, to draw together some other clear examples (besides his age) of the emperor's use of deliberate falsehood and his misrepresentation of facts and recent events which will be discussed in the following chapters.

1   The *Origo Constantini Imperatoris* and Lactantius have differing versions of an invented story that Galerius attempted to get Constantine killed either in battle or on the parade ground (Chapter 3).

2   In his tract *On the Deaths of the Persecutors* (*De Mortibus Persecutorum*), which he wrote c. 315 after he had returned to Bithynia, Lactantius repeats an embroidered version of the death of Maximian (Chapter 4). In 310 Maximian committed suicide under compulsion when his attempt to seize power from Constantine failed; a year or more after his death, a story was invented that he was pardoned by Constantine, but repaid his clemency by attempting to assassinate him as he lay asleep in the palace at Arles; this story was in circulation at the court of Constantine in 311 and 312 when Lactantius heard it (Appendix A) and later repeated it in 314/315 (*Mort. Pers.* 30), even though by this time Constantine was rehabilitating the memory of Maximian. After his death Constantine first vilified Maximian and abolished his memory by ordering statues and images of him to be pulled down and destroyed (Lactantius, *Mort. Pers.* 42.1: *senis Maximiani statuae Constantini iussu revellebantur et imagines ubicumque pictus esset detrahabantur*). After the Battle of the Milvian Bridge on 28 October 312, however, Constantine decided to rehabilitate his memory, and the Roman Senate consecrated his memory so that in 318 coins from Constantinian mints honored him as a *divus* together with Constantine's father and Claudius, his purported third-century imperial ancestor as (I transpose the obverse legend from the dative to the nominative case and expand the abbreviations) *divus Maximianus senior fortissimus* (or *optimus*) *imperator* (*RIC* 7.180, Trier: nos. 200–207; 252, Arles: nos. 173–178; 310–312, Rome: nos. 104–128; 395, Aquileia: nos. 21–26; 429–430, Siscia: nos. 41–46; 503, Thessalonica: nos. 24–26).

3   Maxentius granted the Christians of Italy and Africa the right to practice their religion freely very soon after he came to power in October 306, though

he did not allow Christians to recover confiscated property until some years later (Chapter 4). But he exiled Marcellus and Eusebius, successive bishops of Rome, and the latter's rival Heraclius because Christian factions were fighting one another in the streets of Rome (*Chr. min.* 1.76; Damasus, *Epigrammata* 48, 18 = *ILCV* 962, 963, cf. Barnes 1981: 38, 304 n.106). The see of Rome then remained vacant for almost three years until Miltiades was consecrated bishop on 2 July 311 when war loomed with the pro-Christian Constantine (*Chr. min.* 1.76). These necessary police actions helped to provide a basis for claiming that after a good start Maxentius turned against the Christians and after the Battle of the Milvian Bridge Constantinian propaganda rapidly transformed Maxentius into a textbook tyrant who massacred his subjects, raped the wives of senators and examined the entrails of pregnant women, infants and lions for magical purposes (Eusebius, *HE* 8.14.1–5, cf. Grünewald 1990: 64–71; Barnes 1996a).

4   Constantinian propaganda conflated the two wars against Licinius of 316–317 and 323–324 into one. While many sources correctly distinguish between the two wars, which were separated by an interval of several years (*Origo* 18–28; Victor, *Caes.* 41.6–9; Eutropius' *Brev.* 10.5–6.1), they are conflated in Praxagoras' history of Constantine, which was probably completed in or by 330 (Appendix F), in Eusebius' *Life of Constantine* (1.47–2.18), by Libanius in his double pane-gyric of Constantius and Constans, which he probably delivered in 344 (*Orat.* 59.21, cf. Barnes 1993a: 315–316 n.49) and by the *Epitome de Caesaribus* (41.4–8).[3]

5   After the execution of Crispus in 326, Constantine abolished his memory, even though he had been a member of the imperial college for more than nine years. Hence the historical Crispus 'was not only dead, he was abolished, an *unperson*' – like George Orwell's original *unperson*, who bore the significant name of Syme.[4] Eusebius duly conformed to the new official truth. In a minor revision of the final edition of his *Ecclesiastical History*, which survives only in Syriac translation, he expunged the name of Crispus and excised the two laudatory references to his role in the campaign of 324 (*HE* 10.9.4, 6). The *Life of Constantine*, which Eusebius composed or at least revised after Constantinus, Constantius and Con-stans had been proclaimed Augusti on 9 September 337, predictably presents Constantine as only ever having had three sons, and it makes not the slightest allusion to the existence of the Caesar Dalmatius, whose existence Eusebius had naturally acknowledged when he saluted Constantine as a charioteer driving a four-horse team of Caesars in Constantinople on 26 July 336 (*Panegyric of Constantine* 3.4). Eusebius was writing before Constantinus invaded the terri-tory of Constans in 340, when he was killed, suffered *abolitio memoriae* and officially became, like Crispus, an unperson for a decade or more. Praising Constantius and Constans as joint emperors after 340 (*Orat.* 59, cf. Barnes 1993: 315–316 n.49), Libanius carefully avoids any hint that Constantine might ever have had more than two sons.

An anti-Christian version of the history of the reign of Constantine was adumbrated by Julian the Apostate during his brief period as sole emperor (from November 361 to June 363) and elaborated by others after he was killed in combat in Mesopotamia. But neither Julian nor writers like the Antiochene rhetor Libanius, the rabidly pagan historian Eunapius of Sardis and Ammianus Marcellinus, who adopted a deceptive posture of impartiality in matters of religion (Barnes 1998a: 79–94; G. Kelly 2003), took any pains to discover and reveal truths about Constantine which had been hidden by his Christian admirers. They were more intent on fixing blame for all the disasters of the intervening decades on the first Christian emperor and his adopted religion. Julian blamed Christianity for the dynastic murders of his close relatives in the purge of imperial rivals to the sons of Constantine in the summer of 337, while both Libanius and Eunapius came out with deliberate falsehoods about Constantine's religious beliefs and policies. In particular, when Libanius addressed a plea for the protection of pagan temples to Theodosius in 386, he made the palpably false claim that Constantine 'made absolutely no change in the traditional forms of worship' (*Orat.* 30.6). Not only is the claim false, but Libanius knew that it was false, since his *Autobiography* alludes to Constantine's prohibition of sacrifice: as a student in Athens in the 330s Libanius formed a close friendship with Crispinus of Heraclea whose uncle risked death by his ostentatious paganism and 'mocked that evil law and its impious enactor' (*Orat.* 1.27), who can only be Constantine (Barnes 1989a: 329–330). Unfortunately, Libanius' barefaced lie that Constantine 'made absolutely no change in the traditional forms of worship' (sometimes modified in quotation by modern scholars in order to mitigate its absurdity) has been treated as essentially true by modern historians who have written about Constantine from Edward Gibbon in the eighteenth century and Jacob Burckhardt in the nineteenth to Paul Stephenson in the twenty-first (2009: 56). Indeed, it has often served as the cornerstone of modern interpretations of the emperor's religious policies.

THE PROGRESS OF HISTORICAL RESEARCH

It has recently been asserted that 'the rediscovery of the historical Constantine had to await the arrival of critical scholarship in the Renaissance' (Lieu 2006: 317). That is untrue. It had to wait much longer. For neither Johannes Leunclavius (Löwenklau), who defended Zosimus as an accurate historian in the introduction to his Latin translation of the historian, published at Basle in 1576, nor Cardinal Baronius (1538–1607), whose *Annales Ecclesiastici* was the greatest intellectual achievement of the Counter-Reformation, nor Henri de Valois (1603–1676), the distinguished seventeenth-century editor of Eusebius' *Ecclesiastical History* and *Life of Constantine*, had any knowledge at all of the most important historical source for the 'Great Persecution' initiated by Diocletian in 313 and the political history of the decade 303–313. The historical Constantine only began to emerge from the mists of the emperor's own propaganda, of fourth-century polemic, of distortion by ecclesiastical historians and of sheer myth-making when Étienne Baluze (1630–1718) published the *editio princeps* of Lactantius' *On the Deaths of the Persecutors* in 1679. But Lactantius' authorship and the authenticity of the work were often denied, as by Edward Gibbon, until the beginning of the twentieth century when René Pichon finally put its authenticity and authorship work beyond all possible doubt (Pichon 1901, cf. Moreau 1954: 22–33). Yet Lactantius' trustworthiness as a witness continued to be denied or doubted by many for most of the twentieth century.

A true understanding of Constantine only began to become possible in the 1950s. Quite independently of each other, Jacques Moreau's classic commentary demonstrated Lactantius' accuracy on matters of fact (Moreau 1954: 187–473) while the researches into the coinage of Constantine by the Finnish numismatist Patrick Bruun rescued Lactantius' credit as a historical witness. For almost three centuries from Godefroy's edition of the Theodosian Code (Lyon, 1665), the Battle of Cibalae, the first battle of the first war between Constantine and Licinius, had universally been dated to 8 October 314, which is the date stated in the *Descriptio consulum* (otherwise known as the *Consularia Constantinopolitana*), from which it followed that Lactantius, who cannot have completed *On the Deaths of the Persecutors* before October 314, had deliberately and dishonestly misrepresented the relations between the two emperors by suppressing any mention of the War of Cibalae. In 1953, however, Bruun re-dated the war from 314 to 316/317 (Bruun 1953; 17–19; 1961: 10–22; 1966: 65–67), and, when other numismatists demurred, Christian Habicht weighed in to decisive effect by showing that all the relevant ancient evidence with the sole exception of the *Descriptio consulum* confirmed Bruun's re-dating of the war (Habicht 1958). Hence, when Lactantius wrote *On the Deaths of the Persecutors* in 314/315, the first war between Constantine and Licinius still lay in the future.

A parallel controversy long impugned the reliability of Eusebius' *Life of Constantine* until a magisterial survey of 'the problem of the authenticity of the *Life*' brought it to a sudden end in 1962.[5] In a lengthy and incisive article of more than fifty pages, Friedhelm Winkelmann carefully untangled three separate questions which those who rejected the evidence of the *Life of Constantine* had too often combined and confused (1962b: 187–243). (i) Were the documents quoted in the *Life* authentic? The often bitter controversies over this question were stilled in 1954 when it was shown that a contemporary papyrus preserves part of the long letter of Constantine (*VC* 2.24–42), whose authenticity had been most confidently denied (Jones & Skeat 1954). (ii) Is the *Life* the work of Eusebius of Caesarea or a later hand or has Eusebius' original text been heavily interpolated after his death? (iii) Is the *Life of Constantine* a reliable historical source? Those who have denied Eusebius' authorship too often argue that he could not have written particular passages in the *Life* because they contain errors which a contemporary could not have made (Grégoire 1938a: 562–563, 569–577, 582; 1953: 473–478). Winkelmann showed that most of these supposed errors either reflect Constantinian propaganda or result from modern misunderstanding (1962b: 218–243). Moreover, Winkelmann pointed out that not only had Giorgio Pasquali proved in 1910 that the *Life of Constantine* as we have it is a conflation of two stylistically heterogeneous drafts which someone else put into circulation after Eusebius' death, but also that all who had written about Constantine in the next fifty years, including Grégoire and Norman Baynes had misstated Pasquali's very clear conclusion, apparently at second hand (Winkelmann 1962b: 208–218, cf. Pasquali 1910: 386). Since 1962 the reliability and historical value of the *Life of Constantine* have been enhanced in several ways. In particular, not only has it been established that Constantine's *Speech to the Assembly of the Saints* is authentic (Chapter 6) and that Eusebius does indeed report accurately what Constantine told him about what he and his army saw in the sky (Weiss 1993, 2003 cf. Chapter 4), but Kevin Wilkinson's proof that the epigrammatist Palladas was writing under Constantine has confirmed Eusebius' account of Constantine's aggressively Christian policies in the East after 324 and his often doubted assertion that Constantine founded Constantinople as a Christian city (Wilkinson 2009; 2010a; 2010b).

CONTEMPORARY PERSPECTIVES ON CONSTANTINE

Literary texts survive which were written at different times during the reign of Constantine by authors from widely varying points of view. Four Latin panegyrics delivered in the presence of Constantine in Gaul between 307 and 313 and another delivered in Rome in 321, though not in his presence (Appendix B) reflect a change in the religious atmosphere in 312; an exchange of letters between Constantine and a Roman aristocrat and poet reveals the emperor as an educated man and a patron of Latin literature (Chapter 4); the summary of a panegyrical history of the reign of Constantine down to 324 written by a young Athenian aristocrat shows pagan acquiescence in his achievements (Appendix F); a fragmentary panegyric from Egypt praises Constantine for not despoiling pagan temples (Appendix G); and a handbook on astrology includes largely conventional praises of the emperor written in the last weeks of his life (Chapter 7). But it will be clear from the preceding pages that three writers are of central importance the Latin rhetor and Christian apologist Lactantius, without whose polemical pamphlet *On the Deaths of the Persecutors* we could not write a satisfactory account of the first forty years of Constantine's life; Eusebius, who was metropolitan bishop of Palestine from c. 313 to 338 or 339 and composed, in the last three books of his *Life of Constantine*, an account of the emperor's religious policies after 324 which quotes many documents in full; and the Egyptian poet Palladas who wrote anti-Christian epigrams, some of them in the newly founded city of Constantinople, which confirm Eusebius' veracity in all essentials.

Lactantius

Lactantius came to Nicomedia at the invitation of Diocletian who appointed him to the city's official chair of Latin rhetoric (Jerome, *De viris illustribus* 80). In this capacity (like Augustine in Milan in the 380s), Lactantius will have delivered praises of the emperor – with Constantine not only present, but at the emperor's side as a candidate for the imperial purple. Since Lactantius probably arrived in Nicomedia no later than the mid-290s, he had the opportunity to meet and converse with both Constantine and his mother on less formal occasions. A careful study of Lactantius' philosophical and theological assumptions appears to have established that he was converted to Christianity in the East rather than in his native Africa (Wlosok 1960: 191–192 n.28; 1961: 247). In 303, under the provisions of the first persecuting edict of 24 February, Lactantius was compelled to choose between making a symbolic act of sacrifice in order to retain possession of his official chair of Latin rhetoric or resigning in order to avoid the obligation to sacrifice (Barnes 1981: 13, 22–23). It can hardly be doubted that he chose the latter course of action. But he remained in Bithynia at least until 1 May 305 when Galerius gained control of Asia Minor (*Div. Inst.* 5.2.2, 11.15, cf. Barnes 2006: 15). His movements in the years following 305 are not properly documented, but it seems that he left the East not long after 1 May 305 and was at the court of Constantine in Trier, where he was tutor to Crispus, the son of Constantine, before the Battle of the Milvian Bridge (Appendix A). He probably returned to the East in 313 to resume possession of his chair of rhetoric in Nicomedia: he wrote his tract *On the Deaths of the Persecutors* in Nicomedia and remained there until he died, probably in the summer of 324 (Barnes 1981: 13–14, 290–292 nn.93–100).

On this reconstruction of his career (tabulated in Appendix A), Lactantius was in Nicomedia from the mid-290s until at least May 305, at the court of Constantine in Trier in 311/312 and in Nicomedia again from 313 onwards. Hence he wrote *On the Deaths of the Persecutors*, whose composition is firmly dated to 314/315, in Nicomedia as a subject of Licinius, not of Constantine (Barnes 1973: 39–41). This tract or pamphlet, though a political satire and often grossly tendentious, scores very highly for factual accuracy in what it explicitly states[6] – though its deliberate omissions and silences can be extremely misleading (Barnes 1999a; 2010a: 114–118).

Eusebius of Caesarea

Eusebius of Caesarea, who was born shortly after 260, was primarily a biblical scholar in the tradition of Origen, though far more interested in history than philosophy than Origen ever was, and a Christian apologist and theologian who preferred to use primarily biblical and historical arguments in the defense of his religion (Barnes 1981: 94–188). Eusebius was bishop of Caesarea in Palestine from c. 313 until his death and he wrote in a wide variety of genres (Barnes 2010b). Only two of these are works of contemporary history. The final two books of his *Ecclesiastical History* include the rise of Constantine to sole rule, and his *Life of Constantine* is our most voluminous and informative single source for the first Christian Roman emperor. Eusebius saw the young prince as he traveled through Palestine at the side of the emperor Diocletian as an heir presumptive to the imperial purple in 301 or 302 (*Life* 1.19, cf. Chapter 3) and he died almost forty years later, leaving the *Life* unfinished. It was published by an editor, probably Acacius, his successor as bishop of Caesarea, who added a few brief passages to sew the two disparate drafts together (Pasquali 1910: 386; Winkelmann 1975: xlix–lvii; Barnes 1989b: 98–107; 1994c). But Eusebius only became a subject of Constantine when he was aged more than sixty, and his relationship to Constantine was universally misunderstood until thirty years ago. For Eusebius' presentation of himself as close to the emperor in his *Life of Constantine* was accepted uncritically, even by those who expressed extreme skepticism about his account of the emperor. Hence it was widely, indeed almost universally, assumed that in his later years Eusebius frequented the court of Constantine, that he was 'an adviser of the emperor Constantine,' and an 'elder statesman' (Brown 1971: 82, 90). In fact, Eusebius met Constantine on no more than four occasions, always in the company of other bishops (Barnes 1981: 261–275).[7]

Modern understanding of both Eusebius and Constantine was, for more than a century, derailed by Jacob Burckhardt, whose *Die Zeit Constantin's des Grossen* was first published in 1853 and issued in a revised edition in 1880, in which Burckhardt introduced the concept of a *Reichskirche*, absent from the first edition, under the impact of the unification of Germany in 1871 and its consequences for Christian churches in the united Germany of Otto Bismarck (Barnes 1993a: 168, 292–293 nn.11–15). The introduction to a recent coffee-table reprint of Moses Hadas' English translation of this classic praises Burckhardt for 'his mastery of the ancient sources' (Lenski 2007: xiv). That is an utterly perverse and grossly misleading verdict. For Amadeo Crivellucci pointed out long ago that Burckhardt, no less than Cardinal Baronius in the sixteenth century, evaluated the testimony of Eusebius, not by comparing him with other evidence, but in accordance with his own antecedent preconceptions (Crivellucci 1888: 6–7, quoted by Winkelmann 1962b: 195–196) – a procedure which is entirely appropriate for a historical novelist like Sir Walter Scott, but improper for one who claims to be a serious historian.

Burckhardt set aside the clear and explicit evidence of Lactantius and Eusebius that Constantine gave Christians his political support from the start and began to declare himself a convert to Christianity before the Battle of the Milvian Bridge on 28 October 312. Burckhardt, who was echoed in the twentieth century by Henri Grégoire (1930–31: 270), depicted Constantine as a fourth-century Napoleon, not only a skilful politician (as he indeed was), but essentially irreligious and amoral. His anachronistic interpretation of Constantine owed far more to the modern German philosopher Friedrich Hegel than to the ancient evidence. Hence, in order to sustain his perverse interpretation of Constantine, Burckhardt was obliged to discredit the two main surviving contemporary literary sources by fair means or foul. He denounced Eusebius as 'the most objectionable of all eulogists' and 'the first thoroughly dishonest historian of antiquity,' on the grounds that Eusebius must have known the truth about Constantine, as discovered in the nineteenth century, but deliberately misrepresented it. According to Burckhardt, Eusebius praised

Constantine insincerely, falsified history and indulged in 'contemptible inventions' (Burckhardt 1949: 260, 283, 299).[8] This condemnation also relied on the false assumption that the bishop of Caesarea in Palestine was somehow a habitué of the imperial court who displayed the manners of a courtier and flattered his royal master, often with conscious dishonesty.

Burckhardt's depiction of Constantine inspired two ultimately futile scholarly controversies, whose course Winkelmann surveyed in magisterial fashion: one concerned the authenticity of the Constantinian documents in the *Life of Constantine* (Winkelmann 1962b: 197–202); the other whether Eusebius of Caesarea really was the author of the *Life* in its present form (Winkelmann 1962b: 213–226). The first controversy was suddenly and completely extinguished in the early 1950s when A. H. M. Jones, following up a suggestion by the Oxford Roman historian C. E. Stevens (who owned a copy of the Benedictine edition of Athanasius), showed that part of the text of what critics had assailed as the most obviously inauthentic of all the documents in the *Life* (2.24–42) was preserved on a contemporary papyrus from Egypt (*P. Lond.* 878 verso, edited with supplements from *VC* 2.26–29 by Skeat in Jones & Skeat 1954: 198–199),[9] while the second effectively ended in 1962 when Winkelmann examined and disproved all the arguments ever brought against Eusebius' authorship.

One important observation by Winkelmann requires special emphasis. He pointed out that, although Giorgio Pasquali had solved the literary problem of the *Life* in 1910 (Pasquali 1910), his solution had been almost immediately misreported by Jules Maurice (1913) and that Maurice's misrepresentation had remained unchallenged for almost fifty years. In his classic and influential paper on 'Constantine the Great and the Christian Church,' Norman Baynes not only appeared to repeat Maurice's *canard* that Pasquali had argued that the *Life* contains interpolations added after Eusebius' death, which is the exact opposite of the thesis that Pasquali actually maintained, but then repeated his conclusion as if in opposition to him (Baynes 1931: 42–45, 49, cf. Winkelmann 1962b: 208–213).[10] Unfortunately, when the learned Henry Chadwick supplied a preface to a second edition of Baynes's classic essay in 1972 (Chadwick 1972: iii–viii), he omitted to warn readers not to be misled by Baynes on the central matter of the literary nature of the *Life of Constantine* which Pasquali had proved to be an unfinished work with traces of two separate drafts which a posthumous editor had published together as a unitary work without changing what Eusebius had written (1910: 386) – though he seems to have added some short bridging passages (Barnes 1994c).

The final three books of Eusebius' *Ecclesiastical History* contain an account of the 'Great Persecution' from 303 to 313 (Books VIII and IX) and the new situation of the church after 313 (Book X), with a postscript on the persecution of Licinius (321–324) and his defeat by Constantine (10.8–9). The manuscripts provide clear evidence that Eusebius published at least two editions of the *Ecclesiastical History*, while the allusions to Roman emperors in the text necessitate the postulate of at least three successive editions (Barnes 1980: 191–192, 196–201; 1981: 148–163).

In the present context there is fortunately no need to review the various modern attempts to sort out and date the successive editions; it will suffice to note that Eusebius composed his account of the early years of Constantine's reign (*HE* 8.13.14–15; 9.9.1–12) no later than c. 315.

The *Life of Constantine*, which combines a number of different ancient literary genres (Averil Cameron 1997: 145–179; Bleckmann 2007b: 27–38), had its first origins in Eusebius' unfulfilled intention of continuing his history of the church beyond the end of persecution into the new Christian Empire of Constantine (Barnes 1989b: 111–114, cf. Winkelmann 1962a: 57–66). The work neither is nor claims to be a biography in the normal sense of the word. It comprises three disparate elements:

1   the *Life* itself in four books;
2   the Greek translation of a speech of Constantine addressed *To the Assembly of the Saints*, which several manuscripts present as a fifth book of the *Life*; and
3   two speeches delivered by Eusebius himself on different occasions.

Constantine delivered the speech (2), whose authenticity has often been needlessly doubted, in Nicomedia at Easter 325 and in it he stated that his mission in life was to Christianize the Roman Empire (Chapter 6). Although the manuscripts indicate a break between Chapters Ten and Eleven (p. 223.22 app.), Ivar Heikel printed (3) as a single speech with the title 'Ε'ις Κωνσταντῖνον τὸν βασιλέα τριακονταετηρικός,' which he rendered into German as 'Trikennatsrede,' in his unsatisfactory but still unsuperseded edition of 1902 (*GCS* 7: 193–259). The first ten chapters are a *Panegyric of Constantine* which Eusebius delivered in Constantinople as part of the celebration of the emperor's *tricennalia* on 25 July 336 (p. 195–p. 223.22, cf. Drake 1975). The last eight chapters are an earlier and entirely independent *Speech on the Holy Sepulchre* (11–18, p. 223.23–p. 259), which Eusebius delivered in Jerusalem as part of the ceremonial dedication of that church in September 335 (Barnes 1977). Since I shall have little or nothing to say about either of these speeches, I need to warn readers here that the thesis that the *Panegyric* shows that Constantine was still uncommitted to Christianity in 336 (Drake 1976: 3–79) is completely mistaken, since the speech is thoroughly and deeply Christian in its inspiration, although Eusebius deliberately uses arguments and rhetoric designed to appeal to the pagans in his audience as well as Christians (Barnes 1981: 253–255; Averil Cameron 1983a: 78–82). Equally mistaken, therefore, are the corollaries drawn from that interpretation by its propounder, that 'through his reticence in the *Panegyric*, Eusebius has himself undermined the credibility of his witness in the *Life of Constantine*' and that 'we must therefore abandon interpretations of Constantine's religious policy based on that witness' (Drake 1976: 60).

Eusebius intended the three elements (the *Life* proper, Constantine's speech and his own two speeches) to be read together in order to establish that he was the authoritative interpreter of the Christian emperor Constantine and that emperor and bishop agreed on fundamental theological issues. In the *Speech* Constantine asserts the existence of a first and a second God, two substances (*ousiai*) with one perfection (*Oratio* 9.3), just as Eusebius himself had used the phrase 'second *hypostasis*' of Christ (*Ecl. Proph.* 4.25 [*PG* 22.1240B]). Moreover, although the text of the *Life of Constantine* never names Arius, who died in 336 in embarrassing circumstances, it praises the bishops who readmitted to communion those who had been excluded for heresy or schism, but later showed genuine repentance (*VC* 3.66). It can hardly be an accident that when Eusebius commends those who were readmitted for 'acknowledging their mother the church' (*VC* 3.66.3: τὴν μητέρα, τὴν ἐκκλησίαν, ἐπεγίνωσκον), he echoes words which Arius and Euzoius had used when they submitted a petition to Constantine requesting him to facilitate their reunion with 'our mother, that is the church' (Opitz, *Urkunde* 30.5 = *Dokument* 34.5: τῇ μητρὶ ἡμῶν, τῇ ἐκκλησίᾳ δηλαδή).

Of Eusebius' other works only one needs to be noted in the present context. It is the treatise *On Easter / De sollemnitate paschali*, which Angelo Mai published in 1847 (it is translated in Appendix D). Eusebius' main purpose appears to be to explain and justify the decision of the Council of Nicaea which changed the basis on which the date of Easter was to be computed in the future in Palestine, but what he says also lends weight to the suggestion that it was Constantine who introduced the originally western custom of Lent into the East in 325 (Chapter 6).

The epigrammatist Palladas

Palladas was a poet from Egypt who until recently has been known only through the more than 150 of his poems and epigrams included in the *Greek Anthology*. Three lemmata in the Byzantine manuscripts appear to date Palladas long after the death of Constantine. One declares that an epigram ascribed to Palladas is about 'a certain philosopher who became urban prefect during the reigns of Valentinian and Valens' (on 11.292), and Maximus Planudes identified him as Themistius, a philosopher who became prefect of the city of Constantinople, though in 384 in the reign of Theodosius, not under Valentinian and Valens (on 11.292).[11] Another lemma describes three lines of hexameters as being about the 'house of Marina' (on 9.528), which can hardly be any building other than the palace of Marina, the youngest daughter of Arcadius, who was born on 10 February 403 and died on 3 August 449 and who, therefore, did not have a separate palace or residence of her own in Constantinople before the 420s (*PLRE* 2.723, Marina 1), while a third lemma identifies the subject of another epigram as the philosopher Hypatia, who was brutally murdered in 415 (9.400, cf. *PLRE* 2.575–576, Hypatia 1). Accordingly, the poetic activity of Palladas was traditionally dated between 380 and 450.

This traditional dating of Palladas suddenly collapsed in 1958 and 1959. First, A. S. P. Gow, who had embarked on the monumental task of editing and commenting on the *Greek Anthology*, not as it survives in Byzantine manuscripts, but by reconstituting the earlier collections incorporated in it, such as the *Garlands* of

Meleager and Philip from the first centuries BC and AD respectively, showed that the information in the lemmata to individual poems in the Anthology was frequently false, being normally no more than a guess based on the text of the poem and hence of no independent historical value (Gow 1958: 17–22). In the same year, Georg Luck showed that the poem alleged to praise Hypatia (*Anth. Pal.* 9.400) is an *ekphrasis* on a church dedicated to the Virgin Mary, the word *hypatia* in it being not the name of the female philosopher murdered in Alexandria in 415, but a title of the Mother of God, so that the ascription of poem to the pagan Palladas must be erroneous (Luck 1958: 462–466, cf. Alan Cameron 1993: 322–325). A year later Maurice Bowra identified the man 'whom God loves' in several poems of Palladas (*Anth. Pal.* 9.90, 91, 175) as Theophilus, bishop of Alexandria from 385 to 412 (Bowra 1959, cf. 1960), after which Alan Cameron soon buttressed Bowra's chronology with new arguments and established it as the new orthodoxy (Cameron 1964; 1965a; 1965b). From the mid-1960s, therefore, it has been very widely accepted that Palladas was writing in the 380s and died in the early 390s.[12]

It has now, however, been proved beyond all reasonable doubt that Palladas was writing in the first half of the fourth century (Wilkinson 2009). The impetus to this re-dating of Palladas came from Kevin Wilkinson's preparation of an edition of a fragmentary papyrus codex now in the Beinecke Rare Book and Manuscript Library of Yale University (*P.CtYBR* 4000, cf. Wilkinson 2009: 42). This papyrus manuscript, which was written in the first half of the fourth century, contains a series of Greek epigrams, almost all extremely fragmentary, apparently by a single author, whose name is not preserved in the surviving fragments. But two sequences of four lines in the papyrus codex are also found in the *Greek Anthology* with only very minor verbal variants and while one is anonymous, the other is explicitly ascribed to Palladas. In view of the importance of the latter, I print here (1) what is legible on the papyrus including letters which Wilkinson dots as uncertain ignoring supplements derived from the *Greek Anthology*; (2) the four lines as they are transmitted in the *Greek Anthology*; and (3) Wilkinson's translation in the draft of his forthcoming commentary.

(1)
Φασὶ παροιμι[ακῶς
　　ἀλλ' ἐγὼ οὐχ οὕτ[ω
ἀλλά· 'δάκοι κἄν οἷς¹³ [
　　τοὺς δὲ κακοὺς [(page 21.5–8)
(2)
　　　　　　　ΠΑΛΛΑΔΑ
Φασὶ παροιμιακῶς· "κἄν οἷς δάκοι ἄνδρα πονηρόν."
　　ἀλλὰ τόδ' οὐχ οὕτω, φημί, προσῆκε λέγειν,
ἀλλά· "δάκοι κἄν οἷς ἀγαθοὺς καὶ ἀπράγμονας ἄνδρας."
　　τὸν δὲ κακὸν δεδιὼς δήξεται οὐδὲ δράκων. (*Anth. Pal.* 9.379)

(3)
The old saying goes, "Even a sheep would bite a wicked man." But in my opinion one should not say that. Rather, "Even a sheep would bite good men who are minding their own business. But not even a snake would be bold enough to bite bad men."

It is an almost ineluctable inference that all the poems in this short collection of little more than twenty lacunose pages are the work of Palladas, and at least one poem is datable to the first decade or so of the fourth century since it refers to an emperor ascending the Nile valley and alludes to the imperial victory title *Sarmaticus maximus quater*, which Diocletian took in 299 or 300 and Galerius in 306 or 307 – but which no other emperor took before or after them (page 11.27–35, with Wilkinson's commentary).

Alan Cameron's researches into the genesis and evolution of the *Greek Anthology* provided Wilkinson with an almost equally powerful argument. Cameron showed that a precursor of the *Anthology*, which in its transmitted forms is a product of the middle and late Byzantine periods, existed in the fourth century and was used by Ausonius and authors of poems in the so-called *Epigrammata Bobiensia* when they produced Latin translations of a number of epigrams preserved in the *Greek Anthology*, including some by Palladas (Alan Cameron 1993: 78–96). While the Bobbio collection was assembled c. 400 (and could thus theoretically accommodate a Theodosian date for Palladas, if only with difficulty), the only datable epigrams of Ausonius belong early in his literary career, perhaps as early as the 340s. When a recent commentary argues that Ausonius' epigrams 'span most or all of his literary activity,' the only positive reason stated for dating any of them later than the 360s is the fact that Ausonius translated Palladas (Kay 2001: 13–24). The fourth-century anthology whose existence Cameron detected should not be dated on the assumption that Palladas was writing under Theodosius. Rather, given the fact that the *Greek Anthology* contains more than 150 poems by Palladas, it is reasonable to identify the fourth-century editor as Palladas himself and to date it to the first half of the fourth century (Wilkinson 2009: 41–42, 51–52).

Other arguments too, in which Wilkinson analyzed familiar evidence afresh, situate Palladas' poems either in the first half of the fourth century or, more specifically, in the reign of Constantine. The strongest is derived from the poem in which Palladas laments that he cannot escape from his quarrelsome wife 'because a piece of paper and Roman law prevent me' (*Anth. Pal.* 11.378). Enough is known about the Roman law of divorce to prove that this poem was written between 331 and 362. In 331 Constantine issued an innovatory law which for the first time, at least since the first century AD, placed significant restrictions on unilateral divorce, by allowing a man to divorce his wife against her wishes only for adultery, witchcraft and procuring (*CTh* 3.16.1). Julian rescinded the law (Ambrosiaster, *Quaestiones de vetere et novo testamento* 115.12 [*CSEL* 50.322]) and Constantine's law was not revived until 421, and then only in the West (*CTh* 3.16.2, cf. Arjava 1988: 9–13; Evans Grubbs 1995: 228–232; 2002: 177–183). No less persuasive is Wilkinson's identification of the man 'whom

God loves' as the emperor Constantine (Wilkinson 2009: 43–48): he shows how Palladas not only echoes Constantine's representation of himself in the 320s, but also presents the enemy of the man 'whom God loves' in a fashion which has close parallels in Eusebius' depiction of Licinius (*VC* 2.17–18).

The importance of Wilkinson's re-dating of Palladas cannot be overstated. In 1981 and subsequently I argued at length that after he conquered the East in 324 Constantine pursued aggressively Christian policies which amounted to a religious reformation or even revolution (Barnes 1981: 208–212, 245–250; 1986; 1989a; 1992b). This depiction of a *Constantinus Christianus* failed to overturn the prevailing *communis opinio* that Constantine never deviated from the policy of religious toleration which he had espoused early in his reign (see, e.g., Drake 1982; Averil Cameron 1983b: 187–188; Gaudemet 1990: 451–455). And assertions continue to be made that after 324 Constantine pursued 'a policy of concord, in which forbearance towards the temple cults was intended as a means of achieving ultimate religious unity,' that 'Constantine's own edicts show little evidence that he attempted to suppress the practice of traditional cult' (Digeser 2000: 125), that his religious policies after 324 were 'inclusive,' that the emperor 'preached religious toleration' to the end of his reign (Van Dam 2007: 177) and even that 'Constantine managed simultaneously to project the image of the devout Christian and that of the crypto-pagan down to his dying days' (Lenski 2006a: 276).

The central objection to the interpretation of Constantine set out in 1981 has always been that it relied exclusively upon the partisan and tendentious evidence of Christian writers, especially on Eusebius in his *Life of Constantine*, a 'suspect' source that ought not to be regarded as a trustworthy witness for the religious policies of the emperor. Wilkinson has now proved that it is not Eusebius alone, as Averil Cameron confidently asserted in 1983, who makes the claim that paganism was 'seriously attacked' after 324 (1983b: 189). For the pagan Palladas provides proof, from the other end of the religious spectrum, that Constantine's religious policies after 324 were such that a contemporary believer in the old gods could utter a lament in the that traditional Hellenic religion had already perished:

> We Greeks are men reduced to ashes,
> holding to our buried hopes in the dead;
> for everything has now been turned on its head.
> (*Anth. Pal.* 10.90.4–6, trans. Wilkinson)

COINS, INSCRIPTIONS AND MONUMENTS

The central arguments of the following chapters and my interpretation of Constantine rest primarily on the careful evaluation of primary documents, including the extracts from imperial legislation which survive in the Theodosian Code; and on literary evidence, especially that of Lactantius, Eusebius of Caesarea and Palladas. It thus differs in both scope and documentation from those modern studies of Constantine which devote much space to Constantinian coins, inscriptions and monuments, sometimes resting their interpretation of Constantine's personal beliefs on such inarticulate evidence. I need, therefore, to explain why the coinage of Constantine and inscriptions and monuments honoring Constantine play a secondary role in the development of my interpretation of the emperor. In essence, it is because I regard the inferences often made from coin-legends and from inscriptions whose wording was not dictated by Constantine to the mind and religious beliefs of the emperor as extremely insecure, since on close inspection such inferences usually turn out to be logically dependent on mistaken assumptions about the value of the surviving literary evidence. Accordingly I shall conclude this introductory chapter by discussing five items of non-literary evidence: (i) the supposed manifestation of Constantine's devotion to Sol, the sun god, on his coinage after 312; (ii) the dedicatory inscription on the Arch of Constantine in Rome; (iii) the dossier relating to the granting of city status to Orcistus in Phrygia; (iv) Constantine's rescript to the city of Hispellum in Umbria; and (v) the porphyry column in the city of Constantinople which is claimed to have depicted Constantine as the sun god Apollo.

(i) Coins are an extremely important source of information about the reign of Constantine, since they provide a firm chronological framework for political, dynastic and military events, often add significant details missing from our literary sources, and disclose much about Constantinian propaganda. Coins have, therefore, played an important role in modern research into Constantine. Most conspicuously, as I noted above, it was his analysis of the Constantinian coinage of Arles that first led Patrick Bruun to re-date the War of Cibalae from 314 (a date which no-one had challenged since 1665) to the autumn and winter of 316–317, which permitted a reevaluation of Lactantius' account of the period of the 'Great Persecution' (Bruun 1953, cf. Barnes 1973: 36–41, 43–46). Richard Burgess has now brought numismatic evidence to illuminate the political crisis and dynastic murders that followed the death of Constantine.

The events of 337 will be discussed later (Chapter 7). In the present context, I merely note the important historical conclusions that Burgess derives entirely from the Roman imperial coinage. First, the coinage between late 335 and the death of Constantine consistently presents the two older Caesars, Constantinus and Constantius, Caesars since 317 and 324 respectively, as equals but superior to the two younger Caesars, Constans and Dalmatius, who were proclaimed Caesars on 25 December 333 and 18 September 335 respectively (Burgess 2008: 43–45). Second, between late 335 and the autumn of 337, six mints regularly struck coinage in gold and seven in silver in the names of the emperors, but three of these mints did not strike coins in either precious metal in the name of Dalmatius – Trier, the residence of Constantinus; Rome, the major mint of Constans, who probably resided in Milan, which had no mint; and Antioch, the city where Constantius resided (Burgess 2008: 21). The absence of Dalmatius amounted to an implicit denial of his legitimacy as an emperor, and Burgess deduces that the three sons of Constantine not only regarded

Dalmatius as an interloper in the imperial college, but had agreed among themselves to advertise their disapproval of him to the army officers and civil servants for the payment of whom gold and silver coins were primarily minted (Burgess 2008: 22). Third, technical analysis of the bronze coinage struck in the names of Constantine, his four Caesars and Helena and Theodora, Constantine's mother and step-mother (now posthumously invested with the title of Augusta), establishes (a) that the Caesar Dalmatius died very soon after Constantine, probably in early June 337, (b) that at Trier coins began to be struck in the names of Helena and Theodora almost immediately after the disappearance of Constantine and Dalmatius coinage, and (c) that coins proclaiming *Virtus Augusti* and *Securitas Reipub(licae)* began to be struck in Rome at the same time (Burgess 2008: 33–35, 45–49).

What of the coinage depicting the Unconquered Sun (*Sol invictus*) as the patron and special protector, the *comes* of Constantine, into which great significance has sometimes been read? There are problems on two levels. One is interpretative and was perhaps most pithily put by Andreas Alföldi, when he opined that it was Constantine's 'outbreaks of passion' in angry letters rather than coin types that represented 'his real emotions' (1948: 7, n.2). The other is chronological. When did Sol first appear on the coinage of Constantine, and when did it disappear? Sol appeared suddenly on the coinage of the Constantinian mints of London, Trier and Lyons in the year 310: the date makes it clear that this reflects Constantine's vision of Apollo during his march south to suppress Maximian's attempt to seize power (Sutherland 1967:32, 42, 72, 108, 111, 120). It must, therefore, also be connected with Constantine's new emphasis that he ruled as the son of his father Constantius and with the invention of a fictitious descent from the emperor Claudius, who had ruled from 268 to 270: a series of statue bases from Thamugadi dedicated by Valerius Florus, the governor of Numidia in 303, imply that Sol had been the patron deity of Constantius (*ILS* 631–633, cf. Castritius 1969: 25–30). The disappearance of Sol from the coinage of Constantine began shortly after the conclusion of the first war with Licinius: the latest issues with the legend *Sol invicto comiti* or solar imagery cease by the end of 319 at all of the Constantinian mints except Arles where it continued until 323 (Bruun 1958: 28–37, cf. 1966: 48, 61). Moreover, in the East, Licinius' coinage exclusively featured Jupiter Conservator as the tutelary deity of all the emperors for several years before 324 (*RIC* 7, 547–548: Heraclea 50–55; 605–608: Nicomedia nos. 37–50; 644–646: Cyzicus 8–19; 676–682: Antioch 7–36; 703–708: Alexandria 6–33). The Roman imperial coinage thus provides no support whatever for the modern view that Constantine was a solar monotheist to the end of his life. On the contrary, Sol offered some sort of bridge between paganism and Christians: adherents of the old religions could see Sol as one of their gods, while Christians could identify Sol as Christ, the sun of righteousness (Baynes 1931: 95–103; Alföldi 1948: 55–59) – and Constantine himself had progressed from acknowledging Apollo or the sun as his divine protector to belief in Christ as the redeemer of the human race.

(ii) The Arch of Constantine in Rome was not erected by the emperor, but by the city of Rome (at this date, in effect the Roman Senate). It honored the emperor on the occasion of his *decennalia*, which he celebrated in Rome on 26 July 315, but it is reasonable to assume that the Roman Senate voted to erect the arch while he was in Rome in the weeks following the Battle of the Milvian Bridge on 28 October 312. The arch was dedicated in 315 and the inscriptions on it read (*CIL* 6.1139 = *ILS* 694):

1   On large central rectangular plaques at the top of the arch on both north and south faces

> Imp(eratori) Caes(ari) Fl(avio) Constantino maximo
> p(io) f(elici) Augusto S(enatus) p(opulus) q(ue) R(omanus)
> quod instinctu divinitatis, mentis
> 4 magnitudine, cum exercitu suo
> tam de tyranno quam de omni eius
> factione uno tempore iustis
> rempublicam ultus est armis
> 8 arcum triumphis insignem dicavit

2   Above the friezes depicting the capture of Verona and the Battle of the Milvian Bridge inside the central arch

> liberatori urbis   fundatori quietis

3   Above the pairs of reused and remodeled tondi on the southern and northern façades

> sic X sic XX   votis X votis XX

Lines 1–2 and 5–8 of the dedication and the brief inscriptions seem straightforward: the Senate and People honored Constantine as 'liberator of the city' and 'founder of peace and civil order' on the tenth anniversary of his reign and they dedicated 'an arch resplendent with his triumphs because he had avenged the state by force of just arms on both the tyrant and the whole of his faction.' But by 315 the adjective *iustus* had acquired a specific connotation in addition to its traditional and obvious meaning of 'just': both oracles of Apollo and Lactantius in his *Divine Institutes* had used *iustus* as a virtual synonym of 'Christian' (Chapter IV n.9). Lines 3–4, however, contain a deliberately ambiguous phrase. When Constantine liberated Rome 'together with his army' (*cum exercitu suo*), he did so *instinctu divinitatis, mentis magnitudine*. Analysis of the phrase *instinctu divino* and of instrumental ablative *instinctu* followed by either *deorum* or the name of a god in the genitive case establishes that *instinctu divinitatis* must mean 'through inspiration from (or: at the urging of) a supreme deity' (L. J. Hall 1998: 668–670). It may be inferred that the still predominantly non-Christian Senate modified a recognizably traditional phrase to accord with Constantine's recently proclaimed Christianity. What of *mentis magnitudine*? The inscription does not explicitly state whose mind it is, and Glen Bowersock has argued that the mind in the phrase *mentis magnitudine* 'may be interpreted more plausibly as the *divina mens* than as the *mens* of Constantine himself' (1986: 302–303). But the 'greatness of mind' should surely be that of the emperor, as Baynes forcefully contended (1931: 10, 66–68): the two phrases on the arch are 'contrasted, not parallel' and they juxtapose two almost identical phrases which the panegyrist of 313 had used of the emperor (*Pan. Lat.* 12[9].11.4: *cum tu divino monitus instinctu … iussisti*; 21.5: *tua, imperator, magnitudo animi*). In other words, the inscription on the arch needs to be understood on the basis of literary sources, not the other way round.

(iii) Raymond Van Dam makes the epigraphical dossier relating to the granting of city status to Orcistus in Phrygia and the rescript to Hispellum central to his recent attempt to define what he calls 'the Roman Revolution of Constantine:' he removes Lactantius and Eusebius from their traditional place as the main witnesses to Constantine and bases his interpretation of the emperor's religious policies after 324 primarily on these two well-known inscriptions (Van Dam 2007: 19–220). The first of the three main sections of his book, 'A Roman Empire without Rome,' begins with the latter (*ILS* 705 = Van Dam 2007: 366–367), while the second has the title 'A Greek Roman Empire' and begins with 'Constantine's Dialogue with Orcistus' (*Monumenta Asiae Minoris Antiqua* 7.69–72 no. 305 = Van Dam 2007: 370–371).

The Orcistus dossier has many other fascinating aspects which Van Dam duly explores (2007: 150–162). It makes a significant, if small, contribution to our understanding of the importance of Constantine's Christian beliefs in even routine administrative decisions. When he accorded the village of Orcistus in Phrygia the status of a city, he stated as the crowning justification for his decision that all its inhabitants were said to be 'supporters of the most holy religion' (Document 2.41–42: *sectatores sanctissimae religionis*). Van Dam argues that the people of Orcistus 'wanted to take advantage of Constantine's good will' when they applied this 'perhaps intentionally cryptic' description to themselves shortly after 324 (2007: 176). That analysis paradoxically concedes that the people of Orcistus believed that their new emperor was indeed a Christian.

(iv) The rescript to Hispellum was paraded by Burckhardt as one of the 'very plain indications of un-Christian, even of directly pagan, sympathies' shown by Constantine at the end of his reign (1949: 301–302). Van Dam adopts a much subtler and more sophisticated interpretation, correctly setting the rescript in the context of administrative changes in central Italy and the rivalry between cities for prestige (2007: 23–34). Yet he fails to see the central point of the city's petition or to realize that the emperor who granted it was not Constantine, as everyone since Burckhardt until now has believed, including the present writer (Barnes 1981: 212), but his youngest son Constans.

Hispellum was the principal city of Umbria, which formed part of the province of Tuscia et Umbria, one of the regional provinces into which Italy had been divided, probably by Diocletian (Barnes 1982: 162, 218–219). A *corrector Tusciae et Umbriae* is attested c. 310 (*ILS* 1217 [Atina], cf. Barnes 1982: 100–101). The capital of the double province created some time before c. 310 was the ancient Etruscan city of Volsinii, and the petition from Hispellum arises from one of the consequences of this fact. The inscription calls itself a copy of an imperial rescript (*e(xemplum) s(acri) r(escripti)*), whose text falls naturally into three sections. First comes a conventional proclamation of general imperial beneficence to all cities (lines 8–15), but the bulk of the text comprises a paraphrase or summary of the petition, presumably made by an imperial secretary (lines 15–36), and the imperial reply to the petition (lines 37–59). In order to avoid prevalent misunderstandings, it is necessary to translate in full both the second and third sections of the text.[14] First the report of the petition:

> You assert that you are combined with Tuscia in such a way that according to the tradition of ancient custom priests[15] are selected by both you and the aforementioned in alternate years (*per singulos* [sic] *annorum vices*) and that these <priests> present theatrical shows and gladiatorial games at Volsinii, a city belonging to Tuscia. Because of the hardships of the mountains and the forests on the journey[16] you urgently request that a remedy be granted and that it not be necessary for your priest to travel to Volsinii in order to celebrate the games. Hence <you request> that we give to the city, which now has the name Hispellum and which you recall is adjacent to the Via Flaminia and stretches along it, a name <that is derived> from our cognomen (*ut de nostro cognomine nomen daremus*). In this city <you ask> that a temple of the Gens Flavia be erected in a magnificent construction matching the grandeur of its title, and that in the same place the priest whom Umbria has <in the past> provided in alternate years (*anniversaria vice*) should present the spectacle of both theatrical shows and gladiatorial games, but with the custom remaining that in Tuscia the priest appointed from there should officiate at the festivals of the aforementioned shows, as has been customary at Volsinii.

In other words, the city of Hispellum has requested permission to build a temple of the Gens Flavia, that the annual games associated with the imperial cult of the combined province of Tuscia et Umbria, previously held every year in Volsinii, should in future be held in Volsinii and Hispellum in alternate years, and that the change be marked by conferral on the city of a new name in honor of the imperial house. The requests were granted, but with significant qualifications:

> Our approval has readily been accorded to your prayer and desire. We grant to the city of Hispellum an eternal title and a venerable name <derived> from our own appellation, so that in future the aforementioned city shall be called Flavia Constans. In the heart of this city, we wish, as you desire, a house (*aedem*) of the Flavian, that is, of our family, be built with magnificent construction, <but> with the restriction spelled out that a house dedicated to our name not be polluted by the deceits of any contagious superstition. Hence we also give you permission to put on games (*editionum*) in the aforementioned city, with the proviso that, as has been said, the celebration of games not depart from Volsinii in alternate years (*per vices temporis*), when the festival which you mention is to be celebrated by priests appointed from Tuscia. In this way not very much will be judged to have been derogated from old customs (*institutis*), and you who have appeared before us as petitioners on account of the aforementioned causes will rejoice that those things for which you urgently asked have been obtained.

Between them the petition and imperial response state clearly which member of the imperial college replied to the city of Hispellum. The petitioners asked for a new name derived from the cognomen of the emperor. The new name given by the emperor who received the petition was Flavia Constans, and not Flavia Constantina or Flavia Constantia, even though other cities had been renamed Constantina and Constantia during the reign of Constantine,[17] the emperor who gave Hispellum its new name derived from his cognomen was surely the Caesar Flavius Constans. This deduction, which is inexorable in logic, is confirmed by the fact that the petitioners approached the emperor in person (*nobis supplices extitistis*): Constans resided in Milan from 335 to 337, while after 330 Constantine never ventured further west than Singidunum, Viminacium or Naissus (Barnes 1982: 78–79).[18]

The date of the rescript can now be considered. The heading reads

Imp(erator) Caes(ar) Fl(avius) Constantinus max(imus) Germ(anicus) Sarm(aticus) Got(hicus) victor triump(hator) et Fl(avius) Constantinus et Fl(avius) Iul(ius) Constantius et Fl(avius) Constans.

At first sight, the imperial college is that of the period between between 25 December 333, when Constantine invested Constans as Caesar, and 18 September 335, when he appointed Dalmatius Caesar. But why are the three sons of Constantine not styled *nobbb. Caesss.*, that is, *nobilissimi Caesares*? The natural assumption, made by Hermann Dessau in his annotation to the inscription (*ILS* 705), used to be that the title was accidentally omitted by the stonecutter. As long ago as 1964, however, an Italian deduced the correct date from the absence of the title: the heading lists the imperial college as it officially existed for about three months after the elimination of the Caesar Dalmatius, which followed closely on the death of Constantine (Andreotti 1964: 254–255, cf. Gascou 1967: 617–623). Van Dam brusquely dismisses the correct date as requiring 'too much special pleading' (2007: 364). But since the text of the rescript indicates that it was issued by Constans, while the heading does not give him the title of Augustus, the rescript must belong to the period between the death of Constantine on 22 May 337 and the joint proclamation of Constantinus, Constantius and Constans as Augusti on 9 September, when there was an official pretence that the dead Constantine still reigned (Eusebius, *VC* 4.67.3). Hence the request for a temple of the Gens Flavia and Constans' emphasis on the eternity of the nomen Flavia in the city's new name of Flavia Constans: the petition protests the loyalty of Hispellum to the sons of Constantine during a period of political uncertainty, while Constans' reply reflects the determination of the sons of Constantine not to share their imperial power with any interloper.

It is wrong, therefore, to use the rescript to Hispellum as direct evidence for Constantine himself. Nevertheless, Constans respects and continues his father's policies. The imperial cult was not suppressed after 324, but retained in a modified form as a vehicle for the display of loyalty to the reigning dynasty: in Africa, for example, laws of 415 and 429 mention assemblies of the provincial council in

Carthage (*CTh* 16.10.20; 12.1.186) and the imperial cult appears to have persisted into the period of Vandal rule, with Vandal kings replacing Roman emperors as the focus of loyalty (Clover 1982). But Constans requires that any ceremonies at Hispellum be purged of 'the deceits of contagious superstition,' that is, of sacrifice and other traditional religious rites. Moreover, although imperial funds for building churches had been freely available on request from subordinate officials since 312 in the West and 325 in the East, Constans did not offer to subsidize the building of the new temple of the Gens Flavia, as the petitioners doubtless expected. Further, Constans implicitly discountenances gladiatorial games: the petitioners requested that the provincial high priest of Tuscia et Umbria put on both theatrical shows and gladiatorial games (*spectaculum tam scenicorum ludorum quam gladiatorii muneris*); in reply Constans granted permission for *editiones* – which could be construed tacitly to exclude gladiatorial shows.

(v) Confident assertions about Constantine's religious beliefs have sometimes been made on the basis of inference from purely iconographic evidence. For example, Martin Wallraff deduced from the fact that the Arch of Constantine 'is full of solar symbols' that in 315 there can be no doubt that 'Sol invictus was at least as important to Constantine as Jesus Christ' (2001: 256). Modern historians who have persuaded themselves that Constantine remained an adherent of solar monotheism even after 324 have always appealed to the bronze statue which for nearly eight centuries stood atop a porphyry column in the forum of the city of Constantinople until it was blown down at the beginning of the twelfth century.[19] Thus Wallraff both identified the statue as without any doubt Helios and argued more generally that 'the profile of the new capital on the Bosporus … showed a new and intensified interest in solar symbols' (2001: 261–265).

Both the identity of the lost statue and its attributes have been in dispute. Although some late Byzantine writers state that it was a statue of Apollo or Helios, that is, the sun god, brought from elsewhere and superficially modified to depict Constantine (e. g., Pseudo-Codinus, *Patria Cpl* 2.45 [Preger 1907: 174]; Zonaras 13.3), both John Malalas in the sixth century (13.7 [320 Bonn = 245–246.79–82 Thurn) and Nicephorus Callistus in the fourteenth identify the statue as that of Constantine (*HE* 7.49 [*PL* 145.1325]). More important, so too do the earliest surviving writers who refer to it. Two ecclesiastical historians writing in or shortly after 440 are explicit. According to Socrates, Helena sent a fragment of the True Cross to her son who 'enclosed it in his own statue which stands on a large column of porphyry in Constantine's forum in Constantinople' (*HE* 1.17.8). Philostorgius, at least as reported by Photius, is equally explicit, though he draws a distinction between the original statue and ceremonies at its foot which were added later:

Οὗτος ὁ θεομάχος καὶ τὴν Κωνσταντίνου εἰκόνα, τὴν ἐπὶ τοῦ πορφυροῦ κίονος ἱσταμένην, θυσίαις τε ἱλάσκεσθαι καὶ λυχνοκαΐαις καὶ θυμιάμασι τιμᾶν, καὶ εὐχὰς προσάγειν ὡς θεῷ καὶ ἀποτροπαίους ἱκετηρίας τῶν δεινῶν ἐπιτελεῖν τοὺς Χριστιανοὺς κατηγορεῖ.

> This God-hater also accuses Christians of propitiating the statue of Constantine standing on the porphyry column with sacrifices, honoring it with the lighting of candles and the burning of incense, offering prayers to it as to a god, and performing supplications to ward off evils. (Philostorgius, *HE* 2.17).

Similarly, Hesychius, writing in the reign of Justinian, records the erection of 'the conspicuous porphyry column on which we see Constantine giving dawn[20] light to the citizens like the sun (*Patria Cpl* 41 [Preger 1901b: 17]).

The statue, which Eusebius does not mention, faced east and depicted a standing male figure holding a spear in its left hand and a globe in its right. Although Anna Comnena states that the statue held a scepter in its right hand and an orb in its left (*Alexiad* 12.4.5, p. 66 Leib, cf. Mango 1993b: 3), she was writing many years after it fell down from the top of the column. The *Tabula Peutingeriana*, which is a twelfth- or thirteenth-century copy of a schematic map of the Roman Empire, places the orb in the right hand and a lance or spear in the left.[21] Since the lost original of the *Tabula Peutingeriana* appears to have been a much earlier map of the Roman Empire which was brought up to date in the later fourth century (Kubitschek 1919: 2127–2128, 2139), sound method surely obliges the historian to prefer the visual testimony of a cartographer who drew the statue before it was repaired (the spear fell down in 554 and the globe was dislodged by earthquakes in 477 and again in 869). Cyril Mango, who followed Anna Comnena in placing the spear in the right hand of the statue, opined that before 477 the original globe may have been surmounted by a miniature Victory (Mango 1993b: 2–3). But the *Tabula Peutingeriana* shows the globe in the statue's right hand without any object surmounting it.

The *Tabula Peutingeriana* depicts a naked male with an apparently bare head. Nevertheless, Mango assumed that the figure was clad in military garb, observing that both gods and emperors were often depicted thus (Mango 1993b: 3, with appeal to Kantorowicz 1961: 368–391), and, like most other modern writers both before and after him, he assumed that the original statue wore on its head a radiate crown with the canonical number of seven rays (Mango 1993b: 3, cf., e.g., Fowden 1991: 125–130; Leeb 1992: 12–15; Berrens 2004: 168). But the earliest extant references to the radiate crown come from the chronicle of John Malalas (13.7 [320 Bonn = 245–246.81–81 Thurn]) and the *Paschal* Chronicle (528, 573 Bonn = pp. 16, 65 Whitby & Whitby), who both wrote long after the original globe fell in 477. As it is the only witness to the attributes of the statue before 477, and the radiate crown could have been added when the original globe was replaced after it fell, the testimony of the *Tabula Peutingeriana* surely ought to be preferred on this point too.[22]

In her recent discussion of the statue, Sarah Bassett adduces a classic study of Hellenistic portraits of rulers which observed that the type of the naked statue of a male holding a spear or scepter was characteristic of and specific to kings and rulers (Bassett 2004: 201–204, citing Smith 1988: 33). The bronze statue set atop the porphyry column in the lifetime of Constantine lacked a radiate crown and depicted the emperor, either with or without a diadem, in the traditional guise of a Hellenistic king or Roman emperor. Hence the reason why Eusebius 'fails to mention it' is not because the statue portrayed Helios (Preger 1901a; Wallraff 2001: 267) or because it could not 'be read in a Christian sense' (Mango 1993b: 6), but because it portrayed Constantine as a traditional Roman emperor – which was neither noteworthy nor problematical for Christians.[23]

The persistence of traditional titles and imperial attributes with pagan connotations ought not to seem surprising to the modern enquirer. All the kings and queens of England since Henry VIII have sported the title 'Defender of the Faith' (*Fidei Defensor*), even though Pope Leo X bestowed it on Henry in 1521 for writing a tract attacking Martin Luther and defending a version of Christianity which British monarchs have by law been forbidden to embrace since 1689. Similarly, no Late Roman or Byzantine emperor for centuries – not Constantine, as is well known, and neither Gratian nor Theodosius, as has often been supposed – ever abjured the title of *pontifex maximus*, even though this title, which had been an exclusive imperial prerogative since Augustus became *pontifex maximus* in 12 BC, indicated that its holder was head of the college of *pontifices* which had guarded Roman religious traditions since Rome was no more than a small city beside the River Tiber (Alan Cameron 2007). The only change that occurred is that the adjective *inclitus*, which had previously been used only by authors with literary pretensions, replaced *maximus* in the imperial titulature, probably while the very Christian Magnus Maximus was emperor in the 380s (Alan Cameron 2007: 362–365, 374–376). Both *pontifex inclitus* and victory titles such as *Germanicus inclitus* are attested in the imperial titulature of the emperors Marcian in 452 and Anastasius in 516 (*ACO* 2.3.2.87–88 = 2.3 346–347; *Collectio Avellana* 113 (*CSEL* 35.610.15–16).

The testimony of archaeology and art history can also be invoked to show that there were more wealthy and high-class Christians in Rome and the western provinces than is often believed. Wealthy Christians in the West began to commission sarcophagi with distinctively Christian iconography to receive their bodies after death in surprisingly large numbers after 312: Alan Cameron has drawn attention to a study of sculptured sarcophagi found in or near Rome which are datable on stylistic grounds between 270 and 400 (2011: 183). The percentage of sarcophagi with identifiably Christian themes rises from 8.2% in the three decades 270–300 (71 out of a total of 859) to 59.36% in the three decades 300–330 (463 out of 780) and 96.4% during the rest of the fourth century (325 out of 337) when elaborately carved sarcophagi were passing out of fashion (Dresken-Weiland 2003: 64–65, cf. Sapelli 2005). These are startling figures, but they accord well with the fact that between 317 and 337 there were more Christian aristocrats appointed to the prefecture of the city of Rome than known pagans (Barnes 1995: 143, 144, 146).

Equally significant is the abandonment by one of the oldest religious confraternities in Rome of their sanctuary, which had been in continuous use since at least the middle of the third century BC, within a very few years of the death of Constantine (Scheid 1990: 680, 739–740). Excavations conducted under extremely difficult conditions from 1975 to 1988 at La Magliana, on the right bank of the

Tiber downstream from Rome close to the fifth milestone along the Via Campana (Scheid 1990: 73, Fig. 1), have added immensely to our knowledge of the sacred grove of the *dea Dia*, where the Arval Brethren met and performed their rituals, and of its buildings. The first volume of the final excavation report documented the history of the bath-house of the Arval Brethren, which was built in the first quarter of the third century AD, apparently (given its size) for their use alone and went out of use shortly after 334/335 (Broise & Scheid 1987: 172–173, 244–245, 275–277). Although the names of many individual *Arvales* survive, the religious activities of the Arval Brethren as a confraternity are known only from epigraphy and archaeology. The latest fragment preserved of the *commentarii* in which they regularly recorded their meetings and sacrifices belongs to 241, and it is not clear how long after 241 they continued to inscribe their *acta* regularly (Barnes 1993b: 86). For the existence of a *magister bis* of the college in 304 (*Notizie degli scavi*[6] 16 [1919], 105, cf. Scheid 1992) may indicate not continuity of practice, but an aspect of the restoration of ancient cults by Diocletian and his colleagues, which Aurelius Victor later noted (*Caes.* 39.45: *veterrimae religiones castissime curatae*, cf. Scheid 1990: 738–739). The closure of the baths, dated archaeologically shortly after 334/335 reflects the profound religious changes under Constantine: within a few years of the abandonment of the bath-house, the sacred grove of *dea Dia* was overlooked by a Christian cemetery, and some decades later the stones on which the Arval Brethren had recorded their acts of piety were used in building a Christian oratory.

2

THE SOLDIER AND THE STABLE-GIRL

The birthday of Constantius, the father of Constantine, was remembered long after his death in 306: it was 31 March (*CIL* 1², p. 255).The year of his birth is not recorded, but must be deduced by inference from his career and the age of his son Constantine, who was born in the early 270s (Barnes 1982: 39–40).The *Origo Constantini Imperatoris*, a brief, sober and reliable account of the emperor written very shortly after his death in 337 (Barnes 1989c), which is the most accurate and well-informed non-Christian source for Constantine that survives, lists three posts which Constantine's father held before he was appointed Caesar in 293 (*Origo* 1). Constantius was first a *protector*, then promoted to the rank of tribune, and subsequently 'governor of the Dalmatias.' As a *protector*, Constantius was attached to the mobile central striking force of the Roman army, which was probably created by the emperor Gallienus in the 260s and emerges into view as a real entity in Dexippus' account of Aurelian's reception of an embassy from the Iuthungi, who were suing for peace after he had defeated them in battle:

He drew up his soldiers as if for battle in order to intimidate the enemy. When he considered that the arrangement was good, he ascended on to a high platform and, wrapping himself in the <imperial> purple, he formed the whole array into a crescent around him. Next to himself he stationed all those entrusted with high office, all mounted on horses. Behind the emperor were the standards of the select army – these are eagles fashioned in gold, images of the emperor and lists of the individual bodies of troops exhibited in letters of gold – all these were brandished aloft on poles plated with silver. When this was arranged in this way, he asked the Iuthungi <to come forward> (*FGrH* 100 F 6. 2–3).

When promoted to the rank of tribune, Constantius will either have continued to serve in the corps of *protectores* in the *comitatus* (as it was called) or have been transferred to a provincial army.The *Origo* describes his third known post as 'governor of the Dalmatias' (*praeses Dalmatiarum*).That description is much more problematical than it

Constantine: Dynasty, Religion and Power in the Later Roman Empire, First Edition.Timothy Barnes.
© 2011 Timothy Barnes. Published 2011 by Blackwell Publishing Ltd.

has often seemed to be. Modern works of reference elide a real obscurity when they make Constantius 'governor of Dalmatia' (in the singular) and adduce two other items of evidence in support (*PLRE* 1.227–228, Constantius 12; Thomasson 1984: 95).

The *Origo*, so it is widely held, is corroborated on this point by the *Historia Augusta*, a pseudonymous collection of imperial biographies composed after 360 (how long after remains a topic of dispute), whose author took more delight in inventing fictions than reporting fact (Syme 1968; 1971). The *Historia Augusta* makes two statements about Constantius' career before 293. First, Constantius had been trained as a general together with the future emperors Carus and Diocletian and the future praetorian prefects Asclepiodotus and Hannibalianus (*Probus* 22.3), which could well be true even if the author of the *Historia Augusta* invented it out of his own imagination. Second, Constantius 'administered the governorship of Dalmatia' between the death of the emperor Carus in the summer of 283 and Diocletian's defeat of Carus' son, colleague and successor Carinus at the Battle of the Margus in spring 285 (*Carus* 17.6: *praesidatum Dalmatiae administrabat*). The date is both plausible and doubtless correct, for it allows us to infer that Constantius earned the gratitude of Diocletian by a timely change of allegiance from the ruler of Italy and the West to his eastern challenger, who had been proclaimed emperor outside Nicomedia on 20 November 284. But the *Historia Augusta* should not be preferred to the *Origo* on the title and nature of Constantius' post. The plural in 'governor of the Dalmatias' implies that Constantius held a military command which embraced not merely the Dalmatian coast, but extended into the interior of the Balkans.

The final item of evidence often adduced for the career of Constantius before 293 is a forged inscription which modern scholars have unforgivably continued to quote and use as evidence long after it was exposed as a modern confection. The inscription was published in 1882 in Split by Giuseppe Alačević, the editor of an Italian-language publication devoted to the history and archaeology of Dalmatia. Alačević published the inscription on the authority of a certain Stefan Petković of Knin, recently deceased. Twenty years later Otto Hirschfeld included the inscription in the third volume of the *Corpus Inscriptionum Latinarum* even though it was known only by report. Hirschfeld reproduced the diplomatic transcript and the restorations proposed by the editor of the publication in which it had first appeared: I quote Hirschfeld's presentation of the text, though without making any attempt to reproduce his spacing between letters typographically.

	IVOEX////AIVSAILA	iu[d]ex [d]a[t]us a [F]la/
2	VIO VAIFPIO CONS	vio Va[ler]io Cons/
	IAVIIO/////PPOELM	[t]a[nt]io [v. c.] p(raeside) p(rovinciae) [D]elm(atiae)
4	TIVISIVIEP SALV	[f]i[ne]s i[nt]e[r] Salv/
	I A I ASE I S I PIDO	ia[t]as e[t] S[tr]ido
6	VEV SES OEIE P M	[n]e[n]ses [d]e[t]e[r]m/
	IV A VIIi	[n]avi[t] (*CIL* 3.9860)

When he included the inscription in the *Corpus*, Hirschfeld duly noted that the Croatian editor who published the inscription from the papers of Petković informed him that he had failed to find any record or transcript among the latter's papers after his death.[1] Hirschfeld also voiced suspicions about the authenticity of the inscription, since Mommsen had alerted him to the fact that it gave Constantius the name Valerius, which he acquired (so it seemed otherwise clear) only in 293 when appointed to the imperial college. In a supplement which bears the same date of publication (1902), Hirschfeld confessed that his doubts were more than justified: the inscription is only one of a group of forgeries, and Arthur Stein rightly dismissed it out of hand in his entry for Constantius in the standard guide to Roman imperial prosopography.[2]

There are two reasons for rejecting the alleged inscription apart from its lack of an authenticated provenance and its association with other forgeries. The first is the anachronism already mentioned. Not only is there no good evidence that Flavius Constantius had the second *gentilicium* (family name) Valerius before 293, but there is a strong positive reason for believing that he added the name in consequence of his appointment to the imperial college. Diocletian, who had been born with the *cognomen* Diocles, styled himself C. Valerius Diocletianus immediately on becoming emperor. When he co-opted M. Aurelius Maximianus as his imperial colleague, he added Aurelius to his own nomenclature, while Maximian added Valerius to his, so that they both now had the double family name Aurelius Valerius. In 293 when Flavius Constantius and C. Galerius Maximinus were added to the imperial college with the lower rank of Caesar, each of the pair added Valerius to his name, so that they were thenceforward styled M. Flavius Valerius Constantius and C. Galerius Valerius Maximianus, with the latter modifying his *cognomen* to Maximianus by adding a single letter in order to make it identical with that of the Augustus Maximian (Lactantius, *Mort. Pers.* 18.13).

The second suspicious feature of the inscription is that it not merely provides the sole item of ancient evidence for the precise location of the town where Saint Jerome was born, but puts it in the wrong place. The last chapter of Jerome's work *De viris illustribus* (*On Famous Men*) comprises a list of his numerous writings in chronological order down to the year 392, preceded, as are most of his notices of other Christian authors, by brief biographical details (135). Jerome, whose father was called Eusebius, was born in Stridon. Before the Goths destroyed it, Stridon had been on the border between Dalmatia and Pannonia (*Dalmatiae quondam Pannoniaeque confinium fuit*). If Constantius had determined the boundary between Stridon and Salvia, as the inscription claims, then Stridon was adjacent to Salvia, which lay about fifty miles inland from Salona on the modern road leading from Split on the coast over the mountains to the Pannonian plain (*Barrington Atlas*, Map 20D5). Eighteen years after Hirschfeld and shortly after the creation of the twentieth-century country of Yugoslavia, the Croatian cleric Franjo Bulić (1846–1934), who was not only the curator of the archaeological museum in Split, the excavator of Salonae and a renowned researcher into Croatian antiquities, but also active in politics for most of his life, pronounced the inscription indubitably authentic and claimed that the ancient Stridon was the modern town of Grahovopolje (Bulić 1920: 264, 286, 317–328). Four years later, when a *Festschrift* for Bulić was published, a Belgian monk, who in other matters usually showed himself a careful scholar, flattered the dedicatee by contributing an essay supporting Bulić's identification of the ancient Stridon with Grahovoplje (Morin 1924). But he soon issued a retraction and apologized for being deceived by a modern forgery, though he corrected Hirschfeld in one minor detail, by attributing the forgery to Alačević himself rather than to the dead Petković from Knin (Morin 1926: 217–218). The exact location of Stridon remains unknown.[3]

All four emperors who ruled jointly from 293 to 305 came from Illyricum (Victor, *Caes.* 39.36). But Illyricum is an imprecise geographical term almost as wide in meaning as 'the Balkans' in modern parlance. The only precise evidence of any value for the origin of Constantius comes from the angry pamphlet which his grandson Julian addressed to the populace of Antioch after they mocked him on New Year's Day 363. Julian's *Antiochene Oration* or *Beard-Hater* is a distasteful exercise in ironic self-depreciation in which the emperor presents himself as little more than an uncouth barbarian in contrast to the ever so clever, civilized and sophisticated citizens of Antioch. Julian speaks of Thracians as his fellow citizens and proclaims that his family was Thracian, even if he himself is a true Hellene in his way of life (*Misopogon* 20, 350cd; 40, 367c). But Thrace and Thracians are also terms of wide geographical application. One passage in the *Beard-Hater* is, however, much more precise: it states that the author's family derived from the Moesians who dwell on the banks of the River Danube between the Thracians and the Pannonians (18, 348cd). As Ronald Syme demonstrated, Julian indicates that his grandfather came from the area once known as Moesia and Treballia, which became the province of Dacia Ripensis which Aurelian created in 271 when he evacuated Trajan's Dacia north of the Danube (Syme 1983: 64–65).

Constantius' eldest son, apparently born when his father was in his early twenties, saw the light of day in Naissus (the modern Niš), which lay far south of the Danube in Aurelian's new province of Dacia Mediterranea. The fact is attested in the clearest possible fashion by Firmicus Maternus, who mentions almost in passing in his handbook of astrology that the reigning emperor Constantine was born in Naissus (*Math.* 1.10.13: *apud Naissum genitus*). But Naissus was not the *patria* of Constantius. How then did his eldest son come to be born there? That question can only be answered by asking where and how Constantius met the mother of Constantine.

THE SOCIAL STATUS OF HELENA

Helena, the mother of Constantine, was born into a humble station in life. All the ancient authors who mention her origin are agreed on this basic fact (Drijvers 1992: 15–16). The *Origo Constantini Imperatoris*, which, like Firmicus Maternus, records that Constantine was born in Naissus, calls his mother *vilissima*, which is probably best translated into English as 'very humble' or 'very low-born' (2). A generation later Eutropius stated that Constantine was born 'of a rather obscure marriage' (*Breviarium* 10.2: *ex obscuriore matrimonio*). But the only precise evidence for the social status of Helena before she married Constantius comes from the funerary speech *On the Death of Theodosius*, which Ambrose, the bishop of Milan, delivered on 25 February 395, the fortieth day after the emperor had died in Milan on 17 January 395.

Since the tenor and significance of what Ambrose says about Helena has so often been misunderstood or misrepresented, it is necessary to quote the relevant passage both in the original Latin and in English translation, so that readers may see clearly what is at issue.[4] The passage comes in a section of the speech where Ambrose quotes, embellishes and dilates upon a recently invented story. In the late 320s, as the ground was being cleared for the construction of a new church in Jerusalem, fragments of wood were discovered which were immediately identified as remains of the cross on which Christ had been crucified three centuries earlier. The actual discovery was presumably made by manual laborers and it was Macarius, the bishop of Jerusalem, who reported it to Constantine. The emperor immediately authorized the construction of the imposing Church of the Holy Sepulchre, which was dedicated in September 335 (Eusebius, *VC* 3.30–40, esp. 30.1, 4, cf. Krautheimer 1993: 513–519). About fifty years later a story was invented, which it would be misleading to describe as either a myth or a legend, which credited Helena personally with the discovery of the relics of the True Cross in Jerusalem during her pilgrimage to the Holy Land in the later 320s. The story is found not long after 395 in the translation and continuation of Eusebius' *Ecclesiastical History* which Rufinus of Aquileia completed in 401/402 (*HE* 11.7–8, p. 969.11 – p. 971.8 Mommsen) and in a letter of Paulinus of Nola written in 403 (*Ep.* 31), from which Sulpicius Severus took it in his brief world-chronicle down to the year 400 (*Chronica* 2.33.2–34.2). It is normally held that the story was invented in Jerusalem (Drijvers 1992: 95–145), in which case Rufinus may have taken it from a Greek continuation of Eusebius independent of Ambrose,[5] though Alastair Logan now suggests a Roman origin (Logan 2010). No extant author other than Ambrose alone, however, says anything whatever about Helena's precise social status.

Immediately after he has related the story of how Helena found the True Cross, Ambrose comments on Helena's original status in life, how she met Constantius and her service to the church of Christ (*De obitu Theodosii* 42 [*CSEL* 73 (1955), 393]):

> Stabulariam hanc primo fuisse adserunt sic cognitam Constantio seniori, qui postea regnum adeptus est. Bona stabularia, quae tam diligenter praesepe domini requisivit. Bona stabularia, quae stabularium non ignoravit illum, qui vulnera curavit a latronibus vulnerati. Bona stabularia, quae maluit aestimari stercor<e>a,[6] ut Christum lucrifaceret. Ideo illam Christus de stercore levavit ad regnum, secundum quod scriptum est, quia suscitat de terra inopem et de stercore erigit pauperem.

It is claimed that she was originally a stable-girl, and that it was thus that she became acquainted with the elder Constantius, who afterwards obtained the position of emperor. Excellent stable-girl who so diligently searched for the manger of the Lord![7] Excellent stable-girl, who was not unaware of that famous innkeeper who cared for the wounds of the man wounded by robbers (Luke 10.35)! Excellent stable-girl who preferred to be considered <as one who shoveled> manure in order to gain Christ! For that reason Christ raised her from the manure to the position of an empress, as it is written 'He raised up the beggar from the earth, and lifted up the poor man from the dunghill' (Psalm 112[113].7).

This passage requires careful exegesis, not least because English cannot reproduce Ambrose's play on the ambiguity of the Latin word *stercus*, which means both 'dung,' that is, the excrement of cows, sheep and goats, and 'manure,' the latter in both English senses of 'horse droppings' and of 'manure used in farming and gardening' (*OLD* 1818). In the last sentence of the passage quoted above, the phrase *de stercore* refers on its first occurrence to the manure of horse stables, on its second to a 'dunghill.' Without that double meaning Ambrose could not apply the words of the psalmist to Helena's elevation from her original lowly status to that of Augusta, to which his phrase *ad regnum* alludes.

The central interpretative problem in this passage is exactly what Ambrose means by calling Helena a *stabularia*, which I have translated as 'stable-girl' in order to reflect its primary etymological meaning. The standard scholarly monograph on Helena, while acknowledging that the literal meaning of *stabularia* is 'a woman who comes from or works in the stables,' proceeds to argue that 'because stables are often associated with inns, the word *stabularia* can also mean female innkeeper or servant at an inn' and that 'the life of a *stabularia* was one spent in servitude, very probably including sexual servitude' (Drijvers 1992: 15). That might conceivably be true, but it fails to take account of the fact that the feminine noun *stabularia* not only does not appear to be attested before Ambrose (and hence is not registered in the *Oxford Latin Dictionary*), but also only occurs after Ambrose in authors who repeat, adapt or allude to this passage. An appeal to established linguistic usage, therefore, proves nothing, since the feminine noun *stabularia* is not documented before Ambrose.

In contrast, the masculine noun *stabularius* is relatively well attested down to the early third century in the sense of 'one who keeps or manages stables and lodging for travelers' (*OLD* 1812–1813). Legal texts often speak of *caupones* (tavern-owners) and *stabularii* together: the praetor's edict laid down that neither category could choose their guests or turn away travelers (11.2/49 [*FIRA* 1.347]; Gaius as quoted at *Digest* 4.9.5; Ulpian as quoted at *Digest* 47.5.1.6, cf. 4.9.1.5, 14.3.5.6). At first sight, therefore, it might seem surprising that there is no mention of *stabularii* in either the Theodosian Code or the Codex Justinianus,[8] nor have I succeeded in finding any occurrence of the word *stabularius* in Latin authors of the fourth or fifth centuries except in discussions of the parable of the Good Samaritan to which Ambrose alludes. Luke is the only evangelist to record the parable (10.30–37), and Latin versions of his Gospel use the word *stabularius* to describe the inn-keeper in whose care the Good Samaritan left the wounded man whom he had rescued. But the non-occurrence of the noun *stabularius* in Late Latin texts is due to simple linguistic change. First, the noun *stabulum* acquired a more specific meaning over the course of time which is very relevant to how Helena met Constantius: it came to be used as the equivalent of *mansio*, a staging post of the *cursus publicus* (A. Kolb 2000: 210–213), and this sense of *stabulum* may be attested as early as Apuleius' *Metamorphoses*.[9] Second, when *mansio* established itself as the normal word for *stabulum* in this sense, *stabularii* began to be called *mansionarii* in a parallel linguistic development. Hence, although I have translated Ambrose's *stabularia* as 'stable-girl,' the linguistic facts set out here can be combined with our knowledge of how the *cursus publicus* functioned to suggest another meaning and interpretation, namely that Ambrose means that Helena was the daughter of the inn-keeper at an imperial *mansio* or *stabulum* where Constantius changed horses and lodged overnight.

The owner of an inn or tavern had a much higher status than the servants who worked for him, as Constantine assumed when he ruled that the female owner of a tavern could be guilty of the crime of adultery (which in Roman law only those of a certain social status could commit), but that her barmaid who served customers could not, because sexual promiscuity was only to be expected of a lowborn woman of that status (*CTh* 9.7.1). If Helena was the daughter of a man in charge of an imperial *mansio* or *stabulum*, then her status in life was considerably higher than a mere 'stable-girl.' Ambrose commends Helena by evoking three biblical passages. The logic of his choice of the first and third is clear. The excellent *stabularia* discovered where the infant Christ had been laid in a manger next to horses and other animals (Luke 2.7) and she built a church there; and the excellent *stabularia* was not ashamed of a social status which involved her in dealing with horse droppings (cf. Psalm 112.7). But in the second biblical passage which Ambrose evokes it was the male owner of the inn, not a female slave or servant belonging to him, who cared for the wounded man rescued by the Good Samaritan. Ambrose's biblical allusion becomes clearer, perhaps will only make sense at all, if we suppose that Helena was the daughter of the owner of an inn where Constantius lodged – and where he perhaps had a wound or injury tended.

THE MARRIAGE OF CONSTANTINE'S PARENTS

The preceding discussion is very relevant to the question of whether Constantius formally married Helena or not. The majority of modern scholars deny that Helena was ever legally married to the father of Constantine (Pohlsander 1995: 13–14) and some have described her as a mere concubine without perceiving any need to document the assertion (Vittinghoff 1989: 24). Moreover, 'the illegitimacy of Constantine' is simply assumed in some reconstructions of the emergence of the Diocletianic Tetrarchy in 293 (Leadbetter 1998). The question is sometimes decided on a priori grounds without proper evaluation of the evidence. Legislation from the reign of Augustus prohibited the marriage of a man and woman of highly disparate social status: hence, since a senator or *vir perfectissimus* was not legally permitted to marry a barmaid, the confident asseveration has been made that 'it was impossible for Constantius, who belonged to the provincial aristocracy of Dalmatia (sic!), to become the lawfully wedded husband of the *stabularia* Helena' (Drijvers 1992: 18). But not only does that assertion rely upon an interpretation of what Ambrose meant by *stabularia* which has been challenged above, but there is no reason to believe that Constantius came from any 'provincial aristocracy' no matter where his *patria* lay. Like his imperial colleagues Diocletian, Maximian and Galerius, he was a soldier of relatively humble birth who rose through the ranks on the strength of his military abilities. When Constantius was a young man, therefore, his social status did not constitute a legal impediment which prevented him from formally marrying Helena. And it must not be forgotten that in Roman law no wedding ceremony was necessary to effect a legally valid marriage, since Roman marriages were private civil contracts and could be created by constant cohabitation alone without any formal ceremony (Treggiari 1991: 3–13, 32–80). Thus there is no reason at all in Roman law for doubting that Constantine's parents could have contracted a legal marriage. Did they in fact do so?

The ancient evidence divides, almost entirely along predictable lines. Writers hostile to Constantine deny that Helena was the wife of Constantius and make her a mere concubine. The fifth-century ecclesiastical historian Philostorgius called Helena 'a vulgar woman no better than a common street prostitute' (*HE* 2.16a, p.27.25–26 Bidez: φαύλης τινὸς γυναικὸς καὶ τῶν χαμαιτύπων οὐδὲν διαφερούσης), while Zosimus, writing c. 500, alleged that Constantine was a bastard, the offspring of his father's illicit union with a woman who lacked respectability, and he contrasted him with Constantius' legitimate children by Theodora (2.8.2, 9.1–2). But both Philostorgius and Zosimus are echoing the denigration heaped upon the first Christian emperor by the often inaccurate and wildly tendentious Eunapius, whose violently anti-Christian history asserted that not only Constantine himself, but all of his children were born outside wedlock (Zosimus 2.20.2, 39.1). Such a consistent pattern of distortion discredits the specific allegations about Helena. Somewhat surprisingly, Jerome's *Chronicle* is almost equally hostile when it records the transfer of power from Constantius to his son in the following terms (228[g]):

> Constantius XVI imperii anno diem obiit in Britannia Eboraci. post quem filius eius Constantinus ex concubina Helena procreatus regnum invadit

> Constantius died in the sixteenth year of his reign in Britain at York. After him his son Constantine, who was born by the concubine Helena, seized the position of emperor.

There is a choice between two reconstructions of the relationship between Constantius and Helena. On the hostile view, the young officer picked up a female servant at an inn for his sexual pleasure and kept her as a concubine. On the other view, which is the scenario evoked by Ambrose, Helena was the respectable, though still quite humble, daughter of the owner of an inn where Constantius lodged: the young pair fell in love, married and produced a son, and this marriage entered into out of love on both sides was only dissolved when Constantius, who had risen far in the world, divorced his comparatively lowborn wife in order to marry an emperor's daughter. Everything surely commends the latter view. The issue is not a trivial one. For the standard scholarly monograph on Helena draws important inferences from the supposition that 'Helena and Constantius had not been officially married:' since Constantine was technically a bastard (it argues), he 'had fewer rights than the children produced by the marriage of the lawfully wedded Constantius and Theodora' (Drijvers 1992: 19). That is to put Constantine's career after 293 into a false perspective: with Constantius' appointment as Caesar, his oldest son, who was his legitimate heir, automatically became a candidate for the imperial purple.

Since Constantine was born before c. 275 (Chapter 1), his parents must have met shortly after 270, that is, during the reign of Aurelian, who came to power in 270 and waged energetic campaigns in both East and West to reunite a divided Roman Empire under the rule of a single emperor. If Constantius was attached to the central imperial army, as has been argued above, then he presumably accompanied Aurelian on at least some of his attested journeys, which the emperor will have made along the great military highway that led from Italy across the Balkans to the Bosporus and thence in a southeasterly direction across Asia Minor to Antioch on the Orontes. The movements of Aurelian can be reconstructed approximately as follows (Halfmann 1986: 239–240; Drinkwater 2005: 50–53):

270	Defeats Quintillus at Aquileia and goes to Rome
271	Deals with an invasion of Pannonia, returns to Italy to face an invasion of Alamanni and Iuthungi, defeats the invaders and pursues the Iuthungi as far as the Danube
271/2	Winters in Rome
272	Goes east in the spring, defeats the Palmyrenes near Antioch, then at Emesa, receives the surrender of Zenobia at Palmyra and returns westwards
272/3?	Winters in Byzantium
273	Campaigns against the Carpi, then returns to the East to suppress a rebellion at Palmyra, which he captures again and destroys, after which he goes to Egypt to suppress a rebellion there and returns to Italy
274	Invades Gaul and suppresses the *Imperium Galliarum*
274/5	Holds spectacular triumph in Rome, where he spends the winter
275	Represses lingering elements of disloyalty in Gaul, then proceeds eastwards, but is assassinated in August/September between Perinthus and Byzantium at Caenophrurium

Positive evidence may also exist that Constantius accompanied Aurelian on campaign, though it requires the discussion of a textual crux to yield the desired confirmation. The Gallic orator who praised Constantine in 310 emphasized that the emperor inherited his status and power as the first-born son of his father, who had begotten him in the flower of his youth – unlike (as the orator is careful to avoid the indelicacy of saying explicitly) the six children who were the product of Constantius' second marriage and all much younger than Constantine (*Pan. Lat.*6[7].4.2):

> te enim tantus ille et imperator in terris et in caelo deus in primo aetatis suae flore generavit toto adhuc corpore vigens, illa praeditus alacritate ac fortitudine quam bella plurima, praecipue campi †videris idonei†

> For that great man, an emperor on earth and a god in heaven, fathered you in the first flower of his youth, when he was still completely vigorous in body and endowed with that energy and bravery which very many wars witnessed, especially the fields of <?>.

I have printed the Latin text as transmitted by the archetype of the extant manuscripts marking with the customary obelus the two words in it which are obviously corrupt. The obvious and convincing correction of the first to *videre*, the more polished and literary equivalent of *viderunt*, was duly made in the fifteenth century. But I have chosen to obelise both words rather than only the last one because I believe that the last letter of the transmitted *videris* is in fact the first letter of the corrupt proper name that follows. Modern editors of the speech have had no hesitation in following the emendation of the two corrupt words to *videre Vindonii*, which was proposed in the eighteenth century.[10] This emendation, however, ignores the final letter of the transmitted *videris*. Accordingly, in 1982 I proposed to revive the Renaissance conjecture *videre Sydonii* with the corrected spelling *videre Sidonii* and to see an allusion to service by Constantius under Aurelian on campaign against Zenobia (Barnes 1982: 36–37).

This proposal was rejected by Ted Nixon and Barbara Rodgers, who allowed their acceptance of the emendation *videre Vindonii* to affect their translation of the passage (Nixon & Rodgers 1994: 222–223). With the emendation to *videre Vindonii* the speech must allude to victories won by Constantius after his reconquest of Britain in 296: this Nixon and Rodgers justify on the grounds that the orator 'refers to a youthful energy that was exemplified over a period of time' and that 'an allusion to an important victory in the West would have much more impact on a Gallic audience than one to an obscure episode long ago and far away.' But the emphasis of the whole passage is on the similarity of the Constantine of 310 with his father at the age when his father begat him: the orator goes on to assert that, although people grieve that Constantius is dead, when they gaze on Constantine they cannot believe that his dead father has really departed this life (*Pan. Lat.*6[7].4.5: *dum te cernimus, illum excessisse non credimus*). The passage quoted invokes the energy and bravery of the young Constantius as a soldier, not his prowess as a general, as the orator would surely have done if he had wished to allude to Constantius' victories as a Caesar. Hence the allusion should be to Constantius' service before 293. It is not a valid objection to point out that 'the final battles in Aurelian's campaigns were around Antioch and Palmyra, not Sidon' (Nixon and Rodgers 1994: 223, citing Müller-Rettig 1990: 84). There is no difficulty in supposing that the 'plains of Sidon' can by synecdoche refer to the areas where fighting occurred in the early 270s. Indeed, classical Latin poets employ the adjective *Sidonius* with a variety of wider geographical meanings, not merely 'Phoenician,' but also 'Carthaginian' or 'Punic' and even 'Theban' with an allusion to the Sidonian origin of Cadmus, the founder of the city (*OLD* 1757). In the mouth of the orator of 310, *Sidonii* means merely 'eastern' and, since the quantity of the second vowel can be either long or short, he chose *Sidonii* because it produces a double cretic clausula, which was one of the most common in Latin prose. He may also have chosen *Sidonii* because Sidon produced royal or imperial purple and thus implied a putative allusion to Constantius' subsequent co-optation into the imperial college.

Where and when did Constantius meet Helena? According to Ambrose, it was at a *mansio* where the young Constantius stopped on one of his journeys, and it is a reasonable conjecture that this *mansio* lay on the main military highway in north-west Asia Minor close to the Bosporus. By chance one Claudius Herculanus, a *protector Aureliani Augusti* who died at the age of forty, was buried at Nicomedia: his brother and fellow *protector Augusti* Claudius Dionysius marked his burial place with an epitaph which was published in 1861 (*CIL* 3.327 = *ILS* 2775). Constantius could well have been in the company of Herculanus and Dionysius when Aurelian and his army passed through Bithynia. It is a reasonable surmise, therefore, that Helena came from Bithynia and that Constantius met her at one of the *mansiones* on the great highway which led from the Bosporus to Syria.

In the sixth century, according to Procopius, people said that Helena came from Drepanum (*De Aedificiis* 5.2.1–5), which was situated on the southern shore of the small gulf at whose head Nicomedia lay (*Barrington Atlas*, Map 52F3). This has correctly been called into question (Vittinghoff 1989: 26 n.64; Drijvers 1992: 9–11). For not only does no extant writer before Procopius report Helena's precise local origin, but the early evidence suggests a different connection between Helena and Drepanum, which Constantine elevated in status from village to city, renamed Helenopolis and exempted from taxation (Jerome, *Chronicle* 231[g]; Socrates, *HE* 1.17.1; Sozomenus, *HE* 2.2.5; *Chronicon Paschale* 527 Bonn = Whitby & Whitby 1989: 15.3–9).

Jerome adds the significant detail that Constantine did this in honor of the martyr Lucian of Antioch, who was buried in Drepanum (*in honorem martyris Luciani ibi conditi*), even though Lucian was tried by the emperor Maximinus in Nicomedia and martyred there on 7 January 312 (Barnes 2005c). It is natural to assume that Constantine renamed Drepanum after his mother's death. But that is not a necessary assumption any more than the inference that the emperor's half-sister

Constantia, the widow of Licinius, must already have been dead when Constantine made Maiuma in Palestine, the Christian port of pagan Gaza, into an independent city and renamed it in her honor (Eusebius, *VC* 4.38; Socrates, *HE* 1.18.13; Sozomenus, *HE* 2.5.7, 5.3.6, cf. Barnes 1981: 386–387 n.78). Furthermore, Helena was certainly still alive on 7 January 327, which is the date at which Jerome and the *Paschal* Chronicle imply that Drepanum acquired the status of a city (Vittinghoff 1989: 26 n.64). Now Lucian's remains were already in Drepanum (so Jerome states) before it became Helenopolis. Hence they were presumably either brought to Drepanum for interment in 312 or transferred there after September 324. This suggests that Helena lived in Drepanum, which was an easy fifteen-mile boat ride from Nicomedia, while her son was in attendance at the court of Diocletian in that city and that Constantine made the village into a city in the hope that his mother would reside there again after her pilgrimage to the Holy Land, which probably began in the autumn of 326.

Now, if Constantius met Helena in the way that Ambrose describes, and if Constantius was on hand to acknowledge his son when he was born, then the earliest combination of dates which accommodates the fortuitous meeting of the pair, their falling in love, their consequent liaison and the birth of their son in Naissus on 27 February is a first meeting in the spring of 272 followed nine months or a little more later by the birth of their son Constantine on 27 February 273.[11] Moreover, that will be the only possible date for the birth of Constantine if, after fighting in Syria and further east in 272 and returning to Europe with Aurelian, Constantius continued to accompany Aurelian on campaign, since the emperor probably did not set foot again in the Danubian area until the summer of 275.

CONSTANTIUS' SECOND WIFE

Constantius divorced Helena in order to marry Theodora, who was either the daughter or the step-daughter of the Augustus Maximian (Barnes 1982: 33–34). The date of this marriage is uncertain, and Constantius' divorce from Helena presumably occurred shortly before it precisely in order to enable him to remarry. Later writers implicitly date both the divorce and the remarriage to the spring of 293 when they report that both the new Caesars divorced their wives in order to marry the daughters of the two Augusti (Victor, *Caes.* 39.25; Eutropius, *Brev.* 9.22.1; Jerome, *Chronicle* 225[g]; *Epitome* 39.2). In fact, it seems certain that these writers, who are probably all repeating the same lost source, have reversed the true order of events: in 293 the new Caesars did not marry the daughters of the two Augusti, but 'the existing sons-in-law of the Augusti became Caesars' (Leadbetter 1998: 82). For, while no early and reliable evidence dates the marriage of Galerius to Diocletian's daughter Valeria, the contemporary evidence of two Gallic panegyrics indicates that Constantius was already related to Maximian several years before 293. In the exordium of a panegyric of Constantius which he delivered on 1 March 297 to mark the start of the Caesar's quinquennial year the orator recalls how he had obtained access to Maximian through Constantius 'long ago,' which implies that Constantius was influential and held high office under Maximian before his elevation to the imperial college (*Pan. Lat.* 8[5].1.5). He then refers to events which occurred between his introduction to Maximian and 1 March 293 (2.1–2):

> Yet of necessity I must at present pass over many of those things too, and most particularly those <events> at which I was present because of the office conferred upon me by your divinity, namely, the capture of the king of a most savage nation in the very act of preparing an ambush, and the complete burning and devastation of Alamannia from the Rhine bridge to the crossing of the Danube at Guntia. For not only are they too important to be narrated together with others, but, in order not to appear to boast of my services too, I am satisfied to have witnessed them.
>
> Hence may that divine birth of Your Majesties (i.e., both Constantius and Galerius), invincible Caesar, give me a starting point for today's rejoicing, a birth brighter than the very beginning of spring which gave it light, for which the day was fair, and, as we who celebrated it felt, a summer sun warmed it beyond the expectation of the season, shining with a more august clearness of light than when it gave life to the origin of the world at its birth.

To put matters in more prosaic language: the day on which Constantius was proclaimed Caesar (1 March 293) was a bright, warm and sunny spring day; and before he became Caesar, Constantius had captured a barbarian king and led an army from Cologne to the headwaters of the Danube, perhaps advancing from Mainz up the Neckar Valley, spreading devastation as he went. Unfortunately, neither the route of Constantius' march nor its date is certain. It is difficult to accept the notion advanced recently that in the summer or autumn of 287 Maximian not only crossed the Rhine (*Pan. Lat.* 10[2].7.2–3), but also was in command of the expedition to which the panegyric of 297 refers here and that he therefore 'traversed Alamannia' (Drinkwater 2007: 181, cf. 37 fig. 4).[12] But there seems to be no obstacle to connecting Constantius' march to the crossing of the Danube with Diocletian's attack on 'that part of Germany which lies opposite Raetia' in 288 or 289 (*Pan. Lat.* 10[2].9.1; 3[11].5.4).

It should be Constantius, therefore, to whom the panegyric on Maximian delivered on 21 April 289 alludes when it commends the emperor for binding his highest officials to him by marriage (*Pan. Lat.* 10[2].11.4–5):

> You indeed, emperor, so earnestly hold that harmony is a virtue that you have bound to you by ties of friendship and marriage even those who perform the duties of a most powerful office close to you, thinking it a very fine thing to have held them by your side, not through the obsequiousness inspired by fear, but through pledges inspired by dutiful affection. Under the leadership of such men, although with the aid of your

auspices, that pliant and treacherous race of barbarians was crushed as it deserved. This is to your credit, emperor, yours, for even what is carried out by others originates with you.

To whom precisely does this passage allude? Late Greek and Late Latin authors so often use the generalizing plural when referring to individuals that it would require positive arguments to show that the orator of 289 refers to several persons, not to a single individual. Moreover, the orator refers to a single office, and therefore by implication to a single individual. But what post or office is denoted by the phrase *potissimum officium*, which Nixon and Rodgers translate as 'the highest office in your entourage' (1994: 70)? Otto Seeck long ago decreed that it must be the praetorian prefecture (Seeck 1895: 29, 421 = 1921: 29, 452–453), and Seeck's authority led to the identification of the man to whom the orator alludes as Afranius Hannibalianus, who is attested as praetorian prefect between 286 and 292 (*ILS* 8929); Hannibalianus was then identified as the first husband of Eutropia, the wife of Maximian, on the plausible grounds that several fourth-century writers state that Theodora, the second wife of Constantius, was Maximian's step-daughter (Victor, *Caes.* 39.25; Eutropius, *Brev.* 9.22.1; Jerome, *Chronicle* 225[g]; *Epitome* 39.2, 40.12), while the name Hannibalianus recurs among the grandchildren of Theodora (*PLRE* 1.407–408, Hannibalianus 3).[13]

In 1982 I argued that the testimony of these writers, which derives from a lost Latin source conventionally known as the *Kaisergeschichte*, given to it by the scholar who detected its existence (Enmann 1883),[14] should be rejected in favor of the early and more reliable *Origo Constantini Imperatoris* (1), which states that Theodora was the daughter, not the step-daughter of Maximian, as does the ecclesiastical historian Philostorgius (*HE* 2.16[a]). Hence I deduced that the orator of 289 alludes to Constantius and that Constantius had therefore served Maximian as his praetorian prefect for several years before he became Caesar in 293 (Barnes 1982: 6, 33–34, 37, 125–126).

As formulated, this hypothesis rested on the antecedent hypothesis that between 286 and 305 each emperor had his own praetorian prefect (Barnes 1982: 124–128). That assumption has now been disproved by the publication of an inscription from Brixia in which a college of two prefects comprising Julius Asclepiodotus, who had been ordinary consul in 292 and hence is styled *vir clarissimus*, and Hannibalianus' successor Aurelius Hermogenianus, who was an equestrian and therefore a *vir eminentissimus*, honor the Caesar Constantius (*AE* 1987.456, cf. Chastagnol 1989: 165–168). It follows that Diocletian retained the practice of having a pair of precisely two prefects for the whole Roman Empire after 1 March 293 and, in default of contrary evidence, it must be presumed that he continued to do so down to his abdication in 305 (Porena 2003: 133, 136–152).[15] Asclepiodotus, who was Hannibalianus' colleague both as praetorian prefect before 292 and as consul in that year, still held the office of praetorian prefect in 296, when he commanded one of the two armies which crossed the English Channel and suppressed the rebellion in

Britain which had lasted for nearly a decade (Victor, *Caes.* 39.26; Eutropius, *Brev.* 9.22.2; Jerome, *Chronicle* 227ª). But if Asclepiodotus served as praetorian prefect in the West continuously from before 292 until at least 296, then Constantius cannot have been praetorian prefect immediately before being appointed Caesar. Yet the orator cannot allude to Hannibalianus, as Seeck argued: the new inscription shows that he was praetorian prefect in the East, since he was succeeded as colleague of the western prefect Asclepiodotus by Hermogenianus, the jurist who produced the Codex Hermogenianus, whose contents, which almost entirely comprised rescripts of Diocletian from the years 293–295, indicate that he was *magister libellorum* of the senior Augustus in the East in these years and hence cannot have become Diocletian's praetorian prefect until c. 296 (Corcoran 1995 85–90). The phrase *potissimum officium* need not denote the praetorian prefecture. Since Latin lacks the definite article, the phrase means either 'a most powerful office' or 'the most powerful office': hence, although it alludes to Constantius, it need not allude to him as praetorian prefect (cf. Nixon & Rodgers 1994: 70–71 n.38). In the years before 293, Constantius was rather a powerful and successful general of the western Augustus, as Galerius doubtless was in the East.[16]

The marriage of Constantius and Theodora is known to have produced six children (Eutropius, *Brev.* 9.22.1), none of them yet adults by the time of their father's death in 306 (Chausson 2007: 116–122). Neither their actual nor their relative ages are known for certain. Philostorgius named the three sons of Constantius and Theodora in the order Dalmatius, Hannibalianus and Constantius (*HE* 2.16a = *Passio Artemii* 7 [Kotter 1988: 205.8–12]). Flavius Dalmatius and Julius Constantius were ordinary consuls in 333 and 335, respectively. Hence, although Julius Constantius' name might be taken to imply that he was older than Dalmatius, he was presumably younger, so that the names of the three brothers in Philostorgius may well reflect their relative ages. As for the absolute ages of Theodora's children, Dalmatius' elder son Dalmatius was proclaimed Caesar in September 335 and his younger son was married in 335 or 336 (Chapter 7). Moreover, Constantia married Licinius in February 313, while Anastasia was a married woman in the summer of 315 (Chapter 5). None of these four siblings, therefore, can have been born later than c. 300, which entails that at least one of them must have been born in or before 295. Dalmatius and Constantius may both in fact have been born some years earlier, say close 290, since their parents have been shown to have already been married in 289. Hence the Constantius whom Constantine used as an envoy in secret negotiations in 315 could be Julius Constantius (*Origo* 14, cf. Chapter V n.13). Thus the six children of Constantius and Theodora are in what may be the descending order of their ages:

1   Flavius Dalmatius, consul in 333 (*P. Oxy.* XIV 1716 identifies him as the emperor's brother), was in administrative charge of the Syrian region with the title of *censor* in 333 and 334 (Athanasius, *Apologia contra Arianos* 65.1–2; Socrates, *HE* 1.27.20–21, cf. Barnes 1982: 105).

2   Hannibalianus is no more than a name and presumably died very young (Philostorgius, *HE* 2.16ᵃ; *Chronicon Paschale* 516 Bonn = Whitby & Whitby 1989: 6.12; Zonaras 12.33).

3   Julius Constantius, consul in 335, having previously been given the rank of title of *patricius*.

4   Constantia married Licinius in February 313 (Lactantius, *Mort. Pers.* 43.2, 45.1) and bore him a son c. August 315 (*Epitome* 41.4; Zosimus 2.20.2).

5   Anastasia was married to the Roman senator Bassianus: she is named as his wife in the only surviving account of a puzzling episode which occurred in 315–316 (*Origo* 14, cf. Chapter 5, at nn. 13–19).[17]

6   Eutropia was the mother of Julius Nepotianus, who was proclaimed Augustus in Rome on 3 June 350 (Eutropius, *Brev.* 10.11; *Epitome* 42.3; Socrates, *HE* 2.25.10; Sozomenus, *HE* 4.1.2; Zosimus 2.43.2). The name of her son implies that Eutropia's husband was Virius Nepotianus, consul in 336, about whom nothing else appears to be known for certain (Barnes 1982: 108).

THE LATER LIFE OF HELENA

After her divorce from Constantius, Helena vanishes from the historian's view for more than thirty years. From her connection with Drepanum, it has been deduced above that Helena resided there in order to be near her son while he was at the court of Diocletian in Nicomedia. After Constantine was excluded from the imperial succession on 1 May 305 and joined his father in the West (Chapters 3, 4), it is not clear how long Helena remained in the East.[18] But it has been plausibly argued that Helena resided in Trier and then in Rome between 306 and 326, when she emerges again to historical view (Drijvers 1992: 21, 30–34).[19] For Trier was Constantine's main residence between 306 and 316, and if Helena did not remain in the East, it seems probable that she lived close to the court of her son, at least until he conquered Italy in 312, even if we completely deny both the historicity of medieval legends which locate Helena in Trier and any relevance to Helena of the frescoes which adorned the ceiling of a room, apparently the imperial bedroom, in the palace at Trier, in which Constantine's son Crispus resided as Caesar from 318 onwards (Simon 1986; W. Weber 1990).[20] In contrast, the evidence is strong that Helena took up permanent residence in Rome soon after her son announced his conversion to Christianity (Drijvers 1992: 30–34).

In Rome Helena resided in a palace which she acquired after the defeat of Maxentius. The *Liber Pontificalis* records that while Silvester was its bishop (that is, between 314 and 335), the Church of Rome received as a donation the *fundus Laurentus*, which was a large estate stretching southwards from the Porta Sessoriana (the modern Porta Maggiore) between the Via Praenestina and the Via Latina far beyond the Aurelian city wall, whose previous owner was Helena Augusta

(*LP* 34.27, p. 183.13 Duchesne). The *Gesta de Xysti purgatione* (*CPL* 1682), though fraudulent in what it alleges about the 430s, is impeccable evidence for Roman topography at the time of its composition in the early sixth century: it identifies what is now the Church of Santa Croce in Gerusalemme as the 'basilica of Helena which is called the Sessorium' (*Gesta* 4 [Coustant: 1721, App. 118, whence *PL*, Supp. 3.1250]: *in basilica Heleniana quae dicitur Sessorium*), and fragments of an inscription, datable on internal grounds between 317 and 324, were found near the basilica in the sixteenth century which recorded that baths destroyed apparently in a fire were restored by Helena, 'the mother of our venerable lord Constantine Augustus and grandmother of our most blessed and most flourishing Caesars' (*CIL* 6.1134). Moreover, it was in Rome that Helena's body was laid to rest after she died.

Helena was saluted briefly on the Roman imperial coinage as *femina nobilissima* in 318/319 (*RIC* 7.504–505, Thessalonica: nos. 48, 50), then formally proclaimed Augusta after the defeat of Licinius, apparently at the same time as Fausta, perhaps on 8 November 324 (*RIC* 7.551: Heraclea no. 80; 7.613, 615, 621: Nicomedia nos. 79, 80, 95, 129, cf. Bruun 1966: 26, 77). But it was only in 326 that Helena emerged again into the full light of history. She was in Rome when Constantine's wife Fausta died not long after the emperor had executed his oldest son. After this family tragedy, whose details are obscure (Chapter 7), Constantine sent his mother on an official pilgrimage to the Holy Land. She traveled to Palestine to visit the sites associated with the life, death and resurrection of Jesus with the power (granted by her son) to authorize unlimited expenditures from the imperial treasury in her own right to any person, group or cause she considered worthy (Eusebius, *VC* 3.43.4, 44, 47.3). She visited churches wherever she went adorning them with treasures, she showered gifts on all, but especially the poor and needy, she set men free from prison and the mines, she recalled men from exile (*VC* 3.44–45). But the most spectacular results of her tour of the Holy Land were two magnificent churches, one the Church of the Nativity in Bethlehem, the other on the Mount of Olives marking Christ's bodily ascension into heaven: Helena founded both and her son endowed them even more richly after her death (*VC* 3.42.3–43.1–4).

When Helena left Palestine, she proceeded first to Antioch, where the bishop Eustathius is alleged to have insulted her (Athanasius, *Historia Arianorum* 4.1), then to the imperial court, where she died in the presence of her son aged about eighty (Eusebius, *VC* 3.46.1–2). Her body was transported to Rome with a large military escort (47.1) and laid to rest in an ornate porphyry sarcophagus in the mausoleum attached to the Church of the martyrs Peter and Marcellinus on the Via Labicana which Constantine seems to have had carved to receive his own body (*LP* 34.26, p. 182.11–13 Duchesne, cf. Drijvers 1992: 74–76). Neither the precise date nor the place of Helena's decease is explicitly attested. The *Paschal Chronicle* dates the refoundation of Drepanum as Helenopolis to 7 January 327 (527 Bonn = Whitby & Whitby 1989: 15.3–9), when Helena must still have been alive. Moreover, coinage with the name and obverse of Helena seems to cease abruptly early in 329, which implies that she died in the last months of 328, when Constantine was in

Trier (Drijvers 1992: 13, 73, cf. Barnes 1982: 77–78). It may be, therefore, that Helena died in Trier.

Helena's role in the discovery of the True Cross is demonstrably a later invention of the 380s (Barnes 1981: 248, 382 n.130; Drijvers & Drijvers 1997: 11–29). Although wood believed to have been part of the cross on which Jesus was crucified was indeed discovered in Jerusalem about the time of Helena's visit to Palestine, perhaps even during it, Helena herself had nothing directly to do with the original discovery.[21] Eusebius narrates the discovery of wood that came from the cross on which Christ was crucified entirely separately from Helena's pilgrimage to the Holy Land (*VC* 3.29–40). It was Macarius, the bishop of Jerusalem, who wrote to Constantine to inform him that wood had been found during the clearing of the site of a temple of Aphrodite for the foundations of a church commemorating Christ's death and burial. The emperor wrote to Macarius to thank him most warmly for this important discovery which had brought to light 'the token[22] of the Savior's passion' in the form of 'evidence of his sacred passion, long since hidden under the ground' (Eusebius, *VC* 3.30. 1, 4).

Fragments or alleged fragments of the True Cross were rapidly dispersed far beyond Palestine in the fourth century. Two inscriptions record the dedication of relics of the cross in far-off Mauretania within a few decades of its presumed discovery in Jerusalem. One was found inland near Sitifis, the other is known from a transcript made in the coastal city of Rusguniae (Duval 1982: 1.331–337 no. 157; 351–353 no. 167, previously published as *CIL* 8.20600 = *ILCV* 2068 and *CIL* 8.9255 = *ILCV* 1822).[23] The first records the deposition of earth from the Holy Land on 7 September 359 (*de tera promisionis ube natus est Cristus ... ano provin[ciae tr]ecenti viges(imo) ...*) and, apparently some time later, of wood from the Holy Cross (*de lignu crucis*). The other records that Flavius Nuvel, who had commanded the Equites Armigeri Iuniores, a unit known from the *Notitia Dignitatum* (Occidens 6.37 = 80; 7.198), brought back a piece of the True Cross from the Holy Land and deposited it in a church which he dedicated together with his wife and entire family (lines 1–2, 5–7: *de sancto ligno crucis Christi salvatoris adlato ad(que) hic sito ... basilicam voto promissam ad(que) oblatam cum coniuge Nonnica ac suis omnibus dedicavit*). What makes this particularly significant is that Flavius Nuvel was a Moorish chieftain and the father of Firmus, who led a rebellion against Rome in the reign of Valentinian (Ammianus 29.2.5, 2.44, cf. Matthews 1988 371, 373).[24] Moreover, when Cyril of Jerusalem wrote to Constantine's son Constantius to announce the miraculous appearance of a cross in the sky above Jerusalem on 7 May 351, which had been seen by the whole population of the city, he reminded the emperor that 'the saving wood of the cross' was found in Jerusalem during the reign of his father (*BHG* 413 = *CPG* 3587, cf. Barnes 1993: 107, 272 n.59).

One important question about Helena remains.[25] When did she become a Christian? Eusebius says that it was Constantine who converted his mother (*VC* 3.47.2), and it has normally been assumed that this statement must be true, since Eusebius is presumed to report what he had heard from Constantine or his mother, either on one of the occasions when he visited the imperial court or while Helena was in Palestine. Paul Stephenson, however, has recently advanced a convincing argument that it was rather Helena who led her son towards embracing Christianity (2009: 3, 5–6, 269–270). He discounts Eusebius' statement as inspired by a desire 'to assign all credit to Constantine' and argues that both the toleration of Christians by Constantine's father as Caesar in 303 'despite instructions from his superiors to act otherwise' and Constantine's actions 'in the interests of Christians even before his conversion' correspond to what 'one would expect of the husband and son of a Christian woman,' from which Stephenson deduces that 'Helena was likely a Christian before her son was born.' That is certainly a speculative hypothesis, as is the suggestion made a century ago that Helena was sympathetic to Christianity from her childhood onwards (Couzard 1911: 10–12). But the hypothesis that Helen was a Christian long before her son will explain both Constantine's demonstrable sympathy for Christianity from the moment the he acceded to power in 306 (Chapter 4) and his apparent interest in Christianity before 305 as a crown prince awaiting elevation into the imperial college.

3

CONSTANTINE, THE RUINS OF BABYLON AND THE COURT OF PHARAOH

The two Augusti and the two Caesars of the imperial college as it was constituted between 293 and 305 were bound to one another by both adoption and marriage. While Caesar, as he was briefly in 285–286, Maximian was the adoptive son of Diocletian, but with his elevation to the rank of Augustus in 286 he became Diocletian's adoptive brother and retained this status when the imperial college was enlarged by the addition of two Caesars. On 1 May 293 Constantius and Galerius were co-opted into the imperial college and became the adoptive sons of the two Augusti. Constantius became the adoptive son of the Augustus Maximian and Galerius the adoptive son of Diocletian, but, although Galerius was the Caesar and adoptive son of the senior Augustus, Constantius took precedence over him for a reason which no ancient source states explicitly, presumably either in virtue of a seniority gained through his previous career or because he was the older of the pair.[1]

THE DIOCLETIANIC TETRARCHY (293–305)

The four emperors of the Diocletianic or so-called 'First Tetrarchy'[2] comprised two symmetrical pairs of a senior and a junior emperor, each pair of which governed the eastern and western halves of the theoretically united and unitary Roman Empire. In this respect the appointment of the two Caesars did not in any way change the theoretical assumption that the Roman Empire was an indivisible patrimony. An orator addressing Maximian in 291 assumed the unity of the Empire when he asked 'What full or twin brothers share an undivided inheritance so fairly <between them> as you share the Roman world?' (*Pan. Lat.* 11[3].6.4: *qui germani geminive fratres indiviso patrimonio tam aequabiliter utuntur quam vos orbe Romano?*). The appointment of the Caesars did not change the theory of imperial unity, since each

Constantine: Dynasty, Religion and Power in the Later Roman Empire, First Edition. Timothy Barnes.
© 2011 Timothy Barnes. Published 2011 by Blackwell Publishing Ltd.

emperor always spoke in the name of all, but in practice the administration of the Roman Empire was divided in two, as it had been since 285, and after 293 the Empire was not united politically again until 324, when Constantine defeated Licinius. Between 293 and 305 Maximian sometimes declined to enforce or even to promulgate in the West legislation which the eastern emperor Diocletian had enacted for the whole Empire. Thus he did not promulgate the edict on maximum prices of late 301, whose preamble proclaims that it was issued for the whole world and for all time (*ILS* 642; Barnes 1982: 18–19; 2002: 190–192), and, although he promulgated and enforced Diocletian's edict of 24 February 303 against the Christians, he neither enforced nor promulgated the more severe edict which his senior colleague issued in early 304 requiring universal sacrifice (Barnes 2010a: 111–112, 124–128).

After 293 the eastern Caesar Galerius was not only the adopted son of the Augustus Diocletian, but also the husband of his daughter Valeria; similarly in the West, the Caesar Constantius was both the adopted son of the Augustus Maximian and the husband of his daughter or step-daughter Theodora. Moreover, dynastic connections marked out a line of succession in both East and West. For a full century no emperor who established himself firmly in power (and some who did not) had failed to mark out his son or sons (if he had more than one) as destined to inherit his power after his death by appointing him Caesar and subsequently, if he reigned long enough, as Augustus with legal powers virtually equal to his own. Thus Severus (193–211) promoted his two sons, Caracalla and Geta, to the rank of Augustus in 196 and 209, respectively; the short-lived emperor Macrinus (217–218) his infant son Diadumenianus; Maximinus (235–238) his young son Maximus in 236; Philippus (244–249) his homonymous son Caesar in 244 and Augustus in 247; Decius (249–251) his two sons in 250–251 and Volusianus (251–253) his son in 251. Valerian (253–260) co-opted his son Gallienus (253–268) as his colleague as Augustus almost immediately, while Gallienus made his oldest son Caesar in 255 or 257 and his second son Caesar in 258 and Augustus in 260. Carus (282–283) made his two sons Caesars in 282 and Augusti in 283 before his invasion of Persia in which he died (Kienast 1996: 162–167, 170–171, 185, 200, 210, 221, 260–261).

In 293 only two of the four emperors had sons of an age capable of taking over the reins of power within the foreseeable future. Constantine, who was probably born in 273 (Chapter 2), was already an adult when his father was invested with the imperial purple: he was soon sent to the East, where he became an officer in the army which Galerius led into Persia and then joined the entourage of Diocletian as an heir presumptive to the imperial purple. Maximian, the Augustus of the West, also had a son, who was younger than Constantine, perhaps by as much as a decade, though his precise age is nowhere attested.[3] The orator who praised Maximian on 21 April 289 brought the young Maxentius into his peroration when he looked forward to an imperial visit to Rome with the boy by his father's side as a future emperor, and tactfully suggested he himself was the ideal person to be the boy's tutor (*Pan. Lat.* 2[10].14.1–2):

But surely that day will soon dawn, when Rome sees you (sc. Diocletian and Max-
iminan) victorious, and, alert right at your right hand the son or and alert born with
every endowment of talent for a study of the liberal arts, whom some lucky teacher
awaits. It will be no great labor for him to encourage in this divine and immortal scion
a yearning for glory. It will not be necessary to put forward the examples of men like
Camillus, Maximus, Curius and Cato (*Camillos et Maximos et Curios et Catones*) for
imitation. Rather let him point out your deeds to the youth, and repeatedly and continually display you as best examples for the formation of an emperor.

The dynastic implications of this passage are indirectly reinforced by the orator's
strange selection of Roman Republican heroes whom he need not encourage the
young prince to imitate. Q. Furius Camillus was believed to have defeated the
Gauls in 390 BC; Q. Fabius Maximus Verrucosus, who was consul in 233, 228, 215,
214 and 209 BC, devised the defensive strategy which frustrated Hannibal after
the Battle of Cannae; and M'. Curius Dentatus, who was consul in 290, 275 and
274 BC, defeated King Pyrrhus when he invaded South Italy.[4] Presumably the Cato
in question is Cato the Younger whose suicide at Utica in 46 BC turned him into a
Stoic hero and martyr for political freedom. The one thing that these four Roman
Republican heroes, to whom the orator alludes, have in common is that none of
them produced a son who distinguished himself in any way.

In 293 it was clear what would happen if any of four emperors were to die. If
either the eastern or the western Augustus were to die, then his Caesar would automatically become Augustus in his place, and if a Caesar died, then Diocletian would
co-opt a new Caesar to replace him. The marriage arrangements of the Tetrarchs
marked out who would be the new Caesars if either of the Augusti died. If
Diocletian were to die and be replaced as Augustus in the East by his Caesar
Galerius, then Constantius' son Constantine would replace Galerius as the Caesar
of the new eastern Augustus. Similarly in the West, if Maximian were to die,
Constantius would automatically replace as him the western Augustus with
Maximian's son Maxentius as his Caesar. During the next twelve years the dynastic
situation did not change significantly. To be sure, Constantius and Theodora produced six children in all (Chapter 2), but none of their sons would for many years
be old enough to function as an emperor in an imperial college of four, all of whom
were constantly on military campaign (Barnes 1976a). But Maxentius was soon
betrothed to the daughter of Galerius and presumably married her shortly after she
reached puberty, perhaps c. 300 when he was about twenty. For Maxentius had
certainly married Valeria Maximilla before October 303 (Lactantius, *Mort. Pers.*
18.9) and they produced a son (Valerius Romulus) whom his father was to proclaim ordinary consul in 309. Unfortunately, nothing is known for certain about
the first wife of Constantine, except that her name was Minervina and that she left
him a widower before 307, after bearing him a son (Crispus) who was born no later
than c. 300.[5] Her name, however, encourages speculation.

The goddess Minerva was the daughter of Jupiter, in Greek guise Athena the
daughter of Zeus. Now in the last decade of the third century, Diocletian was the

deputy of Jupiter on earth, sported the title or name Iovius and was likened to Zeus by a contemporary Greek poet who wrote about the imperial campaigns of the late 290s (*P. Argent.* 480 = Page 1941: 542–545 no. 135 = Heitsch 1963: 79–81 no. XXII, 1 verso 1–11, cf. Barnes 1976a: 182–183). Who was Minervina? Constantius, Galerius and Maxentius married daughters of Maximian, Diocletian and Galerius, respectively. The wife of Constantine, whom he married while he was in the East and being groomed as one of the next two Caesars to join the imperial college, ought also therefore to be the daughter or at least a close relative of one of the tetrarchs. Accordingly, I propose to identify Minervina as a niece or other close relative of Diocletian. This is admittedly a bold and speculative hypothesis. But it fills a real void in our evidence. After his proclamation in 306 Constantine distanced himself as far as possible from Diocletian. Hence neither the four Gallic panegyrists who praised Constantine between 307 and 313 nor Lactantius in 314/315 will have wished to record anything that linked the two emperors. Nor did Nazarius in 321 have any occasion to mention Minervina, while Eusebius, who lived in Palestine, far removed from the court of Diocletian, may even have been unaware of her existence. Hence the total absence of Minervina from the surviving literary works from the reign of Constantine is both explicable and predictable – and no explicit evidence contradicts the hypothesis that she was related to Diocletian.

THE APPOINTMENT OF NEW EMPERORS

What formal rules or unwritten conventions governed the nomination of new members to the imperial college? Although it does not seem to be expressly stated by any surviving ancient source or text, only the reigning Augustus who was senior in rank to all his imperial colleagues possessed the right to co-opt or appoint new members to the imperial college. This rule or custom, which can be traced back to Augustus, the founder of the imperial system, came into play in 337 after the death of Constantine (Chapter 7), and remained unbroken until 375, when, after the sudden and unexpected death of Valentinian, his courtiers proclaimed his young son Valentinian as Augustus without consulting Valens, who was now the senior Augustus and who took a long time to acknowledge his nephew as his imperial colleague (Girardet 2004). Hence when Licinius proclaimed an Augustus on his own authority in 316/317 and again in 324, he gave notice that he had ceased to recognize Constantine as in any way a legitimate Augustus. Gregory of Nazianzus gives a hint of other rules and conventions when he complains that the Caesar Julian in 360 put the diadem on his own head and began to style himself Augustus without waiting to receive the title as the reward of his merits either through the passage of time or the vote of the existing Augustus Constantius or, as used to be the case of old, a decree of the Senate (*Orat.* 4.46). Gregory does not 'state in plain language the various ways in which an emperor might be legitimately created' (Jones 1964: 3.60 n.3): he is not talking about the appointment of a new member of the imperial college, but listing the normal ways in which a Caesar was elevated to the higher rank of Augustus. Julian, Gregory complains, disregarded normal procedures and took matters into his own hands when he allowed himself to be proclaimed Augustus by his troops in Paris in early 360: he should have waited until Constantius died and his troops could legitimately salute him as Augustus or until Constantius had promoted him or the Senate had voted him the higher title, as used to be the practice in the past.

What Gregory says can be combined with Lactantius and actual practice to deduce the rules and conventions governing the appointment of new members of the imperial college between 284 and 337. Diocletian intended the tetrarchic system of two Augusti and two Caesars which he devised to be a permanent feature of the administrative structure of the Roman Empire (Lactantius, *Mort. Pers.* 7.2). In other words, he intended the Roman Empire to be divided permanently between an eastern and a western Augustus, each assisted by a Caesar (Lactantius, *Mort. Pers.* 18.5). Diocletian therefore intended that new emperors should always enter the imperial college at the rank of Caesar and that any Augustus who departed from the college, whether because of death or through abdication and retirement, should be replaced by his Caesar, as Diocletian and Maximian were in 305. After 1 May 305, therefore, it was to be expected that, if either Constantius or Galerius were to die or abdicate, then their Caesars would automatically replace them as Augusti, Severus in the West and Maximinus in the East, with a new Caesar co-opted into the imperial college by the senior of the two Augusti at the time of co-optation. But this expectation was very soon set aside and disregarded, not once but twice – not only when Constantine was proclaimed Augustus in place of his father Constantius in July 306, but also when Galerius reconstituted a college of four emperors at the Conference of Carnuntum in November 308 by co-opting Licinius to replace the dead Severus as Augustus of the West. Galerius refused to recognize Constantine's proclamation as Augustus in 306, though he did accept Constantine as a legitimate member of the imperial college with the rank of Caesar. In 308 he summoned the retired emperors Diocletian and Maximian to witness and authenticate his formal proclamation of Licinius as Augustus in a college of four emperors, viz., Galerius and Licinius as Augusti with Maximinus and Constantine as their Caesars.

There has been a widespread modern fancy that Diocletian set the principle of hereditary succession completely aside when he devised the tetrarchic system of two Augusti, each with a subordinate Caesar, with the two pairs of emperors, the Iovii in the East and the Herculii in the West, dividing the government of the Roman Empire between them (e.g., Seston 1946: 193–257; F. Kolb 1987: 139–143, 177–179). But that idea, which appears to derive ultimately from Burckhardt (Leppin 2006: 15–18), is anachronistic and runs counter to the political reality of both the Roman and the Byzantine Empires (Corcoran 2008: 232). More specifically, it is contradicted by both the marriage alliances between the members of the college of four emperors created in 293 and the status of Constantine and Maxentius between 293 and 305. Although no evidence survives for the movements or activities of Maxentius during this period, he probably remained at the court of his father, whose normal residences were Milan and Aquileia (Barnes 1982: 56–60), and he may well have accompanied his father first to Spain and then on campaign in Mauretania, Numidia and Africa in the late 290s. But Maxentius is one of history's losers and nothing at all is known for certain about him between 289 and 305 beyond the fact of his marriage to the daughter of Galerius. In contrast, the surviving evidence allows the reconstruction of the career of Constantine between 1 March 293 and 1 May 305 in some detail.

CONSTANTINE IN THE EAST (293–305)

The outline of Constantine's career is known from three writers independent of one another. The panegyrics of both 307 and 310 evoke his service as an officer in the Roman army. He 'accomplished many things bravely, many things wisely, while <he was> completing <his> first campaigns in the most important tribunates' and he 'serv<ed his> time in the ranks and pass<ed> through all the grades of the military hierarchy' (*Pan. Lat.* 7[6].5.3; 6[7].3.3). By the spring of 305, at the age of thirty-two, he was a *tribunus ordinis primi* according to the transmitted text of Lactantius' *On the Deaths of the Persecutors* (18.10), which Jacques Moreau emended to *tribunus <et comes> ordinis primi*, plausibly arguing that Constantine was both a *tribunus* and a *comes primi ordinis*, in other words that he was a military tribune with the status of a *comes* of the first rank at court (Moreau 1954: 313–314). Whether that is correct or not, a reliable source reports that Constantine fought bravely as a *tribunus* in Asia under Diocletian and Galerius (*Origo* 2).

Constantine himself provides the key to a more detailed reconstruction of his career between 293 and 305. His *Speech to the Assembly of the Saints*, which he delivered in Nicomedia in April 325 (Chapter 6), alludes to his presence in both Egypt and Mesopotamia (16.2, p. 177.1–4):

> τοιγάρτοι καρπὸν ἤραντο τὸν προσήκοντα τῇ τοιαύτῃ θρησκείᾳ Μέμφις καὶ Βαβυλών, ἐρημωθεῖσαι καὶ ἀοίκητοι καταλειφθεῖσαι μετὰ τῶν πατρῴων θεῶν. καὶ ταῦτα οὐκ ἐξ ἀκοῆς λέγω, ἀλλ' αὐτός τε παρὼν καὶ ἱστορήσας ἐπόπτης τε γενόμενος τῆς οἰκτρᾶς τῶν πόλεων τύχης

> Memphis and Babylon have reaped the fruit appropriate to such <false> worship, made desolate and left uninhabited together with their ancestral gods. And this I do not report from hearsay, but having been there myself: I made enquiry and saw with my own eyes the pitiable fate of the cities.

Since Eusebius saw Constantine traversing Palestine at the right hand of Diocletian before he became emperor (*VC* 1.19), Constantine went to Egypt before 305, so that there can be no reason whatever to doubt his claim that he saw the ruins of Memphis. But it has sometimes been deemed 'highly improbable' that he could ever have seen the ruins of Babylon (Hanson 1973: 506). In fact, there is an occasion (and there is only one) when Constantine could have seen the ruins of Babylon, and it is an occasion which fits perfectly into his career before 305 as it is known from elsewhere.

The site of Babylon lay far beyond the boundaries of the Roman Empire, about forty miles almost due south of the city of Ctesiphon, one of the capitals of the king of Persia (*Barrington Atlas*, Map 91F5). The ruins of ancient Babylon, or at least what passed for them, were still standing in the fourth century. In his *Commentary on Isaiah*, which in its present state reflects the Christian Empire of Constantine after 324 (Barnes 1992b: 651–652), Eusebius argues that the prophecy of Isaiah has been fulfilled in that Babylon 'shall be as when God overthrew Sodom and Gomorrah and shall not be inhabited for ever' (1.67, p. 100.3–11 Ziegler, quoting Isaiah 13.19–20 LXX):

> It is necessary to observe that he tells the truth in accordance with what is <now> the case. Babylon is now to be seen uninhabited and completely deserted. Those who come to us from those parts testify to the fact. But, he says, 'nor shall Arabs cross it,' referring (I think) to those who are called Saraceni in our day, who used to pitch their tents on the very site of Babylon when travelling with their caravans. But <now> it is avoided by those who live thereabouts who even go around it as if they were from a distant country to such an extent that not even shepherds of the Arabs allow any of their own flocks to graze there because it has been so completely devastated.

Roman armies penetrated to Ctesiphon twice during Constantine's lifetime. The first was in 283, when he was a boy of ten and his father was probably stationed in Illyricum (Chapter 2). On that occasion, not only was Constantine too young, but the Roman expeditionary army was compelled to retreat almost as soon as it reached Ctesiphon, in front of whose walls the emperor Carus perished (Drinkwater 2005: 57). In 297/298, however, Galerius invaded the Persian Empire through Armenia and entered Ctesiphon in triumph, probably on 28 January 298, a day carefully chosen as the hundredth anniversary of Septimius Severus' entry into the city and the two hundredth anniversary of the accession of Trajan, who had captured Ctesiphon in 115 (Barnes 1996b: 544). Galerius appears to have remained inside Persian territory for a full year. Since Constantine both served in the Roman army under Galerius and was an officer in the Roman army at the date when Galerius took Ctesiphon, it is an ineluctable inference that he was with the army of Galerius and that he therefore had the opportunity to visit the ruins of Babylon. That he availed himself of the opportunity to inspect them is extremely significant. For it implies that in 298 he already had an interest in the Old Testament – which fits well with the hypothesis that his mother Helena was either a Christian or at least a Christian sympathizer (Chapter 2).

One further geographical detail is known of Constantine's military career. According to the *Origo Constantini Imperatoris*, Galerius made repeated attempts to get Constantine killed by exposing him to excessive danger in battle against the Sarmatians, but through remarkable deeds of valor he slaughtered many Sarmatians and won a victory for Galerius (3: *Galerio victoriam reportavit*). The *Origo* explicitly dates the episode after the abdication of Diocletian and Maximian (2). Galerius cannot have attempted to encompass the death of Constantine at the date alleged by the *Origo*, since Constantine left Nicomedia to join his father in the West very soon after 1 May 305 (Chapter 4). Moreover, although Galerius took the victory title *Sarmaticus maximus* for imperial victories in the field over Sarmatians five times in all between 293 and 311, none of these victories occurred in 305 (Appendix B). Lactantius offers a variant of the same story dated earlier than 1 May 305. According to this version, Galerius had already tried to get Constantine fatally wounded by wild animals on the exercise ground before his father requested his return in 305 (*Mort. Pers.* 24.5: *sub obtentu exercitii ac lusus feris obiecerat*). It should be clear that the story of Galerius' attempt to get him killed is an invention of Constantine's propaganda against him (Chapter 1). Its invention, however, presupposes that Constantine did indeed serve under Galerius against the Sarmatians between the end of the Persian War in 299 and 1 May 305.

Constantine presumably remained with Galerius' victorious army in Mesopotamia until Diocletian and Galerius met in Nisibis and jointly negotiated a peace treaty with the Persians in 299 (Petrus Patricius, frag. 14). But after Galerius departed to the Danubian frontier, presumably towards the end of 299, Constantine remained at the court of Diocletian, who resided in Antioch from at least February 300 to 4 July 301, then went to Egypt, where the presence of the senior emperor is attested in Alexandria on 31 March 302 (*Lex Dei* 15.3; *Chr. Min.* 1.290; *Paschal Chronicle* 514 Bonn = Whitby & Whitby 1989: 4, cf. Barnes 1976d: 246–250). For it was either in the second half of 301, while Diocletian was on his way to Egypt, or in the late spring or summer of 302, when he was returning from Egypt, that Eusebius saw Constantine traversing Palestine at the right hand of the senior emperor (*VC* 1.19, cf. Barnes 1982: 41, 42, 55).[6]

Constantine himself reports that he was in Nicomedia when Diocletian, who had moved his court from Antioch to Nicomedia late in 302, launched the 'Great Persecution' towards the end of February 303 (*Speech* 25.2, p.190.24–29). But Galerius too was in Nicomedia in February 303, and it appears that he had recently celebrated a victory over both Carpi and Sarmatians: Constantius and Galerius both took the title *Carpicus maximus* four times between late 301 and January 306; a Christian tore down the first persecuting edict when it was posted up 'declaring mockingly that victories over Goths and Sarmatians were being proclaimed' (Lactantius, *Mort. Pers.* 13.2); and by 'Goths' Lactantius clearly meant Carpi. On the other hand, neither Constantius nor Galerius took the title *Sarmaticus maximus* again before they became Augusti in 305. It may, therefore, have been in autumn 302 or the winter of 302/303 that Constantine fought under Galerius when the latter won a victory over the Sarmatians. However, a victorious Sarmatian campaign during the summer of 304, when both Diocletian and Galerius were on the Danube (Lactantius, *Mort. Pers.* 17.4, 18.6) cannot perhaps be completely excluded.

After the spring of 303, the whereabouts of Constantine are next explicitly attested two years later, when he was in Nicomedia on 1 May 305 (Lactantius, *Mort. Pers.* 18.10, 19.1–4). But he surely accompanied Diocletian to Rome in 303 (Barnes 1981: 25; Hartley 2006: 15). In the autumn of this year the four tetrarchs gathered in North Italy, presumably in Milan, where they discussed plans for the retirement of the two Augusti and for the imperial succession (Barnes 1997a: 102–104). Galerius was unexpectedly called away to deal with a military emergency on the Lower Danube, but the other three emperors proceeded south to Rome where they celebrated the *vicennalia* of the two Augusti and the *decennalia* of the two Caesars on 20 November 303 and held a traditional triumph over the Persians, which was presented as a collective achievement of all four emperors (Barnes 1996b: 544–545).

The status of Constantine at the court of Diocletian has been both misrepresented and misunderstood. After he became emperor in 306, Constantine misrepresented his situation in Nicomedia before 1 May 305 in order to disguise his links with the regime of Diocletian, who had persecuted the Christians, and nearly twenty years later he felt able to tell a brazen lie about his age and to claim that he was a mere boy in 303 (Chapter 1). The misrepresentation of Constantine's status at the courts of Diocletian and Galerius began shortly after his accession to power. It was claimed that before 1 May 305, so far from being a crown prince, Constantine was held as a hostage for his father's good behavior, and a story was put into circulation that Galerius detained him against his will for a full year after 1 May 305 until he contrived to escape, fled to Gaul in peril of his life and found his father on his death-bed (Chapter 4). So early and so prevalent was this false version of history that it is repeated in the *Origo Constantini Imperatoris*, which alleges that Constantine was merely a hostage all the time that he was in the entourage of Diocletian and Galerius (2: *obses apud Diocletianum et Galerium, sub iisdem fortiter in Asia militavit*).

Eusebius offers a very different interpretation which, though couched in biblical language, corresponds much more closely to the reality of Constantine's position at the court of Diocletian. In his *Ecclesiastical History* he had compared Constantine's victory over Maxentius at the Battle of the Milvian Bridge to God's destruction of Pharaoh and his army as they pursued Moses and the Hebrews on their flight out of Egypt and across the Red Sea (*HE* 9.9.5–8, quoting in order Exodus 15.4–5; Psalm 7.15–16; Exodus 15.10, 14.31, 15.1–2, 11). In his *Life of Constantine* Eusebius found a deeper similarity between Constantine and Moses.[7] The heading to the relevant chapter of the *Life*, which was admittedly not written by Eusebius himself, but by a posthumous editor, summarizes its contents as 'That like Moses Constantine was reared in houses of tyrants,' that is, taking account of the generalizing plural, in the palace of a ruler who persecuted God's people (*VC* 1.12: heading). Eusebius himself had written (*VC* 1.12):

> An ancient report relates that terrible generations of tyrants once oppressed the
> Hebrew people, but that God, disclosing himself as well-disposed to those who were

oppressed, decided that Moses, a prophet who was still in his infancy, should be brought up in the very homes and bosoms of the tyrants and learn to share in the wisdom which they possessed. When the passage of time called him forth as a man, and Justice, which aids the wronged, began to pursue the wrongdoers, then the prophet of God left the houses of the tyrants and began to serve the will of the Higher <Power>, diverging in deed and word from the tyrants who had reared him and acknowledging as his friends those who were in truth his brothers and relatives. God then raised him up as the leader of the whole nation, liberated the Hebrews from bondage to their enemies and through him (sc. Moses) pursued the race of tyrants with punishments sent from God ...

Now the same God has granted to us that we should be eye-witnesses of wonders greater than those in myth and see clearly with fresh eyes things that are truer than anything which we have heard. For, while the tyrants who in our time set out to make war on the God of all oppressed his Church, in their midst Constantine, who was soon to be a tyrant-slayer, sat at the tyrants' hearth, still a tender young boy and blooming with the flower of youth like that famous servant of God (παῖς ἄρτι νέος ἁπαλὸς ὡραῖός τ' ἀνθοῦσιν ἰούλοις, οἷα αὐτὸς ἐκεῖνος ὁ τοῦ θεοῦ θεράπων), even though he did not share the character of the godless, young as he was (καίπερ νέος ὤν).

Eusebius had seen Constantine in 301 or 302 and hence knew what his approximate age was. Moreover, the early chapters of the *Life of Constantine* state that he became emperor at about the same age as Alexander the Great (who lived from 356 to 323 BC) was when he died and that he lived twice as long as Alexander (*VC* 1.7.2–8.1). He knew perfectly well, therefore, that Constantine was neither a boy nor an adolescent youth in 303, but a grown man of thirty. Yet in the passage quoted Eusebius repeats Constantine's deliberate misrepresentation of his age in order to dissociate him from the Diocletianic persecution of the Christians. Eusebius also reflects Constantinian propaganda when he uses the Greek word *tyrannos* in the double sense of persecutor and illegitimate ruler, which was invented shortly after the Battle of the Milvian Bridge (Grünewald 1990: 64–71; Barnes 1996a).

One other piece of evidence relates to Constantine in the East before 305. The speech delivered at the double ceremony in Trier c. September 307 at which Maximian both invested Constantine with the rank of Augustus and gave him his daughter Fausta in marriage, just as he had given Theodora in marriage to Constantine's father years earlier, claims that Maximian had long intended to make Constantine his son-in-law, and for proof the orator appeals to a mosaic in Maximian's palace in Aquileia (*Pan. Lat.* 7[6].6.2):

There is no doubt that he who had chosen you of his own accord, long ago, to be his son-in-law, even before you could have sought this, was erecting for you at an early date that sacred pinnacle of divine power. For this, I hear, is what the picture in the palace of Aquileia, placed in full view of the dinner guests demonstrates. In it a young girl already adorable for her beauty, but as yet unequal to her burden, holds up and offers to you, then still a lad, Constantine, a helmet gleaming with gold and jewels, and conspicuous

with its plumes from a beautiful bird, in order that her betrothal present might enhance
your beauty, a result which scarcely any ornaments of clothing can produce.

The orator makes clear that the mosaic depicted a very young Fausta presenting
a youthful Constantine with a plumed helmet, and he indicates that the dramatic
date of the scene depicted must be shortly after 1 March 293. But his interpretation of what the scene signified is anachronistic, even though Julian was later to
claim that the marriage of Constantine and Fausta was arranged by Maximian and
Constantius – at what date he does not specify (*Orat.* 1, 7d). The scene depicted is
one of departure. Hence the helmet is to be interpreted, not as a betrothal gift, but
as a gift from Fausta to Constantine when he departed to the East to attach himself
to the court of Diocletian as a candidate for Empire (Barnes 1981: 9). However, the
orator would doubtless have been pleased at his hint that Fausta, who was born c.
290,[8] was destined to marry Constantine, who was a bachelor when he left for
the East.

THE DYNASTIC COUP OF 305

If Constantine and Maxentius were marked out for co-optation into the imperial
college, how and why were they shunted aside when Diocletian abdicated? The
answer is simple, and Lactantius fathomed it. Galerius vastly increased his prestige
and political influence over the senior Augustus through his spectacular victories in
his second campaign against the Persians, when he did not share command with
him, as he had in the first disastrous campaign, which ended in a Roman defeat
(Barnes 1982: 54, 63). Galerius advanced through Armenia, captured the harem of
the Persian king Narses, occupied his capital of Ctesiphon and negotiated a very
favorable peace (*Mort. Pers.* 9.5–10).[9] But Lactantius' account of the abdication of
Diocletian and Maximian omits an important part of the political equation.
Lactantius, who concentrates his and his readers' attention on Constantine, sup-
presses the very relevant fact that before 305 Maxentius enjoyed an equal status to
that of Constantine. In 305 the new Caesars ought to have been Constantine in the
East and Maxentius in the West. In the event, Galerius replaced Constantine and
Maxentius as the new Caesars with two of his own nominees.

Constantine and Maxentius were both sympathetic to Christianity. The political
ideology of the Diocletianic Tetrarchy, rooted as it was in traditional Roman values
and cultural attitudes, had a religious aspect that found expression in vast numbers
of dedications to traditional deities by provincial governors in office. Hundreds of
these dedications survive from the period 293–305 (Barnes 1992b: 656 n.51), which
to some degree reflect the personal choice of the governors, since Christians were,
at least until 300, excused the traditional obligation to commence public business
with a symbolic act of sacrifice (Eusebius, *HE* 8.2.4). Each of the four emperors had
his own traditional tutelary deity. Panegyrists might occasionally hail Diocletian

and Maximian as gods on earth — an extravagant hyperbole which persisted as late as the reign of Theodosius, when Pacatus saluted this most ostentatiously Christian emperor as a *praesens deus* (*Pan. Lat.* 2[12].4.5: *deum dedit Hispania quem videmus*). Officially, however, neither Diocletian nor Maximian was a *Gottkaiser*, both emperor and god: they were *Kaiser von Gottes Gnaden*, emperors by the grace of God, to use Wilhelm Ensslin's famous distinction (Ensslin 1943). Diocletian and Maximian were the chosen instruments of Jupiter and Hercules respectively, the sons of Jupiter and Hercules, their deputies on earth and under their special protection. The Caesars Constantius and Galerius were the sons of the Augusti and thus the grandsons of their tutelary deities. Thus, as the son of Maximian, Constantius was himself Herculius, son of a Herculius and grandson of Hercules (*Pan. Lat.* 9[4].8.1). But each Caesar also had his own special individual divine protector. In 303 the governor of Numidia dedicated four altars to the tutelary deities of the Tetrarchs (*CIL* 8.2343–2345 = *ILS* 631–633: Thamugadi). The inscriptions of three of them survive: to Jupiter Optimus Maximus the *conservator* of Diocletian, to Hercules Augustus the *conservator* of Maximian and to the *Genius Virtutum Mars Augustus* the *conservator* of Galerius, whom Lactantius ridicules for claiming to be the son of Mars (*Mort. Pers.* 8.9). Originally there must have been a fourth altar dedicated to the *conservator* of Constantius, whose tutelary deity was the Unconquered Sun, otherwise known as Apollo (Julian, *Orat.* 7, 228d, cf. Castritius 1969: 29–30).

Besides being a successful general, Galerius was a fanatical devotee of traditional religion (Lactantius, *Mort. Pers.* 9.9, cf. 11.1). Galerius also had relatives who would be excluded from power if Constantine and Maxentius were to become the next emperors. He therefore decided to mount a political campaign with an ideological aspect. If he could persuade Diocletian to act against the Christians, then it would become difficult for the senior emperor to persist in his intention of nominating Constantine and Maxentius to the imperial college when the time came. Hence Galerius and his political allies exerted themselves against the Christians. The first step, probably taken in 300 (Burgess 1996: 157–158), was to purge the eastern armies of Christians, and by 303 it proved politically possible to launch a general persecution. The 'Great Persecution' that Diocletian decreed on 24 February 303 was not, as has often erroneously been imagined, a titanic struggle for mastery between two religions on a collision course. Christianity had achieved full legal recognition from Gallienus in 260 (Barnes 2010a: 97–105) and Diocletian continued to tolerate Christians as governors and as officers in the eastern Roman armies for fifteen years. The 'Great Persecution' was rather a political maneuver designed to influence the imperial succession. Perhaps Galerius hoped that Constantine would remain loyal to his Christian friends as they suffered martyrdom, as some undoubtedly did. But Constantine was careful not to compromise himself.

The silence of later sources, Eusebius' ignorance of western affairs and Lactantius' allusiveness have conspired to conceal a political event of the highest significance from all modern historians of Constantine until about thirty years ago. In November 303 there occurred what has justly been described as a 'composite political extravaganza' (McCormick 1986: 19–20). Diocletian came to Rome to celebrate his *vicennalia* on the nineteenth anniversary of his proclamation as emperor on 20 November 284 (Lactantius, *Mort. Pers.* 17.1–2). By a transparent fiction, his colleague Maximian celebrated his own *vicennalia* at the same time, even though Diocletian had appointed him Caesar in 285 (probably on 21 July) and promoted him to Augustus in 286: his regnal years in Egypt were increased by one on 20 November 303 to give him parity with Diocletian (Thomas 1971: 171–179) and his presence in Rome is explicitly attested. With the *vicennalia* of the Augusti were combined two other celebrations, the delayed *decennalia* of the Caesars, who had been appointed on 1 March 293 and the joint Persian triumph of all four Tetrarchs, in which the harem of Narses was paraded in effigy before the imperial chariot (*Chr. Min.* 1.148; Eutropius, *Brev.* 9.27.2; Jerome, *Chronicle* 227ᵐ; Zonaras 12.32).

In preparation for the imperial visit a monument was erected in the Roman forum which comprised four columns, each topped by a statue of one of the four Tetrarchs, in a row in front of a column topped by a statue of Jupiter (cf. Kähler 1964: 29 Abb. 6; Taf. 1–3). One of the bases of the columns survives: one face is inscribed *Caesarum decennalia feliciter*, another depicts the four emperors in procession and a third a Caesar in the act of sacrificing. It was André Chastagnol who first made the plausible inference that the Caesars took part in this grand 'political extravaganza' (Chastagnol 1980–81: 189; 1982: 105; 1983: 16). But Lactantius states explicitly that Galerius had never set eyes on Rome before he set siege to the city in 307 (*Mort. Pers.* 27.3). A more nuanced hypothesis is therefore required.

As so often, oblique allusions in Lactantius provide the key to unlocking the puzzle. Lactantius reveals that Galerius met Maximian not very long before May 305, that Maxentius had refused to perform obeisance (*adoratio*) before his father-in-law, and that under pressure from the Goths a tribe of Carpi had surrendered themselves to Galerius at the time when the *vicennalia* were being celebrated (*Mort. Pers.* 18.1, 18.9, 38.6). All the relevant evidence can therefore be accommodated by the hypothesis that the four emperors met and conferred in North Italy before the celebrations of November 303, but that an unexpected military emergency prevented Galerius from accompanying his three imperial colleagues to Rome and compelled him instead to go to the lower Danube (Barnes 1996b: 545).

At the meeting of the Tetrarchs agreement was reached on three central points: first, Diocletian and Maximian would soon abdicate on the same day, although a precise date for their joint abdication may not have been set; second, on their retirement into private life they would automatically be replaced by their Caesars, so that Constantius would become Augustus in the West and Galerius Augustus in the East; and third, on their promotion to the rank of Augustus the two Caesars would be replaced by the closest adult male relatives of emperors in the imperial college, that is, by Constantius' son Constantine, who would become Caesar in the East in place of Galerius, and Maximian's son Maxentius, who would become Caesar in the West in place of Constantine's father Constantius (Barnes 1997a: 102–103). That there was such an agreement is confirmed by the panegyrist of 310, who reprimands the dead Maximian for breaking the oath that he would abdicate which he had sworn to Diocletian in the Temple of Jupiter on the Capitol in Rome (*Pan. Lat.* 6[7].15.4–6, cf. F. Kolb 1987: 143–150).

Diocletian left Rome on 20 December 303 and entered on his ninth consulate on 1 January 304 in Ravenna. During the winter, as a result of traveling in the cold and wet, he contracted a lingering illness. In the spring he joined Galerius and toured the Danubian frontier. By 28 August 304 Diocletian was in Nicomedia again (*CJ* 3.28.26), where he dedicated his new circus on 20 November 304 to complete the celebration of his *vicennalia* on the twentieth anniversary of his accession to power. His illness then got worse and on 13 December a rumor swept Nicomedia that he was dead, with some suspecting that his death was being concealed until Galerius could reach the city. Uncertainty lasted until 1 March 305, when Diocletian appeared again in public, emaciated and scarcely recognizable as the emperor who had departed for Rome in 303, and also, according to Lactantius, showing obvious signs of mental degeneration (*Mort. Pers.* 17.2–9).

Galerius soon arrived in Nicomedia and set about persuading Diocletian to change the arrangement for the imperial succession upon which the Tetrarchs had agreed in North Italy. Lactantius offers a vivid dialogue between the Augustus and the Caesar, which, in accordance with the conventions of historical writing in the Greco-Roman world, he did not intend to be read as an accurate and authentic record of a private conversation, but as an analysis of the political situation and of the motives of the two men (*Mort. Pers.* 18.2–15). It contains the following interchange after Diocletian had agreed to abdicate at once:

> The tired old man … replied in tears: 'So be it, if this is what you have decided.'
>
> It <still> remained for Caesars to be chosen by common agreement of all <four emperors>.
>
> 'But what need is there of an agreement,' <Galerius asked>, 'since the <other> two must of necessity accept whatever we do?'
>
> 'Quite so,' <replied Diocletian>. 'For it is necessary that their sons be appointed.'

After a brief discussion of Maxentius and Constantine, whom Lactantius describes in his own voice as 'a young man of the highest integrity, entirely worthy of the rank of Caesar' whose 'distinguished and becoming presence, military application, upright character and extraordinary affability' made him loved by the soldiers and desired as emperor by civilians (*Mort. Pers.* 18.10), Galerius comes to the point. He urges the appointment of men 'who will be in my power, who will fear me, who will do nothing except on my orders' and names them as Severus, whom he tells Diocletian that he has already sent to Maximian for his formal investiture as Caesar, and his own relative Maximinus, who was his nephew, the son of his sister and hence his closest male relative by blood (*Epitome* 40.1, 18; Zosimus 2.8.1). Since Lactantius tendentiously presents Maximinus as merely an *adfinis* of Galerius, that is, a relative by marriage, he had presumably married a cousin who was the daughter (or possibly granddaughter) of a sibling of Galerius (Barnes 1999a: 460, cf. Mackay 1999: 202–205).[10] The new dynastic arrangements were announced to the world almost at once and caused great surprise.

Lactantius, who was in Nicomedia at the time, gives an account of the military ceremony held on 1 May 305 about three miles outside the city on exactly the spot where Diocletian had donned the imperial purple more than twenty years before (Lactantius, *Mort. Pers.*19.2, as emended by Barnes 1982: 62 n.73), which he presumably obtained at the time from a soldier who witnessed it.[11] Diocletian announced that he was retiring because of old age and illness and was appointing two new Caesars. On hearing this, everyone expected him to proclaim Constantine and Maxentius as the two new Caesars until he actually named Severus and Maximinus and summoned the latter to his side. That all without exception expected Diocletian to appoint Constantine Caesar can hardly be literally true, but there is no good reason to doubt that almost all who were present expected the appointment to follow normal dynastic principles, since they knew that both Constantine and Maxentius had been groomed for the purple since 293.

4

THE ROAD TO ROME

Shortly after the proclamation of the new Caesars, Constantine left Nicomedia and traveled west to join his father. He presumably took with him his mother Helena and his young son Crispus. Constantine deliberately distorted and misrepresented this episode for propaganda purposes, and it is his false version of events that dominates the surviving literary sources. Not only the Latin epitomators of the later fourth century (Victor, *Caes.* 40.2–4; *Epitome* 41.2–3) and Zosimus (2.8.2–9.1), but also Eusebius and Lactantius repeat the story that, when Constantine finally obtained permission to leave his court from Galerius, who had constantly plotted to kill him, he hamstrung all the horses at each *mansio* of the imperial post in order to make pursuit impossible, and that he only reached his father when he was on his deathbed. Eusebius develops the story by comparing Constantine to Moses, who fled the court of Pharaoh in fear for his life (*VC* 1.20–21). Lactantius gives the fullest version of the story, presumably repeating what he had been told at the court of Constantine in 311 or 312 with rhetorical embellishments of his own (Lactantius, *Mort. Pers.* 24.3–8):

> Being seriously ill, Constantius had written to Galerius asking him to send his son Constantine back for him to see, as he had not seen him for a long time. There was nothing that Galerius was less keen to do. Although he dared not take any open action against Constantine, in case this stirred up civil war against himself and (what he feared most) the hatred of the soldiers, he had already often made secret attempts to kill the young man and had exposed him to wild beasts under the pretence of military exercise and sport, but in vain, since the hand of God was protecting him.
>
> It was God who rescued him from Galerius' hands at the critical moment. For, since <Galerius> was unable to refuse a request which had been made rather frequently, he gave Constantine his seal one evening and told him to set out the following morning

after he had received formal instructions with the intention of either holding him back on some pretext or to send letters ahead <ordering> that he be arrested by Severus. Since Constantine anticipated this, he hastened to depart while the Augustus was resting after dinner and sped in flight, removing all the horses of the *cursus publicus* at each of the many staging posts he passed through. The next day the Augustus deliberately slept until midday, then ordered Constantine to be summoned. He was told that he had set out immediately after dinner. He began to fume and rage. He called for horses of the *cursus publicus* so that he could have him dragged back, but it was reported that it had been stripped of its horses. He could hardly restrain his tears.

Meanwhile, Constantine, traveling at amazing speed, reached his already dying father, who commended him to the troops and transmitted the imperial authority to him with his own hands. Thus Constantius died quietly in his bed as he wished.

In fact, Constantine reached Britain before the end of summer of 305, almost a full year before his father's death.[1] Not only the Gallic orator who praised Constantine in 310 (*Pan. Lat.* 6[7].7.5), but also the *Origo Constantini Imperatoris* (4), which again demonstrates its value as an early and reliable source, record that he joined his father at Bononia before they crossed the English Channel together, went north and conducted a military campaign beyond Hadrian's Wall against the Picts. The stray find of a brooch with an inscription commemorating the *vicennalia* of Diocletian has been held to confirm the presence of Roman troops in Dumfriesshire at this juncture (Hassall 1976: 107–108).[2] More important, both Constantius and Galerius took the title *Brittanicus maximus* for the second time before 7 January 306 (*AE* 1961.240), which proves that the western Augustus won a victory on the battlefield in Scotland in the second half of 305 (Barnes 1982: 61, cf. 256–257). Constantius was not the first Roman emperor to campaign in Scotland: almost a century earlier in 209, Septimius Severus had advanced west of the Grampian Mountains far to the north of Perth (Birley 1988: 179–187). Constantine accompanied his father on this campaign and subsequently returned with him to York, which was probably his winter quarters, as the city had been for Severus, who died there on 4 February 211.

CONSTANTINE'S PROCLAMATION AND RECOGNITION AS EMPEROR

As so often with Constantine, the truth has been deliberately misrepresented for purposes of propaganda. But what, in this case, is the truth that was deliberately hidden from the view of both contemporaries and posterity? Although certainty is unattainable, Paul Stephenson has recently and plausibly argued not merely that Galerius could not refuse Constantius' request for the return of his son in 305, but that by complying with the request he effectively acknowledged Constantius' right to appoint Constantine to the imperial college when he felt himself close to death, though of course with the rank of Caesar, since the Caesar Severus would automatically be promoted to Augustus when Constantius died (Stephenson 2009: 116, 330). Stephenson further argues that there was a formal agreement to this effect between Constantius and Galerius which 'was later suppressed by Constantine, who concocted a far more romantic tale of midnight flight.' That is not a necessary hypothesis, but the truth, whatever it was, has certainly been hidden behind an invented story. For it was in the summer of 305, not nearly a year later, that Constantine left the East to join his father. How long after 1 May 305 was it that Constantine departed from the East? The ancient evidence does not yield a precise date, though a novelist's conjecture has him pass through Serdica in late August 305 (Kerboul 1993: 9). That is probably too late, but the exact chronology does not matter. Galerius surely knew what was likely to happen if his senior colleague fell ill and died with Constantine at his side.

By the spring of 306 Constantius was ailing, and it was presumably his medical condition that compelled him to remain in York into the campaigning season of 306. Before he died, however, he exercised his right as the senior of the two Augusti to appoint a new emperor to the imperial college[3] – or at least he was widely believed to have exercised it before he expired, which in political terms amounted to the same thing, as Galerius was quick to recognize. This point requires emphasis since so many recent writers on Constantine claim that he came to power and began his reign as a usurper (e.g., Grünewald 1990: 9, 15, 173, echoed by Van Dam 2007: 83; Humphries 2008). A recent biographer goes so far as to present Constantine's appointment by his father followed by the acclamation at York as a 'veritable coup d'état' (Brandt 2006), and even an otherwise admirably accurate and perceptive historian has succumbed to the false communis opinio (Eck 2007: 79: 'Konstantin war usurpatorisch an die Macht gekommen'). The death-bed appointment of an Augustus occurred again in November 361, when the dying Constantius recognized Julian as his full colleague with the rank of Augustus: he thereby made his Caesar, who had been illegally proclaimed Augustus in Gaul in early 360, his legitimate successor (Ammianus 21.15.3) and removed any danger of continuing resistance to the rebel whom he was traveling west to suppress. In 306 the new senior emperor Galerius accepted Constantine as a legitimate member of the imperial college, though only at the lower rank of Caesar.

Constantius had co-opted his son into the imperial college as an Augustus, disallowing the automatic promotion of his unlucky Caesar Severus to the higher imperial rank which he expected, and as soon as Constantius was dead his appointment of his son was ratified by his troops, who saluted Constantine as Augustus. The new ruler of Britain, Gaul and Spain immediately sent the customary laureled letter to Galerius in which he both announced his appointment by his father and his salutation as Augustus by his father's army and requested recognition from the new senior Augustus as his father's successor. Galerius, who was perhaps on campaign on the Danube, as he so often was in the first decade of the fourth century, was implacably opposed to recognizing as his equal in rank one whom he had excluded from the imperial college fifteen months earlier. But what could he do? He was in no position to dispute Constantine's claim that his father had appointed him to the imperial college. Constantine was in undisputed command of his father's army and already recognized as an emperor in Britain, Gaul and Spain. Lactantius reports that Galerius hesitated long (*Mort. Pers.* 25.2: *deliberavit diu*). Whatever his hesitations, however, he had no choice but to accept the new military and political reality established on 25 July 306 in distant York.

Galerius offered Constantine a compromise. At a date which fell after the beginning of the new regnal year in Egypt on 30 August 306 (Barnes 1982: 28–29), he co-opted Constantine into the imperial college on his own authority, but at the lower rank of Caesar. Constantine made the wise decision to accept this appointment, since it made him a full and undisputed member of the imperial college, acknowledged from September 306 as a legitimate emperor throughout the Roman Empire, from Hadrian's Wall to Mesopotamia, from the Pillars of Hercules to the mouth of the Danube, from the lower reaches of the Rhine to the northern fringes of the Sahara Desert and beyond the cataracts of the Nile. Whatever might happen in the future, therefore, Constantine's legitimacy as an emperor was now indisputable, and he could afford to wait until time or a political opportunity brought promotion to the rank of Augustus – and opened up the possibility of ultimately becoming the senior emperor with the right to shape the imperial college as he wished. For had he not been a fully legitimate emperor from the start, Constantine could never have become master of the whole Roman Empire.

Before he accepted the purple robe of a Caesar sent to him by Galerius, however, Constantine acted to assert his claim to be an Augustus and at the same time to make a significant political gesture. Although he officially sported the title of Caesar from the autumn of 306 until he was invested as Augustus by Maximian c. September 307, Constantine never dropped his claim that he became an Augustus on 25 July 306, and there is no valid evidence for the bizarre modern hypothesis that in the first few years of his reign he regarded some later date as his *dies imperii* – which would have implied that he had not been a legitimate emperor between 25 July 306 and that later date, whenever it might be imagined to fall (Barnes 1982: 5 n.14, 255). It follows that from late July until the early autumn of 306, Constantine claimed to hold the rank of Augustus, and that his subjects in Britain, Gaul and Spain regarded him as an Augustus. How then could he advertise this claim? There were two obvious ways. One would have been to issue coins in his name with the title of Augustus. This Constantine refrained from doing. The imperial mints which he controlled consistently style him Caesar or *nobilissimus Caesar* until the late summer or autumn of 307 (*RIC* 6.127–130, Londinium: nos. 40–100; 202–214, Treveri: nos. 615–787).

The second way for Constantine to advertise his status as an Augustus to his subjects in Britain, Gaul and Spain was to issue legislation, since all Augusti in the imperial college possessed the right to issue innovative legislation which a Caesar lacked. To be sure, it has often been claimed that the senior emperor who held the first place in the imperial college alone had the right to issue such legislation (Chastagnol 1982: 185). But there are indisputable counter-examples which disprove this modern claim.[4] In the heading to the so-called Brigetio Table granting tax exemptions to his soldiers which Licinius issued at Serdica on 10 June 311, Constantine's name precedes his own (*FIRA* 1.93),[5] and Licinius addressed a general law concerning municipal councils to the provincial council of Bithynia in 317 (*CTh* 8.4.3 + 10.7.1 + 10.20.1 + 12.1.5). But legislation of Licinius (it may legitimately be objected) cannot properly be cited as a precedent for what Constantine did in 306. For that, however, there are two documented precedents from the period between 1 May 305 and 25 July 306 when Galerius, as the second-ranking Augustus after Constantius, issued edicts and general laws on his own authority. One law issued by Galerius in 305/306 has long been known from inscriptions in Athens and at Tlos in Lycia (*IG* 2/3². 1121 = *AE* 1996.1403; *CIL* 3.12134 = *AE* 1996.1498), to which some small fragments have recently been added (*AE* 1996.1478a, c, d, cf. Corcoran 2007: 224, 226–227). Simon Corcoran has now identified a second in the famous *edictum de accusationibus* which the Theodosian Code attributes to Constantine and dates to 1 January 314 (*CTh* 9.5.1). Copies of this imperial edict (the Lyttus copy has the heading [*e*]*xemplum sacri edicti*) are now known from no fewer than eight eastern cities, and Corcoran has shown that a fragment of an inscription from Corcyra, unfortunately known only from report (*CIL* 3.578 = *AE* 1995.1386 = *AE* 2002.1302), contains part of the imperial titles of the Augusti Constantius and Galerius immediately followed by the initial letters of first few lines of this imperial edict or letter, which was therefore issued by Galerius, though of course in the joint name of the whole imperial college (Corcoran 2002; 2007: 224, 229–233).

Under the tetrarchic system devised by Diocletian, while a Caesar could make appointments in the area entrusted to his rule and issue instructions to governors under his command (since otherwise he could not govern) and could even make rulings on points of law by issuing rescripts to governors and private individuals, he could not issue edicts and general laws – a prerogative possessed only by Augusti.[6] Writing in 314/315 Lactantius, who had been at the court of Constantine before the emperor declared himself a convert to Christianity, states with emphatic precision that the new emperor issued innovative legislation as soon as he assumed power (Lactantius, *Mort. Pers.* 24.9):

> suscepto imperio Constantinus Augustus nihil egit prius quam Christianos cultui ac deo suo reddere. haec fuit prima eius sanctio sanctae religionis restitutae.

> On assuming the imperial power Constantine's first act was to restore the Christians to their worship and their God. This was the first measure by which he sanctioned the restoration of holy religion (translation by J. L. Creed slightly modified).

Lactantius reiterated his assertion in a passage which he may have composed in 324 before the defeat of Licinius for a second edition of his *Divine Institutes*, which he did not live to complete (1.1.13, cf. Heck 1972: 127–170).[7]

> quod opus nunc nominis tui auspicio inchoamus, Constantine imperator maxime, qui primus Romanorum principum repudiatis errroribus maiestatem dei singularis ac veri et cognovisti et honorasti. nam cum dies ille felicissimus orbi terrarum inluxisset,

quo te deus summus ad beatum imperii columen evexit, salutarem universis et opta-
bilem principatum praeclaro initio auspicatus es, cum eversam sublatamque iustitiam
reducens taeterrimum aliorum facinus expiasti.

This work I now commence under the auspices of your name, Constantine the greatest
emperor: you were the first of Roman emperors to repudiate falsehood and to recog-
nise and honour the greatness of the one true God. For, on that day, which was the
happiest ever to dawn on earth, when the highest God raised you to the blessed peak
of empire, you inaugurated a reign that all desired for their salvation with an excellent
start when you brought back justice [i.e., Christianity], which had been overturned and
removed, and made amends for the most abominable crime of others.[8]

It used to be the standard practice of historians who wrote about Constantine
not merely to disbelieve what Lactantius says about his first act as emperor, but to
discount it so completely that they did not feel obliged even to mention it. In 1973
I protested against the scholarly impropriety of passing over explicit testimony from
a contemporary source in total silence (Barnes 1973: 44). Unfortunately, the habit
of ignoring or disbelieving Lactantius has persisted, even after the careful analysis
and defense of what he reports about Constantine in 306 by Pedro Barceló (1988:
78–83).[9] It is of course legitimate to argue either that Lactantius was mistaken or
that he is deliberately lying. But such a thesis requires better arguments than those
employed so far.[10] For Lactantius scores highly for factual accuracy, no matter how
misleading his glosses and omissions may be, and his tract *On the Deaths of the
Persecutors* treats Maximian in a fashion which reflects Constantinian propaganda of
the period between the summer of 311 and 28 October 312 – and of no later
period (Barnes 1973: 41–43).

On the basis of the ancient evidence that survives (as opposed to modern
assumptions), there is no good reason to doubt that Constantine advertised himself as a protector of the Christian church as soon as he came to power. In 306,
immediately after his proclamation, Constantine also had very strong political
motives for distancing himself from the other three emperors by putting an end
to the persecution of the Christians which was still their official policy, even
though Maximian had ceased to enforce it in Italy, the African provinces and
Spain several months before his abdication. Constantine also had a strong motive
for issuing the law or general edict reported by Lactantius which had nothing
whatever to do with the Christians or the new emperor's religious beliefs, since it
asserted his status as an Augustus and as the heir to his deceased father's domains.

POLITICS AND WARFARE 306–310

Soon after Galerius reconstituted the imperial college as a Second Tetrarchy, with
himself and Maximinus as Augustus and Caesar in the East, Severus and Constantine
as Augustus and Caesar in the West respectively, it ceased to function as it had before

305. Maximinus had from the start persecuted Christians with greater ferocity than either Diocletian or Galerius. In 306, when a census for the purpose of assessing taxation was taken throughout the Roman Empire, Maximinus used the newly compiled census lists to compel the Christian inhabitants of cities in Oriens and Egypt to sacrifice to the traditional gods (Eusebius, *Martyrs of Palestine* 4.8, cf. Barnes 1981: 152). In contrast, Constantine repealed all Diocletian's anti-Christian legislation in the summer of 306, so that from that time the Christians of Britain, Gaul and Spain both regained their freedom to worship God openly and recovered property confiscated from them in 303.

In 306 the imperial college lost control of Italy and Africa. At this period an empire-wide census was conducted on a five-year cycle with censuses due in 306 and 311 (Barnes 1982: 226–237). Galerius introduced two innovations in the census of 306. The first affected the whole of the Roman Empire: the inhabitants of cities who did not own any landed property were compelled to register their persons in the census registers for the first time (Lactantius, *Mort. Pers.* 23.1–9) and it was certainly resented, since Maximinus restored the earlier exemption both in the territories which he had ruled since 305 and in Asia Minor, which he seized after the death of Galerius in the summer of 311 (*CTh* 13.10.2[Seeck], cf. Barnes 1982: 232).[11] In 306, however, this innovation had no observable political repercussions. It was otherwise with Galerius' decision to extend direct taxation, to which Roman provinces had always been subject and which had already been introduced in North Italy (hence its designation as Italia Annonaria), to the Italian peninsula south of the Po Valley including the city of Rome (Italia Suburbicaria). Lactantius describes the policy and its consequences in his own vivid and inimitable way (*Mort. Pers.* 26.1–3):

> Matters seemed to him settled in a way when suddenly another frightening report was brought to him. The cause of this rising was this. When he decided to devour the whole world by instituting censuses, he rushed so far into madness that he did not wish even the people of Rome to be exempt from this virtual enslavement. Census-officials were already being appointed to be sent to Rome to register the populace. At about the same time he had abolished the camp of the praetorian guard. So the few soldiers who had been left at Rome in the camp seized their opportunity, killed some magistrates and invested Maxentius with the imperial purple, with the acquiescence of the Roman people, who had been roused <to indignation>.

Maxentius, who was residing as a private person on the Via Labicana just outside Rome (*ILS* 666, 667; Eutropius, *Brev.* 10.2.3; *Epitome* 40.2), refused at first to accept the title of Augustus, styling himself merely *princeps* or *princeps invictus*, though he soon took the title together with all its normal accompanying sobriquets (*RIC* 6. 367–373, Rome: nos. 135, 137, 138, 143, 144, 147, 148, 152, 153, 162, 163, 166–174). Maxentius was quickly acknowledged as ruler of the Italian peninsula south of Rome and of Sicily, Africa, Sardinia and Corsica, and he formally decreed an end to the 'Great Persecution' in his domains as Constantine had in his: the day on which 'peace' arrived was remembered in Africa decades later (Optatus, App. 1, p. 194.12 Ziwsa, cf. 1.18: *indulgentiam mittente Maxentio Christianis libertas est restituta*). Unlike Constantine, however, Maxentius did not restore confiscated Christian property at the outset. He only took this further step later, possibly in 308 (Kriegbaum 1992: 22–33, cf. Girardet 1998b: 308–309 = 2006a: 36), but more probably in 311 (Barnes 1981: 38–39), when war with Constantine began to loom and he was afraid of losing the political support of the Christians of Italy and Africa, who must have known about the restoration of confiscated property by the ruler of Gaul, Spain and Britain.

A satisfactory narrative of the civil wars of the next seven years, which left Constantine and Licinius in joint control of the Roman Empire, is only possible because Lactantius described in some detail how each of the emperors responsible for the 'Great Persecution' died – in the order of their deaths, Maximian, Galerius, Diocletian and Maximinus – to demonstrate how God always punishes persecutors of the Christians. It is much more difficult to piece together any sort of coherent narrative of wars against external enemies, especially of the campaigns of Maximinus on the eastern frontier or of those of Galerius and Licinius on the Danubian frontier: although campaigns of Constantine are described in panegyrics delivered before him in 307, 310, 311 and 313, only disconnected and sporadic evidence survives for other emperors because Lactantius took no interest in these military activities unless they impinged directly on his main theme. The narrative of the years 306–312 which follows is therefore constructed around Lactantius' account (*Mort. Pers.* 26.4–52.1, cf. Moreau 1954: 346–473) and specific references will for the most part be given only for significant details derived from authors other than Lactantius, from inscriptions or from archaeology.

Upon his accession to power on 28 October 306, Maxentius presumably sought recognition from Galerius, as Constantine had a few months earlier. But Galerius snubbed his son-in-law, who soon began to present himself as the champion of the city of Rome (*conservator urbis suae*) against the empire-wide imperial college (Oenbrink 2006). The senior Augustus summoned Severus, who had automatically advanced in rank from Caesar to Augustus when Constantius died, and instructed him to recover Rome for the imperial college and legitimate government. That turned out to be a risky and unwise move. For the army stationed in North Italy which Severus commanded was the army which had served Maximian for twenty years until 1 May 305. In order to resist Severus, therefore, Maxentius sent the imperial purple to his father, who was living in retirement in Campania, and appointed him 'Augustus for the second time' (*bis Augustus*). Maximian, who had not wished to abdicate in 305, accepted the invitation to help his son with alacrity. He confronted Severus, who had led his army right up to the walls of Rome: on the arrival of Maximian they rapidly deserted their legitimate emperor, the Augustus of the West. Severus fled and took refuge in Ravenna with a few soldiers, who soon decided to hand him over to Maximian. Severus then surrendered himself and returned to Maximian the imperial purple with which he had invested him less than two years before (Lactantius, *Mort. Pers.*26.4–11; Zosimus 2.10.1–2). Both Lactantius and Zosimus state that Severus was either allowed to commit suicide by cutting his veins or executed at once. In fact, Maximian took him to Rome as a hostage and he was put to death later when Galerius invaded Italy, probably on 15 September 307 (*Origo* 10; *Chr. Min.* 1.148, cf. Barnes 1981: 30, 299 nn.12–16).

Since Maximian and Maxentius expected Galerius to avenge Severus and reassert the authority of the imperial college over Italy, they sought and formed an alliance with Constantine. After fortifying Rome and making the city ready to withstand a siege, Maximian traveled to Gaul, where c. September 307 he gave his daughter Fausta in marriage to the western Caesar and elevated him to the rank of Augustus in a double ceremony, which took place in either Arles or Trier (Grünewald 1990: 36–38). The speech delivered on that occasion survives and is a valuable historical document (*Pan. Lat.* 7[6], cf. Rees 2002: 153–184). The speech emphasizes the ties between the old and the young emperor. Constantine, already the grandson of Maximian by adoption through his father and in a sense his son because of his rank, is now also his son-in-law. He resembles his father Constantius both in bodily beauty and moral character as a model of the four cardinal virtues of continence, bravery, justice and wisdom. Moreover, from his adolescence onwards Constantine (who was now thirty-four) had exhibited an *animus maritalis*: as a young man devoted to his wife, he showed himself worthy of the wife he was now marrying. Constantine's first wife was Minervina, who was (I have argued) closely related to Diocletian (Chapter 3) – a connection which it would have been tactless in the extreme for the orator to mention explicitly in the political circumstances surrounding a wedding which cemented an alliance to resist Galerius' invasion of Italy. But Crispus, a boy of ten or twelve and the son of Constantine by his first marriage, was doubtless present to witness the remarriage and promotion of his father.

The alliance of Constantine with Maxentius, his marriage to Maxentius' sister and his investiture as Augustus by Maximian led Galerius to expel him from the imperial college in the autumn of 307: for more than a year thereafter Galerius officially regarded Constantine as no longer an emperor, but merely a private citizen (see the appendix to this chapter). Galerius' exclusion of Constantine from the imperial college and his withdrawal of recognition of him as a legitimate emperor has long been attested by coins and inscriptions (Barnes 1982: 5–6; *SEG* 52.1182 [Alexandria Troas]), but an imperial letter to the city of Heraclea Sintica has recently been discovered from the period between 10 December 307 and 30 April 308 (Galerius is *trib(unicia) p(otestate) XVII imp(erator) III*) in which Galerius writes in the joint name of himself as Augustus and Maximinus as Caesar with no mention of Constantine (*AE* 2002.1293, cf. Lepelley 2004; Corcoran 2006c).

Galerius invaded Italy while Maximian was in Gaul and advanced with ease as far as the walls of Rome. The city was barred against him and his army was not large enough for circumvallation and a siege. Soon the allegiance of Galerius' troops began to waver, and some of them had already deserted to Maxentius when he threw himself at his soldiers' feet, begged them not to betray him and offered enormous rewards for their continued loyalty. Having secured that, he ordered a retreat in which his troops were allowed to pillage, plunder and rape to their hearts' content. He was thus able to cross the Julian Alps and reach his own territory with his army largely intact.

Maximian returned to Italy to find Galerius already repulsed, but also to a diminution of his power, since his son Maxentius was in political control. Several months later, wishing to exercise supreme power once more, Maximian foolishly attempted to depose his son. On 20 April 308 (*Chr. Min.* 1.148) he called an informal assembly of the people of Rome and the soldiers, to whom he delivered a harangue on the ills of the state. Well into this speech Maximian suddenly pointed at his son, denounced him as responsible for the ills and calamities of the state and tore the imperial purple off his shoulders. Maxentius leapt from the tribunal and was welcomed by the soldiers whose angry shouts persuaded Maximian to flee the city at once. Maximian betook himself to his son-in-law in Gaul, from where after a few months he proceeded to a meeting with Galerius to which Diocletian, who had retired to his palace in Split (Spalato) in 305 and was enjoying the salubrious climate of the Dalmatian coast, was also summoned.

In the army camp at Carnuntum on 11 November 308 (*Descriptio consulum* 308) Galerius co-opted Licinius into the imperial college, which was again reconstituted as a tetrarchy, though with the addition of the retired emperors as honorary members. A dedication was then made to the unconquered god Mithras in the name of all six – Diocletian and Maximian the *seniores Augusti*, Galerius and the new emperor Licinius as Augusti, and Maximinus and Constantine as Caesars (*ILS* 657). There is no evidence that Constantine had ever taken any notice of his expulsion from the imperial college by Galerius in 307–308: he consistently presented himself as an Augustus from the moment when Maximian had promoted him from Caesar. On 11 November 308 Galerius readmitted Constantine to the imperial college, though still only as Caesar, but he compelled Maximian to lay his imperial garb aside again, so that he returned to Gaul a private citizen despite his honorific title of *senior Augustus*, which conferred neither power nor authority.

In the East, Maximinus chafed at the elevation of Licinius who had entered the imperial college at the higher rank of Augustus and he refused to be satisfied any more with the lower rank of Caesar. He rebuffed several attempts by his uncle and father-in-law to persuade him to acquiesce, after which Galerius invented the title *filius Augustorum* for both the Caesars (*RIC* 6.513–515, Thessalonica: nos. 28, 32a, 32b, 39a, 39b; *P. Cairo Isidore* 47, 90, 91). But Maximinus soon curtly informed Galerius that his troops had proclaimed him Augustus on the exercise ground. With reluctance Galerius finally conceded the claims of Maximinus and Constantine to be Augusti, not Caesars, with the result that Licinius was demoted from second place in the imperial college to the most junior in a college of four Augusti.[12]

The Conference of Carnuntum did not merely bestow the rank of Augustus on Licinius; it looked forward to a future political division of the Roman Empire into an eastern and a western half with their border at the Julian Alps, which divided

North Italy from Pannonia. Licinius, who was specifically appointed as Augustus of the West, received responsibility for defeating the usurper Maxentius and restoring Italy and Africa to the theoretically united and indivisible Roman Empire. Although Licinius never succeeded in this endeavor, he attempted to do so and invaded Italy at least once. For obvious reasons, Lactantius is silent about these military operations, which are documented only by coins and archaeological evidence. In 309 Maxentius closed the north Italian mints of Ticinum and Aquileia (Sutherland 1967: 276, 308), presumably because he feared that they might fall into the hands of Licinius.[13] In 310 the town of Parentium in Istria honored Licinius as its sovereign, but the fact that his name was later erased may indicate that Maxentius subsequently recovered the peninsula before finally losing it to Licinius in 312 (*ILS* 678 = *Inscriptiones Italiae* 10.2.7, cf. Barnes 1981: 33, 300–301 nn.51, 52). For Maxentius had been distracted by a rebellion in Africa, where Domitius Alexander, *vicarius* in Africa since 303, proclaimed himself Augustus in 308, sought an alliance with Constantine, seized control of Sardinia and cut off the supply of African grain to Rome. Maxentius sent his praetorian prefect Rufius Volusianus to put down the rebellion, which he suppressed with great ferocity, then transferred the rebel's army to Italy as reinforcements against the military threat in the north of the peninsula (Barnes 1981: 33).

Between 306 and the winter of 311/312 Constantine pursued two main political and military aims, which complemented each other. The first was to consolidate his political base in Gaul and Britain, which he certainly visited late in 310 after Maximian's attempted coup (*RIC* 6.134–135, Londinium: nos. 133–145; Eusebius, *VC* 1.25).[14] (Spain seems to have remained totally quiescent during these years.) The second was to make the Rhine frontier completely secure, if necessary by mounting expeditions across the river. Between 306 and 310 Constantine won victories in the field for which both he and his imperial colleagues took the title *Germanicus maximus* twice; he campaigned against the Franci and celebrated a triumph over them; and he built a bridge over the Rhine at Cologne and raided the territory of the Bructeri (*Pan. Lat.* 7[6].4.2; 6[7].10–13; 4[10].16.4–18.6; Barnes 1976a: 191–193; 1982: 69–70, 256–258). Constantine's political and military activities both served the single overriding purpose of preparing for war against Maxentius. The appointment of Licinius as Augustus of the West at the Conference of Carnuntum reconstituted the imperial college on the model of the Diocletianic Tetrarchy, with Constantine as Licinius' Caesar and subordinate. After November 308, therefore, Constantine confronted a serious political danger. If Licinius discharged the task for which he had been co-opted into the imperial college and mounted a successful invasion of Italy, he faced the dismal prospect of being forever restricted to ruling only those territories which he had inherited from his father in 306.

Fortunately for Constantine, Licinius' first attempt to take possession of Italy in 309 failed, and in 310 and 311 he was distracted by political and military events further east. On 27 June 310 Licinius won a victory over the Carpi (*ILS* 660, cf. Appendix B n.2). Galerius was already afflicted by a debilitating illness, probably bowel cancer, which rendered him incapable of commanding troops in the field, and he eventually died in April 311. Maximinus immediately seized Asia Minor, appealed to the inhabitants of its cities by canceling the unpopular requirement introduced by Galerius in 306 that landless city-dwellers be included on the census rolls, and prepared to invade Europe. Licinius responded by blocking any attempt to cross the Bosporus and by bribing his troops. He then met Maximinus on board a ship in the straits of Chalcedon and concluded a treaty of non-aggression with him.

By the spring of 312, therefore, Licinius was ready to recover Italy for the Roman Empire. But so too was Constantine, who had survived an attempted coup which might have cost him his life. In the spring of 310, the Franks near the mouth of the Rhine took up arms. Constantine marched north, leaving a large part of his army behind under the command of his father-in-law. Lactantius alleges that Maximian tricked his young, naive and inexperienced son-in-law into leaving more than one-half of his army behind so that he could supplant him as ruler in Britain, Gaul and Spain while he was being defeated at the mouth of the Rhine (*Mort. Pers.* 29.4–5). That is surely an *ex post facto* invention of Constantinian propaganda designed to blacken the character of Maximian. For in the spring of 310 Constantine must have suspected that Licinius would attempt to enter the Po Valley with an army in order to claim the Italian peninsula for himself. Hence it made sense for him to leave a significant number of troops in southern Gaul to meet this eventuality.

Whether or not Maximian had planned a coup in advance, he seized the opportunity provided by Constantine's absence to attempt to regain power. He suddenly assumed the imperial purple again, took control of the imperial treasury at Arles, distributed lavish donatives and spread a rumor that Constantine was dead. As soon as he learned what had happened, Constantine hurried south from the lower Rhine to Cabillunum (Châlons sur Marne), then transported his army by boat down the Saône and the Rhône to confront his father-in-law. The bulk of his troops returned to their old allegiance, and Maximian took refuge in Massilia. There are two significantly different versions of what happened next.

The orator who delivered the extant panegyric of Constantine in the emperor's presence a few weeks later, either in Trier or in Arles, faced a difficult task (*Pan. Lat.* 6[7], cf. Müller-Rettig 1990). He needed both to present Maximian's attempted coup in a light favorable to Constantine and to gloss over the fact that three years earlier Constantine had accepted promotion to the rank of Augustus from Maximian while marrying his daughter. Accordingly, he depicts the rebellious Maximian as a demented monster of ingratitude, who donned the purple a third time although he had twice been deposed and who finally killed himself rather than accept pardon from his ever-forgiving son-in-law, who had twice given him refuge. When Constantine pardoned the rebels after he took Massilia, Maximian committed suicide because he 'judged himself unworthy to live' (*Pan. Lat.* 6[7].20.3). According to the orator Constantine owed nothing whatever to Maximian. Moreover, he reveals something about Constantine which was hitherto unknown and not even suspected – it had in fact just been invented (Syme 1971: 204–205; 1983).[15] Although most might not know it, Constantine was related to a heroic emperor of the third century, for there flowed in his veins the blood of the deified emperor Claudius who had been the first to rescue the Roman Empire from the disasters of the third century (*Pan. Lat.* 6[7].2.1–2: *a primo igitur incipiam originis tuae numine, quod plerique fortasse nesciunt, sed qui te amant plurimum sciunt. Ab illo enim divo Claudio manat in te avita cognatio, qui Romani imperii solutam et perditam disciplinam primus reformavit*). Claudius, who died in 270 after reigning for only two years (though the orator is predictably silent about the brevity of his reign), had destroyed enormous Gothic forces which invaded through the Bosporus and south of the Danube on both land and sea. Constantine was destined to become a Roman emperor because of his descent from Claudius; alone of the three other Augusti with whom he jointly ruled the Roman Empire in 310, Constantine was born an emperor (*Pan. Lat.* 6[7].2.3, 5: *ab illo generis auctore in te imperii fortuna descendit. … inter omnes, inquam, participes maiestatis tuae hoc habes, Constantine, praecipuum, quod imperator es <natus>*). He was in fact the third emperor in his family after Claudius and his father Constantius. His father had died leaving Constantine as his heir; his father's army at once invested him with the imperial purple; and he showed himself worthy to be emperor by defeating barbarians, giving Gaul peace and security and mounting expeditions across the Rhine.

All other surviving sources, with one exception, similarly place Maximian's death immediately after he surrendered to Constantine (Moreau 1954: 375–376). The version of his death that was put out officially in 310 was that he killed himself (*Pan. Lat.* 6[7].20.3) and that is the version that Eusebius heard in Palestine a very few years later (*HE* 8.13.15, app. 3), although the majority of later writers state that he was executed (Victor, *Caes.* 40.22; Eutropius, *Brev.* 10.3; *Epitome* 40.15). Lactantius has a very different and much more complicated story, which bears the stigmata of a later propaganda invention (Moreau 1954: 376–378). Lactantius agrees with the orator of 310 and Eusebius that after his surrender at Massilia, Constantine stripped Maximian of the imperial purple which he had donned for the third time but spared his life. According to Lactantius, however, Maximian did not thereupon kill himself. Instead, he devised a plot to assassinate Constantine as he slept, presumably in the imperial palace at Arles (Lactantius, *Mort. Pers.* 30.1-5):

He summoned his daughter Fausta and urged her now with entreaties, now with cajolery to betray her husband and promised her another who would be worthier. He asked her to allow their bedroom to be left open and guarded rather carelessly. She promised to do this and immediately reported the matter to her husband. A scenario was set up so that the crime should be caught in the act. A worthless eunuch was substituted to die in place of the Augustus. Maximian rose at the dead of night and saw that everything was ready for his plot. There were few guards and those rather far away; he told them that he had had a dream which he wished to describe to his son. He entered the room armed, slaughtered the eunuch, rushed out exultantly and pro-claimed what he had done. Suddenly Constantine revealed himself in front of him with a band of armed men. The corpse of the murdered man was brought out of the bedroom. The murderer, caught red-handed, stood rooted to the spot and speechless as if he were 'a hard flint or block of Parian marble' (Virgil, *Aeneid* 6.471). He was rebuked for his disloyalty and crime. Finally he was given a free choice of how to die 'and he bound the noose of an unseemly death from a lofty beam' (*Aeneid* 12.603).

In both the original and Lactantius' versions of his death Maximian hangs himself. But Lactantius adds a failed and most improbable attempt at assassination between his surrender at Massilia and his suicide. Why? The answer is supplied by a change in Maxentius' attitude to his father. After his death he began to commemorate him as *divus Maximianus pater* (*RIC* 6.382, Rome: nos. 243, 244, 250, 251; 404, Ostia: nos. 24–26)[16] and he accused Constantine of killing him (Zosimus 2.14.11). In response, Constantine's propaganda started to paint Maximian in the blackest terms possible: hence the invention of the attempt at assassinating Constantine as he slept, which Lactantius doubtless heard constantly reiterated at the court of Trier in 311 and 312 – and which he innocently repeated in his *On the Deaths of the Persecutors* after he returned to Bithynia. Once Maxentius was dead, however, Constantine's propaganda machine instantly went into reverse: Maximian's widow confessed on oath and in public that Maxentius was not in fact her husband's son, but conceived in adultery with a Syrian (*Origo* 12, cf. *Epitome* 40.13), and Maximian himself was rehabilitated to such an extent that he became *divus Maximianus* within half a dozen years (Chapter 1).

THE VISION OF CONSTANTINE

Maximian's attempted usurpation was the historical context of 'the vision of Constantine,' whose date, nature and significance were first properly clarified by Peter Weiss in a classic paper which has transformed the long debate among scholars about the 'conversion of Constantine' by propounding a new and convincing solution to the apparent contradictions in the evidence which had troubled all historians of Constantine (Weiss 1993, 2003). Unfortunately, Weiss's paper met with a frosty reception when he delivered it in 1989 at a colloquium celebrating the eightieth birthday of Alfred Heuss, who during his lifetime enjoyed a high reputation among German historians of the ancient world, in large part because he successfully concealed his membership of the Nazi party, which he joined in 1937, apparently in order to obtain academic preferment.[17] The unreceptive honorand listened to Weiss in stony silence (Weiss 2003: 257), and made no mention whatever of Weiss's paper in the fifty pages which he was allowed to add to the essays honoring him (Heuss 1993: 171–221). Moreover, the historian who edited the volume in which papers from the colloquium were published in 1993 denounced Weiss's paper in print even before it appeared (Bleicken 1992: 27–29).

On its publication in 1993, Weiss's paper was greeted with general skepticism in Germany.[18] In 1998, when Klaus Girardet published a lengthy survey of modern discussions of 'die constantinische Wende' (whatever that slippery phrase is supposed to mean),[19] he mentioned Weiss's paper only in passing and declined to discuss it at all, as if it were irrelevant or of negligible importance (Girardet 1998a: 9–122 at 21 n.35 = 2006a: 51 n.35). Two years later a lengthy German monograph on dreams and visions under the Roman Empire, which promised a systematic and methodologically innovative approach, argued that it was irrelevant whether or not Constantine saw a vision in the sky or dreamed a dream (Weber 2000: 274–294, esp. 281–282), and in the following year an essay appeared in a German *Festschrift* with the uncompromising title 'The Visions of Constantine' (Barceló 2001). Such a dismissive attitude has now spread into academic cultures outside Germany. A French historian of ancient religion has recently rejected the astronomical basis of Weiss's theory (Turcan 2006: 153–156), while some Roman historians in North America have joined in a humming chorus of disbelief: an essay with the provocative title of 'The Many Conversions of the Emperor Constantine' fails to mention Weiss at all (Van Dam 2003), and another with the apparently more irenic title of 'Constantine's Dream' dismisses Weiss's arguments as 'a curious re-warming of an old-fashioned theory' (Harris 2005: 493). Yet the tide of scholarly opinion seems at last to be turning. Noel Lenski has accepted Weiss's theory as proven (Lenski 2006b: 67, 71) or at least as 'perhaps the best resolution to the problem' of the apparently divergent accounts (2008: 261). In a book of more than six hundred pages about Constantine and the Christian bishops published in 2000, Hal Drake contrived to discuss the emperor's 'Vision of the Cross' without any mention of Weiss (Drake 2000: 179–191, cf. xv, 172); he now accepts Weiss's central contention that there is 'no substantive difference' between 'the dream story in Lactantius and the vision story in Eusebius' (Drake 2009: 216).[20] And Stephenson, who still rests his main narrative upon acceptance of traditional and conventional views (2009: 129–131),[21] has pronounced Weiss's interpretation superior to competing interpretations in a bibliographical appendix (2009: 187–189, 339). Moreover, Girardet who in 1998 derided 'astronomical speculations' as no more than an amusing pastime (Girardet 1998a: 42 n.133 = 2006a: 76 n.133),[22] has now belatedly announced his conversion to Weiss's theory (2006b: 72–73), while Reinhart Staats has saluted Weiss as 'the elucidator of the vision of Constantine' (2008: 334).

Weiss did find some early champions. Stephen Mitchell accepted his theory as soon as he read it, as I did when Mitchell drew it to my attention. Mitchell pronounced the theory 'brilliant and convincing' (Mitchell 1999: 124 n.143), and in a review article concentrating on the brusque dismissal of ancient evidence by so many modern interpreters of Constantine, I explained why I found it totally compelling (Barnes 1998b: 287–289). The fundamental reason is that Weiss showed how the hypothesis that Constantine saw a solar halo in 310, to which he only later gave a Christian interpretation, explains all the early evidence in a way which no earlier hypothesis had ever done. For everyone, including the present writer (Barnes 1981: 43), had assumed that, whereas the panegyric of 310 described a pagan vision of that year, what Eusebius described, on the authority of Constantine himself, was another, Christian vision two years later, shortly before the Battle of the Milvian Bridge.[23] For obvious reasons, the notion that Constantine saw two very similar visions caused deep disquiet and suspicion, regardless of what their precise nature was taken to be. Weiss's hypothesis of a single vision which was later reinterpreted removes the need to try to explain either one of them away, as many scholars did, though they disagreed whether it was the pagan vision of 310 or the Christian vision of 312 which was the 'real' one. On the one hand, Henri Grégoire accepted the pagan vision as authentic and dismissed the alleged vision of 312 as a legend unknown to Lactantius and therefore invented much later than 316 (Grégoire 1930–31: 252–258; 1932: 135),[24] while on the other Hans Lietzmann, to whom I appealed in 1981, argued that the pagan vision was an invention of the orator of 310 (Lietzmann 1937: 266; Barnes 1981: 36).

Ancient evidence always deserves priority of esteem over modern preconceptions, but sometimes it needs to be interpreted in the light of modern insights or scientific theories. In this case, any serious analysis of the vision or visions of Constantine must start from Cassius Dio's precise description of the three stars which were seen in the sky in Rome in early April 193 (Dio 73[74].14.4) and draw upon the considerable scientific literature about the solar halo phenomenon (Weiss 2003: 240, 247). Astronomers with no stake at all in 'the Constantinian question' who have discussed his vision simply assume that Constantine saw a solar halo (Weiss 2003: 240–245).[25] By good fortune, Weiss had himself seen a solar halo in Würzburg some years before 1989 (Weiss 2003: 244) – though it is a measure of the extreme skepticism with which many scholars approach Constantine that in 1996 I heard an able German historian of the ancient world famous for his academic quarrels say that he did not believe that Weiss had seen any such thing. But there is no real justification for doubting Weiss's word that it was his personal experience which enabled him to realize that both the orator of 310 and Eusebius, who repeats what he heard from Constantine, report the same solar halo phenomenon, despite the apparent discrepancies in their two descriptions.

Although Eusebius was writing many years later, he specifically states that he is repeating what Constantine had told him, not necessarily in private (as has often been assumed), but rather in the company of many other bishops and most probably on the occasion of the Council of Nicaea, either informally during the banquet in the imperial place to which he invited the bishops or in his formal address to them as the Council was drawing to a close (Eusebius, *VC* 3.15, 21, cf. Barnes 1981: 266).[26] Moreover, Eusebius explicitly places the vision before Constantine became embroiled in war with Maxentius and before he decided to invade Italy in 312, events which he narrated later (*VC* 1.33–38). Eusebius reports that (Eusebius, *VC* 1.28):

> A most remarkable divine sign was revealed to the emperor, which it would perhaps not be easy to accept if anyone else had alleged it. However, since the victorious emperor himself reported it to the author of this narrative many years later, when we were honoured with knowing him and being in his presence, and confirmed his story

with oaths, who could hesitate to believe the account, especially when the following period provided testimony of the truth of the story? In the middle of the day, when the daylight was already beginning to fade (ἀμφὶ μεσημ βρινὰς ἡλίου ὥρας, ἤδη τῆς ἡμέρας ἀποκλινούσης), he said that he saw in the sky with his own eyes a cross-shaped trophy formed from light above the sun with a picture attached which proclaimed:[27] 'By this conquer' (γραφήν τε αὐτῷ συνῆφθαι λέγουσαν· τούτῳ νίκα). Amazement at the spectacle seized both him and the whole army which both was following him on a march somewhere and witnessed the marvellous sight.

This passage needs careful exegesis. The fundamental point from which discussion must begin is that what Constantine described to Eusebius was a cross of light which he saw in the sky together with several thousand soldiers under his command: it was not something which the emperor saw alone in private, which he dreamed or which he imagined.[28] However, the passage contains a worrying contradiction which is evaded by Averil Cameron and Stuart Hall, who translate the two temporal phrases as 'about the time of the midday sun, when the day was just turning' and in their commentary state that 'Constantine sees his vision in the middle of the day' (1999: 81, 206). But the two phrases formally contradict each other: the first (ἀμφὶ μεσημβρινὰς ἡλίου ὥρας) means literally 'around the midday hours' and implies that Constantine and his army saw the celestial phenomenon close to the noon hour (LSJ[9] 1105–1106), while the second (ἤδη τῆς ἡμέρας ἀποκλινούσης), which in Greek authors from Herodotus onwards literally means 'as the day was declining <towards evening>' (LSJ[9] 203, s. v. ἀποκλίνω), implies that the celestial phenomenon occurred in the late afternoon. Which of the two temporal indications is correct, and why do the two contradictory indications stand in juxtaposition? The possibility that one is a later interpolation can be excluded. Both are repeated in the same juxtaposition in the ecclesiastical historians who copy the passage from Eusebius (Socrates, HE 1.2.35; Sozomenus, HE 1.3.2).[29] But they could be author's variants, since the man who edited the Life of Constantine has left substantial doublets elsewhere in a text which Eusebius left unfinished when he died (Barnes 1989b; 1994b). Perhaps Eusebius was uncertain exactly what he had heard from Constantine's lips. Alternatively, the contradiction can be palliated or even removed if it be supposed that Eusebius is trying to say that the celestial phenomenon occurred in full daylight, but somewhat later than noon (say, around two or three in the afternoon). This appears to be the view taken by Weiss, whose German translation Anthony Birley renders as 'about the time of the noonday sun, when the day was already beginning to wane' (Weiss 2003: 246).[30]

What happened next? Eusebius slides over the interval of two years between the vision in the sky and Constantine's interpretation of it as a sign from the God of the Christians. He continues (VC 1.29):

He was, he said, wondering to himself what the manifestation might mean; then, while he meditated, and thought long and hard, night overtook him. Thereupon, as he slept, the Christ of God appeared to him with the sign which had appeared in the sky, and urged him to make a copy of the sign which had appeared in the sky, and to use this as protection against the attacks of the enemy.

When he awoke, Constantine did as he was bidden, summoned goldsmiths and jewelers, described what he had seen and instructed them to produce a copy of it (*VC* 1.30).This became the emperor's personal standard, Eusebius saw it many years later and describes it, carefully marking the anachronism in his narrative (*VC* 1.30–31). The new imperial banner was called the *labarum* and the name is first attested in the chapter heading which the editor of the *Life of Constantine* added very shortly after Eusebius' death (heading to *VC* 1.31: 'Description of the cross-shaped sign which the Romans now call *labarum*').[31] The name is highly significant because it is of Celtic origin and therefore must have been bestowed on it by Constantine's army before the Battle of the Milvian Bridge since this army contained large numbers of Gauls and Germans (Barnes 1981: 43, 306 n.150).

The Gallic orator of 310 gives a rhetorical elaboration of what is recognizably the same celestial phenomenon as that described by Eusebius, though his allusive and figurative language long disguised the fact (*Pan. Lat.* 6[7].21.3–7):

> Fortune herself so ordered this matter (sc. the return of quiet to the frontier) that the success of your affairs prompted you to carry out what you had vowed to the immortal gods at the very spot where you had turned aside toward the most beautiful temple in the whole world, or rather, as you saw, to a god who revealed himself. For you saw, I believe, Constantine, your Apollo accompanied by Victory offering you laurel wreaths, each one of which conveys a portent of thirty years. For this is the number of human ages which are owed to *you*, an old age greater than Nestor's. And – why do I say 'I believe'? – you *saw*, and recognized yourself in the likeness of the one to whom the divine songs of bards had prophesied that dominion over the whole world was due.

Before Weiss it was always assumed that the orator describes a vision which Constantine saw inside the temple to which the speech refers (e.g., Rodgers 1980: 259–261), which would exclude identifying it with the vision in the sky which Eusebius describes. But the orator does not locate the vision in a temple: he locates it at the spot where Constantine turned aside to visit the temple and to which he returned to continue his journey south. In other words, it was the epiphany of the god while his army was on the march that persuaded Constantine to turn aside to the god's temple (Weiss 2003: 247).There may still be room for doubt on the exact meaning of the orator's words: for example, whereas Weiss construes 'the striking *omina tricena* on each crown' as 'the three concentrations of light on each halo-ring' in the sky, I am inclined to include the sun itself among the laurels which Apollo displays to Constantine, so that the sun together with the three other points of light seen in the solar halos portend that Constantine will live four times thirty years, one hundred and twenty years being the canonical extreme limit of a human life in the ancient world (Gudeman 1914: 59–60).

The identity and location of the temple which Constantine visited in 310 are not in doubt. Camille Jullian identified the 'most beautiful temple in the world' as the shrine of Apollo Grannus at Grand in the Vosges, on the border of the Roman provinces of Belgica and Germania Superior (Jullian 1926: 107 n.2) and his identification has only been strengthened by subsequent archeological discoveries at the site (Müller-Rettig 1990: 339–350; Woolf 2003: 139–142). Exegetes differ, however, on the identity of the figure in whom Constantine is said to have recognized himself. The traditional view has been that it is the god Apollo (Barnes 1981: 36; Müller-Rettig 1990: 280–286). But the orator states that Constantine recognized himself in the appearance of 'the man to whom the divine songs of poets proclaimed that rule over the whole world was owed' (21.5: *in illius specie recognovisti cui totius mundi regna deberi vatum divina carmina cecinerunt*). That can hardly be anyone other than the future world ruler prophesied in Virgil's *Aeneid*, who (it was foretold) was aided by Apollo at the Battle of Actium and ruled the whole world (8.705–706; 1.286–291; 6.791–805, cf. Syme 1971: 204; Rodgers 1980: 267–272).

The third writer contemporary with Constantine who alludes to the vision of Constantine is Lactantius. It has normally been assumed that Lactantius says nothing at all about a vision in the sky, but speaks only of a dream which Constantine had the night before the Battle of the Milvian Bridge (*Mort. Pers.* 44.5–6):

> commonitus est in quiete, ut caeleste signum dei notaret in scutis atque ita proelium committeret. fecit ut iussus est et transversa X littera, summo capite circumflexo, Christum in scutis notat.

> Constantine was advised in a dream to mark the *caeleste signum dei* on the shields <of his soldiers> and thus to join battle. He did as he had been ordered and by means of a rotated letter X with its top bent over he marked Christ on their shields.

I have deliberately left the crucial phrase *caeleste signum dei* untranslated. For everyone before Weiss, including the present writer (Barnes 1981: 43), assumed that the words meant 'the heavenly sign of God' and referred to the sign or symbol which Lactantius seems to imply that Constantine saw in a dream. Scholarly discussion focused rather on the question precisely what the sign or symbol put on the shields was. The text transmitted in the sole manuscript of *On the Deaths of the Persecutors* describes a rotated Greek chi with its vertical bent slightly at the top to indicate a rho. On the other hand, it has been proposed to add the letter *I* either before the word *transversa* or after the word *littera* (Sulzberger 1925: 406–408, reporting and developing a suggestion of Grégoire): this makes Lactantius speak of an iota with its top bent over to form a rho superimposed on an X and allows the hypothesis that in 310 Constantine placed a traditional six-pointed symbol of the sun on his soldiers' shields, which he transformed into a Christian symbol in 312 by bending the top of the vertical slightly so that it could be read as a Chi-Rho Christogram (Weiss 2003: 253–255). But that is a minor matter. More important, Weiss argues that Lactantius means 'the sign of God <seen> in the sky' and thus alludes to the celestial phenomenon which Constantine and his army had seen in Gaul (Weiss 2003: 246). If this is correct, then there is no contradiction between Eusebius, the panegyric of 310 and Lactantius: in 310 Constantine and his army saw a solar halo while on the march, which the emperor interpreted as an indication that the sun-god Apollo had revealed himself as his personal protector; in 312 he declared that he had come to the conclusion that the god who had revealed himself was not Apollo, but the God of the Christians.

The consequences of Weiss's analysis are momentous. It explains Constantine's conviction that divine support underlay his successes in war. At a critical time, when he was marching in haste to squash a coup by his father-in-law, which threatened to end his imperial career and even his life, he and his army saw a solar halo which they interpreted as a sure sign of victory under the protection of the sun-god Apollo. Subsequently, either in 311 or 312 (Girardet 2007b: 32–42), Constantine became convinced that his divine protector was not Apollo, but the God of the Christians. Significantly, the emperor's account of the celestial vision and its conse-quences implies that he was already in the habit of conversing with Christian bish-ops in his entourage at court, whom Werner Eck has convincingly identified as Maternus of Cologne, Reticius of Autun and Marinus of Arles (Staats 2008: 365–368, cf. Eck 2007: 76–91).

THE INVASION OF ITALY

The internal psychological process which led to the 'conversion' of Constantine and his public embrace of the Christian religion is not important to the historian because it is undiscoverable – and perhaps was unclear even to Constantine himself. What is important for both history and the historian is that Constantine declared himself a Christian before the Battle of the Milvian Bridge on 28 October 312 when he defeated Maxentius and thus became master of Italy, Africa and the west-ern Mediterranean islands in addition to Britain, Gaul and Spain. But the battle itself has often been misunderstood, partly because historians have trusted Lactantius when he claims not only that Maxentius had the larger army, but also that

> fighting took place and the forces of Maxentius held the advantage until Constantine later, having strengthened his resolve and ready for either outcome (sc. victory or the grave) moved all his forces close to Rome and encamped in the vicinity of the Milvian Bridge. The anniversary was at hand of the day on which Maxentius had taken power, that is, the sixth day before the kalends of November and his *quinquennalia* were com-ing to an end

when Constantine had the dream in which he was instructed to put the *caeleste signum dei* on the shields of his soldiers (*Mort. Pers.* 44.3–4). Hence Norman Baynes, who believed that the rise and triumph of Constantine constituted 'an erratic block which has diverted the stream of history,' presented the Battle of the Milvian Bridge as a fight against fearful odds in which Constantine was heavily outnumbered (Baynes 1931: 3, 8–9). That is totally to mistake the real political and military context of the last battle in a war whose outcome had already been decided (Barnes 1985b: 375–378). Constantine invaded Italy in the spring of 312 in order to forestall Licinius, who was now, after repulsing Maximinus' attempt to seize Byzantium and part of Europe in addition to Asia Minor in the previous year, finally ready to take possession of the territories over which he had been appointed to rule at the Conference of Carnuntum in November 308. To meet this expected invasion from the East, Maxentius' main army was not guarding the Alpine passes in order to repulse an invasion from Gaul: it was stationed far to the east, probably in the vicinity of Aquileia, in order to ward off an invasion of Italy from Pannonia, that is, an invasion under the command of Licinius.[32]

Constantine therefore assembled an expeditionary force of probably 35,000–40,000 and crossed the Alps before Licinius could join battle with Maxentius. In the spring of 312, to use the vivid metaphor of a recent writer, Constantine 'assembled a crack force and vaulted over the Alps' (Lenski 2006c: 69)[33] in order to invade North Italy from the West. The heavily fortified town of Segusio (*Barrington Atlas*, Map 17 I3) shut its gates against Constantine, but it was swiftly stormed, though not sacked or plundered. As the ruler of Gaul next descended into the western part of the Po Valley, he was confronted by a force including heavy mailed cavalry, which he routed. The city of Turin then opened its gates to him, other cities of North Italy sent him embassies of congratulation and he was warmly welcomed in Milan, where he halted for some days (*Pan. Lat.* 12[9].6–7; 4[10].17.3, 21–24). Maxentius had already realized that his only hope of prevailing in what was now a war on two fronts was to defeat Constantine before confronting Licinius, whose army could perhaps be delayed in the mountain passes of the Julian Alps. When Constantine left Milan, the main army of Maxentius was stationed east of Verona, which Maxentius' praetorian prefect Ruricius Pompeianus had entered and garrisoned. The city's situation next to the fast-flowing and rocky River Adige protected it from direct attack and ensured access to fresh supplies. Constantine advanced and defeated a force of Maxentian cavalry near Brixia, then crossed the Adige upstream from Verona and invested the city. After several unsuccessful attempts to break out, Pompeianus escaped the siege and returned with the greater part of his army. Constantine, who, among his many other qualities, was a most capable military commander, decided not to lift the siege of Verona, but divided his forces. The battle against Maxentius' army was desperate and bloody, but decisive. Pompeianus was killed and his army surrendered. Aquileia came over, Verona capitulated and Constantine was the undisputed master of North Italy.

The war was won, and Licinius would never possess Italy – unless he first dispossessed Constantine. All that remained for the victor was to advance slowly southwards and wait for resistance to crumble. The military situation after the Battle of Verona was virtually identical with the military situation in the autumn of 69

immediately after the second Battle of Bedriacum. But the sequel to the north
Italian campaign of 312 was very different. In 69 Antonius Primus had seized control of the Flavian forces in Pannonia and invaded Italy in haste, but failed to prevent his victorious troops from sacking and pillaging Cremona before marching on
Rome. In 312 Constantine had neither reason nor motive for haste, and he did not
reach the vicinity of Rome until six months or more after he had crossed the Alps.
The Battle of the Milvian Bridge in 312 thus resembles the Battle of Actium in
31 BC in two fundamental respects. First, the result of both battles was a foregone
conclusion: Constantine could no more have been defeated by Maxentius than
Caesar's heir and his able lieutenant Agrippa could have been defeated by Marcus
Antonius and Cleopatra. Second, since each of the two battles provided a foundation myth for the victor's reordering of Roman society, culture and ideology, both
Augustus (as he was from January 27 BC) and Constantine claimed that they had
won famous victories whose true nature they misrepresented. Augustus himself and
the Augustan poets tendentiously depicted the campaign of Actium as a war waged
by a united Italy against an Egyptian queen and her Oriental allies with her rene-
gade Roman lover in tow (Syme 1939: 297, 335; Gurval 1995: 19–85, 137–278).
Constantine coolly denied that his defeated adversary was the son of Maximian and
compelled Maximian's widow (who was also his own mother-in-law) to swear on
oath and in public that she had conceived Maxentius in adultery with a Syrian
(*Origo* 12). Constantine then set about transforming Maxentius, who had granted
the Christians of Italy and Africa toleration shortly after he came to power, into a
persecutor. By a masterstroke of propaganda, he combined the traditional meaning
of the Latin noun *tyrannus* as denoting an oppressive ruler, the Christian use of the
word to describe rulers who persecuted God's people and a newly invented meaning which used the word *tyrannus* to designate an illegitimate emperor (Grünewald
1990:64–71; Barnes 1996a): Maxentius was a *tyrannus* because he had never been
recognized empire-wide as a member of the imperial college; he was also a *tyrannus*
because he both oppressed his subjects and persecuted the Christians. Specific cases
were alleged and Maxentius was turned into the textbook tyrant whom the Gallic
panegyrist of 313 systematically traduces (*Pan. Lat.* 12[9], cf. Ziegler 1970: 24, 32,
39–52). More serious, over the course of time Maxentius became as rabid a persecutor as Diocletian, Galerius or Maximinus – the bloodthirsty enemy of God who
appears in so much fictitious hagiography and in the religious art of the Middle
Ages and the Renaissance.

The actual battle at the Milvian Bridge was brief. Maxentius had cut the bridges
over the Tiber intending to withstand a siege of Rome, as he had against Galerius
five years earlier. But by 312 he had lost his political support within the city: there
were riots in which the crowd proclaimed Constantine invincible. Maxentius was
therefore compelled to fight. He justified his change of policy by producing a
Sibylline oracle foretelling that the enemy of the Romans was fated to die. He sent
his wife and son out of his palace to a private house, he buried his imperial regalia
on the Palatine (Panella 2008: 86–91, 611–613), he constructed a temporary bridge

of boats across the Tiber and confronted Constantine. His troops buckled at the first charge and fled back over the temporary bridge, which collapsed under their weight. Maxentius himself descended into the Tiber with his heavy armor and drowned. His body was recovered, mutilated and decapitated; his head was then paraded through the streets of Rome before being sent to Carthage to prove to Maxentius' African subjects that he was dead (*Origo* 12; *Pan. Lat.* 4[10].32.6–7).

CONSTANTINE IN ROME AND CHRISTMAS 312

On the day after the battle Constantine entered Rome in triumph, though he neither celebrated a formal triumph nor ascended the Capitol in order to render thanks to Jupiter Feretrius. This was not primarily because Constantine now regarded and disported himself as a Christian, as has sometimes been argued (Straub 1955, cf. Paschoud 1993), but out of political tact and necessity. Roman emperors did not celebrate triumphs over foes in a civil war: in August 29 BC the victor of Actium held triumphs on three successive days which officially commemorated his victories over the Dalmatae, the defeat of Cleopatra and the conquest of Egypt (*Inscriptiones Italiae* 13.1 [Rome, 1947], 570), and a century later Vespasian and Titus triumphed *de Iudaeis*, making no mention of the defeat of Vitellius and his partisans (Barnes 2005a: 129–131). Constantine had visited Rome in 303 for the joint celebration of the *vicennalia* of the Augusti Diocletian and Maximian, the *decennalia* of the Caesars Constantius and Galerius and the triumph of all four over the Persians. On that occasion he was greeted as an emperor in waiting. Now, nine years later, he entered Rome as the victor in a civil war. Hence, while he needed the political support of the Roman Senate, senators needed to make peace with their new master, especially those who had exerted themselves in the service of Maxentius. It was thus in the interest of both to forget what had happened in Rome and Italy over the past six years and to cooperate in the future for their mutual advantage.

The Senate at once gave Constantine what he most needed: they decreed that he was the senior of the three reigning emperors (Lactantius, *Mort. Pers.* 44.11: *primi nominis titulum decrevit*), thus bestowing on him the sole right of appointing new emperors. Constantine reciprocated by blaming all the evils of the regime which he had overthrown on a few henchmen of Maxentius, and, although he invalidated all of Maxentius' appointments, he carefully preserved the status of several men who had held high office under Maxentius by reappointing them. He retained Annius Anullinus, whom Maxentius had appointed *praefectus urbi* on the day before the Battle of the Milvian Bridge, in office for another thirteen months; his next *praefectus urbi*, Aradius Rufinus, had been Anullinus' predecessor; and C. Ceionius Rufius Volusianus, who had been praetorian prefect, *praefectus urbi* and ordinary consul under Maxentius in 311, was *praefectus urbi* again and held an ordinary consul in 314 during his tenure (Barnes 1982: 100, 111). More generally Constantine reintegrated senators into the imperial administration. Whereas the emperors of the third century from Septimius Severus onwards had preferred equestrians, that is, non-senators, in important posts, Constantine abolished the distinction between senators and *equites* and thus allowed the landed aristocracy of Italy and the West to aspire again to high office and political power.

While he was in Rome in November and December 312 Constantine began to grant privileges and subsidies to the Christian church and to Christian clergy; indeed, before he left Rome, Constantine had already set in motion a religious transformation of the Roman world. In the newly conquered territories of Italy and Africa Constantine was of course committed to an overall policy of religious toleration such as he had practiced in Britain, Gaul and Spain since his accession to power. But religious toleration is perfectly compatible with the granting of special privileges to the practitioners of a particular form of religion, and in the winter of 312/313 Constantine began to grant fiscal privileges to Christian clergy and to raise the status of the Christian church within Roman society (Barnes 1981: 49–52, 56–57).

It was also almost certainly in November or December 312 that Constantine exchanged letters with the Roman senator and poet Publilius Optatianus Porfyrius. The pair of letters, which are preserved in the manuscripts of Porfyrius' poems, reveal that Constantine, so far from being an emperor without intellectual attainments or interests, presented himself as a patron of literature in the mold of Augustus (Barnes 1975c: 185; 1982: 71; Green 2010: 65–71).[34] Porfyrius' letter, which accompanied a poem which he presented to the new ruler of Rome, emphasized Constantine's status as *maximus*, a title which the Senate had recently granted him and it predictably contrasted the smallness and poverty of the poet's talent with the eternal felicity of the emperor who has inspired him. Porfyrius presents Constantine as an emperor who not only wins battles and issues salutary legislation, but also has a keen interest in literature: he applauds the Muses who are his constant companions, so that 'among so many insignia of divine majesty' the splendor of his enthusiasm for literary endeavors shines forth. In reply, the emperor complimented the poet, whom he addressed as his 'dearest brother,' on his originality and technical skill, praised different genres of poetry, and declared that literature was important to him: he assured Porfyrius that in the age of Constantine (he uses the conventional phrase *saeculo meo*) a favorable reception like a gentle breeze awaited orators, poets and authors in general, that literary achievements would not be denied the imperial approval which they deserved. Suetonius reports that the emperor Augustus 'encouraged the literary talents of his period (*ingenia saeculi sui*) in every way' and that he 'listened kindly and patiently to recitations, not only poems and histories, but also speeches and dialogues' (*Div. Aug.* 89.3). Constantine himself presumably intended to evoke comparison with Augustus. Later in the fourth century the Roman Senate greeted emperors with the salutation 'More successful than Augustus, more upright than Trajan' (Eutropius, *Brev.* 8.5.3) – the two imperial models whom Constantine invoked and imitated.

Constantine's presence in Rome during the winter of 312/313 is last certified on 6 January 313 (*CTh* 15.4.3[Seeck]). He therefore took care to remain in the city until the day (now known as Epiphany) on which Christians of the early fourth century normally celebrated the birth of Christ in Bethlehem. By the end of Constantine's reign, however, the Christians of Rome had begun to date the Nativity of Christ to 25 December (*Chr. Min.* 1.71: *kal(endis) Ian(uariis) natus Christus in Betleem Iudeae*), which was the *natalis Invicti*, the birthday of the Unconquered Sun (Usener 1911: 376–378). Is it rash to suggest that it was Constantine who introduced this synchronism in 312, thereby in some way equating the traditional pagan god with his new Christian God?

CONSTANTINIAN CHURCHES IN ROME

It is in this context that it will be most appropriate to discuss both those churches in the city of Rome that Constantine founded or endowed (or both) and those with which his name has been erroneously associated. For recent researches have demonstrated that, whereas Constantine founded the church of Saint John Lateran while he was in Rome in 312, probably on 11 November, he did not found either Saint Peter's on the Vatican or Saint Paul's outside the Walls either in 312 or later.[35]

The *Liber Pontificalis*, as Louis Duchesne showed in the introduction to his classic edition, was first compiled in the sixth century, but incorporates in its entries for Silvester, who was bishop of Rome from 31 January 314 to 31 December 335 (*LP* 34.9–33) and Mark, who briefly succeeded him for a few months from 18 January to 7 October 336 (*LP* 35.3–4), a much earlier document that preserves a list of endowments of churches in Rome and other Italian cities in the reign of Constantine (Duchesne 1886: lvii–lxvii, cxli–cliv). This document lists as founded by or under Constantine the following churches in the following order (pp. 172–187, 202 Duchesne):

1	the Basilica Constantiniana, i.e., the Lateran, with its baptistery;
2	Saint Peter on the Vatican;
3	Saint Paul on the Via Ostiensis;
4	the Basilica Sessoriana, i.e., Santa Croce in Gerusalemme;
5	Saint Agnes with its baptistery;
6	Saint Laurence;
7	Saints Peter and Marcellinus with the mausoleum of Helena;
8	Saints Peter, Paul and John at Ostia;
9	Saint John the Baptist at Albanum;
10	Basilica of the Apostles at Capua;
11	the basilica at Naples with an aqueduct and forum;
12	the *Titulus Equitii*;[36]
13 and 14	under Marcus (336), a basilica on the Via Ardeatina where Marcus was buried and another *iuxta Pallacinis*, on the site of the present San Marco on the Piazza Venezia (Cecchelli 1992: 299–303).

Duchesne produced a convincing demonstration of the reliability of the information which the *Liber Pontificalis* provides about the endowments for these churches (1886: 188–201, 203–204), and Edward Champlin has added an additional proof on the basis of prosopographical arguments (Champlin 1982). After listing benefactions to the Church of Saints Peter, Paul and John the Baptist at Ostia which it attributes to Constantine, the *Liber Pontificalis* adds that one Gallicanus donated three items of silver plate and four landed estates which together produced an annual income of 869 solidi (*LP* 34.29, p. 18.14–22 Duchesne). Champlin showed that all four estates lay in areas where Ovinius Gallicanus, who was curator of Teanum Sidicinum in the closing years of the third century (*CIL* 10.4785), *praefectus urbi* in 316–317 and ordinary consul in 317 (*PLRE* 1.383, Gallicanus), owned property.[37] Another mark of the high quality of the information in the list of endowments which the *Liber Pontificalis* incorporates is that the landed property given to provide income for St Peter's not only consists entirely of property in the East, but also includes one property which can hardly have been donated to St Peter's in Rome until Constantine had been dead for almost thirty years. This is the *domus Datiani* in Antioch, which yielded an annual income of 240 solidi (*LP* 34.19–20, p. 177.6–p. 178.11 Duchesne). The only historical Datianus in the fourth century who was rich and famous was Datianus, the principal adviser of Constantius, who made him consul in 358 and bestowed on him the even higher honor of the title *patricius* before 18 January 360 (*CTh* 11.1.1; Philostorgius, *HE* 8.8, cf. *PLRE* 1.243–244, Datianus 1). Datianus is known to have been a Christian (Libanius, *Ep.* 81.5; Epiphanius, *Panarion* 71.1.5–8, cf. Barnes 1989a: 313–315; 1993a: 91, 109); he owned an estate in Antioch, where he built baths, villas and gardens (Libanius, *Epp.* 114, 435, 441, 1184) – and he was still alive in 365 (Libanius, *Ep.* 1488). Datianus presumably decided to bequeath his villa in Antioch to the Church of Rome after visiting the city in the company of Constantius in 357.

Two recent writers have departed from the venerable tradition of giving primacy of place to the *Liber Pontificalis* and its list of Constantinian endowments. Ross Holloway adopts a thematic approach under the chapter title 'Basilicas, Baptistry, and Burial' (2004: 57–119), and, like Holloway, Alastair Logan accords primacy to the testimony of archaeology and epigraphy (2010). Logan's more systematic and incisive analysis of the evidence for the date and original construction of the Roman churches traditionally associated with Constantine proceeds in chronological order as follows:

1   Saint John Lateran (*LP* 34.9–15) was built on the site of the demolished barracks of the *equites singulares*, the mounted imperial guard which Constantine disbanded after the defeat of Maxentius (Victor, *Caes.* 40.25, cf. Speidel 1994: 152–157). Constantine probably donated the site before the end of 312, and he constructed a large basilica with five aisles and an apse to be the seat of the bishop of Rome (Holloway 2004: 57–61).

2   The second Roman basilica that Constantine constructed (*LP* 34.26–27) was probably the U-shaped ambulatory basilica built on the imperial property

ad duas lauros by the side of the Via Labicana: it was dedicated to the Saints Marcellinus and Peter, two humble Roman martyrs of the 'Great Persecution' (a deacon and an exorcist), and it had subterranean catacombs attached which were expanded in the Constantinian period (Holloway 2004: 86–93, cf. Guyon 1987: 74–25). The siting of this church had a particular symbolic value: it was built over the cemetery of the *equites singulares*, which Constantine ordered to be desecrated and its many magnificent carved and inscribed marble headstones to be used in its construction (Guyon 1987: 30–33, 237–238; Speidel 1994: 114, 157, cf. 1984: 1–3).

3   The third basilica constructed by Constantine appears to be that dedicated to Saint Laurence, a deacon of the Roman church who was martyred on 10 August 258 (S. Lorenzo fuori le mura) on the Via Tiburtina close to the shrine of the saint (*LP* 34.24–25). This church too was a U-shaped basilica, but larger and more ornate than that of Saints Marcellinus and Peter (Holloway 2004: 110–111).

4   The basilica of Santa Croce in Gerusalemme (*LP* 34.22) lay within the Sessorian Palace which Constantine's mother owned and where she lived, apparently from the winter of 312/313 until her pilgrimage to the Holy Land in 326 (Chapter 2). The *Liber Pontificalis* reports that Constantine placed in it some fragments of the True Cross, which may well have been found during Helena's visit to Jerusalem (though not by her), and dedicated the building under the name 'Jerusalem' (*LP* 34.22, p. 179.12 Duchesne). The golden cross engraved with a dedication by Constantine and Helena which refers to a royal house surrounded by a hall may originally have been in this church, although the *Liber Pontificalis* reports that the emperor gave it to Saint Peter's, where it was later located (*LP* 34.17, p. 176.8–9 Duchesne, cf. Bowersock 2005: 10).

5   Another of Constantine's Roman basilicas (though omitted from the *Liber Pontificalis*) was the Basilica Apostolorum at the site *ad Catacumbas* on the Appian Way which had been a cult center of the apostles Peter and Paul since 29 June 258 (Barnes 2010a: 27–31). An inscription attests that it was begun by Constantine and completed by his son Constans (*ICUR* 2 [1888], 248 no. 17 = *ICUR*, N. S. 1 [1922], no. 3900, cf. Marucchi 1921).[38] After Constantine's death the cults of the apostles were transferred to the Vatican and the Via Ostiensis respectively and the church became the basilica of San Sebastiano (Holloway 2004: 105–109, 146–155, cf. Nieddu 2009).

6   The *Liber Pontificalis* records grants of church plate, lamps and land by Constantine to a *titulus* constructed by Silvester, bishop of Rome from 314 to 336 near the baths of Domitian (p. 181.1–17 Duchesne) and to two basilicas built by Silvester's short-lived successor Mark. One of these was a U-shaped cemeterial basilica on the Via Ardeatina where Mark himself appears to have been buried (Fiocchi Nicolai 1995–1996), while the other, which was in Rome near the Pallicinae (*LP* 35.2, p. 202.4–5 Duchesne), has been identified as San Marco al Corso (Krautheimer 1959: 216–247; Cechelli 1992).

7   Although the *Liber Pontificalis* attributes to Constantine the construction of
           Sant'Agnese fuori le Mura, another U-shaped cemeterial basilica beside the
           Via Nomentana (*LP* 34.23), the church seems to have been entirely the
           work of his daughter Constantina, who lived in Rome in the 340s
           (Krautheimer 1937: 14–39).

8

and 9   Although the *Liber Pontificalis* attributes both Saint Peter's (San Pietro in
           Vaticano) and Saint Paul's on the Via Ostiensis (San Paolo fuori le Mura) to
           Constantine (*LP* 34.16–21), it is certain that neither church was completed
           before the emperor's death. Glen Bowersock's critical examination of the
           evidence demolished the notion that Constantine played any part in the
           construction of Saint Peter's several years ago (Bowersock 2005). Even if the
           leveling of the side of the Vatican Hill in order to provide a platform for con-
           struction (which must have taken a long time and cost an enormous sum)
           had begun in Constantine's lifetime, the supply of funds involved no special
           grant for or special interest in Saint Peter's on the part of the emperor, since
           his stated policy from at least 324 onwards was to provide unlimited funds
           from the imperial treasury for building churches to any bishop who requested
           them (Eusebius, *VC* 2.45.2–46.4, cf. Chapter 6).

To Bowersock's proof, Logan has added a decisive piece of evidence to which
attention was drawn in 1953 in a Danish publication and again in 1969, though in
a book whose author failed to appreciate its true significance (Torp 1953: 61;
O'Connor 1969: 135), but which has been generally, perhaps even universally, overlooked even by the most critical (no mention for example, in Barnes 1970). In his
Ecclesiastical History, which he completed in or shortly after the year 439, Socrates
celebrated the early practitioners of monasticism in Egypt (*HE* 4.23). They included
the monk Ammonius (*HE* 4.23.72–74):

> There was also another remarkable man among the monks, whose name was
> Ammonius. This man was so lacking in curiosity that, when he was in Rome with
> Athanasius, he chose to visit none of the sights of the city, but only to see the martyr-
> shrine of Peter and Paul. This Ammonius, when he was being physically coerced into
> becoming a bishop and trying to escape, struck out his right eye in order to avoid
> consecration because of his bodily deformity.

If Ammonius was in Rome with Athanasius, he cannot have visited the city before
the spring of 339, when the bishop of Alexandria fled to Rome in order to avoid
arrest (Barnes 1993a: 45–50). In 339, therefore, there was a single *martyrium* at
which both Peter and Paul were commemorated together. This can only have been
the Basilica Apostolorum on the Appian Way, 'the one important site in Rome of
early Christian times which is known to have been connected with both Peter and
Paul' (Torp 1953: 61). It follows that in 339, two years after the death of Constantine,

the joint cult of the apostles established *ad catcumbas* in 258 had not yet been transferred back to the separate locations of Saint Peter's basilica on the Vatican and the Church of Saint Paul outside the Walls.

APPENDIX: THE STATUS OF CONSTANTINE 306–311

Since some recent writers about Constantine (e.g., Drake 2000: 186; Van Dam 2007: 36, 125; Humphries 2008) seem to have difficulty in understanding the simple fact that Constantine's view of his standing within the imperial college differed from that taken by Galerius for much of the period between his proclamation as Augustus in York on 25 July 306 and Galerius' acceptance of him as an Augustus in 310, it may assist readers in understanding the narrative of this chapter if I tabulate the official views of both emperors. The first column (A) lists the imperial rank which Constantine claimed at different dates between 25 July 306 and Galerius' death in April 311, while column (B) lists Galerius' official view of his junior colleague's status, which differed from Constantine's for much of the period between 25 July 306 and April 311.

	(A)	*(B)*
From 25 July to Constantine's appointment as Caesar by Galerius, probably in September 306	Augustus	Private citizen
Between Galerius' appointment of Constantine as Caesar and his receipt of the formal letter of appointment	Augustus	Caesar
From Constantine's receipt of his appointment as Caesar by Galerius to c. September 307	Caesar	Caesar
From c. September 307 to the Conference of Carnuntum (11 November 308)	Augustus	Not recognized as a member of the imperial college at all
From 11 November 308 to early 309	Augustus	Caesar
From early 309 to mid-310	Augustus	*filius Augustorum*
From mid-310 onwards	Augustus	Augustus

5

BROTHERS-IN-LAW

The weeks which Constantine spent in Rome between his triumphal entry on 29 October 312 and his departure in January 313 were extremely rewarding on the political front. Not only did he secure the future loyalty of the Roman Senate, but the Senate voted him the same status, rights and privileges as his father enjoyed (albeit for less than fifteen months) as the senior Augustus in the imperial college. Lactantius reports the bare fact that the Senate decreed that Constantine was the senior emperor immediately after his entry into Rome (*Mort. Pers.* 44.11). The arguments by which this significant declaration was justified in the Senate are easy to infer: Constantine was held to be senior to Licinius and Maximinus because he had been proclaimed Augustus on 25 July 306, whereas they received that rank only much later (on 8 November 308 and early in 310 respectively). As the senior Augustus in what was now an imperial college of three Augusti, Constantine wrote at once to Maximinus in his own name and that of Licinius ordering him to desist from persecuting the Christians of the East (Lactantius, *Mort. Pers.* 44.11; Eusebius, *HE* 9.9.12, cf. Barnes 1982: 67–68).[1] Maximinus did not heed the warning, so that Constantine became committed to removing the last of the persecutors from power for political as well as for religious reasons.

CONSTANTINE AND LICINIUS IN MILAN

Constantine and Licinius met in Milan in February 313. A chance remark from an ancient veterinary writer on the maladies of horses fixes the exact date with some precision: Theomnestus reported that he left Sirmium with an emperor at the beginning of February to travel posthaste to Milan (*Hippiatrica Berolinensia* 34.12). Although Theomnestus did not name the emperor or specify the year, the emperor

Constantine: Dynasty, Religion and Power in the Later Roman Empire, First Edition. Timothy Barnes.
© 2011 Timothy Barnes. Published 2011 by Blackwell Publishing Ltd.

can only be Licinius and the journey must belong to February 313 (Barnes 1982: 81). The two emperors met for a wedding and to plan for the future. Constantine had betrothed his young half-sister Constantia to the middle-aged Licinius in order to cement their alliance against Maximinus, who had foolishly allied himself to the doomed Maxentius either before or during Constantine's invasion of Italy in 312 (Lactantius, *Mort. Pers.* 43.2–3, 44.10). With Maxentius defeated, Constantine in control of Italy, and Licinius threatened by Maximinus in the East, it was time for the promised marriage to be celebrated and for the brothers-in-law to agree on how to rule the Roman Empire jointly after Licinius had defeated Maximinus. The preamble to the substantially identical letters of Licinius posted in Nicomedia on 13 June 313 and in Caesarea in Palestine some time later, as quoted by Lactantius and Eusebius, confirm what could be inferred on a priori grounds. When the two emperors met in Milan they considered 'all matters concerning the public advantage and safety' (Lactantius, *Mort. Pers.* 48.2: *universa quae ad commoda et securitatem publicam pertinerent*; Eusebius, *HE* 10.5.3). Modern research has with virtual certainty identified two permanent administrative innovations on which Constantine and Licinius agreed in Milan.

The earliest *magistri officiorum* are attested before the final defeat of Licinius in both halves of the empire. Between 313 and 324 Constantine had an official whose title was 'tribune and master of the offices' (Clauss 1980: 7, 12–13, 159, 171, 186): a rescript issued at Serdica during this period concerning the religious implications of imperial and public buildings being struck by lightning mentions the fact that Maximus, apparently prefect of the city of Rome at the time, had written *ad Heraclianum tribunum et mag(istrum) officiorum* (*CTh* 16.10.1: 17 December 320), and an imperial constitution transmitted without addressee, which was posted up at Castulo in Spain, refers to letters sent *ad Proculeianum tribunum et mag(is)trum officiorum* (*CTh* 11.9.1: 31 December 323). On the other hand, the earliest master of the offices known to Peter the Patrician and John the Lydian in the sixth century was the unfortunate Martinianus, whom Licinius promoted to the rank of Augustus after his defeat at Adrianople on 3 July 324 and whom Constantine promptly executed when Licinius surrendered in September (John the Lydian, *De magistratibus* 2.25).[2] When Zosimus writes that Licinius chose as his associate in peril 'Martinianus, who was commander of the forces attached to the court (the Romans call this man "master of the offices"' (2.25.2), a correlation of title and function which he repeats in his account of events of 350 and 363 (2.43.4; 3.29.3), his definition of the main function of the master of the offices, though correct for Anatolius, the *magister officiorum* of Julian who was killed in the same battle as his imperial master (*PLRE* 1. 61, Anatolius 5), need not derive from authentic knowledge of what the post was in 324 or earlier.

According to A. H. M. Jones, the *magister officiorum* was 'a minister whose original functions are obscure and who in the course of time acquired a curiously miscellaneous group of duties' (Jones 1964: 368, cf. 3.74–75 nn.6–8). The original title of the office was *tribunus et magister officiorum*, and a magisterial survey of what is known about both the office and the men who held it infers that its holder had both a military command and a civil office (Clauss 1980: 7–13). On the civil side, the *magister officiorum* was in charge of several *officia* (or bureaux) which had previously been administered separately: the posts of *magister a studiis*, *magister sacrarum cognitionum* and *magister memoriae* are attested in the late third century (Clauss 1980: 10); these or similar titles survived to designate the later *magistri memoriae*, *epistularum* and *libellorum* who were subordinates of the master of the offices (*Notitia Dignitatum*, Oriens 11, 19; Occidens 9, 17; Clauss 1980: 15–18) and he seems to have controlled the *officium admissionum* and thus regulated audiences with the emperor from the outset (Jones 1964: 103). The body of troops which the earliest *magistri officiorum* commanded as their tribune was the *schola* of *agentes in rebus*, who are first attested in 319 (*CTh* 6.35.3[Seeck]). Since a law of 315 speaks of *memoriales* and *palatini* (*CTh* 6.35.2), it is a reasonably secure inference that the *schola* of *agentes in rebus* and the office of *magister officiorum* were created at the same time (Clauss 1980: 12–13, 24). A recent essay on 'Bureaucracy and Government' under Constantine holds that the office of *magister officiorum* 'may perhaps have been created by Diocletian, but on balance it seems more likely that the position was established – in the separate administrations of Constantine and Licinius – sometime soon after 312' (Kelly 2006: 188). Such 'parallel changes' (Kelly 2006: 191) surely belonged to a wider set of administrative reforms on which the two emperors agreed in Milan in February 313.

These included, as Constantin Zuckermann has recently demonstrated, a division of the Roman Empire into twelve dioceses which created a new layer of administration in the form of *vicarii* who were responsible for the dioceses and subordinate to the praetorian prefects (Zuckerman 2002: 620–628).[3] Proof comes from the so-called Verona List (or *Laterculus Veronensis*), which Mommsen published in 1862 under the title 'List of Roman Provinces drawn up in 297' (Mommsen 1908: 561–588), but which subsequent research has shown to date from the year 314 (Kolbe 1962: 65–71; Jones 1964: 1.43, 3.4, 381). Zuckerman further argues that the obvious addition of the words *nunc et maior* added after *Armenia Minor* at the end of the list of the provinces of the diocese of Pontica (Verona, Biblioteca Capitolare II (2), fol. 255 verso, line 4)[4] reflects the incorporation of Greater Armenia as a Roman province by Licinius on the eastern frontier of the empire very shortly after the defeat of Maximinus (Zuckerman 2002: 628–635, cf. Barnes 1982: 81). The twelve dioceses varied enormously in size (Britanniae had four provinces, Oriens seventeen): hence the Verona List bestows a spurious equality on Constantine and Licinius by dividing the empire in such a way that each of them rules precisely six dioceses. Such an arrangement suggests an agreement between the two emperors which they reached in Milan 313 (Zuckerman 2002: 636–637).[5]

In contrast, the division of Severan provinces into smaller administrative units, which Lactantius implies that Diocletian initiated (*Mort. Pers.* 7.4: *provinciae quoque in frusta concisae*), was not the result of a single decision, since the process both began before Diocletian and continued after him. For example, a new province of Phrygia and Caria had already been detached from the old proconsular province of Asia in the middle of the third century (Roueché 1981: 106–120; 1989: 1–4, 11–14 nos. 5–6), and the new province of Hellespontus, which is first attested in 307/308, was probably created not under the Diocletianic Tetrarchy (as Barnes 1982: 158, 215), but by Galerius (Zuckerman 2002: 617–620, with revised texts of *Inschriften von Ilion* 97 and *CIG* 3607 = *IGRR* 4.214). In Egypt, Licinius divided the reduced Diocletianic province of Aegyptus into the Aegyptus Jovia and Aegyptus Herculia of the Verona List: Aegyptus Herculia certainly existed by the end of 315 (*P. Cairo Isidore* 74, cf. Barnes 1982: 211; *P. Oxyrhynchus* LI 3619), and Licinius subsequently (so it appears) renamed it Aegyptus Mercuriana when he ceased to recognize Constantine, who belonged to the Herculian dynasty, as his imperial colleague in 321 (*Corpus Pap. Raineri* V 7, cf. Barnes 1996b: 548–549).[6] This division existed only as long as Licinius ruled Egypt: Constantine immediately recombined Licinius' two Egyptian provinces into a single Aegyptus (Barnes 1982: 151; 2009b: 114–116), perhaps primarily in order to get rid of their theophoric names. Constantine also made Hellespontus part of proconsular Asia again, perhaps as early as 324/325 – and perhaps mainly in order to contrast himself with Galerius who had created it. Over the long term, however, administrative necessity or convenience overrode ideology: Hellespontus was again sliced off proconsular Asia before the death of Constantine (Barnes 1982: 158) and Constantius created the new province of Augustamnica in 341 (Festal Index 13), whose boundaries were the same as Licinius' short-lived province of Aegyptus Mercuriana.

If two of the fundamental administrative reforms which created 'the new empire of Diocletian and Constantine' are correctly attributed to a joint initiative of Constantine and Licinius in 313, then it is clear that 'matters which concerned the public advantage and safety' were at least as important to the two emperors as were religious issues arising from the persecution of the Christians in the East, which was still continuing when they met. Moreover, such are the lacunae in our evidence that it is possible that other administrative reforms besides the two documented here, which are now attributed to Diocletian or Constantine, may be the consequence of the negotiations between Constantine and Licinius in Milan.

WAS THERE AN 'EDICT OF MILAN'?

Christianity was only one of the weighty matters of state which Constantine and Licinius discussed in Milan. What action or actions did they take on this matter while they were in the city? The correct answer to this question is amazingly simple. They agreed to extend to the rest of the Roman Empire the freedom of worship and the restoration of property confiscated in 303 which the Christians of the West already enjoyed. No public pronouncement was probably made in Milan because none was needed. Unfortunately, there is a deeply ingrained scholarly tradition of using the term 'Edict of Milan,' with or without the definite article, with or without quotation marks around the bogus phrase, which contradicts historical reality (Barnes 2007a: 186–189). For the term 'Edict of Milan' as conventionally used (as, for example by Drake 2000: 193–198; Stephenson 2009: 158) entails denying that Constantine granted the Christians of Britain, Gaul and Spain both toleration and restitution of property confiscated in the 'Great Persecution' in the summer of 306 immediately after he was proclaimed Augustus at York. It will, therefore, be worthwhile to explain in detail with reference to recent writing about Constantine why the term is so misleading, even dangerous.

A recent textbook designed for undergraduate students of Roman history states succinctly that in Milan Constantine and Licinius 'issued a decree – known today as the "Edict of Milan" – that proclaimed toleration of all religions' (Boatwright, Gargola & Talbert 2006: 287). In similar vein, the chronological table in the relevant volume of the second edition of the *Cambridge Ancient History* has under the year 313 the entry: 'Edict of freedom of religious belief issued jointly by Licinius and Constantine ("Edict of Milan")' – with a reversal of the correct order of the names of the two emperors that seems scarcely credible in a work of reputable scholarship (Bowman, Garnsey & Averil Cameron 2005: 784). Likewise, essays in the catalogue of an exhibition held in York in 2006 to mark the sixteen hundredth anniversary of the emperor's accession in that city assert that Constantine and Licinius issued a 'statement in favour of toleration' or a 'joint declaration' in Milan in 313 (Averil Cameron 2006a: 24: 2006b: 99). The 'Edict of Milan' (with or without inverted commas) also makes several appearances in the recent *Cambridge Companion to the Age of Constantine*, where it appears in the 'Timeline' of important events during the emperor's reign (Lenski 2006a: 401), though it receives a significantly different presentation from different contributors. One contributor at least knows full well that the document to which the name 'Edict of Milan' is conventionally applied is not an edict and was not issued in Milan, but was issued by Licinius to provide for the return of property confiscated from individual Christians and from Christian communities in the years from 303 onwards in Asia Minor, the Levant and Egypt (Bleckmann 2006: 22). Another refers to 'the so-called Edict of Milan, actually preserved as a letter by Licinius to a governor' (Lenski 2006b: 72), which implies that he believes that there was an antecedent edict issued in Milan which either survives as or is reproduced as an extant letter of Licinius. Harold Drake, who had earlier wrongly asserted that 'recognizing Christianity as a legal religion, the emperors removed disabilities imposed by Diocletian' at Milan in 313 (Drake 1999: 390), now offers an extended discussion of the letter of Licinius acknowledging that 'in the form we have it, it was not an edict and was not issued in Milan' (2006: 121). Nevertheless, he consistently writes as if the letter of Licinius was issued jointly by both emperors, not by Licinius alone in their joint name, and he repeats the erroneous view that 'the document legalizes Christianity' as if it did so throughout the Roman Empire and not merely in territory which Maximinus had controlled until 313. Moreover, Drake makes the further claim that 'the Edict of Milan defines Constantine's religious policy' and that 'by legalizing Christianity, the Edict of

Milan created the necessary conditions for imperial intervention' in ecclesiastical politics (Drake 2006: 121–123, 132).[7]

To understand what Constantine and Licinius decided vis-à-vis the Christians in Milan, it is necessary to eschew the term 'Edict of Milan' completely. There is no ancient evidence whatever that either Constantine and Licinius jointly or Constantine alone issued any edict or general law respecting Christianity either during or immediately after their meeting in Milan. For when the two emperors met in Milan in February 313, the Christians of the West already enjoyed everything that the letter of Licinius posted up in Nicomedia on the ides of June 313 gave the Christians of Bithynia, who had been subjects of the defeated Maximinus. The negotiations between Constantine and Licinius in Milan required only one legal innovation relating to the Christians: it was that Licinius should extend to the territories under his control the restitution of confiscated Christian property which Constantine and Maxentius had previously granted to their Christian subjects before 312, as Noel Lenski now recognizes, despite his retention of the bogus term 'Edict of Milan' (2008: 263–264). Hence, either while he was still in Milan or shortly after he left Italy in the late winter or early spring of 313, Licinius must have issued legislation restoring confiscated Christian property in the Balkans and Greece, even though this happens not to be explicitly attested in our surviving sources. To be sure, if Licinius issued an edict to this effect before he departed from Milan, he issued it in the joint names of Constantine and himself, but that does not legitimize use of the term 'Edict of Milan' in its traditional sense, since such a law, even if it was issued in Milan in February or March 313, would have changed the legal status of property confiscated from Christians and Christian churches only in the territories ruled by Licinius, not in those of Constantine.

Much confusion has been caused by the misleading application of the term 'Edict of Milan' to the letter which Licinius sent to each eastern province after he liberated it from the 'tyrant' Maximinus. Otto Seeck demonstrated the utter impropriety of such a use of the phrase as long ago as 1891, and it is a sad commentary on the quality of most scholarly writing about Constantine since then that it is necessary to repeat what he said then. I translate the opening paragraph and the conclusion of this unjustly neglected article (Seeck 1891: 381, 386):

'In the year 313 Constantine guaranteed legal toleration for the Christians in the Roman Empire through the Edict of Milan.' So have we all learned at our school desks, and yet not a single word of that sentence is true. For the Christians did not obtain legal toleration for the first time in 313, but had already obtained it in 311; the originator of this legal measure was not Constantine, but Galerius; and there never was an 'Edict of Milan' which concerned itself with the question of the Christians. Admittedly, a document which people are in the habit of calling by this name is still preserved in its original wording. But first, this document is no edict; second, it was not issued in Milan; third it was not issued by Constantine; and fourth, it does not grant legal toleration, which the Christians had already possessed for some time, to the whole empire: its content has a much more restricted significance.

The law thus applied, not to the whole empire, but only to the East; it was not issued by Constantine, but by Licinius alone; if one wants to have a name for it, one should in future no longer call it the 'edict of Milan,' but merely the 'directive of Nicomedia' (wenn man dafür einen Namen haben will, so darf man es künftig nicht mehr das Edikt von Mailand, sondern nur den Erlass von Nikomedia nennen).

In his famous essay on Constantine and the Christian church, Norman Baynes opined that 'the Edict of Milan may be a fiction, but the fact for which the term stood remains untouched' (Baynes 1931: 11) and he subsequently reiterated this opinion, arguing that, while 'technically, it may be true that there was no edict of Milan,' nevertheless 'the facts for which the "Edict of Milan" once stood are still facts' (Baynes 1939: 686). These assertions are both false and grossly misleading, since they implicitly deny the well-attested fact that both Constantine and Maxentius issued legislation in favor of the Christians of the West before the Battle of the Milvian Bridge.

The surviving document often falsely called the 'Edict of Milan' is in fact a letter which Licinius sent successively in 313 to the governor of each province of Asia Minor, the Syrian region and Egypt as they came under his control after he defeated Maximinus. Lactantius quotes the Latin text of the version addressed to the governor of Bithynia which was posted up in Nicomedia on 13 June 313 (Lactantius, *Mort. Pers.* 48.2–12), while Eusebius quotes a slightly fuller Greek version which reads like an edict and which was posted up in Caesarea in Palestine somewhat later (Eusebius, *HE* 10.5.2–14). The preamble to both versions of the document, which was of course issued in the name of both emperors, refers to their meeting in Milan in February 313 (Lactantius, *Mort. Pers.* 48.2 = Eusebius, *HE* 10.5.4):

> Cum feliciter tam ego [quam] Constantinus Augustus quam etiam ego Licinius Augustus apud Mediolanum convenissemus atque universa quae ad commoda et securitatem publicam pertinerent, in tractatu haberemus, haec inter cetera quae videbamus pluribus hominibus profutura, vel in primis ordinanda esse credidimus, quibus divinitatis reverentia continebatur, ut daremus et Christianis et omnibus liberam potestatem sequendi religionem quam quisque voluisset, ...

> When both I Constantine Augustus and I Licinius Augustus auspiciously met together in Milan and held a discussion of all matters pertaining to the public advantage and safety, we decided that, among the other things which we saw would benefit the majority of men, these arrangements above all needed to be made by which reverence for the divinity is comprised, namely, that we should grant both to Christians and to all the free power to follow the religion which each may wish, etc.

This preamble makes it clear that Constantine and Licinius discussed the legal status of Christians and the restitution of Christian property and came to an agreement on a joint policy regarding these matters in Milan, but it does not state that either emperor separately or both emperors together issued an edict or any sort of public pronouncement in that city. The main purpose of the letters of Licinius was to ensure the restitution of property confiscated both from individual Christians and from Christian congregations as corporate bodies (Barnes 1998b: 277–280). For it contains an explicit statement that Christian congregations owned property as corporate entities before 303 (Lactantius, *Mort. Pers.* 48.9):

> Et quoniam idem christiani non [in] ea loca tantum ad quae convenire consuerunt, sed alia etiam habuisse noscuntur ad ius corporis eorum id est ecclesiarum, non hominum singulorum, pertinentia, ea omnia lege quam superius comprehendimus, citra ullam prorsus ambiguitatem vel controversiam isdem Christianis, id est corpori et conventiculis eorum reddi iubebis ...

> And since these same Christians are known to have possessed not only the places in which they normally assembled but other property too which belongs by right to their corporation – that is, to churches, not to individual persons – you will order that all this property, in accordance with the law which we have set out above, be given back without any equivocation or dispute at all to these same Christians, that is to their corporation and to their conventicles.

It was the emperor Gallienus in 260 who had granted Christian churches, or perhaps Christian bishops as heads of Christian communities, the right to own property and thereby recognized Christianity as one of lawful religions of the Roman Empire (Barnes 2010a: 97–105). When Constantine and Licinius conferred in Milan, the Christians of the West already enjoyed freedom of worship and had obtained the restitution of property confiscated under Diocletian's persecuting legislation of 303. The most damaging consequence of loose talk about an 'Edict of Milan' has been to blind modern historians of Constantine to the fact that Gallienus legalized Christianity more than a dozen years before the first Christian emperor was born – and allowed Christian churches to own property of all types as corporate bodies four decades before the 'Great Persecution.'

TOWARDS WAR

While Constantine and Licinius conferred in Milan, Maximinus prepared for war. He marched an army rapidly from Syria across Asia Minor and anticipated the expected attack from the West by invading Europe and capturing Byzantium after a siege of eleven days before Licinius could bring up enough troops to relieve the city. He then advanced into Thrace, took Perinthus, again after a brief siege, and advanced a further eighteen miles with 70,000 troops. Licinius confronted him near Adrianople with an army that numbered barely 30,000. The two Augusti prepared for battle. Maximinus made a vow to Jupiter that he would, if victorious, utterly destroy the name of Christian; Licinius circulated and ordered his army to recite a monotheistic prayer to the Supreme God, bidden according to Lactantius by an angel who appeared to him during the night before battle. As the two armies faced each other on 30 April 313, the soldiers of Licinius bared their heads, laid aside their shields and followed Licinius in reciting the prayer. Maximinus refused an offer from Licinius to parley, hoping in vain that the latter's army would desert to him. In the event his own army buckled and Maximinus fled, first to Nicomedia, thence to Cappadocia, after which he took up position beyond the Cilician Gates. When Licinius' troops broke through the pass, Maximinus committed suicide at Tarsus (Lactantius, *Mort. Pers.* 45–47, 49).

A purge of persecutors followed in which Christians took revenge on their tormentors (Eusebius, *HE* 9.11.5–6). Hundreds who had prospered under Maximinus were killed, with or without a formal trial. As curator of Antioch, Theotecnus had organized a cult of Zeus Philios with initiations, mysteries and oracles and harried the Christians of his city; as a reward Maximinus had appointed him governor of Galatia, where he used his official position to hunt down and execute Christians, including Theodotus of Ancyra (Eusebius, *HE* 9.2–3; *Passio Theodoti* [*BHG* 1782], cf. Barnes 2010a: 155–159). Licinius came to Antioch and put on what amounted to a 'show trial:' Theotecnus and his associates were tortured until they confessed that their theosophy was nothing but fraud and trickery, and the emperor then presided over their trial and supervised their execution (Eusebius, *Praeparatio Evangelica* 4.2.10–11). Licinius then campaigned on the Persian frontier and presided over the formal adoption of Christianity by the ruler of Armenia as the official religion of his kingdom,[8] after which he returned to Europe, where he campaigned against the Goths in 314 or 315 and took up residence in Sirmium (Barnes 1981: 65; 1982: 80, 81–82).

When Constantine departed from Milan, he returned to Gaul (Barnes 1982: 71). In the summer months of 313 his presence is attested at Trier, on the lower Rhine and again in Trier, where an unknown Gallic orator recited a panegyric which survives in the late summer or autumn (*Pan. Lat.* 12[9]). The speech naturally concentrates on Constantine's invasion of Italy and his defeat of Maxentius in the preceding year. The orator compares Constantine with Alexander the Great and with Julius Caesar. In 312 Constantine had crossed the Alps into North Italy, defeated the main army of Maxentius near Verona and advanced slowly and deliberately on Rome determined to avoid the sort of bloodshed in the city which had marred the victory of Vespasian's forces in the civil war of 69. There was a battle outside Rome, but only after the political situation inside the city compelled Maxentius to fight rather than to stand the siege for which he had prepared. But the orator waxes as eloquent at Constantine's victory at the Milvian Bridge as any Augustan poet had on the Battle of Actium in 31 BC, which had been an equally easy victory.

The orator is clearly not a Christian, since he says nothing explicit about Constantine's new religion or about the Christian emblem which he had emblazoned on his army's shields before battle (Lactantius, *Mort. Pers.* 44.9). But he maintains an extremely eloquent silence on the religious plane, on which his speech offers a striking contrast to the speeches of 307, 310 and 311 (Rosen 1993: 857–861).

The orator of 313 completely avoids any explicit reference to pagan gods. Constantine is no longer Herculius or the descendant of Hercules, as in the speech of 307 (*Pan. Lat.* 7[6].2.5: *imperatores semper Herculii*); there is no mention of Apollo, who had been the emperor's especial patron and protector in 310 (*Pan. Lat.* 6[7].21.4–22.2), or of Mother Earth and Jupiter, invoked by the orator of 311, who describes a visit of Constantine to Autun during which the banners of all the city's corporations and the cult-statues of all its gods were paraded before him (*Pan. Lat.* 5(8).8.4: *omnium signa collegiorum, omnium deorum nostrorum simulacra protulimus*).[9] Even the peroration of the speech of 313 lacks the conventional invocation of the traditional deities. Instead, the orator appeals to a supreme power whose names are as varied as the languages of mankind and whose real name is beyond human knowledge (*Pan. Lat.* 12[9].26.1):

> te, summe rerum sator, cuius tot nomina sunt quot gentium linguas voluisti (quem enim te ipse dici velis, scire non possumus). sive tute quaedam vis mensque divina es, quae toto infusa mundo omnibus miscearis elementis,[10] et sine ullo extrinsecus accedente vigoris impulsu per te ipse movearis, sive aliqua supra omne caelum potestas es quae hoc opus tuum ex altiore naturae arce despicias: te, inquam, oramus et quaesumus ut hunc in omnia saecula principem serves.

> You, supreme creator of matter, whose names are as many as you <once> willed the languages of the nations to be (for we cannot know what you yourself wish to be called), whether you are some force and divine mind and, spread through the whole world, you mingle with the elements and move of your own accord without any impulse of force acting on you from the outside, or whether you are some power above every heaven and look down upon this your creation from a higher pinnacle of Nature – you, I say, we pray and beseech to preserve this prince for all ages.

This peroration, whose echoes of Virgil description of the universe are obvious, has attracted frequent and sometimes lengthy comment (see Baglivi 1984: 32–67). What is less obvious (and appears to have escaped scholarly attention entirely) is the Christian tinge which has been imparted to the passage.[11] The divinity whom the orator invokes is the supreme creator of all things, who decided that every nation should speak its own language – just as the God of the Christians did when he saw the Tower of Babel reaching up towards heaven (Genesis 11.1–9, cf. Gera 2003: 127–134).[12]

When this speech was delivered, the religious ambience of the imperial court had clearly changed from what it was before 312 (Brosch 2006: 85) – though it should not be deduced from the fact that the orator's account of Constantine's triumphant entry into Rome on 29 October 312 omits any mention of an ascent to the Capitol to pay homage to Jupiter Feretrius that the emperor refused to ascend the Capitol because he was a Christian (Straub 1955). For Constantine's entry into Rome on the morrow of the Battle of the Milvian Bridge was not technically a triumph, since triumphs were celebrated after the defeat of a foreign enemy, not after victory in a civil war. Moreover, since the story that Constantine refused to ascend the Capitol is found only in Zosimus, who dates it to 326 (2.29.5), while Zosimus' hostile narrative of Constantine closely follows the hostile and notoriously inaccurate account of his reign by Eunapius, which contained demonstrable errors and inventions, it is unwise to place implicit trust in the story.

In the autumn of 313 Constantine may have made a brief visit to Britain before returning to Trier for the winter, where he remained until June 314. In the summer of 314, however, he traveled south to Arles, where he attended the council of bishops which he had convened in an attempt to put an end to the Donatist controversy (Eusebius, *VC* 1.44; Optatus, App. 4, p. 208.16 Ziwsa, cf. Barnes 1982: 72). This controversy, which was to produce a widespread and long-lasting schism throughout Roman Africa, had begun with a disputed episcopal election in Carthage while Maxentius ruled Africa (Barnes 1975a). In the winter of 312/313 Constantine had unwittingly stepped into the middle of the controversy when he sent three letters to Africa in which he restored property confiscated during the persecution to 'the catholic church of the Christians in every city,' supplied funds to be distributed to 'ministers of the lawful and most holy catholic religion' and instructed the proconsul Anullinus to release the clergy 'of the catholic church over which Caecilianus presides' (Eusebius, *HE* 10.5.15–17, 6.1–4, 7.1–2). Presumably acting on the advice of bishops at court, Constantine thereby excluded the followers of Maiorinus whom a council of African bishops, which probably met in 307 or 308, had chosen as bishop of Carthage to replace Caecilianus, whom they had deposed on the grounds that his consecration by Felix of Abthungi was invalid because they considered Felix a *traditor* and that his surrender of the scriptures in 303 disqualified him from holding office as a bishop (Barnes 1981: 54–56).

In 315 Constantine celebrated his *decennalia* in Rome. It was perhaps during his presence in the city from 18 (or 21) July to 27 September (Barnes 1982: 72) that he devised a plan to expand the imperial college in a way of which he soon repented – with fatal consequences for the Roman aristocrat whom he had proposed to co-opt into the imperial college.[13] The episode is known only from the *Origo Constantini Imperatoris*, which reports it in an obviously incomplete and distorted form. Any attempt to penetrate the smokescreen created by Constantine's propaganda and to understand what really happened must start from the account which the *Origo* gives of the whole period from the meeting of Constantine and Licinius in Milan to the outbreak of war between them three and a half years later (13–15):

> After the celebration of the marriage, Constantine repaired to the Gauls and Licinius returned to Illyricum.
>
> Some time later, Constantine sent Constantius[14] to Licinius to persuade him that Bassianus, who was married to Constantine's other sister Anastasia, should become Caesar,[15] so that, following the precedent of Diocletian and Maximian, Bassus should hold Italy in the middle between Constantine and Licinius.
>
> When Licinius frustrated such plans, Bassianus was armed against Constantine through the agency of Senecio, his brother, who was loyal to Licinius. However, he

was caught in the attempt and on the orders of Constantine convicted and killed. When the surrender of Senecio, the instigator of the assassination plot, was requested so that he could be punished, Licinius refused and concord was shattered. There were additional causes because he [sc. Licinius] had cast down images and statues of Constantine at Emona. Open war was then decided on by both <emperors>.

There is much in this passage to arouse suspicion and much that requires supplement or correction, for it shows tell-tale marks of Constantinian propaganda.

Bassianus' alleged attempt to assassinate Constantine appears to replicate in outline the invented story that the pardoned Maximian attempted to murder Constantine in 310 as he slept (Chapter 4), and the claim that Licinius provoked war by tearing down images and statues of Constantine in the city of Emona (*Barrington Atlas*, Map 20 B3) is equally or even more suspicious. The first battle of the war (on 8 October 316) was fought at Cibalae (*Barrington Atlas*, Maps 20F4, 21A4), over a hundred and fifty miles inside Licinius' territory and only fifty miles short of Sirmium, where the eastern emperor was residing in 316 (*Origo* 16–17; [Julian], *Ep.* 181, 449a, cf. Barnes 1978b: 100–101). Constantine's claim that he was provoked is uncomfortably reminiscent of excuses made in the modern world by the leaders of powerful countries which invade their weaker neighbors or even distant lands of which they know little.

The episode of the tearing down of images and statues of Constantine has often been misunderstood because received opinion erroneously situates Emona in the territory of Constantine by assigning Emona to the province of Venetia et Istria and hence locating it in the newly created diocese of Italia rather than in the diocese of Pannoniae,[16] which belonged to Licinius' portion of the Roman Empire. But Emona lies underneath the modern Slovenian city of Ljubljana, and the view that it ever belonged to Pannonia depends solely on an incidental remark in the historian Herodian (8.1.4), whose narrative of the 230s contains various misconceptions and inaccuracies (Syme 1972: 146, 173, 178, 184–185, 188–189). There is no clear and reliable evidence that Emona ever belonged administratively to Italy. Under the early empire it certainly lay in Pannonia, first in the undivided province, then in Pannonia Superior when it was divided (Pliny, *Natural History* 3.147; Ptolemy, *Geography* 3.14.5, p. 296.1–3 Müller = p. 74 Cuntz).[17] Immutable facts of geography make it improbable that Emona was ever transferred to Italy before the loss of Roman territory in Pannonia after 395. There can be little doubt, therefore, that Constantine was the aggressor. He had decided to attack Licinius and hence needed to manufacture a reason for going to war.

What then are we to make of the story which the *Origo Constantini Imperatoris* serves up? The first step in analyzing it is to ask what rank in the imperial college Constantine is said to have proposed for Bassianus, the husband of his half-sister Anastasia, who is otherwise completely unknown to history (*PLRE* 1.150, Bassianus 1). Now the *Origo* applies the word *Caesar* both to Valens, whom Licinius appointed Augustus in 316 (17), and to Martinianus, whom he appointed Augustus in 324 (25). Hence the proposal which the author of the *Origo* intended to ascribe to Constantine was probably that Bassianus should become a third Augustus (not a Caesar) governing Italy as a buffer between his territories and those of Licinius. For, if he held the rank of Caesar, Bassianus would have been legally the subordinate of Constantine and hence incapable of acting either independently of him or as a buffer between the two Augusti. But the notion that Constantine proposed to appoint a third Augustus who was not related to him by ties of blood is implausible in the extreme. Moreover, the *Origo* states that Constantine's proposal appealed to the precedent of Diocletian and Maximian (14: *exemplo Diocletianu et Maximiani*). It seems probable, therefore, that the *Origo* preserves a muddled and incomplete account of a plan under which Bassianus was to be co-opted into the imperial college at the rank of Caesar together with Constantine's son Crispus.

If this hypothesis be granted, then both Constantine's proposal and his subsequent *volte face* make perfect sense in terms of dynastic politics. By the autumn of 315 Constantine had been married to Fausta for eight years, but Fausta, although of child-bearing age at the time of the marriage in 307, had not yet produced any children, and perhaps had never even become pregnant. In contrast, Constantine's sister Constantia, married to Licinius only since February 313, produced a son and heir for the eastern Augustus in the late summer of 315 (*Epitome* 41.4; Zosimus 2.20.2). In September 315, therefore, Constantine was faced with the very real prospect of fathering no more legitimate children, unless he were to divorce Fausta and marry for a third time, which could have cost him political support among his Christian subjects.[18] Accordingly, in order to secure the imperial succession for his own family, he proposed a new tetrarchy on the Diocletianic model: his son Crispus and his brother-in-law Bassianus were to be appointed as Caesars, Bassianus in the West as the subordinate of Constantine and Crispus in the East as the Caesar of Licinius and his eventual successor as Augustus. Licinius demurred: as matters stood in late 315, he could expect, provided that he lived a few more years, to be succeeded as Augustus of the East by his son Licinius Licinianus.

Constantine's hopes of founding a dynasty which might some day rule the whole Roman Empire were suddenly rekindled when Fausta was discovered to be pregnant. The child turned out to be a boy, to whom Fausta gave birth in the summer of 316 (*Epitome* 41.4; Zosimus 2.20.2).[19] With the birth of another son, Constantine's proposal to add Bassianus to the imperial college became not only outdated, but potentially dangerous for the encouragement that it gave to Anastasia's siblings, the offspring of Constantius and Theodora. Constantine therefore acted with calculated ruthlessness. He eliminated Bassianus, sent Julius Constantius and Flavius Dalmatius to provincial cities as virtual exiles, and turned his misstep to his political advantage. Bassianus was alleged to have attempted to assassinate Constantine, presumably while he was in Rome in the summer of 315, and his brother Senecio,[20] who is otherwise unknown, but whom Constantine (it must be supposed) had used as an emissary to Licinius, was accused of instigating the attempted assassination. Senecio fled for his life to the territory of Licinius, who refused to hand him over for certain execution when Constantine demanded his surrender. Constantine now had the *casus belli* which he wanted, perhaps as early as the spring of 316. But for obvious dynastic reasons he waited to make sure that his unborn child was a boy. Within a few weeks of the birth of Constantinus, his father led an invading army into the territory of Licinius.

FROM CIBALAE (316) TO CHRYSOPOLIS (324)

The first battle of the war occurred at Cibalae on 8 October 316 (Barnes 1973: 36–38; 1982: 73, 82, cf. *Descriptio consulum* 314). The *Origo Constantini Imperatoris* alone among our extant sources gives any sort of detailed account of the first war between Constantine and Licinius (16–19). Its course illustrates both the driving ambition of Constantine and the military skill of Licinius. At Cibalae, if the figures which the *Origo* gives are correct, the invading army comprised 20,000 infantry and cavalry, doubtless all crack troops. They were confronted by an army of 35,000, of which a large number were presumably *ripenses* or frontier troops. The battle was long and hard fought, but in the end decisive. According to the *Origo*, Licinius lost 20,000 infantry and a large part of his armed cavalry. He fled with his wife, son and treasury towards Dacia, appointing Valens, a *dux limitis* on the Danube, to be his colleague as Augustus (*PLRE* 1.931–932, Valens 13). Valens collected a second large army at Adrianople and sent an envoy with an offer to negotiate with Constantine, who had advanced beyond Serdica on the great military road which led from North Italy across the Balkans to Asia Minor over the Pass of Succi and was now in Philippopolis. Constantine spurned the offer. A second long and doubtful battle on the Campus Ardiensis[21] lasted until darkness came to the rescue of Licinius' army, which was beginning to wilt under pressure. Licinius and Valens guessed what Constantine would do next. He advanced rapidly on Byzantium, but they withdrew to the north towards Beroea and cut off his rear. Negotiation was now in the interest of both sides, though as the weaker party after two defeats on the field of battle Licinius was compelled to accept the terms which Constantine offered. Valens was stripped of the imperial purple (and later put to death); Licinius surrendered most of his European territory, retaining only Thrace, Moesia and Scythia Minor in addition to Asia Minor and Oriens (which included Egypt); and on his return to Serdica Constantine officially proclaimed three new Caesars – his sons Crispus and Constantinus and Licinius' son Licinianus.

Licinius himself, though surrendering territory, did not, as has sometimes been assumed, lose the right to issue laws and general edicts in the name of the new imperial college which were, at least in theory, valid for the whole of the Roman Empire. The legislation of Licinius has until recently been 'hidden from history' because of his defeat in 324 and the subsequent retrospective annulment of his 'unjust' decisions (Corcoran 1993: 97–119). But some evidence survives of his administration of the eastern empire after the War of Cibalae. Four separate fragments preserved in the Theodosian Code carry the date of 21 July 317 and are addressed *ad Bithynos*, that is, to the provincial council of Bithynia (*CTh* 8.4.3 + 10.7.1 + 10.20.1 + 12.1.5). They must therefore derive from a letter or edict of Licinius, not Constantine. They regulate possession of equestrian rank, and there is no need to postulate that Licinius was merely repeating an earlier law of Constantine (Seeck 1919: 54, 165; Habicht 1958: 369–370), especially since the extract from Constantine's western law published on 19 January 317 (*CTh* 12.4.1[Seeck]), which Licinius is alleged to have repeated for the East on 21 July (Seeck 1919: 54, 165), has a different focus and purpose. Whereas Constantine was concerned to protect the status of decurions by preventing the usurpation of their privileges, Licinius mentioned decurions as among those whose entitlement to the higher rank of *vir perfectissimus* needed to be strictly regulated (Corcoran 1993: 110–111).[22] The treaty of 317, however, did not bring lasting peace between the imperial brothers-in-law.

Soon after 1 March 317, if not before, Crispus, who was now a young man of twenty or more, began to reside in Trier, where a new palace was built for the Caesar and his wife (Weber 1990). Unfortunately, nothing is known for certain about Crispus' wife other than that her name was Helena and that she gave birth to a child in 322, and these two facts are known only because the compilers of the Theodosian Code in the 430s included an extract from an amnesty granted on 30 October 322 on the occasion of the recent birth of a child to Crispus and Helena (*CTh* 9.38.1).[23] Crispus governed Gaul and Britain from Trier, and from Trier he conducted military campaigns independently of his father (Barnes 1982: 83). But Constantine provided his son with an adviser and counselor. Junius Bassus, who was to become consul in 331, served as praetorian prefect for fourteen years (*AE* 1964.370 = 1975.370: Aqua Viva in Etruria). Many laws addressed to Basssus as praetorian prefect were included in the Theodosian Code (though some extracts survive only in the *Codex Justinianus*) and their dates run from 1 March 320 (*CJ* 7.57.7) to 20 October 331 (*CTh* 1.5.3), so that it is easy to infer, first, that Bassus was in office as prefect from 318 or 319 to early 332 (Palanque 1966: 838) and, second, that as praetorian prefect he was attached to the Caesar Crispus (Barnes 1982: 129). For towards the end of his reign, Eusebius reports that Constantine established his sons by Fausta as rulers of different areas of the Roman Empire, each with his own court and an administration headed by trusted advisers whom he himself had appointed (Chapter 7).

Tension between the two Augusti began again within four years. For each of the four years from 321 to 324, East and West had different consuls. In 321 Licinius held the consulate for the sixth time with his son Licinius Caesar as his colleague and consul for the second time. Constantine may initially have recognized Licinius and his son as consuls (*ICUR* I 34), but by the middle of March at the latest he had proclaimed his sons Crispus and Constantinus as consuls for the year (*ILS* 6111: Rome). In each of the following three years Licinius did not recognize the ordinary consuls whom Constantine appointed: Egyptian documentary papyri from the beginning of 322 to the defeat of Licinius consistently use dating formulae which define the year with reference to the consulate of the two Licinii in 321 (Barnes 1982: 96; *CLRE* 176–183).

Constantine's desire for control over the whole Roman Empire and his consequent need to prepare for war against Licinius produced effects outside the political and military spheres. In Constantine's view, the rights and wrongs of the Donatist schism had been finally decided by November 316, when he issued a law that the places where the Donatists assembled for worship were to be confiscated (Augustine, *Ep.* 88.3, cf. Barnes 1982: 245). In 317 repression began and soon produced Donatist martyrs (Barnes 2010a: 152–153); it continued until December 320 when Zenophilus, the *consularis* of Numidia, conducted an official enquiry in Cirta into the conduct of the Numidian bishops during the 'Great Persecution' in 303 (Optatus, App.1, pp. 185–197 Ziwsa). On 5 May 321, however, Constantine suddenly reversed his policy and allowed exiled Donatist bishops to return from exile (Augustine, *Contra partem Donati post gesta* 31.54, 33.56 [*CSEL* 53.154–156, 158–159]; Optatus, App. 9, p. 212.27–p. 213.26 Ziwsa). For, if he was to depict Licinius as a persecutor of Christians, he could not afford to be persecuting Christians himself, even if they were schismatics. This conciliatory policy Constantine maintained until October 324, when he sent a delegation of eastern clerics to Africa (Eusebius, *VC* 2.66, cf. Barnes 1982: 246). But the Donatists were already strong enough to resist imperial attempts at coercion. They took possession of the basilica at Cirta, and on 5 February 330 Constantine was compelled to acknowledge that he could not eject them and hence reduced to the expedient of offering to build another basilica for the catholic Christians of the city (*CTh* 16.2.7; Optatus, App. 10, p. 213.28–p. 216.7 Ziwsa).

On the military front, Constantine constructed a large harbor at Thessalonica and prepared a fleet in the Aegean so that, when the time came, he could attack Licinius on both land and sea (Zosimus 2.22.1). On the political front he waited until he could depict himself as a liberator of his imperial colleague's Christian subjects from persecution. Licinius unwisely obliged by adopting some repressive policies. He expelled Christians from his palace, he required all members of the imperial administration to perform a symbolic act of sacrifice, he prohibited assemblies and councils of bishops, he forbade men and women to worship together or women to receive instruction from male clergy, and he cancelled the clerical exemption from curial duties which Constantine had granted (Eusebius, *HE* 10.8.10–11; *VC* 1.51–53; 2.20.2, 30.1). Moreover, in the extant first ten books of his *Proof of the Gospel*, which he was probably writing c. 320–322, Eusebius complains that Roman magistrates and governors are again treating Christianity as a crime, even if not a capital one (*DE* 2.3.155–156; 3.5.78–80; 3.7.36–39; 5.3.11; 6.20.17–20; 7.1.131–132; 8.1.61–62, cf. *HE* 10.8.15–18). On Christmas Day 323 Constantine issued a law with obvious propaganda intent (*CTh* 16.2.5[Seeck], cf. Barnes 1981: 321 n.87). He had heard that clergy and other Christians had been compelled to participate in *lustrorum sacrificia*, that is, sacrifices marking Licinius' completion of fifteen years or three *lustra* of five years of rule since his appointment as emperor in Carnuntum on 11 November 308 (Seeck 1919: 98–99).

Constantine had already, it seems, deliberately provoked Licinius in the summer of 323. When Sarmatians raided and ravaged Thrace and Moesia, Constantine took the field in person, pursued the invaders beyond the Danube, took the victory title *Sarmaticus maximus* and sent some of his troops to infringe Licinius' territory (*Origo* 21; Zosimus 2.21). Licinius protested at the violation of his territory and prohibited the circulation of the coins which Constantine minted to celebrate his Sarmatian victory (*Origo* 21; Petrus Patricius, *Excerpta Vaticana* 187 = Anon. post Dionem, frag. 14.1 Müller). But he did not venture to take any military action. He could only wait for the inevitable onslaught from the West.

As war approached ever closer, Constantine made overtures to the Christians of the East. Lactantius appears to have responded by adding a passage to his *Divine Institutes*, finished fifteen years earlier, which reads like an invitation to Constantine to come to the rescue of Licinius' Christian subjects (*Div. Inst.* 1.1.13–16 [*CSEL* 19.4], cf. Heck 1972: 127–170). On the eastern frontier, which abutted Christian Armenia, some Christians may have committed treasonable acts or entered into treasonable correspondence with Constantine: at all events, the bishop of Amaseia and other bishops in Pontus were put to death and churches in that region were destroyed (Eusebius, *HE* 10.8.15; *VC* 2.1–2). Constantine had probably intended to wage a second war against Licinius ever since the first ended with the proclamation of three new Caesars on 1 March 317. When he began the war of 324, he was able to present the war against Licinius as a virtual crusade on behalf of the Christians of the East and himself as a liberator of Licinius' Christian subjects from persecution.

Constantine invaded Licinius' territory again. The story of the campaign is easily told (*Origo* 23–28; Zosimus 2.22–28). An expeditionary force on land accompanied by a large fleet advanced along the northern coast of the Aegean Sea to the River Hebrus, along whose left bank Licinius had taken up a defensive position inland near Adrianople (*Barrington Atlas* Map 51H1). After the two armies had faced each other for some days, Constantine forced a crossing and defeated the opposing army on 3 July (*CTh* 7.20.1; *CIL* 1², p. 268; *Descriptio consulum* 324.1). Licinius fled to Byzantium and his army surrendered on the following day. Constantine had assembled a second fleet at the Peiraeus and placed it under the command of Crispus. After the Battle of Adrianople, this fleet won a decisive victory over Licinius' fleet under his admiral Abantus, sailed through the Hellespont and forced Licinius to abandon Byzantium and take refuge in Chalcedon. Constantine forestalled a prolongation of the war by transporting his army across the Bosporus twenty miles to the north of Chalcedon. The armies of Constantine and Licinius met again at Chrysopolis outside Chalcedon on 18 September (*Descriptio consulum* 324.2; *CIL* 1², p. 272; Socrates, *HE* 1.4.2) and Constantine was again victorious. Byzantium and Chalcedon opened their gates. Licinius fled to Nicomedia, from where he sent his wife Constantia and Eusebius the bishop of the city to plead with Constantine for his life. On the morrow of his defeat he came before the victor, laid down his imperial insignia and swore fealty to the new master of the whole Roman world.

6

THE TRANSFORMATION
OF THE EAST

After his victory over Licinius, Constantine lost little time in demonstrating to the inhabitants of Asia Minor, the Levant and Egypt that their new ruler was indeed the convinced and determined Christian that he claimed to be (Pietri 1983: 73–90). He sent two letters to each of the provinces which he had conquered from Licinius (Eusebius, *VC* 2.23). One was addressed to the Christian churches within each province, the other to its inhabitants in general. Constantine issued the letters in both Greek and Latin and he underlined the importance of what he said by subscribing each copy in his own hand. Eusebius quotes in full the text of the letter 'to the provincials of Palestine' (*VC* 2.24–42) and part of a copy of an identical letter sent to Egypt is preserved on papyrus (*P. London* 878). It was a long letter, containing both a confession of faith and a series of provisions rescinding Licinius' legislation regarding the Christians and restoring confiscated property, and it had a profoundly different tone from the letters issued in his name and that of Licinius eleven years earlier. The letters of 313 had granted the Christians of the East both freedom of worship and the ability to reclaim confiscated property, and they had made compensation from the imperial treasury available on petition to private citizens who were obliged to surrender property confiscated from the Christians, whether the present owners had acquired it by gift, by inheritance, by purchase or by direct grant from the imperial treasury. In 324 the victor over Licinius adopted a much more aggressive stance.

Constantine's letter falls naturally into the two normal sections of Late Roman imperial legislation. The first is an unusually extended preamble, in which the emperor sets out his belief that God has ordained his successes in war and made him master of the whole Roman Empire (24–30), the second a series of legal rulings which systematically undo the effects of Licinius' recent persecution (31–42). Constantine argues that recent events have confirmed the truth of Christianity and

Constantine: Dynasty, Religion and Power in the Later Roman Empire, First Edition. Timothy Barnes.
© 2011 Timothy Barnes. Published 2011 by Blackwell Publishing Ltd.

shown how persecution leads first to war, want and disaster and then to death or shameful imprisonment for its wicked perpetrators, who have now received punishments befitting their crimes. The allusion is to Licinius, now imprisoned in Thessalonica (*Origo* 28–29; *Epitome* 41.7),[1] and to his supporters who had probably been killed in their hundreds when Licinius fell from power, as Eusbius records in his own voice in very similar language (*VC* 2.22).

Constantine presents himself as both the servant of God and his avenging angel on earth (Eusebius, *VC* 2.28.2):

[God] examined my service and judged it fit for <the achievement of> his wishes, while I, beginning from that <famous> sea around Britain and the parts where it has been laid down by some higher necessity that the sun should set, have thrust aside and scattered the terrors that held everything under their sway, so that the human race, taught by my service, might restore observance of the most solemn law and at the same time the most blessed faith might be increased under the protective hand of the supreme power.

The detailed provisions of the new law follow.[2] The emperor restores the original status, personal liberty and confiscated property of all Christians who had lost them under Licinius, and he grants to their surviving kin the property of martyrs and those Christians who had forfeited property through being sent into exile. What of martyrs and confessors who had no surviving kin? Constantine departed from the traditional practice of claiming such property as *bona vacantia* or *bona caduca* for the imperial treasury (Millar 1977: 159–163). Instead, in a significant innovation, he allowed the local church of the deceased to receive the inheritance. Finally, Constantine made it clear to his new subjects that they were now living under a Christian regime. In sharp distinction to Licinius in 313, Constantine ordered all who possessed former Christian property to take the initiative in surrendering it voluntarily and without any compensation. For he ruled that the mere possession of confiscated Christian property, however acquired, now constituted a criminal offense, though one for which he would grant pardon provided that the property in question was rapidly surrendered. Even the imperial treasury was to restore all confiscated property to the churches from which it had been taken. Moreover, the emperor transferred the ownership of all places where martyrs were commemorated to the churches, again apparently without compensation for their existing owners.

This long letter, posted up in public in every province that he had conquered from Licinius, was Constantine's first communication with his newly acquired eastern territories (*VC* 2.20–21, 43). It was very soon followed by more positive measures to enhance and entrench the place of Christianity in the public life of the eastern provinces of the Roman Empire. Constantine began to give preference to Christians wherever possible in appointments to administrative office in the East from provincial governors to praetorian prefects (*VC* 2.44, cf. Barnes 1994a; 1995). This was a policy which he appears to have initiated several years earlier when he appointed a man who was both a blue-blooded Roman aristocrat and a Christian to an ordinary consulate in 317 (Champlin 1982). Now he also prohibited the traditional practice of performing a symbolic act of sacrifice before commencing public business, including both criminal trials and civil lawsuits, by burning incense on an altar (*VC* 2.44). This practice had played such a prominent role in the 'Great Persecution' (Barnes 2010a: 111–150) that it was politically necessary for an emperor who proclaimed himself a Christian to end it, at least in the East.[3] Next, so Eusebius records, Constantine issued two transformative laws (*VC* 2.45):

> One prevented the disgusting pollutions of idolatry which had since ancient times been practised in towns and countryside, so that no-one should dare to erect cult-statues, attempt to <consult> oracles <or use> the nonsense attached to them, or sacrifice at all (ὡς μήτ' ἐγέρσεις ξοάνων ποιεῖσθαι τολμᾶν, μήτε μαντείαις καὶ ταῖς ἄλλαις περιεργίαις ἐπιχειρεῖν, μήτε μὴν θύειν καθόλου μηδένα). The other gave orders to raise the height and increase the width and length the buildings that were homes of prayer,[4] as if virtually everyone in future would attach themselves to God since the madness of polytheism has been removed.

Eusebius immediately quotes the copy of the imperial letter which Constantine sent to bishops urging them to enlarge existing churches and build new ones and granting them unlimited access to imperial funds through governors of provinces and the office of the praetorian prefects whom he had instructed 'to cooperate wholeheartedly' with whatever the bishops proposed (*VC* 2.46). Archaeological and other evidence documents the building of large numbers of new and larger churches throughout the Roman Empire after 325 which transformed the appearance of cities.[5]

During most of the twentieth century, however, serious historians of Constantine and the Later Roman Empire found it impossible to believe that Constantine could have prohibited the traditional practice of sacrificing animals before the temples of the gods – and the habit has persisted into the twenty-first century (e.g., Turcan 2006: 223–224; Veyne 2007: 180–183). In 1981 I argued that Eusebius should be believed because the law which he reports is independently attested by a law of Constans in 341 in which the western emperor confirms that his father Constantine had indeed issued such a law for the East when extending it to the West (Barnes 1981: 210, 246, adducing *CTh* 16.10.2). This apparently cogent argument was countered by the absurd claim that the lost law to which both Eusebius and the emperor Constans was merely a 'posited law,' which Constans and Eusebius invented independently of each other (Drake 1982: 465). Eusebius and Constans (it was maintained) were less credible than Libanius, who claimed in the 380s that Constantine 'made absolutely no alteration in the traditional forms of worship' (*Orat.* 30.6, trans. A. F. Norman). I was scolded for 'a surprising willingness' to trust Eusebius' *Life of Constantine*, when I ought to have treated it as a suspect source and for believing Eusebius' assertion that Constantine forbade the traditional practice of sacrificing animals to the gods (Averil Cameron 1983b: 189). Unexpected vindication of my assessment of the evidence is now to hand. For Kevin Wilkinson has shown that the anti-Christian epigrammatist Palladas was writing under Constantine, not under Theodosius or later, as I had previously assumed in agreement with my critics (Chapter 1). Hence Palladas' lament that Hellenism is dead (*Anth. Pal.* 10.90.3–6) confirms the substance of Eusebius' report. On the correct dating of Palladas to the early decades of the fourth century, no reason whatever remains to doubt either that Constantine prohibited animal sacrifice, which had also played an important role in the 'Great Persecution,' especially in the areas ruled by Maximinus (Eusebius, *Mart. Pal.* 4.8, 9.2), or that he prohibited it very soon after the defeat of Licinius, as Eusebius reports, when pagans were cowed and incapable of resistance. The most that they could do was to submit a petition to the emperor pleading with him to reconsider.

Constantine's reply was brutal and uncompromising. He wrote a long letter 'to the provincials of the East' (Eusebius, *VC* 2.48–60). This has often been misinterpreted as an 'edict of toleration' (Dörries 1954: 330–332)[6] and it has even been construed as a license for pagans to practice their traditional cults as they had before 324 (Gaudemet 1990: 453: 'une lettre de 324 ... proclame la liberté du culte des idoles'). That is very far from the truth. Averil Cameron and Stuart Hall come much closer to understanding the purpose of the letter when they head this section of their translation of the *Life of Constantine* 'letter against polytheistic worship' (Cameron & Hall 1999: 111). For the emperor roundly condemns traditional forms of worship in what he calls 'shrines of falsehood' (56.2). Constantine's letter must be read in the context of his recent prohibition of new cult statues, consultation of oracles and animal sacrifice which Eusebius reports and of the protest at which he himself hints. It was doubtless also in 324/325 that the emperor had made it a capital crime to possess a copy of Porphyry's polemical *Against the Christians*, which the philosopher appears to have composed c. 300 to provide an intellectual justification for the 'Great Persecution' (*Urkunde* 33 = *Dokument* 28, cf. Barnes 1981: 211, 377 n.14; 1994c; 2009b: 127–128).

Against this background, Constantine's open letter is not a document of toleration, but rather the opposite. The emperor coolly informs non-Christians that they may retain possession of their shrines, temples and holy places, but his silence about cult practices implicitly reiterates their prohibition. No longer may non-Christians practice their traditional ceremonies in honor of the gods: in their sacred places they can only worship and pray to their gods in the same manner as Christians do to their God. Constantine denounces Apollo and his oracles for their part in encouraging Diocletian to launch the 'Great Persecution' in 303 (*VC* 2.50–51, 52),[7] and he concludes by informing his pagan subjects that he is only restrained from destroying their cult places by his unwillingness to shed blood (*VC* 2.60.2):

> I have said and explained these things at greater length than the aim of my clemency requires because I did not wish to conceal my belief in the truth, especially since some people, as I hear, say that the customs of the temples and the power of darkness have

been completely removed. I would <indeed> have recommended that to all, were not the violent rebelliousness of vile error so immeasurably implanted in the minds of some that it would harm the salvation of all.

This is not the peroration of a tolerant man. It is the fulmination of one who feels frustrated because he has been compelled to recognize that political conditions are not yet ripe for him to enforce a policy dear to his heart.

THE FOUNDATION OF CONSTANTINOPLE

Within a few weeks of the surrender of Licinius, Constantine took a decision which was to have consequences almost as great as his conversion to Christianity. He decided to build a city on the site of the ancient Greek city of Byzantium which would, when completed, become his customary residence and capital, and he decided to found it as a Christian city. It has been normal since Byzantine times to envisage what Constantine did as 'the renaming and reconstruction of Byzantium' (Lenski 2008: 267).[8] But that formulation of what Constantine did is both factually mistaken and deeply misleading in its historical implications. Constantine did not, as has so often been supposed, rename or refound an ancient Greek city; he did something far more radical and revolutionary – he wiped it off the face of the earth. Constantine razed the existing city of Byzantium to the ground and destroyed its temples, shrines and public buildings. Only when the old Byzantium had been completely destroyed, did Constantine build a completely new city on an empty site which now had no non-Christian temples, no other non-Christian buildings or monuments and no pre-Christian history.

The first step was to consecrate the land on which Byzantium had stood as the site of a new city. Praising Constantius thirty years later Themistius reveals the care with which Constantine chose the day for the ceremony. The emperor linked it with the proclamation of his third son as Caesar on 8 November 324. The *dies imperii* of Constantius is well attested (*Descriptio consulum* 324.3, cf. Barnes 1982: 8), but it is only Themistius who synchronizes his investiture as Caesar with the foundation of the new city. He states that Constantius' reign is exactly the same age as the city because on the same occasion 'his father clad the town with its circuit and his son with the purple' (*Orat.* 4, 58b). The ritual performed on 8 November 324 was also described by Philostorgius, whose account was summarized by Photius and incorporated in a later hagiographical life of Constantine (*BHG* 365): Constantine marked out the periphery of his new city by marching on foot with spear in hand making it clear that he was acting under divine inspiration (Philostorgius, *HE* 2.9, 9ª). In doing this he adapted an ancient Roman ceremony, probably that of *lustratio*, which could be performed by the circumambulation of priests (and Constantine was of course *pontifex maximus* in virtue of being an Augustus) and in which, according to Cicero, the founder of a *colonia* had the privilege of naming those who produced victims for sacrifice (*De Divinatione* 1.102).[9] Constantine eschewed the sacrifice of animals (which he had perhaps already prohibited by law), but he used the rituals and procedures of traditional Roman religion to make it clear that he was inaugurating a Christian equivalent of the city of Rome. For the date of 8 November had a particular significance. The Roman antiquarians Varro and Ateius Capito related that the *mundus*, 'a subterranean vault' which marked the earliest remembered settlement on the Palatine Hill in Rome (Wissowa 1912: 234; *OLD* 1144), was opened on three days of the year and that on these three days no public or sacral business could be done (Macrobius, *Saturnalia* 1.16.18; Festus, *De verborum significatu*, pp.144, 145 Lindsay). One of these three days was 8 November. By his actions on 8 November 324, therefore, Constantine both associated the founding of Constantinople with the founding of Rome more than a millennium earlier and dissociated his new city from traditional religious taboos.

The history of Byzantium between 196 and 324, once it is correctly understood, explains why Constantine destroyed the ancient city of Byzantium rather than simply refounding it as Constantinople or New Rome. Unfortunately, a long series of Byzantine writers, starting apparently with Hesychius in the sixth century, falsified the history of their city in the third century in a way which deceived modern enquirers until very recently. In this false history, the Late Antique and medieval city of Constantinople had three founders in the shape of the mythical Byzas, the historical Septimius Severus and finally Constantine, who renamed an existing city which included Severan buildings such as the Baths of Zeuxippus (Hesychius, *Patria Cpl* 15; *Parastaseis* 73; Pseudo-Codinus 1.39; 2.33 [Preger 1901b: 15.13–17.6, 67.14–18; 1907: 136.15–19, 168.5–6]). Hence the modern belief that the Baths of Zeuxippus were 'first built by Septimius Severus (*ca.* A. D. 196) and later enlarged by Constantine the Great' (Mango 1959: 37) and that there was a 'monumental urban renewal' under the Severan dynasty (Bassett 2004: 18–22, with a plan of post-Severan Byzantium drawn by Brian Madigan). However, in separate volumes on the real and the imaginary Constantinople, Gilbert Dagron exposed the falsity of the Byzantine belief that Septimius Severus restored Byzantium after tearing its walls down (Dagron 1974: 13–19; 1984: 61–97). On the basis of Dagron's work, Paul Stephenson has now penetrated behind the façade of legend to discover what later Byzantine patriotism has hidden from view (Stephenson 2009: 192–194, 339, cf. Dagron 1974: 15–19). The emperor who rebuilt Byzantium after its walls were razed in 196 was not Septimius Severus at all, but Constantine's defeated rival Licinius.

Constantinople, as Stephenson rightly stresses, was among other things a victory city (*Origo* 30), its location chosen for its proximity to the battlefield of Chrysopolis as much as for its geographical situation, close to the River Danube and equidistant from the Rhine and the Euphrates. In 196, after the city had supported his imperial rival Pescennius Niger and withstood a three-year siege, which lasted long after Niger had perished, Septimius Severus destroyed not only the walls of Byzantium, but also its public buildings such as theaters and baths, and reduced it to the status of a village within the territory of Perinthus (Dio 74.14.4–5; Herodian 3.6.9). Admittedly, Byzantium regained its municipal status before the death of Severus through the intercession of Severus' elder son (*Historia Augusta, Caracalla* 1.7) and in his honor the city took the Latin title *Antoniniana* and its Greek equivalent *Antoninia* (Dagron 1974: 17). But the walls were not rebuilt: around the middle of the third century the historian Herodian commented that 'even now anyone who sees the ruins and remains <of the walls> is amazed at both the skill of those who originally built them and the power of those who destroyed them' (3.1.7). By 324, however, not only had the walls had been rebuilt, but the city had acquired new baths and a hippodrome. Since the city walls were rebuilt after c. 250, Septimius Severus can have had nothing to do with their rebuilding. Which emperor, therefore, was responsible? The walls may have been rebuilt in the 250s, when the city was menaced by Gothic raiders (Mango 1985: 14–15, 19, 26), but the construction of a hippodrome suggests the hand of Diocletian or a later emperor. Now Diocletian chose nearby Nicomedia as his residence and built basilicas, a circus, a mint, an arms factory and palaces for his wife and daughter there (Lactantius, *Mort. Pers.* 7.9–10),[10] while Galerius' main residences after his campaigns in Egypt and the East were Thessalonica and Serdica (Barnes 1982: 61–64). Maximinus can also be excluded, since he resided in Nicomedia for little more than six or seven months before returning to Syria along the south coast of Asia Minor (Barnes 1982: 65–67, cf. Mitchell 1988: 108). That leaves Licinius, who resided in Sirmium until he lost Illyricum to Constantine in the autumn of 316 (*Origo* 8, 16–17; [Julian], *Ep.* 181, 449a, cf. Barnes 1978b: 100–101; 1982: 80–82). Stephenson suggests that after 1 March 317 Licinius, who had fortified Byzantium against Maximinus in 311, chose to make Byzantium his capital in preference to Nicomedia (cf. Barnes 1982: 82), since he had good reason for suspecting that Constantine would invade his territory a second time – as indeed he did in 324.

AN IMPERIAL SERMON

The *Speech to the Assembly of the Saints* was for a long time deliberately excluded from some important scholarly discussions of Constantine because their authors believed that the *Speech* was either not by Constantine or at least of doubtful authenticity. Thus Norman Baynes, in his influential essay on Constantine and the Christian church, felt debarred from using the *Speech* in the same way as he used the Constantinian documents in Eusebius' *Life* and the appendix to Optatus, because he believed that he could not distinguish between the work of the emperor himself and the 'redactor' who produced the Greek version which Eusebius preserves (Baynes 1931: 50–56 n.19).[11] And as late as 1973 Richard Hanson, who was in many ways a fine patristic scholar, claimed that 'a careful survey of the work' showed that the improbability of Constantine being its author was so great as virtually to exclude what he called the 'conjecture' that it 'really did come from his pen or from the pen of one of his staff' (Hanson 1973: 505–511). Hanson based his argument on a series of a priori assumptions and misunderstandings of the historical allusions in the *Speech*: he supposed that it shows more knowledge of Platonic philosophy than we could expect Constantine to have acquired; he considered it 'highly improbable' that Constantine could have seen the ruins of Memphis or Babylon (cf. Chapter 3); he accused the *Speech* of confusing Licinius with Maxentius and Maxentius with Maximinus in passages where the confusion resulted from his own misreading of the text; and he detected an allusion to Julian the Apostate's consultation of the oracle of Apollo at Daphne close to Antioch in 362 – from which he deduced that someone composed a fictitious speech for Constantine between 362 and 382 in order 'to supply thereby a gap which Eusebius had left in his biography of that emperor' (Hanson 1973: 511). Unfortunately, Hanson failed to discuss the evidence that anti-Christian oracles were produced in Antioch at the time of the 'Great Persecution,' which may have been circulated as emanating from the oracle of Apollo at Daphne (Eusebius, *HE* 9.2–3; Theodore Lector p. 158.9–14 Hansen, cf. Barnes 1976c: 251–252; Digeser 2004: 63–73).

Denials that Constantine delivered the speech have always, like Hanson's, rested principally on failure to elucidate its historical allusions correctly. In the last generation, however, an almost universal consensus has emerged among scholars that the *Speech* is authentic, by which I mean that what the manuscripts of the *Life of Constantine* present as a fifth book, following the four by Eusebius himself, is the speech which Eusebius promised to append to the *Life* (*VC* 4.32), and that this speech is an official or officially authorized Greek translation of a speech which the emperor delivered in Latin and subsequently put into circulation (Barnes 1976b; 1981: 73–76, 324–325 nn. 129–149).[12] But controversy continues over when and where Constantine delivered the speech.

That Constantine composed the *Speech to the Assembly of the Saints* in Latin, as Eusebius states, whether or not he actually delivered it in Latin rather than Greek, was proved by Anton Kurfess in a series of articles published over the course of nearly four decades, in which he demonstrated that whoever translated the passages of Virgil's *Fourth Eclogue*, to which the *Speech* gives a messianic exegesis, has adjusted the Greek translation of Virgil to fit Constantine's exegesis (Wigtil 1981, cf. Kurfess 1950).[13] The city and the year in which Constantine delivered the *Speech* at Eastertide must both be deduced from the emperor's allusions to recent events. The following passages limit the possibilities considerably (25.4, p. 191.24–27; 192.1–6):

πᾶν γὰρ τὸ τοῦ προειρημένου βασιλέως στράτευμα, ὑποταχθὲν ἐξουσίᾳ τινὸς ἀχρήστου βίᾳ τε τὴν ʿΡωμαίων ἀρχὴν ἁρπάσαντος, προνοίας θεοῦ τὴν μεγάλην πόλιν ἐλευθερούσης, πολλοῖς καὶ παντοδαποῖς πολέμοις ἀνήλωται ...

ἀλλὰ μὴν καὶ αἱ πρὸς τὸν θεὸν ἐκφωνήσεις τῶν πιεζομένων καὶ τὴν ἔμφυτον ἐλευθερίαν ποθούντων, καὶ οἱ μετὰ τὴν ἀπαλλαγὴν τῶν κακῶν τῆς εὐχαριστίας πρὸς τὸν θεὸν ἔπαινοι, ἀποδοθείσης τῆς ἐλευθερίας αὐτοῖς καὶ

τῶν μετὰ δικαιοσύνης συμβολαίων, πῶς οὐ παντὶ τρόπῳ τὴν τοῦ θεοῦ
πρόνοιαν καὶ τὴν πρὸς τοὺς ἀνθρώπους στοργὴν χαρακτηρίζουσιν;

For all the army of the aforementioned emperor, becoming subject to the authority
of a good-for-nothing who had seized the position of Roman emperor by force, was
destroyed in many battles of every sort as the providence of God liberated the great
city. ...

Moreover, both the loud appeals to God of those who were oppressed and longed for
freedom, which is an innate right, and their thankful praises to God after their release
from misfortunes, when freedom and the exercise of legal rights had been restored to
them – surely these in every way express the providence of God and his love towards
humanity.

The 'aforementioned emperor' is Diocletian, who is named in the immediately
preceding passage (25.1, p. 190.19). It follows that the 'unworthy person' who
inherited his whole army after becoming emperor improperly must be Licinius,
who ruled the whole of Diocletian's eastern half of the Roman Empire from 313
to 324, and that Constantine must be speaking in a city which he has liberated by
defeating Licinius in war (Mazzarino 1974: 112–116). This completely rules out of
court any attempt to identify the 'unworthy person' as Maxentius and to deduce
that the *Speech* was delivered at any time earlier than the spring of 317. Hence it is
pointless to waste space assessing the often specious arguments deployed in support
of any of the dates earlier than Easter 317 which various scholars have proposed for
the *Speech* – Easter 313 in Rome (Kurfess 1950: 164–165), Easter 314 in Trier
(Girardet 2006b: 76–80), Easter 314 or Easter 315 in Rome (Edwards 1999: 268;
2003: xxiii–xxix).[14]

In 1976 I proposed that Constantine delivered the *Speech to the Assembly of the
Saints* on 12 April 317 in Serdica, which he had won in his first war against Licinius
(Barnes 1976: 423), though I later accepted André Piganiol's date of 5 April 323
(Piganiol 1932: 370–372), from which it followed that the liberated city could be
either Serdica or Thessalonica (Barnes 1981: 73; 1982: 73). In 1998 Bruno Bleckmann
produced a more satisfying and convincing identification of the liberated city as
Nicomedia (Bleckmann 1997: 186–188). When Constantine recalls the disasters
which attended the onset of the 'Great Persecution' in 303, he exclaims: 'Nicomedia
<still> talks <about them>, and those who saw them, of whom I happen to be one,
are not silent; for I saw' etc. (25.2, p. 190.24–26). He compliments the city where he
is speaking and remarks that it had been the residence of a persecuting emperor
who came to grief soon after it welcomed him (22.1, p. 187.28–188.7):

Ἐγὼ μὲν τῆς εὐτυχίας τῆς ἐμαυτοῦ καὶ τῶν ἐμῶν πάντων αἰτιῶμαι τὴν σὴν εὐμένειαν.
μαρτυρεῖ δὲ καὶ ἡ ἔκβασις τῶν κατ᾽ εὐχὰς ἁπάντων, ἀνδραγαθίαι, νῖκαι, κατὰ τῶν
πολεμίων τρόπαια, σύνοιδεν δὲ καὶ μετ᾽ εὐφημίας ἐπαινεῖ καὶ ἡ μεγάλη πόλις,
βούλεται δὲ καὶ ὁ δῆμος τῆς φιλτάτης πόλεως, εἰ καὶ πρότερον[15] ταῖς σφαλεραῖς
ἐλπίσιν ἐξαπατηθεὶς ἀνάξιον ἑαυτῆς προείλετο προστάτην, ὃς παραχρῆμα ἑάλω

προσηκόντως τε καὶ ἀξίως τοῖς ἑαυτῷ τετολμημένοις, ὧν οὐ θέμις ἀπομνημονεῦσαι, μάλιστα ἐμοὶ τῷ διαλεγομένῳ πρὸς σὲ καὶ πᾶσαν ἐπιμέλειαν ποιουμένῳ, πῶς ἂν ἁγναῖς καὶ εὐφήμοις διαλέξεσι προσείποιμί σε.

I consider your goodwill [sc. of Piety] responsible for my own success and the success of all my <endeavors>. The result of everything according to my prayers bears witness – deeds of valor, victories, triumphs over my enemies. The great city acknowledges this and praises it with acclamations; and also the people of the dear city wish <to do the same>, even if formerly, deceived by false hopes, they chose a champion unworthy of the city, who was immediately caught in a manner appropriate to and worthy of his rash deeds, which it is not right to recall, especially for me as I speak you and take every care how I may address you with pure and auspicious utterances.

The chapter heading, which here may have been added by Eusebius himself rather than by the posthumous editor of the *Life*, identifies the champion who was unworthy of the city as Maximinus (p.153.2). In 1976, I proposed to emend the transmitted Μαξιμίνου to Μαξιμιανοῦ, since the two names are so often confused in manuscripts, and to see an allusion to the death of Galerius, who after 299 resided in both Serdica and Thessalonica and could therefore be described as the champion of either city (Barnes 1976b: 420–422). But what Constantine says fits Maximinus far better than Galerius, who never resided in Nicomedia, although he was certainly in the city during the winter of 302/303 and again in the spring of 305, on both occasions to exert pressure on Diocletian (Lactantius, *Mort. Pers.* 10.6–14.6–7, 18.1–19.6; Eusebius, *HE* 8.5, 8.6.2). In contrast, Maximinus was welcomed in Nicomedia when he arrived there in the summer of 311 after seizing control of Asia Minor on the death of Galerius, and he resided in Nicomedia for several months until January 312 (Lactantius, *Mort. Pers.* 36.1; Eusebius, *HE* 9.9a.4; Barnes 1982: 66).

In the *Speech* Constantine expounds a Christology which uses language that he could not possibly have used in front of bishops or any other Christian audience after the Council of Nicaea. In particular, he commends Plato for distinguishing between two gods in a way that corresponds to the Christian notions of God the Father and God the Son (9.3, p. 163.15–25, cf. J. M. Rist 1981: 155–158):[16]

αὐτός τε ὁ ὑπὲρ πάντας τοὺς ἄλλους †ἠπιώτατος† Πλάτων, [καὶ] τὰς διανοίας τῶν ἀνθρώπων πρῶτος ἀπὸ τῶν αἰσθήσεων ἐπὶ τὰ νοητὰ καὶ ἀεὶ ὡσαύτως ἔχοντα ἐθίσας ἀνακύψαι ἀναβλέψαι τ' ἐπὶ τὰ μετάρσια διδάξας, πρῶτον μὲν θεὸν ὑφηγήσατο τὸν ὑπὲρ τὴν οὐσίαν, καλῶς ποιῶν, ὑπέταξε δὲ τούτῳ καὶ δεύτερον, καὶ δύο οὐσίας τῷ ἀριθμῷ διεῖλε, μιᾶς οὔσης τῆς ἀμφοτέρων τελειότητος, τῆς τε οὐσίας τοῦ δευτέρου θεοῦ τὴν ὕπαρξιν ἐχούσης ἐκ τοῦ πρώτου· αὐτὸς γάρ ἐστιν ὁ δημιουργὸς καὶ διοικητὴς τῶν ὅλων δηλονότι ὑπεραναβεβηκώς, ὁ δὲ μετ' ἐκεῖνον ταῖς ἐκείνου προστάξεσιν ὑπουργήσας τὴν αἰτίαν τῆς τῶν πάντων συστάσεως εἰς ἐκεῖνον ἀναπέμπει.

Plato himself, who surpassed all others in <sagacity>[17] and was the first to accustom human intellects to raise their eyes from the <physical> senses to what the mind perceives and is always the same and taught <us> to look up to things above, correctly posited a god who is above being, and subordinated to him a second <god> and separated the two beings numerically, with both having a single perfection and the being of the second god having its essence[18] from the first <god>. For he (sc. the first god) is the maker and ruler of the universe because he clearly transcends it, while the one <who comes> after him obeys his commandments and owes to him the cause of the cohesion of all things.

Eusebius of Caesarea had been sympathetic to Arius from the very start of the controversy over his views and continued, even after Arius' death, to assert his right to assert theological propositions with which he himself did not necessarily agree, provided that they fell within the bounds of what he called 'the teaching of the church' or 'the theology of the church' (*Contra Marcellum* 1.3.18; *De ecclestiastica theologia* 1, pr.). On the criteria which Eusebius applied, the theological views of Arius fell within these bounds, in contrast to Marcellus, whose attack on himself, Arius and their allies expressed views that were demonstrably heretical (Barnes 1981:264–263, cf. 240–242; 2010b:254–255). After the Council of Nicaea, Eusebius began studiously to avoid terminology implying that God the Son was secondary or subordinate to God the Father, even though he had earlier used it without inhibition. In his *General Elementary Introduction*, written during the 'Great Persecution,' Eusebius called the Logos 'God and Lord of all, second after the Father and Lord of creation' existing 'secondarily (δευτέρως) after the Father' and 'the second cause of creation after the first God' (*Eclogae Propheticae* 1.12, 3.1 [*PG* 22.1068, 1121]). Similarly, in the *Preparation for the Gospel* and *Proof of the Gospel* which Eusebius composed sequentially in fifteen plus twenty books between c. 314 and c. 323, he equates the Logos with the second cause as defined by Plato, Plotinus and Numenius (*PE* 11.14–18; *DE* 5.1.20, 24) and with 'a second *ousia* and divine power' separate from the '*ousia* without beginning and unbegotten of the God of the universe' (*PE* 7.12.2, cf. 7.15.1), and states that God the Son has a second *ousia* after the Father (*DE* 6, pr. 1). Among Eusebius' ecclesiastical opponents, Marcellus of Ancyra latched on to the use of the words 'first and second god' by Narcissus of Neronias as proof manifest that Narcissus was a heretic (frag. 80 Klostermann = Eusebius, *Contra Marcellum* 1.4.53). For the phrase 'second god' became completely unacceptable as soon as the Council of Nicaea declared that God the Father and God the Son shared the same *ousia* and made the word *homoousios* the touchstone of orthodoxy. Although Eusebius did not change his basic theology, he carefully avoided language that could be construed as implying the inferiority of the Son after the Council. Constantine, therefore, delivered the *Speech to the Assembly of the Saints* at Easter 325: he cannot have delivered it in Nicomedia at any earlier Easter, and his use of the phrase 'second God' excludes any date after the Council of Nicaea met in the early summer of that year.[19]

In 325 Easter Sunday fell on 18 April. Constantine, therefore, delivered the *Speech to the Assembly of the Saints* on either 16 or 17 April: although it has been traditional to style the *Speech* Constantine's 'Good Friday sermon' (e.g., Barnes

1976b), Stuart Hall has observed that, since liturgical celebration of Good Friday is first attested in Jerusalem in the 380s (*Itinerarium Egeriae* 35–37), the *Speech* may well have been delivered on the following day, Easter Eve (S. G. Hall 1998: 96). Furthermore, Constantine cannot have been addressing an audience comprised mainly of bishops, as has often been argued or assumed (e.g., by Bleckmann 1998: 197–200). At Easter every bishop was expected to celebrate Easter in his own church in the city of which he was bishop and to baptize cathecumens (S. G. Hall 1998: 86). The 'saints' whom Constantine addressed were Eusebius, the bishop of Nicomedia, whom he saluted as a 'sea-captain who possesses holiness and virginity,' and his church (2.1, p. 155.21),[20] Eusebius' assembled clergy, whom he complimented as 'those who understand the divine mysteries' (p. 155.31), and the Christian congregation of Nicomedia, including those newly baptized, whom he greeted as 'you who truly worship God' (p. 155.24–25). The contents of the *Speech* perfectly reflect its place and time of delivery: Constantine had become sole ruler of the Roman Empire through God's aid and he knew that in a few weeks he would preside over the opening of an empire-wide gathering of bishops.

The *Speech to the Assembly of the Saints* has attracted several illuminating exegeses from different points of view (esp. Pfättisch 1908; 1913; Lane Fox 1986: 642–653; Pizzani 1993; Drake 2000: 292–305; Cristofoli 2005: 17–28, 116–120; Stephenson 2009: 171–172, 269–270). It has three main sections (Barnes 1981: 74–75). The first (3–10) is philosophical with many quotations of and allusions to Plato (Pfättisch 1910). It insists on the equivalence of Platonic metaphysics and Christian theology: God the Father is the Good, the First God, the Demiurge, while the Second God of Plato's *Timaeus* is God the Son, Christ and the Logos. Constantine appears to draw heavily on the second century Platonist Numenius of Apamea, who had posited a 'first god' and a 'second god' and identified the latter as the demiurge of the *Timaeus*, who created the universe (frags. 12–22 des Places), but he consistently modifies Platonic ideas in a Christian direction (J. M. Rist 1981: 155–159).

The second section (11–21) equates virtue with Christian belief and vice with refusal to believe in the Christian God. Constantine first argues that throughout history idolatry has led to disaster, and appeals to the ruins of Memphis and Babylon, which he has seen for himself (Chapter 3), as proof of the fall of the powerful who offended God. He then develops and amplifies arguments which Lactantius had used to show that Old Testament prophecies had come true (*Divine Institutes* 7.16–25). Like Lactantius, whom he knew in Nicomedia before 305 and employed as tutor to his son Crispus before the Battle of the Milvian Bridge, and with whom he may have conversed at length in Nicomedia during the preceding winter, Constantine quotes the Sibylline Oracles and Virgil's *Fourth Eclogue*, but he goes much further than his intellectual mentor. He quotes a thirty-four line acrostic from the eighth book of the Sibylline Oracles which spells out in Greek the words 'Jesus Christ, Son of God, Savior, Cross' (18, p. 179.19–p. 181.2),[21] and he gives a detailed exegesis of the 'messianic' eclogue of 'the most outstanding of the poets of Italy' (p. 181.23), as prophesying the birth of Christ (19–21, cf. Bolhuis 1950).[22]

The third section of the *Speech* (22–26) shows how God punishes persecuting emperors like Decius,Valerian and Aurelian and Diocletian, all of whom Constantine invokes by name (24), but rewards those who worship him. Some of Constantine's references to recent history appear unduly allusive to the modern reader, but that is at least partly because the original audience of the speech in 325 knew perfectly well what had happened in their city since 303, even though it has proved a long and difficult task for modern scholars to establish with certainty what that city was. The original audience will have had no difficulty in understanding Constantine's reference to his victory over Maxentius at the Battle of the Milvian Bridge (22.2, p. 188.8–12):

υπερβάλλων μέντοι μανία καὶ ὠμότητι προκεκήρυκτό σοί ποτε, ὦ θεοσέβεια, καὶ πάσαις ταῖς ἁγιωτάταις σου ἐκκλησίαις ὑπὸ τυράννων πόλεμος ἄσπονδος, καὶ οὐκ ἐπέλειψάν τινες τῶν ἐν τῇ Ρώμῃ τηλικούτοις ἐπιχαίροντες δημοσίοις κακοῖς, παρεσκεύαστο δὲ καὶ πεδίον τῇ μάχῃ

Once a relentless war, excessive in its madness and savagery, had been declared by tyrants against you, Piety, and all your most holy churches, and there were not lacking some in Rome who rejoiced at such public misfortunes. But a field[23] had been prepared for the battle!

Maxentius was unknown to the Christians of Nicomedia. Constantine, therefore, saw no point in expatiating on the allegation that Maxentius had persecuted Christians in Rome, which he knew to be false. But he wished to refer to his famous victory at the Battle of the Milvian Bridge, which had very quickly become known in the East as a victory attributable to the Christian God (Eusebius, *HE* 9.9.2–11). Hence he alludes to Maxentius as one who sympathized with the tyrants who persecuted Christians in the East. Although in reality Maxentius allied himself only with Maximinus (Lactantius, *Mort. Pers.* 44.10), Constantine's plural tyrants include both Diocletian and Galerius. The former confessed his folly and madness in launching the 'Great Persecution,' which led inexorably to Constantine's victories in civil war and the liberation of Nicomedia (25).

The peroration of the *Speech to the Assembly of the Saints* is flat, general and almost platitudinous. But a passage in the middle of the speech contains both a remarkably explicit statement of its author's imperial mission and an allusion to his conversion to Christianity when he was approaching the age of forty (11.1, p. 165.30–p. 166.10):

We strive to the best of our ability to fill those who are uninitiated in such teachings with good hope, having summoned God to assist us in the endeavor. For it is no mean task for us to turn the minds of our subjects[24] to piety if they happen to be <already> good, or, if they are wicked and unfeeling, to lead them to the opposite, making them useful <citizens> instead of good-for-nothings. Taking pleasure in these very endeavors, therefore, and believing that it is the task of a good man to sing the praises of the Savior, I dismiss everything that an accidental inferior condition has unreasonably laid upon the misfortune of ignorance, considering repentance the most important <route to>

salvation, and I wish that this revelation had been vouchsafed to me long ago, since[25] happy is he who from childhood has been steadfast and rejoiced in the knowledge of things divine and the beauty of virtue (cf. Genesis 48.15; Psalm 70[71].5).

In other words, as Johannes Straub put it, Constantine had a genuine sense of mission (Straub 1942): he believed that God had entrusted him with the task of converting the Roman Empire to Christianity.

THE COUNCIL OF NICAEA

Constantine's conquest of the East pitched him into the middle of an acute theological controversy. The so-called 'Arian controversy' – the polemical title attached by the victors to a Christological debate that is more fairly described as a 'search for the Christian doctrine of God' (Hanson 1988) – started c. 318, when Alexander, the bishop of Alexandria, excommunicated the priest Arius for propounding ideas about the relationship between God the Father and God the Son which he considered heretical. Arius appealed to Christian bishops outside Egypt whom he believed to be sympathetic, and they supported his right to hold and express his opinions – whatever they in fact were, since Arius very soon modified the words or ideas which had caused the initial offense and his expulsion from the church of Alexandria. The controversy spread throughout the East with the convening of councils and counter-councils of bishops until Licinius forbade them (Eusebius, *VC* 1.51.1). In the present context, it is fortunately not necessary to try to unravel the theological subtleties at issue, which have given rise to a large modern bibliography.[26] It is more important to note Constantine's instinctive intellectual attitude towards them, which he expressed in the letter that he sent to Alexander and Arius almost as soon as he became aware of the controversy (*VC* 2.64–72).[27] He told the bishop and the priest that they 'were quarrelling over small, indeed exceptionally trivial points' (*VC* 2.71.1: ὑμῶν γὰρ ἐν ἀλλήλοις ὑπὲρ μικρῶν καὶ λίαν ἐλαχίστων φιλονεικούντων), that they should behave in a civilized way like philosophers, who disagree on small matters while remaining in total agreement on basic principles (71.2), that it was wrong to set brother against brother for the sake of 'a few pointless verbal disputes' (71.3: δι' ὀλίγας καὶ ματαίας ῥημάτων ἐν ὑμῖν φιλονεικίας), that they should resume Christian fellowship with each other even if they decided to continue to differ over 'that very silly question, whatever it is' (71.6: τῇ λίαν εὐήθει, καὶ οἵα δήποτέ ἐστιν ἐκείνη, ζητήσει).

Constantine attempted to mediate the controversy in the autumn of 324 by sending Ossius of Corduba to Egypt with the letter in which he urged Alexander and Arius to compose their differences in a civilized manner (Eusebius, *VC* 2.63; Socrates, *HE* 1.7.1; Sozomenus, *HE* 1.16.5). The attempt failed. In Alexandria Ossius presided over a council of bishops which made some firm decisions about the Melitian schism, which had started about 306 and was to divide the Egyptian church for several decades, but it referred the doctrinal problems to a great council to be held at Ancyra. Moreover, during his return journey to court, Ossius presided over a council in Antioch, whose synodical letter, preserved only in Syriac, was published in 1905 (*Urkunde* 18 = *Dokument* 20). This letter contains a long, awkward and intricately phrased creed which in no way anticipates the creed adopted at Nicaea a few months later (Abramowski 1975: 365–366), followed by the provisional excommunication of the bishops Theodotus of Laodicea, Narcissus of Neronias and Eusebius of Caesarea for refusing to subscribe to it: they were pronounced heretical, but given an opportunity to recant their errors at the forthcoming 'great and holy council at Ancyra.' Before the bishops converged on Ancyra, however, Constantine transferred the venue to Nicaea (*Urkunde* 20 = *Dokument* 22). The reason which he gave was that Nicaea had a more salubrious climate. This was (and is) true, but the emperor's real motive was to participate in the debates of the council, as he had at the Council of Arles in 314 (Chapter 5).

Much will always be obscure about the Council of Nicaea.[28] No stenographic record of the proceedings was taken and no minutes were produced by anyone. It is true that we have reports of different parts of the debates from four men who attended the council – Constantine himself, Eustathius the bishop of Antioch (frag. 32 Spanneut = Theodoretus, *HE* 1.8.1–5, cf. Barnes 1978a: 57–59), Eusebius of Caesarea (*VC* 3.6–22) and Athanasius, who attended as the deacon and assistant of Alexander of Alexandria and composed a very selective account of the council nearly thirty years later in a long letter which he probably addressed to Liberius, who became bishop of Rome on 17 May 352 (*De decretis Nicaeni synodi* [*CPG* 2120], cf. Barnes 1993a: 110–112, 198–200). And later writers who were not at the council provide isolated snippets of information about it, such as that the creed was actually written by the Cappadocian priest Hermogenes (Basil of Caesarea, *Epp.* 81, 244.9, 263.3). But neither singly nor collectively do any of these provide more than discontinuous glimpses of the course of the debates.

The opening ceremony, which Eusebius describes, was held in the judgment hall of the imperial palace with appropriate pomp. In a departure from normal court etiquette, however, Constantine did not sit on a throne: he sat on a stool and he asked permission from the bishops before he sat down. Eusebius of Nicomedia delivered an address of welcome, to which Constantine replied briefly urging the bishops to resolve their disagreements peacefully to please God and show gratitude to the emperor who had released them from oppression. He then turned the debate over to the bishops (Eusebius, *VC* 3.10–13.1).[29] The first item of business must have been whether to admit Theodotus of Laodicea, Narcissus of Neronias and Eusebius of Caesarea as members of the council. It is plausibly reported that Ossius of Corduba, who presided over the doctrinal debates, and Alexander of Alexandria had agreed in advance that the philosophically dubious term *homoousios* ('of one substance') should be the touchstone of orthodoxy (Philostorgius, *HE* 1.7, 7a): Eusebius of Nicomedia, the most prominent and influential of Arius' supporters, had declared it unacceptable (*Urkunde* 21 = *Dokument* 23 = Ambrose, *De Fide*

3.15.125) and Arius himself had repudiated the use of the term to define the relationship of God the Son to God the Father as Manichean (*Urkunde* 6.2 = *Dokument* 1.2). Eusebius of Caesarea had arrived in Nicaea with a statement of his beliefs designed to demonstrate his orthodoxy. When he read it out, Constantine commended it and avowed that Eusebius' beliefs were virtually identical with his own: all that Eusebius needed to do was to add that God the Son was of one substance with the God the Father (Opitz, *Urkunde* 22.2-7 = *Dokument* 24.2–7). Faced with an unpalatable choice between swallowing something which appeared to contradict his Christology and immediate excommunication, Eusebius accepted the novel term *homoousios* and salved his conscience with the hope that he could find some way to reconcile it with what he really thought.

Constantine's intervention was decisive. Debate dragged on for days, but in the end the council adopted a creed which incorporated the new term *homoousios* as a belief required of all Christians. Philumenus, the *magister officiorum* supervised the signing ceremony in which imperial notaries carried the creed around for all to add their names (Philostorgius, *HE* 1.9a). Ossius of Corduba, who had presided over the debate, subscribed first, then two representatives of the bishop of Rome to indicate that the creed of Nicaea was intended to be valid throughout the Roman Empire, after which the other bishops present added their names, about 270 in all. Only two Libyan bishops who had been associated with Arius from the start refused to subscribe, as did Arius himself and some priests. All the recusants were sent into exile at once (Philostorgius, *HE* 1.9a, 10, cf. Barnes 2009b: 125).

The second main problem debated by the Council of Nicaea was the date of Easter.[30] Liturgical practice was not uniform throughout Christendom, and different groups of Christians continued to observe Easter at different dates long after the Council of Nicaea. Indeed, they still do, since some churches continue even now to use the Julian calendar, whereas the majority, Protestants and Catholics alike, have adopted the calendaric reforms introduced by Pope Gregory XIII in 1582 (Blackburn & Holford Strevens 1999: 682–692, 791–800, 862–867). Both before and at the Council of Nicaea the underlying issue in disputes which entailed technical calculations was not primarily chronological, but ideological: should or could the Christian Easter either normally or ever coincide with the Jewish Passover?

Jesus was crucified on 14 Nisan, the day before the start of the Jewish Passover, as the fourth gospel correctly states (John 18.28, 19.14, cf. Barnes 2010a: 1–2).[31] The very earliest Christian congregations accordingly commemorated the anniversary of their master's death on 14 Nisan (Strobel 1977: 17–69), and Easter was still celebrated on 14 Nisan in second-century Asia Minor regardless of what day of the week that might be (Eusebius, *HE* 5.23.1). Hence the characterization 'Quartodecimans' for those who celebrated Easter on 14 Nisan, though the term is best avoided in scholarly analysis, since it was applied polemically to those who always celebrated Easter on a Sunday, but used a calculation of its date which allowed the Christian Easter to coincide with the Jewish Passover (Blackburn & Holford Strevens 1999: 791–792, 883). The three synoptic gospels reflect an early modification of the original practice, since they make Jesus eat Passover with his disciples on the evening before his arrest (Matthew 26.17–20; Mark 14.12–17; Luke 22.7–16), and it was this divergence of practice that led to a situation where the Christians of Asia Minor celebrated Easter on 14 Nisan, while Christians elsewhere marked the anniversary of Christ's resurrection, not his death, by always celebrating Easter on a Sunday, specifically on the Sunday following 14 Nisan (Lohse 1953: 10–20; Strobel 1977: 17–69).

Towards the end of the second century, apparently c. 190, Victor the bishop of Rome tried to achieve uniformity of practice, but his attempt, which is known from Eusebius (*HE* 5.23–25),[32] ended in failure. Eusebius reports the contents of letters in which Victor, bishops from Palestine, Pontus, Gaul and Osrhoene, the bishop of Corinth and many others declared that 'the mystery of the Lord's resurrection from the dead should never be celebrated on any day other than the Lord's day' (*HE* 5.23.2–4). Polycrates, the bishop of Ephesus, retorted with a spirited defense of the Asian custom which appealed to the authority of the apostle Philip and his daughters and of Asian bishops and martyrs like Polycarp of Smyrna (24.1–8). Victor thereupon broke off communion with the churches of Asia, but other bishops declined to follow his lead and urged him to be more charitable. Irenaeus of Lyon circulated a letter urging peace, and the controversy died down. Eusebius closes his account by quoting from a circular letter in which the leading bishops of Palestine and southern Syria claimed that the church of Alexandria celebrated Easter as they did and proclaimed a desire that all Christians everywhere 'keep the holy day in concord and at one time' (25). It was perhaps this controversy which encouraged several Christian scholars of the third century to produce Easter cycles for the calculation of the correct date of Easter for years ahead (Schmid 1905: 14–28; Mosshammer 2008: 109–161).

It was probably Constantine himself who placed the date of Easter on the agenda at Nicaea. In August 314 the Council of Arles, which Constantine attended in person (Barnes 1982: 72), had laid down that Easter should be observed 'on the same day and at the same time throughout the whole world' and that the bishop of Rome should circulate this decision to everyone (314 Arles, Canon 1 [*CCSL* 148.9]: *de observatione Paschae dominicae: ut uno die et uno tempore per omnem orbem a nobis observetur*). Until 324, however, no mechanism existed for enforcing such conformity of practice in the parts of the Roman world ruled by Licinius. After he conquered the East, Constantine discovered that not all his new Christian subjects celebrated Easter on the same day as he had celebrated it for more than a decade. Since he regarded such divergence of liturgical practice as improper and equivalent to schism, he set out to achieve uniformity of liturgical practice. In contrast to the theological debates, over which Ossius of Corduba had presided, Eusebius reports that the emperor led discussion of the date of Easter, though not sitting in the normal place of a presiding officer, but sitting in the middle of the bishops (*On Easter* 8).

The primary evidence for the debate over the date of Easter and the decision of the council comprises Eusebius' tract *On Easter* (translated in App. D) and Constantine's letter 'to the churches' announcing the decision (Eusebius, *VC* 3.17–20 = *Urkunde* 26 = *Dokument* 30). According to Eusebius, the debate pitted the bishops of the North, South and West against eastern bishops who defended what they believed to be the ancient custom (*On Easter* 8). Constantine is more precise: the Council decided that the liturgical custom observed in the whole of the West, in Africa and Egypt including Libya, in Greece, in the dioceses of Asiana and Pontica and in Cilicia, should become the norm (Eusebius, *VC* 3.18.3).[33] Eusebius wrote *On Easter* to explain and justify his acceptance of the majority position which the emperor supported. What precisely therefore was the ancient custom which Eusebius was compelled to abandon? It can hardly be the celebration of Easter on the fourteenth day of the lunar month, since the churches of Palestine had long before adopted the practice of always celebrating Easter on a Sunday (Eusebius, (*HE* 5.23.2–4) and Eusebius classed himself as one of the easterners who were compelled to yield. Moreover, the ancient custom allowed Easter to be celebrated at the same time as the Jewish Passover, which was forbidden at Nicaea: in Eusebius' offensive formulation, 'a single festival of Christ came about' when the easterners 'separated themselves from the murderers of our Lord and adhered to those who shared their beliefs.' The ancient custom, therefore, was to use a calculation of its date which allowed Easter to coincide with the Jewish Passover, that is to say, which allowed Easter to fall on 14 Nisan if 14 Nisan was a Sunday, which had the corollary that it could fall before the vernal equinox, which between Julius Caesar and 325 had advanced from 25 to 22 March (Blackburn & Holford Strevens 1999: 792–793, 683).

The anti-Semitic reasoning behind the Nicene decision is clear, and Constantine gave it prominence in the letter in which he announced it to Christian churches. He argued that it was immoral for Christians ever to allow Easter to be celebrated on the same day as the wicked Jews celebrated the Passover (Eusebius, *VC* 3.18.2–4, 19.1):

> First it was decided that it is unworthy to accomplish that most holy festival following the custom of the Jews, who having sullied their hands with a lawless crime are predictably polluted and spiritually blind. Since their nation has been rejected <by God>, it is possible by a truer arrangement (ἀληθεστέρᾳ τάξει), which we have preserved from the first day of the Passion until the present, for the fulfillment of this observation to be extended also to future ages. Let there be nothing in common between you and the detestable mob of Jews. We have received another way from our Savior; a course lies before our holy worship which is both lawful and proper. Let us with one accord, respected brothers, take hold of this and tear ourselves away from that shameful complicity. For it is most bizarre for them to boast that we would not be capable of observing this without instruction from them. What could they calculate correctly, who after the murder of the Lord, that <veritable> parricide, have taken leave of their senses and act out of uncontrolled impulse, not according to any rational calculation, wherever their innate madness leads them? In this matter too, therefore, they do not see the truth so that, always going astray for the most part, instead of the appropriate calculation they <sometimes> celebrate Easter twice during the same <astronomical> year.

Hence, since it was proper that this matter be set right so that there is nothing in common with the race of those parricides and murderers of the Lord, while there is a suitable calculation which all the churches of the western, southern and northern parts of the world observe, and also some <churches> of the eastern areas, for which reason all have at the present <time> decided that it is right (and I myself have promised that it will please your good sense), that what is observed by common and harmonious consent in the city of Rome, in Italy and all Africa, in Egypt, in the <provinces of> Spain, Gaul and Britain, in the Libyas, in the whole of Greece, in the dioceses of Asiana and Pontica, and in Cilicia, your intelligence will also gladly accept, reasoning that not only is the number of churches in the areas specified greater, but also that it is supremely holy for all in common to want precisely what seems both to be required by accurate calculation and have no association whatever with the perjury of the Jews.

Constantine (and therefore the Council of Nicaea) assumed that all Jews were for-ever polluted by the crime of deicide committed by the Jews in Jerusalem on the day when Jesus was condemned to death and crucified. This doctrine of ancestral guilt was not new in 325: it goes back to the very early days of Christianity and is enshrined in Matthew's gospel, which makes the crowd in Jerusalem curse the whole Jewish nation in future ages by shouting 'His blood be on us and our chil-dren' (27.23). And in Severan Carthage Tertullian had sneered that even if Jews wash all over every day, they are never clean, for their hands are 'eternally covered in the blood of the prophets and of the Lord himself' (*De Oratione* 14).

Constantine's participation in the Council of Nicaea was probably also instru-mental in the introduction into the East of the custom of Lent, that is, a pre-Easter fast of forty days (Barnes 1990: 261–262). A pre-Easter fast was certainly already being observed before the end of the second century in the West, since Irenaeus recorded disagreement over whether the fast should last one day, two days or longer, with some maintaining that 'day' meant forty continuous hours (quoted by Eusebius, *HE* 5.24.12–13), and while in Africa in the second decade of the third century Tertullian alluded to fasting between Good Friday and Easter Day (*De Ieiunio* 2.2, 13.1, cf. Funk 1897: 248–250). But the custom of a forty-day fast was unknown in the East in 325. For, when the fifth disciplinary canon of the Council of Nicaea refers to *tesserakoste*, the word does not designate a fast of forty days before Easter, as has often been assumed (e.g., Funk 1897: 258; Duchesne 1920: 231; Barnes 1981: 217),[34] but the period of forty days between Easter and Ascension, during which the canon mandates that the annual spring gatherings of provincial bishops shall be held (Salaville 1910; 1911, cf. Holl 1923: 19).[35]

The practice of a forty-day fast before Easter was introduced into Egypt between 329 and 339. For the earliest Easter Letters which Athanasius wrote after his election as bishop of Alexandria in June 328 for the Easters of the years 329–333 prescribe or assume a six-day fast before Easter (Barnes 1993a: 188–189; Camplani 2003: 217–280). On the other hand, Athanasius complained in 340 that soon after Gregory arrived in Alexandria on 22 March 339 to replace him as bishop (*Festal Index* 11), he entered a church in the city with the prefect of Egypt on a Friday in Lent (*Epistula Encyclica* 4.3, developed later in the *Hist. Arian.* 65.3). Louis Duchesne, therefore, identified Lent as a western custom introduced into Egypt by Athanasius after his return from his period of exile in Trier between late 335 and 337 (Duchesne 1920: 255–256). Duchesne's assumption that Lent was originally a western custom is doubtless correct, even if the earliest explicit evidence for a forty-day fast before Easter in the West is Athanasius' allusion to services during Lent in 345 at Aquileia (*Apology to Constantius* 15.3–4; *Festal Index* 17, cf. Holl 1916: 848–849; Barnes 1993a: 82, 114, 225).

The exact date in the 330s when the forty-day fast before Easter was introduced into Egypt is in dispute. The question turns on whether the dates of 334 and 335 which the late fourth-century editor of a corpus of Athanasius' Easter letters from 329 to 373 assigned to *Festal Letters* VI and VII are correct. If the transmitted dates of these two letters are correct, then Athanasius was already in 334 prescribing a forty-day fast before Easter instead of the previously customary six-day fast (Holl 1916: 849; Camplani 2003: 281–318). But Eduard Schwartz and Rudolf Lorenz dated them later, the former to 356 and 340 respectively, the latter to 345 and 346 (Schwartz 1935: 133, 134 ; Lorenz 1986: 31, cf. Barnes 1993a: 188–189), and, while in theory Athanasius could have replaced the six-day fast with a forty-day fast between the Easters of 333 and 334, it seems far more plausible to assume that he made the change for Easter 338 when he returned to Alexandria on 23 November 337 (*Festal Index* 10), after spending eighteenth months in exile in Trier, where he would have observed the western practice of Lent before the Easters of 336 and 337 (Barnes 1993a: 190–191).

In sum, the observance of Lent was in origin a western custom that was completely unknown in the East in 325. Shortly after the Council of Nicaea, however, Eusebius alludes to a 'spiritual training of forty days' before Easter (*On Easter* 4) and the observance of a forty-day fast before Easter was introduced into Egypt for either the Easter of 334 or the Easter of 338. The simplest explanation for this sudden and rapid change in eastern liturgical practice is that Constantine told the bishops at Nicaea in 325 that he intended to observe the western custom of Lent wherever he happened to be in the East before every Easter from 326 onwards. The eastern churches soon followed the emperor's lead and reorganized their liturgical year.

A CHRISTIAN CAPITAL FOR A CHRISTIAN ROMAN EMPIRE

By 330 Constantine was ready to take up residence in his new city of Constantinople (Barnes 1982: 78). The official dedication took place on the eleventh day of May 330 (*Descriptio consulum* 330; *Chronica Gallica ad annum LXI* [*Chr. min.* 1.643, 466];[36] Hesychius, *Patria Cpl* 42 [Preger 1901b: 18.2–5]; Delehaye 1902: 673). Constantine chose this day to emphasize the Christian nature of the new city, and perhaps also as a personal tribute to the martyr Mocius, whom he may have known when he was a crown prince at the court of Diocletian – and whose execution he could have witnessed (Barnes 1981: 222).[37] The official calendar of the church of Constantinople celebrated Mocius on 11 May and continued to do so centuries later when the foundation of the city was no longer linked to this humble martyr, but to the Theotokos, who saved the city from the Persians in 622 (Delehaye 1902: 673–676). Mocius was a priest at Amphipolis, who refused to sacrifice in the Diocletianic persecution and overturned an altar; after being cruelly tortured, he was sent to Herclea/Perinthus and finally beheaded at Byzantium. Constantine constructed a splendid church one mile outside his new city next to the place where Mocius was buried (Delehaye 1902: 676.5–8).

Although James O'Donnell has recently asserted, on the authority of another, that Constantinople 'was determinedly traditional in form and decoration, with statues of the ancient gods and heroes lining its streets' and that 'Christianity was visibly present in only about a dozen churches' (2009: 181),[38] Constantine's new city was a Christian city, totally free of any trace of paganism until Julian introduced such rites into Constantinople in December 361 (Himerius, *Orat.* 41.1, 8–15, cf. Barnes 1987b: 221–222; Penella 2007: 44, 59 n.64, 62 n.69). Eusebius is explicit on this central point (*VC* 3.48.2):

> Completely inspired by God's wisdom, which he judged that a city bearing his name should display, he saw fit to purify it of all idolatry, so that nowhere in it are to be seen those images of those considered to be gods and worshipped in shrines, altars defiled with the blood of slaughter, sacrifices consumed by fire, festivals of demons, or anything else customary with the superstitious.

Eusebius' testimony has often encountered outright disbelief among modern scholars who chose in preference to repose their trust in much later evidence, much of it obviously fictitious. John the Lydian reports that Vettius Agorius Praetextatus was at the side of Constantine (and the philosopher Sopater) at the foundation ceremonies of his new city (*De Mensibus* 4.2). On the basis of this story from the reign of Justinian, Santo Mazzarino asserted that Praetextatus took part in the ceremonies of 8 November 324 (Mazzarino 1974: 122–131), Lellia Cracco Ruggini that he officiated as a *pontifex Vestae* or *pontifex maior* in 'all the pagan ceremonies of the religious foundation of Constantinople,' which in her view extended from 26 November 328 to 11 May 330 (Cracco Ruggini 1980: 610).[39] Refutation would be unnecessary even if the *Carmen contra paganos* did not prove that Praetextatus was born in 324 (Alan Cameron 2011: 273–309, 612).[40] Even the much later and still more absurd claim by a historian writing in the twelfth century that the second-century astrologer Vettius Valens cast the horoscope of the city (Zonaras 13.3) has sometimes deceived the credulous: a prosopographical manual published in 1971 has an entry for the *Doppelgänger* of the real Vettius Valens, an 'astrologer, consulted by Constantine, who foretold that Constantinople would last for 696 years' (*PLRE* 1.930, Valens 3). The most extreme view was taken by Cyril Mango, who for once dropped his critical guard and asserted that 'it has been proved that the foundation of Constantinople was accompanied by purely pagan rites' (Mango 1963: 56, with appeal to Frolow 1944).[41] But Wilkinson has now rescued Eusebius' credit, for he has proved that several epigrams of Palladas were written in the newly founded Constantinople and mock its Christian character (Wilkinson 2010a).

Two of Palladas' epigrams are of special importance. One, which is preserved only in Planudes' anthology (Cameron 1993: 16, 47), reads as follows (*Anth. Plan.* 282):

Νίκαι πάρεσμεν, αἱ γελῶσαι παρθένοι,
νίκας φέρουσαι τῇ φιλοχρίστῳ πόλει.
ἔγραψαν ἡμᾶς οἱ φιλοῦντες τὴν πόλιν
πρέποντα Νίκαις ἐντυποῦντες σχήματα.

Here we are, the Victories, the laughing maidens, bearing victories to the Christ-loving city. Those who love the city fashioned us, stamping figures appropriate to the victories (trans. Wilkinson).

In the second line φιλοχρίστῳ (Christ-loving) is the reading of the only manuscript and should be retained. Most editors have emended to φιλοχρήστῳ), but the adjective φιλόχριστος was already current in the 330s: it first occurs, so it seems, in the so-called *Testament of the Forty Martyrs* (2.4 [*BHG* 1203], p. 358.10 Musurillo), which is a letter from Christians in prison awaiting execution in the last years of Licinius (Franchi de' Cavalieri 1928: 155–184); the bishops Eusebius of Nicomedia and Theognis of Nicaea used it in the winter of 327/328 in a conventional phrase (*Urkunde* 31.5 = *Dokument* 36.5: καταξιώσατε γοῦν, ὡς ἁρμόζει τῇ φιλοχρίστῳ ὑμῶν εὐλαβείᾳ); and the editor of the *Life of Constantine* used it in a chapter heading (heading to *VC* 1.17, p. 3.25 Winkelmann: τοῦ αὐτοῦ περὶ τῆς φιλοχρίστου προαιρέσεως). Wilkinson argues cogently that the 'Christ-loving city' is Constantinople and that the epigram alludes to coins minted in Constantinople which depicted an armed Nike (Victory) standing on the prow of a warship and commemorating the naval defeat of Licinius in 324 (*RIC* 7.579, 582: Constantinople nos. 63, 79, 86).

The last couplet of Palladas' longest epigram in the Greek Anthology appears to mock Constantine's Church of the Holy Apostles in Constantinople (Eusebius, *VC* 4.58–60). The subject of the epigram is the hackneyed male theme of the supposed infidelity of women, but Palladas gives the theme a twist of his own (*Anth. Pal.* 10.56). He allows that happy, cheerful and beautiful women may be chaste – 'if any woman is completely chaste.' For sixteen lines, Palladas concentrates his scorn on ugly women who are sexually insatiable: even the most outwardly respectable lady may be a secret wanton, and not even old age brings women release from lustfulness. Then a final jibe (*Anth. Pal.* 10.56.17–18):

ὅρκοις λοιπὸν ἄγει τε πεποίθαμεν· ἀλλὰ μεθ᾽ ὅρκον
ζητεῖν ἔστι θεοὺς δώδεκα καινοτέρους[42]

We are left to trust in oaths and religious scruples; but after their oath <women> can seek out twelve newer gods.

In Palladas' mouth, as Wilkinson correctly argues, the 'twelve newer gods' whom unfaithful women can seek out must be the twelve apostles and the last line and a half make a barbed allusion to the Christian idea of the forgiveness of sins after repentance (Wilkinson 2010a: 11–13). Moreover, the phrase 'twelve newer gods' contains a topical reference to the mausoleum which Constantine constructed for himself in Constantinople and dedicated to the Twelve Apostles so that he could there be laid to rest as the equal of the apostles (Eusebius, *VC* 4.60.2, cf. Staats 2008: 358–361):[43] Nicephorus Callistus reports that it was built over a site on which an altar of the twelve gods of traditional paganism had formerly stood (*HE* 8.55 [*PG* 146.220]).

The building and beautification of Constantinople was funded by a massive program of confiscations (Bonamente 1992). Constantine suppressed cults and their shrines which Christians considered immoral and oracles which had encouraged Diocletian to embark upon a policy of persecution. Eusebius records the suppression of the shrine of Aphrodite at Heliopolis, where sacred prostitution was practiced, the destruction of the grove and precinct of Aphrodite at Aphaca, high in the mountains of Phoenicia, and the razing of the temple of Asclepius at Aegeae, famous for its association with Apollonius Tyana, with whom both the philosopher Porphyry and the polemicist Hierocles had compared Jesus to the disadvantage of the latter (Eusebius, *Panegyric of Constantine* 8.5–7, p. 216.26–p. 217.16; *VC* 3.58, 55–56, cf. Lactantius, *Div.Inst.* 5.2.2, 15–17; [Eusebius], *Contra Hieroclem* 1.1–2, 2.2). Constantine probably also took action against two of the three most famous oracles of Apollo for their encouragement of persecution (Barnes 2002: 201–204).

In the winter of 302/3 Diocletian sent a *haruspex* to consult the oracle of Apollo at Miletus and the god gave a reply hostile to the Christians, which may in part survive (Lactantius, *Mort. Pers.* 11.7; *Inschriften von Didyma* 306, cf. Rehm 1939). It has sometimes been assumed that Constantine openly tolerated the continued functioning of the oracle after 324 (Athanassiadi 1991: 271–274). But the philosopher who was also the prophet of Apollo had already been put to death in 313 (Eusebius, *HE* 9.11.3; *Praeparatio Evangelica* 4.2.11), and Constantine complained in a letter intended for publication throughout the East that Apollo had encouraged the persecution of Christians and that Diocletian had listened to him (*VC* 2.50–51). Moreover, archaeological and literary evidence indicates that the Christians appropriated the space and built martyrs' shrines in the sacred enclosure (Sozomenus, *HE* 5.20.7, cf. Athanassiadi 1991: 274). Diocletian had also consulted the oracle of Apollo at Delphi (Cameron & Hall 1999: 245). According to Constantine, 'the oracles of the Pythian' and 'false oracles from the tripods' had encouraged persecution when Apollo, speaking from a cave or dark recess, had declared that he was being prevented from uttering true prophecies by 'the just on earth' (*VC* 2.50–51). The sacred tripods of Apollo at Delphi, the statue of the god and the serpent column commemorating the Greek victory at Plataea in 479 BC were confiscated and taken to Constantinople to grace the new hippodrome (Eusebius, *VC* 3.54.2; Socrates, *HE* 1.16.3; Zosimus 2.31.1; Bassett 2004: 224–227 no. 141; 230–231).

Constantine conducted a systematic confiscation of temple treasures through-out the territories which he conquered in 324, though not in those which he ruled before his final victory, where he had committed before 324 himself to a policy of toleration: the prohibition of sacrifice, for example, was only extended to Italy and Africa by his son Constans in 341 (*CTh* 16.10.2, cf. Barnes 1981: 246; 1984b; 2002: 201–205), and temple treasures in the West were still untouched in 343 when Firmicus Maternus urged Constans to seize them (*De errore profanarum religionum* 16.2–4; 20.7; 28.6–29.4, cf. Barnes 1978a: 68, 75 n.100; 1993a: 225). Constantine sent specially chosen *comites* to tour each province in the East and to scour both cities and the countryside for objects of value which could be melted down and turned into coin (Eusebius, *Panegyric of Constantine* 8.1–4, p. 216.1–23; *VC* 3.54.4–7). They tore the doors and roofs off temples for the metal that they contained, they ordered the custodians of pagan temples and shrines to produce their gold and gold-plated statues; they then took the gold and smelted it into ingots. Statues of bronze they simply seized and removed to adorn the new impe-rial city (Eusebius, *VC* 3.54.2–3). The activities of these commissioners were alluded to in a panegyric, which survives in a very fragmentary form on papyrus (Appendix G). Its unknown author perhaps composed it for delivery in Constantinople during the festivities marking the official dedication of the city in May 330, for which Praxagoras of Athens may have composed his history of Constantine (Appendix F). The speech praises the instructions given to men who are sent out 'to avoid the spoliation of shrines and ill-gotten gains from the admin-istration of their offices' (Guida: 1990.49, Pag. IX. 13–22). Constantine's policy was clear and unambiguous: he forbade traditional forms of worship of the tradi-tional gods throughout the Greek East, but he left most pagan holy places untouched except for the confiscation of the riches that they had accumulated over the centuries, and he allowed worship in these 'shrines of falsehood' in the Christian manner.

Palladas again confirms Eusebius when he alludes to the melting down of the statues of the Olympian gods to mint coins, apparently in Constantinople (*Anth. Pal.* 9.528):

Χριστιανοὶ γεγαῶτες Ὀλύμπια δώματ' ἔχοντες
ἐνθάδε ναιετάουσιν ἀπήμονες· οὐδὲ γὰρ αὐτοὺς
χώνη φόλλιν ἄγουσα φερέσβιον ἐν πυρὶ θήσει

Having become Christian, owners of Olympian palaces dwell here unharmed; for the melting-pot that produces the life-giving *follis* will not put them in the fire (trans. Wilkinson, slightly changed).

To put the matter more plainly, Palladas is saying that the inhabitants of Mount Olympus are safe in Constantinople provided that they become Christian; other-wise they are melted down to produce coins. Palladas thus refers to the same two procedures as Eusebius: the statues of pagan deities were either placed in a Christian context in the Christian city of Constantinople or turned into coin.

These massive confiscations were used to finance a transformation of the urban fabric in Asia Minor, the Roman Near East and Egypt. Large new churches were constructed in the centers of cities, which immediately and inevitably gave their bishops a prominent place in civic life. The emergence of Christian bishops to prominence in the life of Greek cities throughout the East was not a slow and gradual process, as has often been imagined (e.g., Rapp 2005), but a rapid one. It progressed far and fast under the Christian Empire of Constantine and his son Constantius. Already by 359 the bishop of Bezabde anticipated what was to become common in the sixth century: he negotiated with the Persian king Shapur on behalf of and as the main representative of his besieged city (Ammianus 20.7.7–9, cf. Barnes 1998a: 87–88, 137).

PRO-CHRISTIAN LEGISLATION

Constantine introduced significant changes in Roman law in order to refashion Roman society in a Christian direction. Of course, since Constantine often needed to deal with administrative matters or urgent practical problems which had nothing at all to do with religion, much of his legislation was cast in a traditional mold. As a Roman emperor, Constantine's role 'as a giver of justice and distributor of benefits, whether largesse, offices or immunities' remained what it had been since the days of Augustus (Corcoran 2006: 49, summarizing one of the basic theses of Millar 1977). Hence it is quite appropriate to preface any assessment of Constantine's legislation with the observation that 'before Constantine was a Christian emperor, he was a typical emperor' (Van Dam 2007: 11). But it is quite wrong to minimize the changes that Constantine wrought in Roman law. Specialists in Late Roman law, or at least those writing about it in English, tend to question whether Constantine's legislation marked 'the beginning of a new era in imperial law-making.' Caroline Humfress has recently argued that Constantine normally built 'upon a legal framework already in existence' rather than innovating (Humfress 2006: 208, 210) and Jill Harries, with an explicit appeal to Humfress, has asserted of Constantine that 'it is becoming increasingly clear that the emperor was basically a traditionalist, a legislator who on the whole worked within the established juristic tradition' (Harries 2010: 74). But in any society radical innovation can occur, and often does occur, within an 'established juristic tradition.' The most obvious example of such changes that comes to mind is the evolution of the constitution of the United States of America to embrace equality under the law for women and non-whites – a development unimaginable to those who framed the constitution in the eighteenth century. Constantine was able to introduce radical changes or innovations in Roman law without in any way challenging the existing legal framework.

From November 312 onwards Constantine gave Christian clergy special privileges, and began to change Roman law and traditional customs in a Christian direction. Since there are recent surveys of Constantine's legislation as it related to pagan society (de Giovanni 2003), of Christian influence on it in general (Chiusi 2007), and of the possible inspiration of specific laws by the letters of Saint Paul (Staats 2008: 339–354), which complement an extensive and often contentious modern bibliography on other aspects of the emperor's legislation,[44] I shall avoid lengthy argumentation on issues about which I have nothing new to say, and merely comment quite briefly on the most important innovations by Constantine in legal matters where Christian inspiration or influence seems to me most obvious and undeniable.

(1) *Sunday as a day of rest from official business*

Eusebius praises Constantine for establishing Sunday as a day of prayer and a day of respite from official business for all and for making the observance of Sunday obligatory for his soldiers (*Panegyric of Constantine* 9.10, p. 219.20–29; *VC* 4.18 with Cameron & Hall 1999: 317–318). Two fragments in which Constantine lays down that the *dies solis* shall henceforth be a day of rest on which no legal business shall be transacted are preserved in the Theodosian Code and the Codex Justinianus. Both are addressed to Helpidius, *vicarius* of the city of Rome, and have the consular date of 321. But, while the fragment in the Codex Justinianus has a subscription stating that it was issued on 3 March 321, at which time Constantine was in either Serdica or Sirmium (*CJ* 3.12.2, cf. Barnes 1982: 74), the subscription in the Theodosian Code states that the law was posted up in Caralis (Cagliari) in Sardinia on 3 July (*CTh* 2.8.1). Neither date needs to be emended to sustain the hypothesis that both fragments come from a single law issued on 3 March 321 in the Balkans and sent to Rome, but not forwarded from Rome to Sardinia until the summer. Both fragments make an exception for manumissions and emancipations, whose rationale is obvious, though not stated in the preserved fragments: Constantine means manumissions and emancipations performed in church in front of a bishop and his congregation (see (4) below). Klaus Girardet has recently published a searching investigation of the law, its background and its observable consequences (Girardet 2007b): he argues cogently that the two fragments dated 321 reiterate an innovative law which Constantine issued in the winter of 312/313.

(2) *Exemption of Christian clerics from curial obligations*[45]

Constantine granted Christian clergy in the territories which he controlled exemption from curial obligations in the winter of 312/313 (Chapter 4) and Licinius presumably extended this exemption to the whole of the Roman Empire during 313, though he later cancelled it (Chapter 5). Constantine reinstated it in the East in 324, but he had been compelled several years earlier to restrict the ordination of decurions in order to avoid the depletion of city councils: on 18 July 320 he reminded Bassus, praetorian prefect in Gaul that an edict already forbade decurions, the sons of decurions and anyone else with sufficient wealth to undertake public liturgies from being ordained except to replace clerics who died (*CTh* 16.2.3):

> *cum constitutio emissa praecipiat nullum deinceps decurionem vel ex decurione progenitum vel etiam instructum idoneis facultatibus adque obeundis publicis muneribus opportunum ad clerico- rum nomen obsequiumque confugere, sed eos de cetero in defunctorum dumtaxat clericorum loca subrogari,* etc.).[46]

(3) *The legal status of church councils*

Constantine believed, or at least declared, that the decisions of councils of bishops were divinely inspired (Optatus, App. 5, p. 203.25–25 Ziwsa [314]; Rufinus, *HE* 10.5, p. Mommsen = Anon., *HE* 2.27.10 [325]). Hence, as Eusebius reports, he gave these decisions legally binding force (*VC* 4.27.2):

> He put a seal of approval on the rulings of bishops declared at councils, so that gover- nors of provinces were not allowed to rescind what they had decided, for he said that the priests of God were more trustworthy than any magistrate.

Constantine's belief in the probity of bishops was a naïve delusion which caused him endless problems in his dealings with the eastern churches (Barnes 1981: 224– 244; Drake 2000), but it was nevertheless genuine.

(4) *The right of bishops to trial by their peers*

Alone among the inhabitants of the Roman Empire Christian bishops enjoyed the privilege of trial by their peers, whatever the crime might be of which they stood accused, even murder. Moreover, when a council condemned, it could impose no penalty more severe than deposition and excommunication, though the emperor then normally enforced the council's verdict without further enquiry, as the pagan emperor Aurelian had in the early 270s in the case of Paul of Samosata (Eusebius, *HE* 7.30.19). Such enforcement usually took the form of exiling a deposed bishop to a distant part of the Roman Empire.[47] Admittedly the bishops' privilege of trial by their peers is not explicitly attested before 355 (*CTh* 16.2.12, cf. Barnes 1993a: 174). But the vicissitudes of Athanasius in the 330s show that it already existed. Constantine referred charges against Athanasius which included violence and conspiracy to murder to church councils in 334 and 335, and in the winter of 337/338 a council of bishops met in Antioch pronounced him guilty of murder and embezzlement (Barnes 1993a: 28–45). The case of Priscillian, who was tried and executed by a praetorian prefect in the 380s, is not a counter-example, since he was not regarded as a validly consecrated bishop (Girardet 1974: 578–587; Barnes 1990: 162–163).

(5) *The quasi-judicial powers of bishops*

Constantine conferred on bishops the right to preside over the freeing of a slave in church (*manumissio in ecclesia*). The ecclesiastical historian Sozomenus, who was writing in 450 (Barnes 1993a: 205–206), knew of three laws of Constantine on the subject (*HE* 1.9.6), which implies that the Theodosian Code originally contained three. All three stood in the first five books of the Code, which are transmitted in a very incomplete form (Matthews 2000: 85–118), but only two have survived. The innovative law has unfortunately been lost. The Codex Justinianus, however, preserves extracts from two subsequent laws which reaffirmed and extended the original grant. One was addressed to the bishop Protogenes, who must surely be the bishop of Serdica (Millar 1977: 591). The extract assures Protogenes that he had the right to preside over the manumission of slaves by their masters provided that they were manumitted in a catholic church before the congregation and that bishops produced a written and duly authenticated record of the manumission, and probably comes from a rescript issued on 8 December 316 extending the right of *manumissio in ecclesia* to the territories which Constantine won from Licinius with his victory at Cibalae on 8 October 316 (*CJ* 1.13.1[Barnes]).[48] Subsequently, on 18 April 321, in a letter or rescript addressed to the bishop Ossius, who must be Ossius of Corduba, Constantine both confirmed and extended the law: first, he ruled that slaves freed by *manumissio in ecclesia* possess full Roman citizenship provided that their manumission has been duly witnessed by bishops; second, he allowed bishops to manumit their own slaves on their deathbed by a mere verbal expression of their wishes (*CJ* 1.13.2 = *CTh* 4.22.1, cf. Barnes 1981: 311–312 n.76).

The institution of *episcopalis audientia* has attracted a large and contentious bibliography of its own (Selb 1967; Drake 2000: 321–352). As with *manumissio in ecclesia*, the original innovatory law has been lost. Moreover, not only do scholars disagree fundamentally about the precise nature of the innovation, but the authenticity of Constantine's rescript to Ablabius dated 5 May 333, which is preserved in full in a small ecclesiastical compilation of laws apparently made both independently of and earlier than the Theodosian Code (*Constitutio Sirmondiana* 1), has often been denied, as by Élisabeth Magnou-Nortier (2001). In the present context, fortunately, it is not necessary to linger over details. Abundant evidence shows bishops presiding over judicial cases (Elm 1989, cf. Barnes 1993a: 295 n.34; Lamoreaux 1995); its precedents are purely Christian, specifically the letters of the apostle Paul (esp. 1 Corinthians 6.1–6); and there is no dispute that it was Constantine who introduced *episcopalis audientia* into the Roman legal system (*CTh* 1.27.1: transmitted date 23 June 318).[49] In this area too, however, Constantine built on an existing framework: one of the complaints against Paul of Samosata, the bishop of Antioch in the late 260s, was that he accepted bribes from litigants for deciding cases corruptly (Eusebius, *HE* 7.30.7).

(6) Bishops as conduits of imperial largesse

When Constantine exempted the Christian clergy from civic liturgies and initiated a policy of systematic donations to the Christian church from imperial funds, he channeled his generosity through bishops and specifically metropolitan bishops, who thereby acquired the power to decide which individuals should benefit. Constantine's letter to Anullinus, the proconsul of Africa in the winter of 312/3, defines those exempt from curial duties as 'those persons who, in the province entrusted to you, provide their personal service in this holy worship within the catholic church, over which Caecilianus presides, whom they are accustomed to call "clerics"' (Eusebius, *HE* 10.7.2). Similarly, shortly after October 324, when Constantine extended his policy of providing imperial funds for building and enlarging churches to the East (Eusebius, *VC* 2.45.3–46, cf. 1.42.2), he wrote to metropolitan bishops[50] throughout the East encouraging them to build churches telling each of them that (*VC* 2.46.3):

> you may yourself request, and the rest may request through you, what is needed from governors and the prefect's office. For these have been given instructions that they are to lend their assistance to communications.

The imperial largesse which Constantine channeled through the metropolitan bishops of each province and through them provincial bishops in general included grants of food and clothing for widows and the poor. Athanasius reveals that he was part of the distribution process when he reports one of the charges on which he was condemned by a Council of Antioch in 337/338 (*Apol. c. Ar.* 18.2):

> A supply of grain was given by the father of the emperors for distribution to widows, separately in the Libyas and to certain <bishops> from Egypt. All the bishops have received this until now, with Athanasius getting no benefit therefrom, except the trouble of helping them. But now, even though they receive it, have made no complaint, and acknowledge that they receive it, Athanasius has been falsely accused of selling all the supply of grain and embezzling the proceeds.

Whether true or false, the accusation assumes that Athanasius in some way controlled the supply of grain for widows throughout the Egyptian provinces. The mysterious affair of the linen tunics can also only be understood as related to imperial subsidies channeled through the bishop of Alexandria. According to Athanasius, the first charge ever concocted against him c. 330 was 'an accusation by Ision, Eudaemon and Callinicus concerning linen tunics, to the effect that I had imposed a requisition on the Egyptians, and demanded it from them' (*Apol. c. Ar.* 60.2). The charge presupposes an imperial grant of supplies in kind to the church on terms which permitted the bishop of Alexandria to ask individuals to give him tunics to discharge what was, strictly speaking, an obligation to the state or the emperor. The charge which made Constantine lose his temper and send Athanasius to Trier in 335 is also to be understood against the same background. His enemies accused Athanasius of 'threatening to prevent the grain being sent from Alexandria to Constantinople' (*Apol. c. Ar.* 87.1). Athanasius was being accused of wishing to divert grain needed to supply food in the imperial city.

The charge was only plausible because Athanasius had legitimate access to the Egyptian grain supply for charitable purposes. Twenty years later when the Councils of Arles and Milan confirmed the deposition of Athanasius as the metropolitan bishop of the Egyptian provinces, instructions were sent to the prefect of Egypt that 'the supply of grain be taken away from Athanasius and given to those who hold the views of Arius' (*Apol. c. Ar.* 31.2).

Constantine thus acted on the assumption that, as a Christian and an emperor, he had a moral obligation to alleviate the distress of the poor. As Évelyne Patlagean has emphasized, one of the most striking differences between the *mentalité* of the old pagan Roman Empire down to Diocletian and the *mentalité* of the Roman and Byzantine Empires under Christian rulers was the acknowledgment by the rich and powerful that they had a duty of Christian charity, an obligation to help the poor (Patlagean 1977). Constantine did not initiate this fundamental change of attitude, which derives from the New Testament,[51] but he gave bishops a legal and administrative role in the distribution of imperial subsidies to the poor.

(7) *The prohibition of certain punishments previously acceptable under Roman law.*

Crucifixion was one of the normal and traditional methods of executing criminals of servile or very low status, and it was still in use in Licinius' territories after 320 (Lactantius, *Epitome* 46[51].3, cf. Barnes 1981: 292 n.99). Constantine prohibited it – probably well before 320 (Victor, *Caes.* 41.4; Sozomenus, *HE* 1.8.13). For, as early as 21 March 316 he ordered that the crimes of a convicted criminal be tattooed on his hands or lower legs to avoid disfiguring the face which mirrors the beauty of God (*CTh* 9.40.2[Seeck]: *quo facies, quae ad similitudinem pulchritudinis caelestis est figurata, minime maculetur*).

(8) *The rescinding of the Augustan marriage laws*

The marriage legislation of Augustus was designed to encourage the senatorial and equestrian classes to marry and to produce children. In particular, the *Lex Julia de maritandis ordinibus* (which means effectively 'the Julian law on fostering marriage in the upper orders of society') of 18 BC and the *Lex Papia Poppaea* of AD 9, which later jurists treated as a single law, instituted rewards such as career advancement for marrying and producing legitimate children and imposed penalties on the unmarried which restricted their ability to receive large legacies from relatives and friends (Biondi 1945: 166–198 no. 28: *Leges Iulia et Papia Poppaea*, cf. Treggiari 1991: 60–80,

453–456). In contrast, Christians of the fourth century not merely regarded lifelong chastity as one of the highest of moral virtues, but praised perpetual virginity as vastly superior to the married state. Constantine too believed that it was wrong to penalize either those who were married but had no children or those who chose celibacy over marriage (Eusebius, *VC* 4.26.2–4; Sozomenus, *HE* 1.9.1–3). Hence he issued an edict on 31 January 320 which both invalidated the main provisions of the *Lex Papia Poppaea* and denounced its deleterious effects (*CTh* 8.16.1):

> qui iure veteri caelibes habebantur, inminentibus legum terroribus liberentur adque ita vivant, ac si numero maritorum matrimonii foedere fulcirentur, sitque omnibus aequa condicio capessendi quod quisque mereatur. nec vero quisquam orbus habea- tur: proposita huic nomini damna non noceant

> Let those who were considered celibate (*caelibes*) under ancient law be freed from the legal terrors that menace them and let them live as if they were numbered among the married <and> protected by the marriage bond, and let all have an equal opportunity of receiving as legacies what each deserves. Let no-one be considered childless (*orbus*); let the <financial> penalties attached to this designation do no harm <in future>.

Judith Evans Grubbs has argued pertinaciously that this law was intended 'mainly to benefit the upper classes of Rome (especially the senatorial aristocracy), who had always hated the restrictions of the Augustan law, rather than Christian adherents of asceticism (self-denial and sexual abstinence), who were still very rare in the west- ern Empire' (Evans Grubbs 1993: 122–126; 1995: 118–139; 2002: 103). But the antithesis invoked is an imperfect one, and Evans Grubbs fails to recognize the political genius of Constantine in this matter as in others. Since some Christians objected to the Augustan laws on ideological grounds, while rich Christian widows gained significantly from the change in the law, Constantine was able to satisfy a desire for change on the part of both ideologues and many of the wealthy without needing to ask whether the theoretical reasons for change were more or less impor- tant than the personal advantage of women with important political connections.

(9) *Restrictions on unilateral divorce*

In Roman law marriage had the status of a private contract between a man and a woman. Unilateral divorce, where one spouse wished to end the marriage while the other did not, was another matter. In 331 Constantine changed the law signifi- cantly. Henceforth, a wife could only divorce her husband against his wishes if he were a murderer, a poisoner or a tomb violator, while a husband could only divorce his wife against her wishes for adultery, poisoning or running a brothel (*CTh* 3.16.1: transmitted with a consular, but without a diurnal date). The law specifically denied women the right to divorce their husbands for drunkenness, gambling or persistent philandering. It had an immediate effect: the epigrammatist Palladas complained bitterly that he could not be rid of his quarrelsome wife because of 'a piece of paper and Roman law' (*Anth. Pal.* 11.378, cf. Wilkinson 2009: 49–51). Constantine had introduced into Roman law a basic distinction between consensual and non-consensual divorce, and it was not until 542 that Justinian, in a systematic revision of the Roman law relating to divorce, first restricted divorce *communi consensu*, though even then social pressures led to the lifting of these restrictions by Justinian's successor in 566 (*Novella* 140; Schöll & Kroll 1895: 701–703).

How far this law reflects Christian influence has been a matter of dispute (Evans Grubbs 1993: 126–130; 1995: 253–257). The vocabulary used in this law is unusual, so unusual in fact that Eduardo Volterra inferred that it was composed by a cleric rather than anyone in the imperial chancellery (Volterra 1958: 76–80, cf. Evans Grubbs 1995: 257–259) and Antti Arjava has opined that 'the constitution was obviously not drafted by anyone well versed in Roman legal tradition' (Arjava 1996: 179). Evans Grubbs explained the linguistic peculiarities of the law by the hypothesis, first suggested by Manlio Sargenti, that the law was proposed and perhaps drafted by the praetorian prefect Flavius Ablabius to whom it is addressed, on the grounds that, as an easterner 'of rather humble origins,' Ablabius 'was not likely to be familiar with classical Roman law, nor perhaps with egalitarian concepts of marital ethics' (Evans Grubbs 1995: 258, cf. Sargenti 1975: 277–281). But, while the hypothesis that Ablabius proposed the law and suggested its contents could well be correct, it is irrelevant to the question at issue. Constantine issued the law and must therefore be presumed to have approved its contents before he authorized someone else, as was normal imperial practice, to compose the actual text of the law and to express his intentions in suitably ornate and rhetorical prose. The significant point about the law is that it is difficult, indeed probably impossible, to discover a non-Christian origin in the disapproval of divorce which motivated it.

(10) *Legislation concerning the Jews*[52]

Constantine regarded Jews as 'murderers of the Lord' and believed that it was wrong for any Jew to have power over a Christian who had been liberated by the death and resurrection of Christ (Eusebius, *VC* 3.18.2, quoted above). Hence 'he also made a law that no Christian was to be a slave to Jews, on the ground that it was not right that those redeemed by the Savior should be subjected by the yoke of bondage to the slayers of the prophets and the murderers of the Lord' (VC 4.27.1, trans. Cameron & Hall 1999: 163). An extract from the law, which was addressed to Evagrius who was praetorian prefect from 326 to 336 and perhaps into 337, is included in the Theodosian Code, though with the erroneous date of 13 August 339 (*CTh* 16.8.6 + 9.2, cf. Barnes 1982: 131–132).[53] Constantine in fact went further than forbidding Jews to own Christian slaves. In other laws also addressed to Evagrius, he prohibited Jews from circumcising non-Christian slaves as well as from seeking or accepting Christian converts to Judaism and from attempting to prevent their fellow-religionists converting to Christianity (*CTh* 16.8.1[Barnes] [18 October

329];[54] *Constitutio Sirmondiana* 4 = *CTh* 16.8.5 + 9.1[Barnes] [21 October 335], cf.
Linder 1987: 138–144).

These laws represent a significant change in the long-standing Roman policy of
toleration of the Jewish religion (Linder 1987: 60, 125–126). For Constantine
regarded the Jews of his own time as purblind deniers of the truth of Christianity.
Hence, when he was approached by Joseph of Tiberias, who had been an adviser to
the Jewish patriarch before he converted to Christianity, he gave him the rank of
comes and granted him imperial funds to build churches in the predominantly
Jewish towns of Galilee (Epiphanius, *Panarion* 30.4.1, cf. *PLRE* 1.460, Josephus).

(11) *Legacies to the church*

The Theodosian Code contains a brief extract from an edict which either introduced a significant change in testamentary law or possibly reaffirmed an innovation
which Constantine had already introduced (*CTh* 16.2.4).[55] The edict was posted up
in Rome on 3 July 321 and addressed generally *ad populum*: its date has never been
challenged for the simple reason that no criteria exist for evaluating it, though that
does not necessarily mean that its transmitted date is certainly correct.[56] The edict,
whose text requires an emendation which does not seriously affect its meaning,[57] is
central to the question of how innovative Constantine's legislation was in regard to
the Christian church:

> habeat unusquisque licentiam sanctissimo catholicae <ecclesiae> [venerabilique]
> concilio decedens bonorum quod optavit relinquere. non sint cassa iudicia. nihil est,
> quod magis hominibus debetur, quam ut supremae voluntatis, post quam aliud iam
> velle non possunt, liber sit stilus et licens, quod iterum non redit, arbitrium.

> Let every person on his deathbed have the freedom to leave what he wishes of his
> property to the most holy council of the Catholic Church. Let the judgments <of
> such persons> not be ineffectual. There is nothing which is owed more to people than
> that the expression of their last wishes, after which they cannot wish anything else, be
> free and that their power of choice, which will not return again, be untrammeled.

My translation differs significantly from the translation which appeared over the
name of Clyde Pharr in 1952 and which is assumed in recent discussions of what
innovation in testamentary law Constantine is here introducing (Pharr 1952: 441):

> Every person shall have the liberty to leave at his death any property that he wishes
> to the most holy and venerable council of the Catholic Church. Wills shall not become
> void. There is nothing which is more due to men than that the expression of their last
> will, after which they can no longer will anything, shall be free and the power of
> choice, which does not return again, shall be unhampered.

Humfress follows convention in seeing here no more than an extension of the
right of bequeathing gifts by will to pagan temples to 'the recently legitimised

Christian religion' (2006: 218, cf. Jones 1964: 895). But, as Humfress herself acknowledges, 'Christians had manifestly made many gifts to the church long before Constantine,' and what the text actually says when translated correctly is much more radical than is conventionally admitted. Constantine permitted a dying man (Pharr's version misses the force of the present participle *decedens*) to bequeath to the church by a verbal expression of his wishes *bonorum quod optavit*, that is to say, as much of his property as he wished. Two central principles of Roman testamentary law are relevant here. First, Roman society and Roman ideology accorded special respect to the wishes and statements of testators as expressions of a dead person's final wishes (Champlin 1991: 5–29). Second, the stringent formal criteria for making a valid will had long been relaxed for serving Roman soldiers: whereas a civilian needed an elaborate ceremony with several witnesses or at least a written document, the simple expression of a soldier's intention was sufficient for a valid will, and he could make a will in his vernacular tongue, even if that happened not to be either Greek nor Latin (Champlin 1991: 56–58, cf. Amelotti 1966: 81–110; Campbell 1984: 210–229). What Constantine did was to put the deathbed wills of Christians, expressed otherwise than in the customary legal formulae, into the same category as the informal yet binding wills of soldiers (Barnes 1981: 50).

CONSTANTINE AND ECCLESIASTICAL POLITICS

Ecclesiastical politics after the Council of Nicaea have always bulked very large in modern discussions of Constantine, and a recent study of the emperor's dealings with Christian bishops weighs in at more than six hundred pages (Drake 2000). Consequently I can be very brief here, especially since brevity is commended by the enormous lacunae in our knowledge. We know virtually nothing, for example, about the precise circumstances in which prominent bishops of important sees were deposed and exiled between the Council of Nicaea and the death of Constantine – Eustathius of Antioch, Asclepas of Gaza, Euphration of Balaneae, Cymatius of Paltus, Cymatius of Gabala, Carterius of Antaradus and Cyrus of Beroea, all named by Athanasius (*De Fuga* 3.3; *Historia Arianorum* 5.2). To be sure, the vicissitudes of Athanasius between his disputed election as bishop of Alexandria in June 328 and his dispatch into exile in Gaul on 7 November 335 are very well documented, despite some deliberate silences, because Athanasius retained original documents, quoted them in his own defense on many occasions and described his own experiences in works which have survived (Barnes 1993a: 19–135). It is also to Athanasius that we owe the preservation of important documents concerning Arius and the bishops who supported him (*Urkunden* 27, 28, 33, 34 = *Dokumente* 31, 32, 28, 27). In addition, the *Life of Constantine* both preserves a good number of the emperor's letters and pronouncements relating to ecclesiastical affairs and discloses some important items of information, although Eusebius of Caesarea, like Athanasius, is deliberately selective. Not without reason, therefore, has the period after the Council of Nicaea been characterized as 'the lost years of the Arian controversy' (Parvis 2006).

Recent investigations have established that from the very start the so-called 'Arian controversy' has a close structural resemblance to modern party politics. Two cohesive groups of eastern bishops and theologians were pitted against each other and, although not all members of either group by any means shared identical theological views or perspectives, they nevertheless cooperated with other members of their group in acting together in ecclesiastical politics in opposition to the other group (Barnes 1981:225–244; Parvis 2006: 96–133). Both Arius and several of his original allies were disciples of Lucian of Antioch, who was martyred in Nicomedia on 6 January 312 (Chapter 2), and his supporters in ecclesiastical politics included, besides the court bishop Eusebius of Nicomedia and Eusebius of Caesarea, bishops from several parts of Asia Minor, from Libya and from c. 330 the dissident Melitian bishops of Egypt (Parvis 2006: 39–50). Alexander of Alexandria, who originally excommunicated Arius, and his successor Athanasius not only effectively controlled the votes of the bishops of Egypt, but also had some powerful allies outside Egypt – Philogonius and Eustathius, successive bishops of Antioch, Macarius of Jerusalem, Hellanicus of Tripolis (Barnes 1993a: 16, 17, 61, 123), Alexander who was bishop of Byzantium, then of Constantinople until his death in 336 (Barnes 2009b: 119–124), and the belligerent Marcellus of Ancyra, who set out in the 330s to expose the intellectual leaders of the Arian party as manifest heretics (Parvis 2006: 50–68). Indeed, it seems that, through the efforts of Alexander of Alexandria nearly two hundred bishops had condemned the views of Arius before 325 (Parvis 2006: 38 n.2).

There is also a serious psychological obstacle for many modern historians of Constantine whose Christian beliefs have hampered them from seeing (or at least from proclaiming) an obvious truth. The real Constantine as revealed in the primary evidence differs in a fundamental way from the Constantine presented in the three ecclesiastical historians of the 440s and all their followers. Socrates, Theodoretus and Sozomenus, who wrote in that order (Barnes 1993: 205–206, 209, 304 n.1, 306–307 nn.1–3), all present Constantine as unimpeachably orthodox in his theological views. In fact, Constantine was sympathetic to the views of Arius and found it hard to understand why he should be treated as a heretic: on two occasions, in the winter of 327/328 and again in 336, he accepted a written statement from Arius as proof of his orthodoxy and on the basis of it recommended the readmission of the 'heretic' to communion (*Urkunde* 32 = *Dokument* 37; Athanasius, *Ep. ad Serapionem / De Morte Arii* 2.1–3.3, cf. Barnes 1981: 229, 242; 1993: 17–18; 2009b: 121–127).

By the criteria employed by Athanasius and his ecclesiastical allies, the emperor Constantine was an 'Arian' and it is an offense to history to pretend that his personal beliefs were orthodox in the later sense of that term. If we wish to understand Christianity in the Roman Empire, we must respect ancient evidence, not ride roughshod over it because of our own predilections. Even the greatest scholars sometimes succumb to the temptation. Thus Henry Chadwick, who admired Origen very deeply, could not bring himself to believe that his hero castrated himself. He therefore rejected Eusebius' report on the grounds that Eusebius 'depends on an unwritten tradition' (Chadwick 1966: 67–68) and even claimed quite falsely that Eusebius reported the story 'expressly from oral tradition, not from documents' (2000: 139), even though Pierre Nautin had shown that Eusebius derived his information from a letter written c. 231 in which the bishops of Caesarea and Jerusalem protested against an encyclical letter in which Demetrius, the bishop of Alexandria, maintained that Origen's self-castration disqualified him from ordination as a priest (*HE* 6.8.1-6, cf. Nautin 1961: 121–126; 1977: 45–47). It is equally mistaken to deny or play down Constantine's well-attested sympathy for Arius.

EAST AND WEST IN THE FOURTH CENTURY

For the greater part of Constantine's lifetime, the Roman Empire was not a unified or unitary state, and it is misleading to assume a stark contrast between a unified empire in the fourth century and the divided empire of the fifth century (Millar 2007: 3–7). Between 285 and 395 there was a single Augustus whose word held sway everywhere in the empire for a total of fewer than sixteen years: Constantine from 19 September 324 to 22 May 337; Constantius in 354–355 between the removal of Gallus and the appointment of Julian as Caesar on 6 November 355; Julian, then Jovian, then Valentinian from 3 November 361 to 28 March 364; and Theodosius from late August 388 to summer 392 and again from 6 September 394 to 17 January 395.[58] When there were two or more Augusti ruling jointly, the laws and general edicts of one were not valid in or applicable to the territory of the other or others unless he or they ratified and endorsed them (Libanius, *Orat.* 1.144e145, cf. Barnes 2002: 190e192).[59] And on deeper levels than the merely political, such as language, culture, *mentalités* and religion, the differences between East and West were still sharper and more profound.

Constantine came to power at different times in different areas. He was committed, therefore, to different religious policies in different parts of the Roman Empire. At the one extreme, he had proclaimed full toleration for all religions in Britain, Gaul and Spain in 306 (Chapter 4);[60] at the other he acted decisively to curtail the practice of traditional cults in Asia Minor, the Syrian region and Egypt, even if he did not succeed in stamping out pagan practices in remote rural areas.[61] A damaged inscription from Delphi illustrates the situation in the territories which Constantine acquired in his first war against Licinius in 316/317. It preserves portions of two letters written by the college of three praetorian prefects in 341 to Flavius Felicianus, a former *comes*, which have been known for fifty years and used by several scholars to elucidate the evolution of the praetorian prefecture under the sons of Constantine (Chastagnol 1968: 336; Barnes 1981: 377 n.16; 1987: 17; 1992a: 252). Although the inscription has even now still not been formally published (*Inv. Delphi* nos. 1647 + 4077), a helpful French colleague once gave me a copy of the handwritten transcript of the Greek text as reproduced by Claude Vatin in 1962 in his typescript thesis (Vatin 1962: 258–259). The second letter is too fragmentary for a translation of any part of it to be attempted, though it is worth noting that it contains the following phrases separated by lacunae: 'to have been consecrated to Pythian Apollo;' 'to be performed through your [...];' and 'things done by you.' But the heading, the salutation of the first letter and much of its text survive, enough in fact to permit Vatin to make secure restorations in several lines and for me to offer the following translation:

> Letters sealed and engraved in the public archives by decision of the *damiourgoi*
>
> Fl(avius) Dom(itius) Leontius, Fa(bius) Titianus, Fur(ius) Placidus to the former *comes* Fl(avius) Felicianus greeting.
>
> Believing that it is unseemly that you, who have successfully performed the priest-hood of Pythian Apollo and have been both increased with all honours by the [emperor] who is with the gods and praised by our lords the [...], should be harassed by anyone, since we venerate [...] and so that you may remain untroubled for all time, we decree that, if anyone [...], setting condemnation for him so that he be found to have been [...] and punished. We pray that you are well and flourish.

Constantine honored Flavius Felicianus and his sons protected him from harass-ment by Christians: even if Pythian Apollo had ceased to utter oracles, individual pagans could still flourish and prosper in the Constantine Empire without abandoning their traditional beliefs.

7

DYNASTIC POLITICS AFTER THE COUNCIL OF NICAEA

Constantine celebrated his *vicennalia* at both the beginning and the end of the twentieth year of his reign. The celebrations of 25 July 325 were held in Nicomedia very shortly after the conclusion of the Council of Nicaea, for whose principal decisions the emperor claimed a large degree of credit (Chapter 6). The celebrations of 25 July 326 were held in Rome, which Constantine visited for the fourth time in his life and third time since he became emperor. It was in Rome during this visit, so it appears, that his wife Fausta perished in circumstances which present a puzzle and a mystery.

THE DEATHS OF CRISPUS AND FAUSTA

The death of Fausta was closely linked to Constantine's earlier execution of his oldest son Crispus, the only one of his known children whose mother was not Fausta. The the two deaths are explicitly linked in the comments which Sidonius Apollinaris makes on a satirical distich which he quotes (*Ep.* 5.8.2):

> ut mihi non figuratius Constantini domum vitamque videatur vel pupugisse versu gemello consul Ablabius vel momordisse disticho tali clam Palatinis foribus appenso:
>
> Saturni aurea saecla quis requirat? / sunt haec gemmea, sed Neroniana
>
> quia scilicet praedictus Augustus isdem fere temporibus extinxerat coniugem Faustam calore balnei, filium Crispum frigore veneni.

> It seems to me that no greater power of satiric suggestion was shown by the consul Ablabius when in a couple of verses he punctured the life and family of Constantine and bit them with this distich posted up secretly on the doors of the palace!

Constantine: Dynasty, Religion and Power in the Later Roman Empire, First Edition. Timothy Barnes.
© 2011 Timothy Barnes. Published 2011 by Blackwell Publishing Ltd.

Who would now want the golden age of Saturn?
Ours is a diamond age – of Nero's pattern.

<He wrote this> of course because the aforesaid Augustus had almost simultaneously got rid of his wife Fausta with a hot bath and his son Crispus with cold poison (trans. Anderson 1965: 197, slightly amended).

Sidonius can hardly be correct in attributing the distich to Ablabius, the praetorian prefect of Constantine, though he may well have taken it from a fourth-century anti-Christian writer who did attribute it to Ablabius for subversive reasons, since it makes the first Christian emperor the moral equal of the first emperor to put Christians to death. But what was the precise connection between the deaths of Crispus and Fausta? Modern theories diverge widely, and the evidence available will probably never suffice to establish the whole truth. But progress can be made towards unraveling the mystery if close attention is paid to both logic and the evidence.

The first step is to avoid falling into the trap of assuming the two deaths to be exactly parallel. For example, it has often been assumed that both were executed (Jones 1964: 85; Barnes 1975b: 49) or that both were murdered (Clauss 1996: 50; Staats 2008: 362–363, 364).[1] Admittedly, Sidonius was neither the first nor the only ancient writer to assimilate the two deaths to each other. Jerome coupled the death of Crispus with that of Licinius, stating that both were 'most cruelly killed' (*Chronicle* 231[d]: *crudelissime interficiuntur*), and he uses exactly the same verb for the death of Fausta (*Chronicle* 232[a]: *Constantinus uxorem suam Faustam interficit*). The anti-Christian historian Zosimus similarly presents both deaths as murders (2.29.2):

He killed Crispus, who had been deemed worthy of the rank of Caesar, as I have said before, when he incurred suspicion of having sexual relations with his stepmother Fausta, without taking any notice of the laws of nature. Constantine's mother Helena was distressed at such a grievous event and refused to tolerate the murder of the young man. As if to soothe her <feelings> Constantine tried to remedy the evil with a greater evil: having ordered baths to be heated above the normal level, he deposited Fausta in them and brought her out when she was dead.

Zosimus doubtless took the story from the anti-Christian Eunapius of Sardis, but he may have modified it. For another writer also dependent on Eunapius, the anonymous author of the *Epitome de Caesaribus*, who was writing in or shortly after 395, offers a very similar account which nevertheless diverges in its wording and emphasis (42.11–12):

But Constantine, having obtained rule over the whole Roman Empire by remarkable success in wars, ordered his son Crispus to be put to death, at the behest (so people think) of his wife Fausta. Later he locked his wife Fausta in overheated baths and killed her, because his mother Helena blamed him out of excessive grief for her grandson.

In fact, Crispus was not murdered. A generation before Eunapius, who was here the source of both the *Epitome* and Zosimus, a Latin author recorded that Crispus was put to death after a formal trial. Aurelius Victor was writing, so he states, in the twenty-third year after Constantius became Augustus, that is, in 360 (*Caes.* 42.20). Victor was well informed about the reign of Constantine and he correctly reports some important facts which Constantinian propaganda deliberately obscured, for example, that the two wars between Constantine and Licinius were separated by an interval of six years (*Caes.* 41.6–9, cf. Chapter 1). According to Victor, Crispus perished as the result of a judicial verdict rendered by his father (*Caes.* 41.11: *cum natu grandior, incertum qua causa, iudicio patris occidissset*). The only interpretation that can be placed on the word *iudicio*[2] is that the emperor formally sat in judgment on his oldest son and condemned him to death. When Victor adds that the reason for the condemnation of Crispus was uncertain, the cause of the general ignorance of precisely what happened seems clear: Constantine tried his son with only his most trusted advisers present, as had long been normal in politically sensitive cases, especially those involving a member of the imperial family. Moreover, it is illegitimate simply to assume without argument that Crispus was the only defendant whom Constantine tried on that occasion; indeed, it can be established that a young Roman noble aged twenty-three was exiled at approximately the same time as Crispus was sentenced to death – only to be suddenly summoned back from exile and launched on a resplendent career (below at nn. 7–9).

Constantine tried and executed Crispus in North Italy while he was en route to Rome to celebrate his *vicennalia* in July 326: in his continuation of Eusebius' *Chronicle*, which had concluded with the celebration of 325 (*Chronicle* 231[d-f]), Jerome explicitly places the Caesar's death before his notice of Constantine's double celebration of his *vicennalia* in Nicomedia in 325 and in Rome in the following year. After his trial Crispus was executed at Pola in Istria. This detail is known only because Ammianus Marcellinus recorded in passing that when the Caesar Gallus was similarly stripped of office in 354, then tried and condemned to death by high officials of Constantius, he too was executed at Pola (14.11.20). Can the date be determined any more precisely within the year 326?

Constantine spent the winter of 325/326 in the vicinity of Nicomedia, and his presence in Heraclea/Perinthus is attested with certainty on 3 February 326 (*CTh* 9.3.2; 9.7.1). By the beginning of April Constantine was in Aquileia (*CTh* 9.24.1[Seeck]; 9.8.1), where he may only just have arrived after his journey of nearly a thousand miles,[3] and he remained in North Italy until at least 6 July (*CTh* 9.21.3) before setting out for Rome, which he entered on 18 or 21 July (*CIL* 1[2], p. 268; Jerome, *Chronicle* 231[e]). When he arrived in North Italy, Constantine presumably intended to hold a joint celebration to mark both his *vicennalia* at the end of his twentieth year as Augustus and the *decennalia* of his two Caesars during their tenth year. Such a joint celebration of *vicennalia* and *decennalia* had occurred in 303, when it was originally intended that both the two Augusti and the two Caesars present should be present (Chapter 3). More recently, when Nazarius delivered a panegyric in

Plate 1 Imperial bust of the tetrarchic period from Nicomedia; probably Diocletian
Source: The Art Archive/Alamy

Plate 2 Constantius liberating London as the 'Restorer of Eternal Light' (Arras Medallion)
Source: © Musée des Beaux-Arts d'Arras, inv. 927.6.1

Plate 3   Head of Constantine from early in his reign; found in the Stonegate, York
Source: Angelo Hornak/Alamy

Plate 4 Constantine in front of the Roman monument commemorating the *vicennalia* of
Diocletian and Maximian and the *decennalia* of Constantius and Galerius in 303 (Arch of
Constantine)
Source: Alinari/Topfoto

Plate 5   Fragments of the colossal statue of Constantine in the Capitoline Museums in Rome
Source: Russell Kord/Alamy

Plate 6 The 'Great Cameo' showing a Victory crowning Constantine
Source: Photo and collection Geldmuseum (Money Museum), Utrecht

Plate 7 The Ada-Cameo from Trier
Source: Stadtbibliothek Trier, book cover of the Ada-gospels, Ms 22

Plate 8 Coin of Constantinople c. 327: obverse Constantine; reverse labarum with medallions of three emperors (British Museum: *RIC* 7.572 no. 19)
Source: © The Trustees of the British Museum

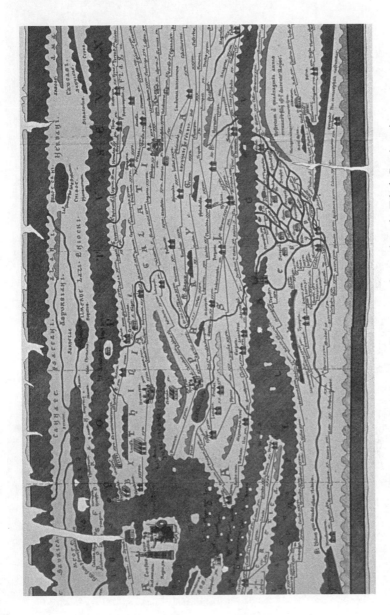

Plate 9A The city of Constantinople and surrounding areas as depicted on the Tabula Peutingeriana

Source: Photo: akg-images

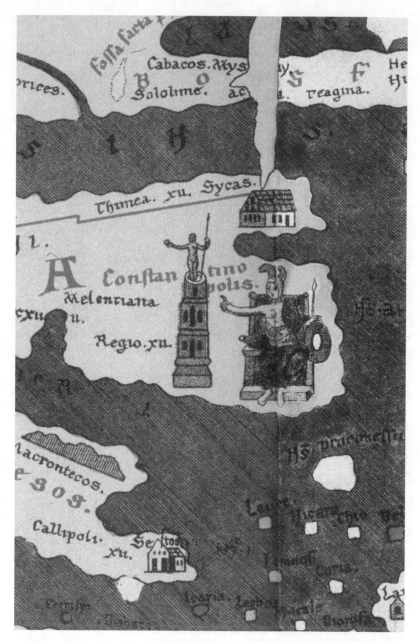

Plate 9B Detail of 9A: the porphyry column with the statue of Constantine and the Tyche of Constantinople

Source: Photo: akg-images

Rome on 1 March 321 on the occasion of the fourth anniversary of the proclamation of Crispus and Constantinus as Caesars, he linked their *quinquennalia* to the
quindecennalia of their father, whose fifteenth year of rule ran from 26 July 320 to 25
July 321 (*Pan. Lat.* 4[10].1.1, 2.1–5). If Crispus, who normally resided in Trier, was
not arrested in Gaul, he must have come to North Italy in order to proceed in the
company of his father (and his young half-brothers) to Rome for the celebrations
of July 326. His downfall and death occurred between early April and early May.

If Crispus was formally tried by his father and then executed, as seems certain,
how did Fausta die? In her case, there seems to be no reason to doubt that she
expired in the imperial baths from which she was carried out no longer alive or to
reject the report that she died by suffocation (*Epitome* 41.12; Philostorgius, *HE* 2.4,
4a; Zosimus 2.29.2). But if Fausta died of suffocation in overheated baths, then her
death can hardly have been an execution, since such a mode of judicial execution
was unknown to Roman law. Admittedly, Fausta could in theory have been drowned,
strangled in the baths or 'poached to death' (Drake 2000: 237) on Constantine's
orders or with his connivance. But it is not likely that Constantine would have had
Fausta murdered in this way, despite the *Epitome* and Zosimus, since in that case her
death would have been open to public scrutiny: those who serviced the baths,
including those who stoked the fires, would have known what happened and would
surely not have refrained from gossiping about the death. Roman emperors who
wished to have close relatives killed normally employed assassins or poisoners.

Elimination of execution and murder leaves open two possible explanations of
Fausta's death. It was either suicide, as has often been supposed, or an accidental
death caused by an abortion gone wrong, as David Woods argued a few years ago
(1998: 75–77, 83). The new hypothesis has a certain initial plausibility. For a hot
bath was one of the standard ways of inducing an abortion in the ancient world
(Soranus, *Gynaecia* 1.61–65, cf. Woods 1998: 76–78) and the problem of an imperial
adulteress who became pregnant was not unprecedented: Augustus exiled his granddaughter Julia after she became pregnant by her lover in AD 8 and presumably
refused to abort the child, which Augustus ordered to be exposed at birth (Suetonius,
Divus Augustus 65.4, cf. Barnes 1982).[4] But if Fausta died in an attempted abortion,
then she must have been pregnant, *ex hypothesi* with the child of Crispus, from
which it would follow either that stepmother and stepson had an illicit love affair
or that Crispus raped Fausta. For the ancient allegation that Fausta tried unsuccess-
fully to seduce Crispus, then accused him of attempted rape in the same way as
Euripides' Phaedra had accused Hippolytus (Philostorgius, *HE* 2.4, 4a, 4b), will not
explain her pregnancy. However, it is difficult to suppose that Crispus and Fausta
conducted a clandestine affair when he was residing in Trier (Barnes 1982: 83–84,
cf. 76–77), while Fausta was presumably with her husband and young children in
the East. Moreover, it would have been both contrary to law and politically dangerous for Constantine to execute his son and spare his wife immediate execution for
sexual acts in which the pair had engaged willingly.[5] The one hypothesis which
remains, therefore, is that Fausta chose to commit suicide rather than face a more

unpleasant alternative. What might that alternative have been? The *Epitome* and the *Passio Artemii*, which is normally believed to derive from Philostorgius, give an answer: Fausta had instigated the death of Crispus on a false charge (*Epitome* 41.11: *Fausta coniuge, ut putant, suggerente Crispum filium necari iubet*) and Constantine put her to death when he discovered the truth (*Passio Artemii* 45.12–18 [Kotter 1988: 227] = Philostorgius, *HE* 2.4b, p. 17.35–27 Bidez).[6] Fausta had a clear dynastic motive for getting Crispus disgraced and executed. For his removal secured the imperial succession for her own sons (Guthrie 1966).

What then was the role of Helena in all this? On the scenario outlined here, she must have approached Constantine when he arrived in Rome and convinced him that he had been wrong to execute his son. Fausta will therefore have decided that voluntary suicide was the only way for her to escape trial by her husband, presumably for calumny or false witness – a trial which could have been followed by a brutal form of execution (Barnes 1975b: 48; 1982: 221). For if Constantine believed that he had executed his oldest son for a crime which he did not commit, he would surely not have flinched from executing his wife for persuading him to sentence Crispus to death.

It remains to ask what Crispus' alleged crime was that merited a sentence of death. Again an easy assumption must be rejected. It might seem obvious that Crispus' alleged crime or crimes had something to do with Fausta. That is not necessarily so. The sequence of events and Helena's blaming of Constantine imply only that Fausta made or supported a false accusation. Tacitus provides an example of how an emperor's wife could ensure a condemnation on false charges without herself either being the accuser or in any way herself affected by the alleged criminal activity. In 47, the emperor Claudius tried Valerius Asiaticus, who was accused of plotting rebellion, adultery and moral depravity, in his private apartments. Claudius' wife Messalina both instigated the accusation of Asiaticus, whose luxurious gardens she coveted, and played a part in securing his condemnation by manipulating her husband (Tacitus, *Annals* 11.1.1–3.2). Manfred Clauss has canvassed the possibility that the charge against Crispus was high treason and that he was accused of participating in a conspiracy against his father (Clauss 1996: 51).[7] That hypothesis might be partly true – and it should lead us to consider the possibility that Constantine tried Crispus together with others who were also accused.

Many years ago I suggested that the vicissitudes of the aristocrat Ceionius Rufius Albinus might be relevant to Crispus and Fausta (Barnes 1975b: 48). In 337 Firmicus Maternus revealed and interpreted the horoscope of a Roman aristocrat who can only be Ceionius Rufius Albinus, consul in 335 (*Math.* 2.29.10–20, cf. Barnes 1975b: 40–43, 47–49). The horoscope establishes that Albinus was born in the evening of 14 March 303 (Beck 2007: 96),[8] while Maternus' detailed exegesis of the horoscope states that its owner succumbed to the attacks of his enemies and was exiled (*Math.* 2.29.12, 14), that he was tried by the emperor Constantine in person for adultery and magic (10, 14, 17, 18): he might therefore have met a violent and untimely death in exile, had the stars not ordained otherwise (16). He was snatched from exile (16), governed Campania and was successively proconsul of Achaea and Asia before he became *praefectus urbi* (10). Albinus had also become ordinary consul on 1 January 335 before being appointed to the urban prefecture,[9] an office which he held from 30 December 335 to 10 March 337 (*Chr. Min.* 1.67). I suggest, therefore, a series of hypotheses to explain the fall and sudden recall of Albinus. First, that Crispus was, at the instigation or through the agency of Fausta, accused of wild and outrageous behavior of the sort which so many sons of monarchs have perpetrated through the ages. Second, that Constantine condemned Ceionius Rufius Albinus at the same time as Crispus for his involvement in some way in whatever criminal offenses Crispus was deemed to have committed. Third, that when Firmicus Maternus, who knew very well the legal dangers of practicing astrology (*Mathesis* 2.30), mentions magic, he may alludes to the criminal act of casting the emperor's horoscope, which was always a capital crime under the Roman Empire (Cramer 1954: 248–281).[10] And fourth, that Constantine recalled Albinus when he decided that Crispus had been wrongfully condemned.

The political context of the fall of Crispus is suggestive. In the spring of 326 the three sons of Fausta were mere boys aged nine, eight and probably two or three. The two elder were Caesars, but Crispus was senior to both of them and thus destined to inherit at some future date his father's right to co-opt new members into the imperial college. Were Constantine to die soon, therefore, it would be possible for Crispus, who was now approaching the age that his father was when he was saluted Augustus in 306, to arrogate to himself his father's political control of the whole Roman Empire and to exclude his half-brothers from power as his father Constantine had consistently excluded his half-brothers. It is therefore not merely an inference *post hoc ergo proper hoc* argument that Fausta's hand lay behind the liquidation of Crispus and that, when the truth about her role in his death came out, she killed herself to protect the succession of her sons. For the six children of Theodora, the widow of Constantine's father Constantius, the half-brothers and half-sisters of Constantine, were lurking in the background, all doubtless eager to press their dynastic claims should the opportunity arise. They could remember that a decade before Constantine had proposed that the husband of one of them, Bassianus the husband of Anastasia, should receive imperial purple, although he subsequently found it necessary to liquidate him (Chapter 5). It would only have needed Constantine to fall seriously ill (if only briefly) to provoke such a dynastic crisis.

After the death of Fausta, Constantine mounted what would now be called an exercise in public relations in order to distract attention from his domestic scandals. If Fausta had played an important part in the condemnation of Crispus (as is argued above) and if it was his mother Helena who revealed to Constantine that he had been wrongly accused, then Fausta killed herself when Constantine was in Rome, that is, between mid-July and mid-August 326 (Barnes 1982: 77). Shortly thereafter Helena set off on an ostentatious pilgrimage to the Holy Land to advertise the piety and imperial munificence of both herself and Constantine (Chapter 2). Nor was Helena the only imperial lady to do so. Eusebius quotes a letter of Constantine to the bishops of Palestine ordering the construction of a basilica on the site of the Oak of Mamre, where God once spoke to Abraham (*VC* 3.52–53, cf. Sozomenus, *HE* 2.4.6), in which the emperor begins by saying that his mother-in-law, that is Eutropia, the widow of Maximian and mother of Fausta, who was a woman of sixty or more, had written informing him that this holy place had been spoiled by super-stitious persons. Constantine may have had a grandiose and well thought out plan for the systematic building of churches in all the places in the Holy Land which Christians considered sacred (Telfer 1955),[11] but Helena's pilgrimage (and perhaps that of Eutropia) had a political context and purpose, about which Eusebius and later ecclesiastical historians are for obvious reasons completely silent.

A THIRD WIFE FOR CONSTANTINE?

It has recently been argued that Constantine remarried after the death of Fausta. There had previously been a universal assumption that he did not, on the reasonable grounds that no surviving source, literary or legal, documentary or epigraphic, records a third wife of Constantine. François Chausson, however, has argued that Constantine had a third daughter named Constantia in addition to the well-attested Constantina and Helena and that, while Constantina, who died in 354, was the daughter of Fausta, she had two younger sisters born after 326 who were daughters of a wife whom Constantine married after the death of Fausta (Chausson 2007: 107–116).

Chausson produced what he claimed to be overlooked evidence for Constantine's third marriage (2007: 109). In a passage of his speech against the Cynic Heraclius, Julian the Apostate attacked Constantine for failing to bring up his sons as he ought to have done and thus becoming responsible for the dynastic bloodbath of 337, in which Julian's father and oldest brother had been killed (*Orat.* 7.22, 227d):

> He had many wives and sons and daughters by them (ἐγένοντο δὲ αὐτῷ γυναῖκες πολλαὶ καὶ παῖδες ἐξ αὐτῶν καὶ θυγατέρες), among whom he divided his wealth before he died, although he had taught them nothing about how to manage it, not even how any of them could acquire the same amount if it was lost or preserve what they had. In his ignorance he thought that mere numbers would suffice, since he himself had acquired <his wealth> with little understanding of that sort of skill, but rather by habit and experiment, like quack doctors, who try to cure their patients by experience alone, as a result of which they fail to detect most diseases (cf. Plato, *Charmides* 156e). Accordingly, thinking that a multitude of sons would be enough to preserve his estate, he gave no thought to how they would become competent.
>
> This turned out to be the beginning of their lawless behavior to one another. For each of them, desiring to have great wealth like his father and to have it all for himself, turned against <the brother> who was his neighbor. This continued for a time, and their relatives also shared in the folly and ignorance of the sons, since they too had not been educated well. Then everything was filled with slaughter, and the tragic curse was brought to fulfillment by divine power. For 'by the blade of the sword they

divided' their patrimony,[12] and everything was thrown into confusion. The sons demolished ancestral temples which their father had previously despised and stripped of their votive offerings which had been placed in them by many others, not least by his own forebears.

But vague generalities in such a tendentious passage must always be suspected of exaggeration. What is the specific evidence that Constantine had three daughters rather than two and that two of them were the daughters of a third wife of Constantine who happens to be otherwise unknown to history?

Two daughters of Constantine are well attested. Evidence from the fourth century leaves no doubt that the name of the older was Constantina, not Constantia (*PLRE* 1.222, Constantina 2). She lived in Rome in the 340s (*CIL* 6.40790), an inscription records her construction of a basilica of St. Agnes and her foundation of a monastery where she was buried after her death in 354 (*ICUR* 2, p. 44 = *ILCV* 1768), and Ammianus Marcellinus paints a hostile and damning account of her conduct as the consort of the Caesar Gallus in Antioch (14.1.2–3, 7.4). Both the *Origo Constantini Imperatoris* and Ammianus Marcellinus state that Constantina was married to Hannibalianus, the son of Constantine's half-brother Flavius Dalmatius, on the occasion when Constantine proclaimed him 'king of kings' (*Origo* 35: *Hannibalianum, data ei Constantina, filia sua, regem regum et Ponticarum gentium constituit*; Ammianus 14.1.2: *quam Hannibaliano regi fratris filio antehac Constantinus iunxerat pater*).[13] Since it can hardly be supposed that Constantine married his daughter off before puberty, Constantina must have been born before 326; indeed, she is commonly taken to be older than Constantine's youngest son Constans, who was born in 320 or 323 (Barnes 1982: 43). After Hannibalianus was killed in the summer of 337, Constantina remained a widow for more than a dozen years until she married Gallus, the older son of Julius Constantius, when he was appointed Caesar on 1 March 351.

Constantina's sister Helena married Julian when Constantius appointed him Caesar on 6 November 355 (*PLRE* 1.409–410, Helena 2). The twelfth-century historian Zonaras states explicitly that she was the daughter of Fausta (13.3).[14] Now it is indeed, as Chausson correctly observes, highly improbable for the daughter of an emperor to be allowed to remain unmarried until the age of thirty. But what follows from that for Helena? Chausson argues that, since Julian is Helena's only attested husband, she must have been born some years after the death of Fausta in 326, in fact c. 336 (2007: 115). It is far more plausible to deduce that Helena had been married before her father's death to a husband who perished in 337, and that after 337 her imperial brothers kept her unmarried like her elder sister for dynastic reasons. An obvious candidate for Helena's hand in 335 or 336 is available – the Caesar Dalmatius, whose brother Hannibalianus married Constantina (Table 7.2).

Despite Chausson, there is not one single clear, explicit and unambiguous item of ancient evidence that Constantine had a daughter named Constantia in addition to the well-attested Constantina. For the ancient references to a Constantia, daughter of Constantine, are sheer mistakes for Constantina (*PLRE* 1.222, Constantina 2).

Thus Photius' summary of Philostorgius records that Constantia, who was the oldest sister of Constantius and Constans (and whom, so he states, her father had created an Augusta[15]), installed Vetranio as a temporary emperor in 350 in order to forestall a genuine challenge to the Constantinian dynasty in the Balkans. But, since Photius identifies Constantia as the widow of Hannibalianus and calls the wife of Gallus Constantia (Philostorgius, *HE* 3.22, 28), he is speaking of Constantina and his 'Constantia' is merely a verbal slip. Similarly, when Peter the Patrician reports that in 350 the usurper Magnentius asked Constantius for the hand of his sister Constantia in marriage, he too misstates the name of Constantina as Constantia (frag. 16). The one reference to Constantia where the context excludes a merely verbal confusion of the names Constantina and Constantia occurs in the *Liber Pontificalis*, which reports that when Liberius returned to Rome from exile in 357 (that is, three years after the death of Constantina) he resided with a sister of the emperor Constantius, who had intervened on his behalf to secure his return. Louis Duchesne prints the passage as follows (*LP* 37.4, p. 207.10–13):

> rediens autem Liberius de exilio, habitavit in cymeterio sanctae Agnae apud germanam Constanti Augusti, ut quasi per eius interventionem aut rogatu redire Liberius in civitatem. tunc Constantia Augusta, quae fidelis erat domino Jesu Christo, noluit rogare Constantium Augustum germanum suum, quia senserat consilium.

> On his return from exile Liberius lived at the cemetery of St Agnes with the emperor Constantius' sister, in the hope that her intervention or request might gain him admittance to the city. Then Constantia Augusta, who was faithful to the Lord Jesus Christ, refused to ask her brother the emperor Constantius, as she had realized what the scheme was (trans. Davis 1989: 28, who, however, changes Duchesne's *Constantia* to *Constantina*).

Since Constantina died in 354 and Liberius returned from exile in 357, Chausson pounces on this passage as proof that this Constantia cannot be identical with Constantina (2007: 115–116), but he fails to note either the textual or the historical difficulty involved. Duchesne's critical apparatus reveals that some manuscripts read *Constantina*, and the content of the passage indicates that the imperial lady who supported and succored Liberius is intended to be Constantina (Duchesne 1886 208–209). Hence it has been suggested that Constanti(n)a in the *Liber Pontificalis* is a 'mistake for Helena,' the wife of Julian, who died in 360 (*PLRE* 1.222). That is less plausible than the hypothesis that the story is a later invention which has no value as evidence for the fourth century.

In brief, there is no good evidence that Constantine had more than two daughters who survived infancy. Hence there is no positive reason whatever to suppose that Constantine, who was fifty-three in 326, married again after the death of Fausta, and as a sincere Christian he will presumably have considered himself debarred from taking a concubine to comfort his old age as Marcus Aurelius had done after the death of his wife Faustina (*Historia Augusta, Marcus* 29.10).

THE ORGANIZATION OF THE EMPIRE

It is notoriously difficult to decide how much Constantine contributed to the structural changes in the administration and governance of the Roman Empire except where the fortunate survival of a contemporary document such as the Verona List dissipates the darkness (Chapter 5).[16] For the literary evidence is partial and contradictory, the non-literary for the most part fragmentary and inadequate. The two fullest literary sources, the Christian Eusebius and the anti-Christian Zosimus, give accounts of Constantine's government which are almost completely antithetical. Eusebius praises the emperor to the skies: he gave freely, bestowing status, land and money on all who asked; he never refused any request; he reduced the land tax by one-quarter, he appointed officials to ensure fairness in the census, and when he sat in judgment on civil cases, he always compensated the loser to the full amount of his claim (*VC* 4.1–4). Zosimus in contrast blamed Constantine for hastening, perhaps even directly causing the decline of the Roman Empire: he ruined both its civil and its military organization; he transferred the troops which Diocletian had stationed on the frontiers to repel invaders to cities where they were corrupted by luxury and indiscipline and thus lost Roman territory; he wasted public funds on useless buildings (that is, Christian churches); he introduced oppressive taxes on both the inhabitants of cities and on senators; in brief, he ruined the majority of cities in the empire (2.32–34). Modern research has revealed a very different reality, which André Chastagnol neatly encapsulated in the title of his study of 'The Political, Social and Economic Evolution of the Roman World from Diocletian to Julian' (Chastagnol 1982). On the one hand, it is possible to identify and describe fundamental differences between the administration and governance of the Roman Empire before Gallienus' recognition of Christianity as a lawful religion in 260 (Barnes 2008; 2009a)[17] and the quarter of a century between 353 and 378, for which the full narrative of Ammianus Marcellinus survives (Matthews 1988. But to detect, describe and analyze the process of change in detail during the intervening nine decades is possible only in a few areas.

(1) *Constantine and the Roman army*

In the military sphere not only is it hard to distinguish reforms initiated by Constantine from those initiated by Diocletian (Fischer 2006), but it has long been recognized that the reforms which between 284 and 337 created 'the new empire of Diocletian and Constantine' were merely part of a process that began under Marcus and continued into the sixth century (Tomlin 1987: 107). Zosimus alleges that Constantine created the new posts of *magister militum*, *magister equitum* and *magister peditum* and transferred the military functions of the praetorian prefects to them, and permitted the barbarians to invade the Roman Empire by withdrawing the troops which Diocletian had stationed along the frontiers and relocating them to cities in the interior where they were soon corrupted (Zosimus 2.33.3, 34, cf. John the Lydian, *De magistratibus* 2.10 = 3. 40). It has been customary to start modern discussions of Constantine's military reforms from these two assertions (Demandt 1970: 560–562; Elton 2006: 331–332). Indeed, one well-regarded book on the Roman army in the early fourth century argues that Constantine reorganized it roughly along the lines pilloried by Zosimus (van Berchem 1952: 75–111). New evidence indicates otherwise.

Although *ripenses* are first attested in our surviving evidence in a law whose transmitted date is 17 June 325 (*CTh* 7.20.4), archaeological excavations of the fortified palace which Galerius built for his retirement in the years 308–311 at Gamzigrad (ancient Romuliana) have brought to light a series of brick-stamps which record the participation of two military officers and five cohorts of a single legion in its construction. As was customary with such stamps, names and titles are highly abbreviated, but the identifications are clear (Christodoulou 2002: 275–278, whence *AE* 2002.1237bis):

the *praefectus legionis* of the legion V Macedonia from Oescus
the *praepositus ripae* of the legion V Macedonia from Varinia
cohorts I–V of the legion V Macedonia.

This shows that by 311 at the latest the legions stationed along the Danube were each divided into two halves: cohorts I–V of the legion V Macedonia were stationed at Varinia, cohorts VI–X at Oescus, each group commanded by a *praepositus ripae*, with both *praepositi ripae* under the command of the *praefectus* of the whole legion, who was stationed at Oescus (Christodoulou 2002: 277). It follows that it was Diocletian who permanently divided the Roman army into field armies who accompanied emperors (*comitatenses*) and garrisons stationed along the imperial frontiers (*ripenses*) – as Lactantius claimed (*Mort. Pers.* 7.2).

As for the creation of the new post of *magistri militum* as commanders of the central armies, with *duces* commanding the frontier troops, which might seem to be a necessary corollary of this division (Elton 2006: 331–332), the first *magister militum* is in fact not attested until several years after the death of Constantine. He was Hermogenes whom Constantius sent to Constantinople to expel the bishop Paul in 342, but who was lynched when he attempted to carry out his orders (Socrates, *HE* 2.12–13, cf. Barnes 1993a: 213–214). Authors from the late fourth century onwards describe Hermogenes as a *magister militum* (Jerome, *Chronicle* 235[f]) or specifically as a *magister equitum* (Ammianus 14.10.2; Socrates, *HE* 2.12; Sozomenus, *HE* 3.7.6). But the text which Scipione Maffei published in 1738 under the descriptive title *Historia acephala ad Athanasium potissimum ac res Alexandrinas pertinens* (conventionally known by the abbreviated title *Historia acephala*) calls Hermogenes simply *comes*, which implies that he served at the imperial court. Modern discussions tend to ignore this fact, even though the

Historia acephala was originally composed in 368 and the title which it gives for Hermogenes is not likely to be one of the later additions to the original document (Barnes 1993a: 4).

One significant innovation in the military sphere has been confidently ascribed to Constantine. In the first years of his reign (306–312), when he ruled only Britain, Gaul and Spain, he could not raise new troops from the traditional recruiting areas in the Balkans. He therefore recruited *laeti*, that is, Franci who had submitted to Rome and whom Maximian settled on derelict land in Gaul in the late 280s (*Pan. Lat.* 8[5/4].9.1–2, cf. Tomlin 1987: 110–111), and perhaps also Germans from beyond the Rhine, if some of Constantine's troops are correctly so identified in the reliefs on the Arch of Constantine in Rome depicting the Battle of the Milvian Bridge (Alföldi 1959, but see Rummel 2007: 197–198).

It was probably also under Constantine that for the first time a significant number of non-Romans were promoted as officers and generals in the Roman army. Barbarian kings or chieftains leading their own troops into battle alongside Roman emperors were no novelty. Among those who acclaimed Constantine Augustus at York on 25 July 306 was said to be Crocus *rex Alamannorum*, who had brought a contingent of troops to Britain to serve under Constantius as auxiliaries (*Epitome* 41.3, cf. Drinkwater 2007: 146, 153, 159, 163),[18] and in 324 the Gothic leader Alica assisted Licinius in the defense of Chrysopolis after he had lost Byzantium at the head of his own troops (*Origo* 27). Between 306 and 324, although Constantine waged many military campaigns, the names are known of only three generals who commanded troops under him: while one was his eldest son and the origin of another is completely unknown, the third was a barbarian. Crispus conducted campaigns against the Franci and on the Rhine as an independent commander before he took command of Constantine's fleet in the Aegean and destroyed the fleet of Licinius at the Dardanelles (*Origo* 23, 26–8). A certain Aelianus was the recipient of an imperial constitution issued on 28 April 323 concerning military matters (*CTh* 7.1.1 + 7.12.1, cf. Seeck 1919: 173).[19] Bonitus, who fought on Constantine's side against Licinius, was the father of Constantius' general Silvanus and a Frank (Ammianus 15.5.33). If this Bonitus is the Bonitus who served as a *praepositus legionis* at Viminacium in Moesia Prima, apparently in the fourth century (*AE* 1910.90, cf. *PLRE* 1. 163, Bonitus 1, 2), then he entered the Roman army at a much lower rank.

After 324 our narrative sources for Constantine's military campaigns peter out, but it is clear that non-Roman generals of high rank who appear in our narrative sources for the 350s must have begun their service before 337. There are several obvious and attested examples of such men. Magnentius was a military *comes* commanding two palatine legions when he was proclaimed Augustus in Gaul on 18 January 350 (Zosimus 2.42.2; Zonaras 13.6, p. 191.17–18 Dindorf): he served in the Roman army under Constantine (Zosimus 2.46.3), having been born a *laetus* c. 303 (*Epitome* 42.6–7; Zosimus 2.54.1). Julian makes a point of emphasizing that Magnentius was of German origin (*Orat.*1, 33d–34d; 2, 56bc);

in fact, a scholiast on Julian offers the precise and credible statement that he was born at Amiens of a Breton father and a Frankish mother (Bidez 1925: 312–318). Silvanus, the son of Bonitus, *magister equitum* in Gaul from 353 to 353 after a timely desertion from Magnentius to Constantius, was of Frankish origin (Ammianus 15.5.16, cf. *PLRE* 1.840–841, Silvanus 2). Flavius Salia, *magister equitum* at least from 344 to 348 and consul in 348, whose military career must have begun before 337, has a name which suggests German origin,[20] as does that of Gaiso, who went to Spain with especially selected troops to kill Constans early in 350 (*Epitome* 41.23; Zosimus 2.42.5) and became ordinary consul with Magnentius in 351 in the latter's domains (Waas 1965: 99). Agilo, *magister peditum* from 362 to 364, first appears in Ammianus' account of events of 354 as a *tribunus stabuli* suspected of passing military information to his fellow Alamanni (14.18.10, cf. *PLRE* 1.28–29): he too may have enlisted in the Roman army before the death of Constantine.

To this list another name can perhaps be added, albeit by a frankly speculative argument. The so-called Sevso Treasure, which has received a spectacular and richly illustrated publication (Mundell Mango & Bennett 1994), is notoriously embroiled in serious legal disputes over its origin and ownership. I first heard of the treasure when a London journalist telephoned me in Toronto in the early 1980s and asked me about a silver plate in the treasure which he told me had raised busts of a group of emperors comprising one Augustus and four Caesars – which would date the plate with certainty to the brief period between 18 September 335 and 22 May 337 and imply that the treasure contained valuable items given to its original owner on the occasion of Constantine's *tricennalia* in 336. I do not know what the journalist with whom I spoke on the telephone did with this information, but this precisely datable plate is absent from the treasure as published. The question therefore inevitably arises: was such a piece ever part of the treasure? On the one hand, the journalist may have been misinformed. On the other hand, the dish may have been removed and deliberately destroyed in order to sustain the false claim that the treasure had an origin outside Europe: a recent book about the theft and illegal export of looted antiquities from Italy documents similar vandalism in pursuit of financial gain (Watson & Todeschini 2006). I do not wish to enter into arguments on a legally fraught matter, just to state what I believe to be the case as simply as possible, even though a full disclosure of the relevant facts about the treasure could show that I am badly mistaken. First, the treasure was found in the former Jugoslavia by a young man who was subsequently murdered when he tried to sell it. Second, at least some of the items in the treasure were given by Constantine on the occasion of his *tricennalia* to a general of non-Roman origin whose name was Seuso.[21] The magnificent Hunting Plate (Mundell Mango & Bennett 1994: 56–57, 77–78, 81–83) identifies the lake which it depicts as Lake Pelso, and inscribed in its central medallion is a christogram followed by a couplet partly in accentual meter (the last syllable of *posteris* being counted as short):

H<a>ec Seuso tibi durent per saecula multa
Posteris ut prosint vascula digna tuis

May these vessels, Seuso, endure for you through many centuries so that they worthily serve your descendants.

(2) Quaestors and praetorian prefects

One important innovation in the civil administration is explicitly attributed to Constantine. In his account of events in 408, Zosimus explains that the *quaestor sacri palatii*, an official who played a central role in the Roman imperial bureaucracy in the first half of the fifth century (Honoré 1998), is 'the man appointed to communicate the emperor's decisions' and that he has had this title since Constantine (5.32.6). Now, in the last section of his history (5.26–6.13), Zosimus is no longer dependent on the unreliable Eunapius, whose narrative ended in the year 404, but closely copies Olympiodorus of Thebes, who visited Rome and used official titles with precision and accuracy (Matthews 1970). On this matter, therefore, the evidence of Zosimus merits serious consideration. On the other hand, no *quaestores sacri palatii* are attested either under Constantine or until the mid-350s. Three quaestors appear in Ammianus Marcellinus' narrative of the year 354 (viz., Montius Magnus, Flavius Taurus and Flavius Leontius) acting as representatives of the emperor entrusted with delicate missions (14.7.12–18, 11.4, 11.14). But nothing that is reported about their activities relates to the discharge of what was later the central function of the *quaestor sacri palatii* (Bonfils 1981: 133–163; Harries 1988: 155–159, 171), though that may be because this function was performed in the imperial *consistorium* when the emperor was closeted with his closest advisers to discuss issues of policy. The *Notitia Dignitatum* defines the sphere in which the imperial quaestor has jurisdiction as *leges dictandae* and *preces* (Oriens 12; Occidens 10). In the first half of the fifth century, the primary role of the quaestor lay in the framing of imperial legislation: he composed a preliminary draft of a new law or general edict after its general tenor and content had been decided in the imperial *consistorium*, he submitted his draft to the *consistorium* for approval, then prepared a final text exhibiting suitable rhetorical polish to which the emperor gave final approval and issued on his authority in the name of the whole imperial college (*CJ* 1.14. 3 [426], cf. Harries 1988: 164–169). The *quaestor sacri palatii* thus combined three functions which had been separate under the early Roman Empire: that of the *quaestor Augusti*, who read an emperor's speeches in the Roman Senate, those of the *ab epistulis* and those of the *a libellis* (Harries 1988: 153–154).[22]

The question of whether *quaestores sacri palatii* of the type Zosimus describes in his narrative of the year 408 existed already under Constantine cannot be answered with any confidence, since our evidence for the last dozen or more years of the reign is so lacunose. The question is not solved even by the contemporary panegyric of Constantine of which fragments are preserved on papyrus (Appendix G), since its date is uncertain and could be as early as 325, when some in Egypt expected an imperial visit in the near future (*P. Oxyrhynchus* X 1261, XIV 1626). One passage, less fragmentary than most, but still full of lacunae, enumerates several high officials (XI.9–17, 19–40 Guida):

> ... entrusting to their foresight, he released ... on them, appointing one as treasurer of the imperial finances, setting up another as judge in charge of cases of murder, and ordering one to deal with embassies and another to receive and in turn to reply to letters ...
>
> of the emperor's foresight that to each of these is assigned the administration to which each seems suited by nature. Since nature has taken care that through one emperor ... I can show [you] by way of supplement also that ... and ... the others. There is no matter great or small which receives a decision according to another's judgment, but every treasurer, prefect, judge in cases of murder, arbiter in disputes over contracts, commander of fighting men, answerer of letters, [dispenser] of outgoings, appraiser of embassies, evaluator of ... and whomsoever else in addition to these you might name takes a single leader as if for some journey, whom they follow, while they themselves ... of their business, ...

Admittedly, the Greek word which I have translated 'treasurer' (ταμίας) is the standard Greek equivalent for the Latin *quaestor*, but the context makes it clear that an official with the duties attested for the *quaestor sacri palatii* cannot be meant.

About the praetorian prefecture, it is possible to be much more precise. Eunapius, duly followed by Zosimus, later complained that Constantine had divided the Roman Empire into the four regional praetorian prefectures of the late fourth century, with disastrous consequences (Zosimus 2.33.1–2). But regional prefectures only started to become a permanent feature of the administration of the Roman Empire in the 340s (Barnes 1987; 1992a: 252, 256–260), while the system of four regional prefectures, which Zosimus alleges that Constantine created, came into existence under the joint rule of the brothers Valentinian and Valens in the late 360s (*PLRE* 1.1050). What happened under Constantine between 324 and 337 is more complicated, and has been the subject of a lengthy recent discussion (Porena 2003: 339–562). Constantine's innovations in relation to earlier practice were two: a praetorian prefect was attached to each emperor who had a separate court to act as his deputy; and praetorian prefects were appointed to govern defined geographical areas, first as a temporary measure until Constantine's three sons by Fausta were old enough to have separate courts and administrations of their own, and also in Africa apparently on what was intended to be a permanent basis. But the evidence for the praetorian prefects of Constantine after 324, though relatively abundant, presents problems of interpretation that need to be discussed in detail.

The Caesar Crispus had governed Gaul and Britain since 317 or 318 with the praetorian prefect Junius Bassus as his deputy to guide him, and Bassus presumably took charge of the administration of Gaul and Britain (and perhaps more) when Crispus departed to the East to take part in the second war against Licinius. Hence no fundamental change was needed when Crispus was disgraced and executed: Bassus continued to provide routine administration for Gaul and Spain as he had been doing for eight years, though no longer under the nominal control of a prince. What of the rest of the Roman Empire? Constantine intended to found a dynasty and the plan for the imperial succession which he started to execute at the end of his reign was to divide his monarchy into a tetrarchy of four emperors, who were still all Caesars at the time of his death. Since Fausta had produced only three sons for Constantine (Julian, *Orat.* 1, 9d, cf. Barnes & Vanderspoel 1984), a fourth Caesar was needed and available in the shape of Dalmatius, the son of Constantine's half-brother Flavius Dalmatius, who was probably born c. 315 (Kienast 1996: 307) and hence approximately the same age as the two oldest sons of Fausta (born in 316 and 317). For several years after the death of Crispus, Constantine had no close relatives of a younger generation whom he could place even in nominal charge of separate administrations. It was only in 335, when he appointed Dalmatius Caesar that Constantine began to put his permanent plans into place. In the interim, he increased the number of praetorian prefects and made some of them responsible for governing specific geographical areas.

Before 324 the only structural innovation in the praetorian prefecture which is attested with certainty was the appointment of Junius Bassus as a third prefect. It was an innovation for the Roman Empire as a whole to have three prefects rather than two (though there had been three prefects between 306 and 312, since Maxentius, who was not recognized outside Italy and Africa, had a praetorian prefect of his own), and Bassus was the first praetorian prefect whose competence was limited to a restricted geographical area.[23] After 9 September 337, in contrast, the three sons of Constantine each had a praetorian prefect: the father of Ambrose was prefect of Constantinus when he invaded Italy in 340, at a time when Antonius Marcellinus, consul in 341, was prefect of Constans and the prefect Septimius Acindynus, consul in 340, was in Antioch and therefore praetorian prefect of Constantius (Augustine, *De sermone domini in monte* 1.50 [*PL* 34.1254]).[24] After the death of Constantinus in 340, the college of praetorian prefects still numbered three, although there were now only two Augusti (*ILS* 8944: Traiana in Thrace; Delphi, Inv. nos. 1647, 4077). It follows that, while Constantius had a single prefect throughout the decade 340–350 (Acindynus until 340 or 341; Domitius Leontius, consul in 344, from 341 to 344; Flavius Philippus, consul in 348, from 344 to 351), Constans had two prefects in the early 340s and added another in 343 or shortly thereafter, so that in the later 340s there were three praetorian prefects in Constans' portion of the empire each of whom administered different geographical areas: one governed Gaul, Britain and presumably Spain, another Italy and Africa, and the third Illyricum (Barnes 1987: 17–22; 1992a: 252).

From this it follows that Constantine instituted no permanent reform of the praetorian prefecture. He retained one praetorian prefect at his court to serve as a deputy emperor, though without the military functions discharged by prefects before and after him, such as Asclepiodotus, who commanded an army when

Constantius recovered Britain in 296 (Chapter 2), and Salutius Secundus, who accompanied Julian on his invasion of Persia in 363 (Ammianus 23.5.6: *praefectus Salutius praesens*). But after the defeat of Licinius Constantine also began to appoint praetorian prefects who were active in different geographical areas of the empire. When Crispus was executed in 326, Junius Bassus continued to serve as praetorian prefect in Gaul until 331, and several other prefects are attested in the late 320s (Barnes 1982: 131–134). Flavius Constantius, consul in 327, appears to have been appointed prefect with responsibility for the diocese of Oriens by 16 December 324 (*CTh* 15.14.1[Seeck]) and to have resided in Antioch (*CTh* 1.5.1[Seeck]); he seems to have dedicated a building at Aqaba between November 324 and the early summer of 326 (*AE* 1989.750c), and he remained in office until at least 11 June 327 (*CTh* 2.24.2). Extracts of laws in the Theodosian Code attest Evagrius, who never held the ordinary consulate, as a praetorian prefect in May and November 326 (*CTh* 12.1.13; *CJ* 2.19[20].11), on 18 October 329 (*CTh* 16.8.1[Barnes]), in August 331 (*CTh* 7.22.3 + 12.1.19, 20) and on 22 August 336 (*CTh* 12.1.22), and Valerius Maximus on 21 January 327 (*CTh* 1.5.2), on 27 September 328 (*CTh* 1.4.2[Seeck]), on 29 December 328 (*CTh* 1.16.4 + 7.20.5), in May 332 (*CJ* 7.36.7) and May 333 (*CTh* 8.1.3).[25] Since Valerius Maximus was one of the ordinary consuls of 327, he must have been appointed prefect before 31 December 326. The heading to an imperial constitution read at Rome on 9 May 328 addresses Aemilianus as praetorian prefect (*CTh* 11.16.4): Aemilianus is otherwise completely unknown, but he appears to have been succeeded by L. Papius Pacatianus, consul in 332, who received laws specifically concerned with the city of Rome in March 334 and April 335 (*CTh* 14.4.1; 8.9.1). Although Pacatianus is not attested as praetorian prefect in the Theodosian Code before 12 April 332 (*CTh* 3.5.4 + 5), he too, like Valerius Maximus, must have been appointed to a praetorian prefecture before he entered on his consulate. Flavius Ablabius, consul in 331, is unambiguously attested as prefect before his consulate (*CTh* 16.8.2: 29 November 330) and the dates of three laws have been emended to show him prefect in 329 (Barnes 1982: 132).

Our understanding of the praetorian prefecture in these years has been considerably enhanced by the discovery of an inscription at Ain Rchine in Tunisia which records a college of five praetorian prefects (all in the genitive case) which included men of both senatorial (*viri clarissimi*) and equestrian status (line 4: –] *cccc et i[llus] trium vvvv[v* –) while Domitius Zenophilus was proconsul of Africa (*AE* 1981.878, cf. Chastagnol 1986: 86–88; Salway 2007: 1283). Zenophilus, who became consul on 1 January 333, was probably proconsul of Africa for the quadriennium 328–332 (Barnes 1982: 106–107, 171). Admittedly, it has been argued that the man who held the proconsulate for four years (*AE* 1917/18.99 = *Inscriptions latines d'Afrique* 456: Bulla Regia) was Antonius Marcellinus (consul in 341) and that Marcellinus was proconsul for the quadriennium 332–336 (Chastagnol 1986: 81–86), which would indirectly imply that Zenophilus was proconsul in 330–331 (Chastagnol 1986: 86–88). In the present context, however, it does not matter whether Zenophilus was proconsul in 330–331 or 331–332.

Only the name of the first of the five prefects is fully preserved on the inscription from Ain Rchine, but there is no doubt about the identities of the second and third prefects, while the fourth and fifth names can be supplied from the preceding discussion (Barnes 1992a: 249 n.2). The prefects are (in the nominative case):

Valerius Maximus (consul 327)
Ju[nius Bassus] (consul 331)
[F]lavius Ablabius (consul 331)
Va[lerius Evagrius]
[Papius Pacatianus] (consul in 332: the name is completely lost).

The order of the first three names does not reflect seniority within the college of prefects, since Bassus had entered it in 318 several years before Valerius Maximus, who precedes him. Hence the first three prefects are listed according to their seniority as ordinary consuls: Maximus had been consul four years before Bassus and Ablabius, and Bassus was the *consul prior* of 331, as all known consular dates from that year and all later calendars make clear (*CLRE* 196–197). It follows that the inscription cannot be earlier than 1 January 331. The order of the fourth and fifth names on the other hand must reflect the order in which Evagrius and Pacatianus entered the college of prefects. For Pacatianus, whose name is supplied with certainty, became consul on 1 January 332, after which date he would have preceded, not followed, Evagrius, who never held an ordinary consulate. The inscription belongs, therefore, to the year 331, probably to the early months of the year, since it seems that at this period a new proconsul will have replaced Zenophilus in April (Barnes 1983: 256–260; 1985c: 144–147).

What were the functions or spheres of operation of these five prefects? Ablabius was at the court of Constantine in the winter of 331/332 when Athanasius had an audience with the emperor (Athanasius, *Festal Letter* 4.5), from which it may be deduced that he was in constant attendance on Constantine from his appointment as prefect until 335 or 336.[26] In 331 Bassus was still prefect in Gaul and Pacatianus was active in Italy. Evagrius had remained in the East in 326 when Constantine went to Italy, but there is no indication anywhere of his sphere of activity in 331, or of that of Valerius Maximus.

As the time approached when the sons of Constantine would reach the age at which they could begin to function as rulers apart from their father, the emperor created a short-lived regional praetorian prefecture in Africa. It was created while L. Aradius Proculus, who was to become consul in 340, was proconsul of Africa for the proconsular year 332–333 (Barnes 1982: 133, 171) and simultaneously praetorian prefect (*ILS* 1240, 1241). Immediately after the end of Proculus' proconsulate in April 333 (Barnes 1982: 133), Felix became praetorian prefect, in which office he is first attested on 18 April 333 (*CTh* 3.30.5). Felix held office for three years and was succeeded by Gregorius (Barnes 1982: 133), who is attested as prefect on 9 October 336 (*CTh* 11.1.3). That Felix and Gregorius were prefects in and of the diocese of Africa is not merely 'an article of faith' (Salway 2007: 1284), but well attested by evidence. First, the nature of the identical dedications to Constantinus Caesar at Tubernuc and Antioch discussed below locate two of the five prefects as physically present in Africa and Syria. Second, two laws addressed to Felix state that he administered Roman Africa: one, posted in Carthage on 27 August 334, contains the injunction 'let your sublimity enforce this in the provinces of Africa' (*CTh* 13.4.1), while another, issued on 21 October 335 and published at Carthage on 9 March 336, is still more explicit: 'we desire that your excellent sublimity advise magistrates by dispatching letters throughout the diocese entrusted to it' (*Constitutio Sirmondiana* 4 = *CTh* 16.8.5 + 9.1). The prefecture lapsed or disappeared in 337 when Constantine's three surviving sons divided the Roman Empire between them.

Constantine's sons Constantinus and Constantius had been Caesars since 317 and 324 respectively. Late in his reign Constantine added two more Caesars to the imperial college, in each case choosing a day with Christian significance for their proclamation: he appointed his youngest son Constans Caesar on Christmas Day 333 and his half-nephew Dalmatius Caesar on 18 September 335, a date which coincided with the dedication of the new and magnificent Church of the Holy Sepulchre in Jerusalem. A pair of inscriptions, one found at Tubernuc in Tunisia and published in 1924 (*AE* 1925.72 = *Inscriptions latines de la Tunisie* 814), the other from Antioch and published in 1985 (Feissel 1985: 421, whence *AE* 1985.823 = *SEG* 35.1484), preserve a dedication to Constantinus Caesar made jointly by a college of prefects whose names are preserved in full (except that the third name has been erased on the African copy). The date must be earlier than 9 October 336, when Gregorius had replaced the prefect Felix, who is third on the list. Chastagnol, followed by Dennis Feissel in his publication of the Antioch text, dated the dedication to 336 and identified the precise occasion of the dedications by the five prefects as the *vicennalia* of the Caesar Constantinus on 1 March 336 (Chastagnol 1983: 88–92; Feissel 1985: 434). But, since Felix was certainly prefect in Africa, far from any imperial court, that would leave one of the four Caesars of 336 without a prefect, which is implausible since Constantine gave each of them a separate court and administration (*VC* 4.51.2–3).[27] The occasion of the dedication may therefore be identified as the marriage of Constantinus in the summer of 335, shortly before Constantine added Dalmatius to the imperial college (Barnes 1992a: 250).[28]

The college of prefects in the summer of 335 numbered five, as had the college of 331, but the later quintet did not necessarily perform the same functions as the earlier. The names are in the order (i) L. Pap(ius) Pacatianus, (ii) Fl(avius) Ablabius, (iii) Val(erius) Felix, (iv) C. Annius Tiberianus and (v) Nestorius Timonianus. Since Pacatianus was consul in 332, one year after Ablabius, the order of names must here reflect solely seniority within the prefectorial college.[29] The functions of at least some of the five prefects are indirectly attested. Jerome's *Chronicle* registers Annius Tiberianus as praetorian prefect of Gaul in the thirtieth year of Constantine (233[m]):

hence Tiberianus must be the prefect assigned to the Caesar Constantinus, and there is no difficulty in supposing that C. Caelius Saturninus, who was praetorian prefect in the reign of Constantine, and whose prefecture, which is attested only epigraphically, was the culmination of many years of service to the emperor (*ILS* 1214, 1215: Rome), followed Bassus and preceded Tiberianus as prefect in Gaul (Barnes 1982: 134; Porena 2003: 442–448). Eunapius reports that Constantine placed Constantius under the guidance of Ablabius (*Vit. Phil.* 6.3.8), which implies that Ablabius was sent to Antioch with Constantius when the Caesar took up residence there. Valerius Felix was a regional prefect administering the diocese of Africa, and the westerner Pacatianus, whom the Theodosian Code attests as praetorian prefect in Italy in 334 and 335 was presumably attached to the Caesar Constans when he was set up with a court and administration of his own. By elimination, therefore, the otherwise unknown Nestorius Timonianus must be the new prefect in attendance on Constantine, replacing Ablabius: since nothing else whatever is known about Timonianus except this dedication of 335, it may be assumed that he lost his life in 337. These inferences will be clearer when presented in tabular form, together with the probable city of residence of each prefect. In summer 335 the college of prefects comprised in order of seniority:

L. Pap(ius) Pacatianus	prefect of Constans	in Italy or Illyricum
Fl(avius) Ablabius	prefect of Constantine	in Antioch
Val(erius) Felix	prefect in Africa	presumably at Carthage
C. Annius Tiberianus	prefect of Constantinus	in Gaul, probably at Trier
Nestorius Timonianus	prefect of Constantius	in Constantinople

The praetorian prefecture has been discussed at some length in order to show that what might seem to be reforms motivated by administrative considerations were in fact changes made by Constantine primarily in order to facilitate his plans for the imperial succession.

CONSTANTINE'S DYNASTIC PLANS

Constantius and Theodora had six children (Table 7.2, cf. Chapter 2). Of their three daughters, Constantia married Licinius in 313, produced a son in 315, and appears to have lived on at Constantine's court after the defeat and subsequent execution of her husband, though it is not clear for how long.[30] Anastasia married the Roman senator Bassianus before the end of 315 (Chapter 5). Of Eutropia (*PLRE* 1.316, Eutropia 2) nothing is known during the lifetime of Constantine except that she must have married Virius Nepotianus, consul in 336, who is equally unknown (Barnes 1982: 108), since her son Nepotianus was proclaimed Augustus in Rome on 3 June and killed on 30 June 350 (*RIC* 8.261, 265–266, Rome: nos. 167, 198–203; Eutropius, *Brev.* 10.11; *Epitome* 42.3; *Descriptio consulum* 350.4, 5). Of the three sons of Constantius and

Theodora, nothing whatever is known about Hannibalianus, who must therefore have died young. About Flavius Dalmatius and Julius Constantius very little is known before they emerged into prominence late in Constantine's reign. Ausonius reveals that both of them lived in Toulouse for a period as virtual exiles, that the rhetor Exsuperius taught Dalmatius and Hannibalianus, the sons of Flavius Dalmatius, at Narbo (as a reward for which he received a governorship in Spain in 335 or 336), and that Ausonius' uncle Arborius taught Dalmatius in Constantinople before he became Caesar and that he perished there in the bloodbath of 337 (Ausonius, *Commemoratio Professorum Burdigalensium* 16.11–12, 17.9–13, 16.13–16, cf. Green 1991: 352–354). Constantius may have been employed by Constantine on a delicate diplomatic errand in 315/316 (Chapter 5), and after the winter of 316/317 he resided in Corinth (Libanius, *Orat.* 14.29–30 = Julian, *Ep.* 20 Bidez-Cumont). But the fact that Gallus, the son of Constantius, was born in 326 at the Massa Veterensis in Etruria suggests that the two brothers may have joined the imperial court in Italy for the celebrations of Constantine's *vicennalia* in Rome (Ammianus 14.11.27, cf. Barnes 1981: 251) – though their recall from quasi-exile in provincial cities far from the imperial court may well have been later than and unconnected with the execution of Crispus.

In the 330s Constantine bestowed consulates on both his half-nephews and revived two ancient titles for new dynastic and political purposes. Flavius Dalmatius held the ordinary consulate in 333, received the title *censor* (which made him higher in rank than a praetorian prefect) and began to reside in Antioch with important military and administrative duties: he suppressed a rebellion in Cyprus, executed its leader at Tarsus and investigated a charge of murder against Athanasius (*PLRE* 1.240–241, Dalmatius 6; Barnes 1982: 105). Julius Constantius, who became consul two years after his brother in 335, received the obsolete title of *patricius*, which excluded him from the imperial college but made him superior in rank to all other holders of high office. But Constantius was not the first *patricius* in the revived or Constantinian patriciate.[31] That honor went to Flavius Optatus, consul in 334 (Zosimus 2.40.2), whose career is described in satirical terms by Libanius, according to whom he was a *grammaticus* who taught the son of Licinius, 'married the daughter of a Paphlagonian innkeeper, and after the fall of Licinius, through her charms, obtained high position and great wealth, becoming consul' (*Orat.* 42.26–27). Libanius' reference to a 'Paphlagonian innkeeper' and the fact that Optatus became a *patricius* before Constantius suggest that he was a relative of Constantine's mother (Barnes 1981: 251; 1982: 107), who probably came from Bithynia (Chapter 2).

On 18 September 335 Constantine added Dalmatius, the elder son of Flavius Dalmatius to the existing imperial college and made a territorial division of the Roman Empire between the four Caesars, except for the African provinces, which remained under a regional praetorian prefect. Constantine himself retained overall control and appointed praetorian prefects to advise and supervise the young Caesars – precisely the same function as Junius Bassus had discharged when Crispus resided in Trier. In this division of 335, the Caesar Constantinus ruled Britain, Gaul and Spain from Trier; the Caesar Constantius ruled Asia Minor and the diocese of Oriens (which included Egypt) from Antioch; the Caesar Constans probably resided in Milan and ruled Italy together with the diocese of Pannoniae; and the Caesar Dalmatius, who may have resided at Naissus, probably ruled the dioceses of Moesiae and Thracia (*Origo* 35; *Epitome* 41.20, cf. Barnes 1982: 198–200). Constantine also married off the four Caesars as soon as the age of each permitted. Constantinus, who was born in 316, was married first (Eusebius, *VC* 4.49); no source discloses the name or identity of his wife, but she was surely a member of the Constantinian clan, possibly a daughter of Flavius Optatus. Constantius, who was born in 317, married a daughter of Julius Constantius during the celebration of his father's *tricennalia* in 336 (Eusebius, *VC* 4.49; Julian, *Letter to the Athenians* 272d; Athanasius, *Historia Arianorum* 69.1). Constans, who was too young to marry before his father died, since he was probably born in 323, was betrothed to Olympias, the daughter of Flavius Ablabius (Athanasius, *Historia Arianorum* 69.1–2; Ammianus 20.11.3, cf. Barnes 1982: 45).[32] And it may legitimately be conjectured that Dalmatius, who was probably of an age with Constantinus and Constantius, married Helena, the daughter of Constantine.

As the dynastic marriages of 335 and 336 make clear, Constantine's plan was that after his death the Roman Empire should be ruled by a college of four emperors. But what form of tetrarchy did he envisage? The obvious precedent was the Diocletianic Tetrarchy of two Augusti and two Caesars. Hence what Constantine envisaged after his death was that the Roman Empire, which he had united under his sole control in 324, should again be ruled by an imperial college comprising two Augusti and two Caesars, thus reintroducing (and potentially rendering permanent) the political and administrative division of the Roman Empire into an eastern and a western half. Heinrich Chantraine divined the precise composition of the imperial college which Constantine intended to rule after he was gone (Chantraine 1992; Burgess 2008: 7–9): his eldest surviving son Constantinus, who would automatically be the senior emperor, was to be Augustus in the West with Constans as his Caesar, while his second eldest surviving son Constantius was to be Augustus of the East with Dalmatius as his Caesar.

This dynastic plan required Constantine to promote either Constantinus or Constantius to the rank of Augustus in order to ensure an orderly transmission of power (Burgess 2008: 8–9). He did not do so. Why? The answer is perhaps partly to be sought in his explicit emulation of the emperor Trajan. In 328 Constantine built a fort at Daphne on the north bank of the Danube opposite the existing fortress of Transmarisca and constructed a stone bridge from Oescus to Sucidava on the *ripa Gothica* in preparation for the sustained military operations north of the river which he conducted several years until his *tricennalia* in 336. In particular, he campaigned against the Goths at the request of the Sarmatians in 332 and against the Sarmatians in 334, when he exploited social conflicts north of the Danube (Eusebius, *VC* 4.5–6; *Origo* 31–32; *Descriptio consulum* 332, 334), and he took the victory titles *Gothicus maximus* in 332, *Sarmaticus maximus* in 334 and *Dacicus maximus* in 335 or 336 (*AE* 1934.158, cf. Barnes 1982: 79, 80) – the last a title taken by no emperor before him except by Trajan for his conquest of Dacia.

Constantine's campaigns may have left archaeological traces which confirm the statement of the emperor Julian that he re-established Roman control over territory conquered by Trajan, which had been evacuated in the third century, and created a new province north of the Danube, even though it was lost again immediately after his death (Tudor 1941–1942; Demougeot 1983: 100–112).[33] In his *Symposium* or *Kronia* (the Greek translation of the Latin *Saturnalia*, though the work is often styled *Caesares*) Julian makes Constantine claim equality with Trajan or even possible superiority over him on the grounds that reconquest is greater than conquest, to which Silenus replies: 'Constantine, do you really offer the gardens of Adonis as your <finest> achievement?' (*Caesares* 30, 329c). Like Trajan, Constantine then turned his gaze to the East.

Religion had influenced Constantine's actions as emperor from the start (Chapter 4). After 324 he brought religion into his dealings with those who lived outside the Roman Empire. Shortly after 324 the Caucasian kingdom of Iberia embraced Christianity and a Roman alliance (Gelasius of Caesarea, frag. 21 Winkelmann, cf. Peeters 1932), and Constantine wrote a personal letter in his own hand (not dictated), which Eusebius quotes, to the Persian king asserting his patronage of Shapur's Christian subjects (Eusebius, *VC* 4.9–13). Shapur, however, desired to recover what Persia had lost in the treaty of 299 after its crushing defeat by Galerius (Chapter 3). Border raids began in the early 330s (Eutropius, *Brev.* 10.8.2; Festus, *Brev.* 26) and in 336 a Persian army under the command of the royal prince Narseh installed a Persian nominee on the throne of Armenia, which had been officially Christian since 314 (Chapter 5 at n. 9). Constantine seized the opportunity to conduct a holy war to rescue the Christians of Persia, who were disposed to welcome him as a liberator, as the fifth treatise of Aphrahat proclaimed in unambiguous terms (Barnes 1985a). He also (it appears) decided to install Hannibalianus, the brother of the Caesar Dalmatius, as a monarch in Ctesiphon. Constantine had already given Hannibalianus the titles of *nobilissimus* (Zosimus 2.39.2) and king and the hand of his daughter Constantina in marriage (Ammianus 14.1.2; Philostorgius, *HE* 3.22), probably intending to set him up as a monarch in the region of the Caucasus: that at least seems to be the implication of the sources which state that he was 'king of the Pontic races' or that he received 'Armenia and the surrounding nations (*Origo* 35; *Epitome* 41.20). But he now styled Hannibalianus *rex regum* ('king of kings'), which was Shapur's title, and coins were minted in Constantinople with *Regi Hannibaliano* on the obverse and the River Euphrates on the reverse (*RIC* 7.584, 589–590, Constantinople: nos. 100, 145–148).

Constantine planned his invasion of Persia from ideological motives and he advertised it to his soldiers, his subjects and the Christians of Persia as a religious undertaking. He invited bishops to travel with his army, he prepared a tent to serve as a mobile church and accompany him everywhere, and he declared his intention of being baptized in the River Jordan before beginning the actual invasion (Eusebius, *VC* 4.56, 62.2). He presumably also proposed to promote Constantius to Augustus when he reached Antioch. A Persian embassy came to Constantinople during the winter of 336/337 seeking peace, but Constantine repulsed them (heading to

Eusebius, *VC* 4.57, whose text is lost; Festus, *Brev.* 26). In the spring of 337, however, as Constantine prepared to depart on his last expedition, death caught him unawares, and in a final, though doubtless this time unintended, imitation of Trajan,[34] he died on 22 May 337 without making the necessary legal arrangements to secure a peaceful succession. Even more disastrously, Constantine left the Christian subjects of the Persian king exposed to the charge of disloyalty. The Syriac writer Aphrahat had welcomed the invasion before it even started (*Demonstration* 5, cf. Barnes 1985a: 130, 133–135). Shapur, therefore, who now embarked on what was to prove a protracted war in Mesopotamia, began to view the Christians of Persia as actual or potential traitors. In March 340 Shapur ordered the confiscation of church treasures to help fund the war, the destruction of churches and the arrest and detention of Christian clergy (Sozomenus, *HE* 2.9.2; *Acts of Simeon* [BHO 1117] 12; [BHO 1119] 18 [Kmosko 1907: 737/738.15–24, 815/816.16–817/818.7]), in 344 he executed Simeon, the metropolitan bishop of Seleucia-Ctesiphon, and another hundred or so Christians in the new city of Karkha de-Ledan near Susa (*Barrington Atlas* 92D4), and in 345 there was a ten-day pogrom, known as the 'Great Massacre' (Burgess 1999b), which concentrated on Christians in Bet Huzay (*Barrington Atlas* 93E2).

At his death Constantine left the Roman Empire under the rule of an imperial college which comprised four Caesars, but no Augustus – that is, in the unprecedented situation where no emperor possessed the legal right either to promote any of the Caesars to the higher rank of Augustus or to issue general edicts or laws. Constantius, who had hurried across Asia Minor from Antioch as soon as he learned of his father's final illness, failed to reach his father before he died. Since there was now no living Augustus, it was officially pretended that Constantine continued to rule after his death. This is attested on the documentary level in Egypt by the written acknowledgment of a loan dated 13 August 337 which refers forward to the Egyptian year due to begin on 29 August 337 as 'the coming year 32, 22, 14, 5, 3,' where the first numeral refers to the regnal years of Constantine, the last to the regnal years of Dalmatius Caesar, news of whose death had therefore not yet reached Oxyrhynchus (*P. Oxyrhynchus* XLV 3266).[35] The heading of the imperial rescript which Constans issued to the Italian city of Hispellum has an imperial college of Constantine as Augustus and his sons Constantinus, Constantius and Constans whose status is not spelled out (*ILS* 705): that, combined with the omission of Dalmatius, dates the rescript to the period between Dalmatius' death and 9 September 337 (Chapter 1 at nn.13–17). Nor did his status as a mere Caesar prevent Constantinus in Trier from restoring the Athanasius to the see of Alexandria in the name of all three sons of Constantine (Athanasius, *Historia Arianorum* 8.1) – and presumably also their father, since Constantinus' personal letter of recommendation of the exiled bishop is dated 17 June 337 (Athansius, *Apologia contra Arianos* 87.4–7).

Eusebius claimed that the unprecedented situation of the sons of Constantine ruling in their father's name represented a blessing of God on Constantine (*VC* 4.67.3) and the posthumous editor of the *Life of Constantine* added the detail that court officials maintained the pretence (heading to *VC* 4.67):

Alone of mortals the Blessed One reigned even after death, and ordinary business was carried on just as if he were alive, God having granted this to him uniquely since time began

That even after death he was honored by *comites* and the rest as he had been during his lifetime.

The political vacuum could not be allowed to continue. Constantius saw that action was needed – and he acted ruthlessly. First, he dismissed Ablabius, whom Constantine had intended to continue as praetorian prefect in constant attendance on his son and in this capacity to serve as a wise counselor guiding the young man in affairs of state (Eunapius, *Lives of the Philosophers* 6.2.7–8). Then he set about removing anyone who might challenge the right of the three sons of Constantine to rule jointly in place of their father (Burgess 2008).[36] He drew upon dynastic loyalties in a way which recalls the appeal of Caesar's heir to the soldiers of Julius Caesar after his assassination in 44 BC (Syme 1939: 112–161) in order to overturn Constantine's attempt to integrate his half-brothers and their progeny into the imperial family. During the summer of 337, the praetorian prefect Ablabius and six imperial relatives were done to death – the Caesar Dalmatius and his brother Hannibalianus; Dalmatius' father Flavius Dalmatius and the latter's brother Julius Constantius; the oldest son of Julius Constantius, whose name is not known (Julian, *Ep. ad Athenienses* 3, 270cd); and the *patricius* Flavius Optatus (Zosimus 2.40.2), whose relationship to the imperial house is not explicitly attested. (The future Caesars Gallus and Julian, the young sons of Julius Constantius were spared because of their age.) The three sons of Fausta then met in Pannonia, where on 9 September they were saluted as Augusti by the Roman army.

AN ASTROLOGER'S PRAISE OF CONSTANTINE

In the very last months of Constantine, the senator Julius Firmicus Maternus Junior composed a handbook of astrology which he dedicated to Q. Flavius Maesius Egnatius Lollianus *signo* Mavortius. Maternus had first promised the work when Lollianus was *consularis* of Campania some years earlier, but he discharged his promise after Lollianus became proconsul of Africa and had been designated ordinary consul for 338 (*Mathesis* 1 pr. 8; 8.15). Towards the end of the last chapter of the first book of the *Mathesis* (1.10.13–14), Maternus speaks of Constantine in a laudatory passage which is less well known than it might be, perhaps because no English translation was published until 1975 and the translation which was published then is full of inaccuracies and outright errors. A translation is therefore offered here.

We shall produce examples of this not from far away nor from ancient books: the lord and our Augustus, emperor of the whole world, the pious fortunate and far-seeing

Constantine, the oldest son of the deified Constantius,[37] a prince of august and venerable memory, who was chosen to rescue the world from the rule of tyrants and to suppress evils at home by the favour of his own majesty, so that through him the squalor of servitude might be washed away and the gifts of secure freedom restored to us, and so that we might cast off the yoke of captivity from our already tired and oppressed necks. Always fighting for our liberty he was never deceived by the fortune of war, that most uncertain thing among human vicissitudes. Born in Naissus, from the first stage of his age he held the rudders of empire, which he had acquired under favourable auspices, and he sustains the Roman world by the salubrious moderation of his rule so that it enjoys an increase of its everlasting good fortune.[38]

Maternus then beseeches the sun, the moon and the planets Saturn, Mars, Mercury and Venus to aid God in protecting the imperial family:

Make Constantine the greatest prince and his most unconquerable children, our lords and Caesars, through the agreement of your moderation and obeying the judgement of the Supreme God who decrees perpetual rule to them rule even over our descendants and the descendants of our descendants through an infinite succession of ages, so that, with all bitterness of evil driven away, the human race may attain the rewards of undisturbed and perpetual good fortune.

Maternus was writing in Rome or at least in Italy. It is not surprising, therefore, that his specific praises of Constantine concentrate on his liberation of Rome nearly a quarter of a century earlier. Moreover, it was obligatory to pray for the ruling dynasty to reign in perpetuity. What is most significant about this passage is that Maternus subordinates the planetary influences to a Supreme God who can only be the God of the Christians. When Maternus wrote on astrology, he was not yet the rabid Christian that he had become by 343 when his violent tract *On the Error of Profane Religions* urged the emperors Constantius and Constans to suppress pagan rites in the western parts of the Roman Empire (Chapter 6). Indeed he was not yet a Christian at all, since he protests to Lollianus that the latter is mistaken if he thinks that he is trying to lead men away from attending to the gods and their cults with profane madness (*Math.* 1.6.1: *unde, quod tu per nos fieri posse definis, ut homines a cultu deorum religionumque profano mentis furore revocemus ... falleris*). Yet he felt obliged or compelled to acknowledge one supreme God.

In the event Constantine died on 22 May 337 and Lollianus did not become consul until 1 January 355, when he replaced Constantius' minister Eugenius, who died unexpectedly in the later months of 354 (Barnes 2007b: 387–389). Lollianus had continued his career under Constans, holding the urban prefecture of Rome in 342 and being awarded the title of *comes ordinis primi intra palatium* for the second time (*ILS* 1225), and his delayed consulate must have been a reward for his loyalty to the Constantinian dynasty during the usurpation of Magnentius, who controlled Italy from the end of June 350 to late September 352 (Barnes 1993a: 101–102, 105–106, 221). In 337, however, after Constantine died on 22

May, Lollianus was deprived of the consulate of 338 to which he had already been formally designated in the political turmoil which followed the death of Constantine. The two ordinary consulates of 338 went, not to two of the three of the new Augusti, as might have been expected, but to two generals.[39] They presumably received their consulates as a reward for services rendered to the sons of Constantine in 'the summer of blood' which has ever since retrospectively tarnished their father's memory and encouraged skeptics to doubt the sincerity of his conversion to Christianity.

TABLES: DYNASTIC ALLIANCES AND CHILDREN OF EMPERORS 285–337

Table 7.1   Marriage alliances and children: members of the imperial college 293–311

Diocletian (died 311)		= Prisca → daughter Valeria = Galerius
		Minervina (precise relationship to Diocletian unknown) = (1) Constantine
Maximian (died 310)		= (1) ?
	→	daughter Theodora = (2) Constantius = (2) Eutropia
	→	son Maxentius (c.282–312) = Valeria Maximilla, daughter of Galerius
	→	daughter Fausta (c.290–326) = (2) Constantine
Constantius (died 306)		= (1) Helena → son Constantine = (2) Theodora, daughter of Maximian
	→	three sons and three daughters (listed in Table 7.2)
Galerius (died 311)		= (1) unknown
	→	daughter Valeria Maximilla = Maxentius (Barnes 1982: 38; 2010d: 321–322) = (2) Valeria, daughter of Diocletian (no issue) = concubine (name unknown)
	→	Candidianus, adopted by Valeria and executed in 313 (Lactantius, *Mort. Pers.* 20.4, 35.3, 50.2–4, 51)
Severus (died 307)		= unknown
	→	son who was an adult in 313 when he was executed (Lactantius, *Mort. Pers.* 50.4)
Maximinus (died 313)		= daughter of a sibling of Galerius (Barnes 1999a)
	→	son Maximus, born 305/306, killed 313 daughter, born 306/307, betrothed to Candidianus, killed 313 (Lactantius, *Mort. Pers.* 50.6; Zonaras 13.1)
Constantine (died 337): Table 7.2		
Licinius (died 325)*		= Constantia, daughter of Constantius and Theodora
	→	Licinianus Licinius, born c.315, killed in 325

Note: * The *Liciniani filius* who was deprived of his rank and sentenced to serve in the *gynaeceum* of Carthage (*CTh* 4.6.2–3) has often been identified as a bastard son of Licinius (*PLRE* 1.510; Barnes 1982: 44). I no longer consider this at all plausible.

Table 7.2   Children and grandchildren of Constantius, the father of Constantine

```
(1) = Helena   →   son Constantine (273–337)
                        = (1) Minervina
                        → son Crispus (c.295–326)    = Helena
                                                        →    child born in 322
                        = (2) Fausta, daughter of Maximian
                        → sons
                        Constantinus (316–340) = ? daughter of Flavius Optatus
                        Constantius (317–361)   = (1) daughter of Julius Constantius
                        Constans (?323–350)
                        → daughters
                        Constantina (died 354)   = (1) Hannibalianus (killed 337)
                                                 = (2) Gallus Caesar (executed 354)
                        Helena (died 358)         = (1) ?Dalmatius Caesar (killed 337)
                                                 = (2) Julian, Caesar 355, died 363

(2) = Theodora, daughter of Maximian
      → sons        Flavius Dalmatius, consul 333, killed 337
                    → sons    Dalmatius, Caesar 335, killed 337
                              Hannibalianus rex, killed 337
                              Hannibalianus (died young)
                    Julius Constantius, consul 335, killed 337
                        (1) = ???                →    son, killed in 337
                        (2) = Basilina
                                                 →    sons Constantius (Gallus), Caesar 351
                                                      Julian, Caesar 355, Augustus 360
                                                 →    daughter (name unknown)

      → daughters   Constantia = Licinius, Augustus 308–324, killed 325
                    Anastasia = Bassianus (executed 316)
                    Eutropia = Virius Nepotianus, consul 336
                                                 →    son Julius Nepotianus, Augustus in
                                                      Rome, June 350
```

APPENDIX: THE DYNASTIC MARRIAGES
OF 335 AND 336

Eusebius, who was in Constantinople at the time, reports that Constantius Caesar was married with great ceremony during the celebrations of his father's *tricennalia* in July 336, and that his older brother Constantinus had been married earlier (*VC* 4.49). Constantius' wife was a daughter of Julius Constantius, consul 335 (Athanasius, *Historia Arianorum* 69.1; Julian, *Ep. ad Athenienses* 272d). Constans, the younger brother of Constantinus and Constans, was betrothed to Olympias, the daughter of the powerful praetorian prefect Flavius Ablabius (Athanasius, *Historia Arianorum* 69; Ammianus 20.11.3), but the marriage never took place. Constantina, the sister of Constantinus, Constantius and Constans, married Hannibalianus, the brother of Dalmatius Caesar (*Origo* 35; Ammianus 14.1.2). If Constantina's sister Helena was married before she married the Caesar Julian in 355, as seems likely, then her first husband was surely her first cousin, the Caesar Dalmatius. The marriages, which were presumably all celebrated during Constantine's thirtieth year of rule (25 July 335–25 July 336), and the betrothal of Constans, who was probably born in 323 and therefore too young to be married before his father's death, are part of a coherent dynastic plan for the imperial succession.

These marriage arrangements may be tabulated as follows:

	w(ife) or *b(etrothed)*
335	
Constantinus Caesar	Probably a daughter of Flavius Optatus, consul 334 (w)
Constans Caesar	Olympias, daughter of Flavius Ablabius, consul 331 (b)
336	
Constantius Caesar	Daughter of Julius Constantius, consul 335 (w)
Dalmatius Caesar	Probably Helena, daughter of Constantine (w)
Hannibalianus	Constantina, daughter of Constantine (w)

8

EPILOGUE

Constantine was one of those rare monarchs who both inherited power from his father and possessed the ability to preserve and enhance his inheritance. He was also supremely fortunate that his religious convictions and his political interests coincided so completely. Constantine was a political genius of the highest order, to whom events presented no obstacle, as they have so often for less able leaders, but rather a launching pad for continual successes. At the age of twenty, as the legitimate son of his father Constantius, he became in effect a crown prince, since Maximian and Constantius were the only two members of the college of four emperors created on 1 March 293 who had legitimate sons and all recent precedent indicated that emperors with sons were expected to transmit their imperial power to them. Constantine spent the years between 293 and 305 either on campaign with the eastern Caesar Galerius or at the court of Diocletian, and he married a woman who was probably a close relative of the eastern Augustus (Chapter 3).

In 305 both Constantine and Maxentius, the son of Maximian, were denied the appointment as Caesar which their status since 293 had led them and almost everyone else to expect. Constantine then joined his father in Gaul, went on campaign with him into Scotland and was at his side when he died in York. The dying Constantius appointed his son to the imperial college with the rank of Augustus, and as soon as he died his army acclaimed him Augustus on 25 July 306. When Galerius, who had automatically become the senior emperor on the death of Constantius and hence now possessed the sole right to appoint a new emperor, offered Constantine the lower rank of Caesar, he astutely accepted the appointment. He thereby entered the imperial college and acquired immediate recognition as a legitimate ruler in the eyes of all the inhabitants of the Roman Empire – and it was and is a gross distortion of history when later writers and modern students

Constantine: Dynasty, Religion and Power in the Later Roman Empire, First Edition. Timothy Barnes.
© 2011 Timothy Barnes. Published 2011 by Blackwell Publishing Ltd.

of Constantine stigmatize him as a usurper like Maxentius, who was never accepted as a member of the imperial college which jointly ruled the Roman Empire.

For the first few years of his reign Constantine fulfilled his imperial obligations to protect his subjects from barbarian invasion by campaigning on the Rhine and waited for opportunities to improve his standing in relation to his imperial colleagues. In 307 he allied himself with the usurper Maxentius and his father Maximian, who had abdicated as emperor two years earlier, in order to frustrate Galerius' attempt to bring Maxentius to heel and to restore Italy to his political control. Galerius expelled Constantine from the imperial college, but his invasion of Italy failed and in 308 he was compelled to acknowledge the unpalatable fact that Constantine had established himself securely and permanently as the ruler of Britain, Gaul and Spain. Galerius therefore reconstituted the college of emperors. On 11 November 308, at the Conference of Carnuntum, Galerius appointed Licinius as Augustus of the West with Constantine as his Caesar. Constantine refused to kowtow, as did Galerius' Caesar Maximinus in the East, so that by 310 Galerius presided over an imperial college of four Augusti, all technically equal in rank (Chapter 4, Appendix).

The years between 309 and 312 were the most perilous politically for Constantine during his whole reign. Licinius attempted to assert his claim to Italy in 309: had he invaded Italy successfully, Constantine could never have become sole master of the whole Roman Empire. But Licinius' attempt failed, as perhaps did a second attempt in the following year, and Constantine's luck held. Although Maximian attempted a coup against him in 310, Constantine was able to suppress it, while Licinius needed to deal with the political and military consequences of Galerius' debilitating illness (probably bowel cancer), which was obviously terminal. When Galerius died in late April 311, Maximinus immediately seized Asia Minor and Licinius concluded a treaty with him on board a ship in the Bosporus. By the spring of 312, however, Licinius was ready to invade Italy again, this time with massive forces. Constantine saw the political necessity of forestalling him, whatever the military risk. He took his chance and invaded Italy with a mere quarter of the total of troops under his command while Maxentius' main army awaited an invasion from Pannonia. This army Constantine was able to overcome in a desperate battle outside Verona, which gave him control of the Po Valley.

It was at this point, when he saw his way clear to sole mastery of the Roman Empire, that Constantine announced his conversion to Christianity and began to exploit his proclaimed religion in his political interest. He advanced slowly and deliberately on Rome, which he reached some days after the middle of October; then he defeated Maxentius at the Battle of the Milvian Bridge on 28 October, entered Rome, won over the Roman Senate and its leaders, and began to grant privileges to the Christian church and its clergy in Rome itself, throughout Italy, in Africa and in the territories which he had ruled for the past six years.

By the summer of 313 the Roman Empire was divided between two emperors, Constantine in the West and Licinius, who ruled the provinces of the Roman Empire that lay east of the Julian Alps in Europe and east of the boundary between Tripolitania and Libya in Africa. Constantine soon embarked upon a scheme to diminish Licinius' political power over the long term, then abandoned the scheme and invaded his territory (Chapter 5). This first attempt to defeat Licinius militarily failed and sons of both Augusti were formally added to the imperial college on 1 March 317. But after some years of increasing political tension, Constantine invaded the territory of Licinius again in 324, defeated him and immediately seized the opportunity to carry through a religious reformation in the East, which quickly developed into something closer to a revolution as the beneficiaries of change consolidated their grasp on political power and influence (Chapter 6). Constantine forbade central practices of traditional religious cult (animal sacrifice, the consultation of oracles and the erection of cult statues), he systematically confiscated temple treasures throughout Asia Minor, the Levant and Egypt, together with any other objects of value in the temples, including doors and roofs of valuable metal, and he used the vast proceeds of these confiscations to beautify the Christian city of Constantinople and to subsidize the construction of magnificent churches in every place whose bishop requested funds from the imperial treasury. This amounted to an enormous transfer of wealth from traditional cults to the Christian church. However, by preserving the ancient temples and shrines, apart from those implicated in the 'Great Persecution' or deemed to shelter disgusting and immoral practices, Constantine avoided provoking the resistance of fanatical adherents of the old religions. Isolated pagans might mutter and rail against the 'impious law' prohibiting traditional sacrifice and its enactor (Barnes 1989a: 330), and a Roman aristocrat, who became consul in 325 only to have his name was removed from the consular fasti in April or May, may have voiced disquiet or even ventured an open protest (Barnes 1981: 214), but no serious resistance is known. Constantine was aware that the time was not yet ripe for suppressing temples or converting them into churches, as he openly informed non-Christians, while confessing his desire to do so. Constantine declined to take that step, not because of any ambiguity in his religious beliefs, not because he lacked the courage to offend diehard pagans, but out of political calculation. As Constantine correctly saw, he was doing enough to ensure that the Roman Empire would with the passage of time become a completely Christian empire, so that an attempt to bring that result about more quickly by using compulsion could be counter-productive – and was therefore politically unwise.

Modern historians of the fourth century have too often interpreted the ancient evidence for Constantine and his age on the basis of anachronistic assumptions and misconceptions, and they have too often denied the validity or distorted the meaning of ancient evidence that has not conformed to their own predilections. In this book I have tried to set the record straight.

APPENDIX A

THE CAREER OF LACTANTIUS

Jerome included a brief account of the career of L. Caecilius[1] Firmianus *signo* Lactantius in his work *On Illustrious Men* (*De viris illustribus* 80), which he modeled on Suetonius' work of the same title. The men in question were literary figures and Jerome's main aim was to survey Christian literature from the Crucifixion to the time of writing, which he states as the fourteenth year of the emperor Theodosius, that is, the calendar year 392 (Barnes 2010a: 172–173, cf. 1971: 235–236). Jerome not only enumerates Lactantius' writings, including several that do not survive, but provides precious details of his career which supplement (and in one particular contradict) what Lactantius' surviving works disclose about his location at various dates.

Lactantius was a pupil of Arnobius, who taught rhetoric at Sicca in Africa Proconsularis and wrote seven books *Against the Pagans* in the context of the 'Great Persecution,' which in Africa commenced in the late spring of 303 and petered out towards the end of 304 (Barnes 2010a: 124–138). Arnobius appears to have started the work in late 302 before persecution began and to have completed it before 305 (Simmons 1995: 47–93). Lactantius himself was summoned, together with the *grammaticus* Fabius, by Diocletian Nicomedia, probably no later than the mid-290s, to hold the municipal chair of Latin rhetoric.[2] In this capacity Lactantius will have delivered panegyrics of the emperor, as Augustine later did in Milan, before an audience which included Constantine at Diocletian's side as a candidate for the imperial purple (Chapter 3). Under the provisions of the first persecuting edict of 24 February 303, Lactantius was compelled to choose whether to make a symbolic act of sacrifice in order to retain possession of his official chair of Latin rhetoric or to resign it in order to avoid the obligation to sacrifice (Barnes 1981: 13, 22–23). It can hardly be doubted that he chose the latter course of action.

Lactantius nevertheless remained in Nicomedia until at least 1 May 305 when Galerius gained control of Asia Minor (*Div. Inst.* 5.2.2, 11.15, cf. Barnes 2006: 15).

Constantine: Dynasty, Religion and Power in the Later Roman Empire, First Edition. Timothy Barnes.
© 2011 Timothy Barnes. Published 2011 by Blackwell Publishing Ltd.

His movements in the years following 305 are not explicitly documented and modern scholars have espoused radically different reconstructions. At the one extreme, it is argued that he remained in Nicomedia throughout the decade of the 'Great Persecution' (303–313) and went to Trier no earlier than the winter of 313/314, where he remained until the end of his life (Wlosok 1989: 376–379; Heck 2005: 209–215; 2009: 118–130).³ At the other extreme, Lactantius' travels have all been dated between 305 and 313, when it is argued that he returned to Nicomedia and lived out his life there (Barnes 1973: 40–41; 1981: 13–14, 290–292 nn.93–100).

The reconstruction of Lactantius' movements depends very much on the date at which Constantine appointed him tutor to his son Crispus in Gaul. Jerome, who alone reports this important fact, states that Lactantius taught Crispus 'in extreme old age' (*De viris illustribus* 80: *extrema senectute magister Caesaris Crispi filii Constantini in Gallia fuit*) and the fact that in his much earlier *Chronicle* he attached the note that 'Lactantius instructed Crispus in Latin letters' (*Crispum Lactantius Latinis litteris erudivit*) to his entry for the proclamation of Crispus, Licinius and Constantinus as Caesars on 1 March 317 (*Chronicle* 230ᵉ) has conventionally been taken to imply that he was tutor to Crispus in 317–320 or thereabouts (e.g., Stevenson 1957: 665–666) or at least that Constantine summoned him to teach his son c. 314/315 (Wlosok 1989: 377). But a date after 313 only appears plausible if Crispus was born c. 305 (as *PLRE* 1.233, Crispus 4; 338, Firmianus 2). In fact, however, Crispus was born no later than 300 and perhaps as early as c. 295 (Chapter 3) and he was already commanding armies in the field as early as 318 or 319 (*RIC* 7.185, Trier 237–241; *Pan. Lat.* 4[10].17.1–2, cf. Barnes 1982: 83), so that Lactantius should have instructed him in Latin literature and Latin rhetoric some years before 317. Now, while Jerome presumably had good evidence for his statement that Lactantius taught Crispus in Gaul, his statement that he did so as an extremely old man need rest on nothing more than a mere guess.

What indications are there in Lactantius' own writings that help to locate him in a specific place at a specific time? Opinions differ here too. Eberhard Heck has recently re-argued the case that *On the Deaths of the Persecutors* itself shows that Lactantius remained in Nicomedia until at least 313, when he read the *litterae Licinii* posted up in the city on 13 June and learned about the defeat and death of Maximinus at close hand (Heck 2009: 122–123, cf. Wlosok 1989: 377). But the vividness and detail of Lactantius' narrative of eastern events in 311–313, on which Heck bases his inference, need prove no more than that he had good informants in Nicomedia while he was writing *On the Deaths of the Persecutors* in 314/315 (Barnes 1973: 40). In my view, incidental remarks in the *Divine Institutes* (5.2.2, 11.15) indicate that Lactantius left Nicomedia in or shortly after May 305. The next firm chronological pointer is Lactantius' account of Maximian's alleged attempt to assassinate Constantine while he slept (*Mort. Pers.* 30), which repeats a propaganda story invented in 311, but only current as the official story of Maximian's death until the Battle of the Milvian Bridge on 28 October 312, after which Constantine's propaganda machine went into reverse and began to rehabilitate the memory of his father-in-law which had been abolished in 311 (Lactantius, *Mort. Pers.* 42, cf. Barnes 1973: 41–43; Chapter 4). From this it follows that it was in 311 and 312 that Lactantius was teaching Crispus, and doubtless conversing frequently with his pupil's father.[4]

What of the intervening period, between Lactantius' departure from Bithynia and his arrival in Gaul? Perhaps he returned to his native Africa in 305 or 306 and completed his *Divine Institutes* there, but was compelled to flee to Gaul when generals of Maxentius suppressed the rebellion of Domitius Alexander in 309 (Barnes 1981: 13, 291 n.96). But other reconstructions of his movements between 305 and 311 which have subsequently been offered cannot be excluded (Digeser 2000: 133–135; Garnsey 2003: 2–3).

Lactantius certainly did not accompany Constantine to Rome in 312. Moreover, under the terms of the agreement which Constantine and Licinius reached in Milan in February to extend to the Roman Empire east of Italy the full restoration of the rights and property of Christians of which they had been deprived in 303, but Constantine had restored in 306 (Chapter 4), Lactantius became entitled to resume possession of the municipal chair of rhetoric in Nicomedia which he had forfeited in 303. Since Lactantius was a poor man (Jerome, *Chronicle* 230[e]: *adeo in hac vita pauper, ut plerumque etiam necessariis indiguerit*), he surely availed himself of the opportunity to recover a secure income, returned to Nicomedia in 313 and remained there until the end of his life (Barnes 1981: 13). For his works from *On the Deaths of the Persecutors* onwards locate him in Bithynia or, more generally, in the East after 314 (Barnes 1981: 292 n.99).

The chronology argued here for the career of Lactantius may be tabulated as follows:

? c. 260–270	born in Africa
before 300	pupil of Arnobius in Sicca
c. 295	appointed professor of Latin rhetoric at Nicomedia
c. 295–305	resides in Nicomedia
after 1 May 305	leaves Bithynia after Asia Minor becomes subject to Galerius
? c. 306	returns to his native Africa
309 or 310	goes to Gaul, where Constantine appoints him tutor to his son Crispus
311–312	at the court of Constantine
313	goes to Nicomedia, where he resumes his official chair of Latin rhetoric in accordance with the provisions of the imperial letter posted up in Nicomedia on 13 June
314/315	writes *On the Deaths of the Persecutors* in Nicomedia
315–?324	continues to reside in or near Nicomedia until his death

APPENDIX B

GALERIUS' SARMATIAN VICTORIES

The chronology of major military operations between 285 and 311 is largely deduced from the victory titles of the Augusti Diocletian and Maximian in 301, of Constantius and Galerius in 306 and of Galerius in 308–311 as attested in the headings of a series of documents which state or stated the titles of the emperors in full or almost in full (Barnes 1976a). The following documents attest the number of times that Galerius had assumed the title *Sarmaticus maximus* since 1 March 293 at various dates between late 301 and April 311:

1   Diocletian's edict on maximum prices issued between 20 November and 9 December 301 (*CIL* 3, pp. 802–803; Lauffer 1971: 90; Barnes 1982: 18–19 no. 2);

2   a military diploma dated 7 January 306 (*AE* 1961.240; Barnes 1982: 20 no. 4);

3   a letter of Galerius granting civic status to Heraclea Sintica, which was apparently written in early 308 (*AE* 2002.1293, cf. Corcoran 2006c: 231–232);

4   a fragment from Tlos in Lycia with the first 2–5 letters of the names and titles of Galerius and three other Augusti (Barnes 1982: 21 no. 6 = *CIL* 3.12133 as supplemented in Barnes 1976d: 277);[1]

5   a fragmentary inscription from Sinope, dated to 310 or early 311, which preserves (a) part of the name of Galerius and part of his victory titles, (b) an erasure, which must conceal the name of Maximinus, and (c) the beginning of the name and titles of Constantine (*CIL* 3.6979; *ILS* 660; Barnes 1982: 21 no. 5; *AE* 1999.1502, from Christol & Drew-Bear 1999: 49);

6   Galerius' edict of April 311 rescinding Diocletian's persecuting edict of 24 February 303 (Eusebius, *HE* 8.17.3–5 as supplemented in Barnes 1982: 22–23 no. 7).

Constantine: Dynasty, Religion and Power in the Later Roman Empire, First Edition. Timothy Barnes.
© 2011 Timothy Barnes. Published 2011 by Blackwell Publishing Ltd.

In these documents, Constantius and Galerius are *Sarmatici maximi II* in late 301 and *Sarmatici maximi III* on 7 January 306, while Galerius is *Sarmaticus maximus V* in the early months of 308, in 310 or 311 and in April 311 (Corcoran 2006c: 233). Combining these firm attestations with other relevant evidence indicates that Galerius took and reiterated the victory title *Sarmaticus maximus* in the following years (Barnes 1976a: 187, 191–192, 194; Corcoran 2006c: 233[2]):

I	294
II	299 or 300
III	302 or 304
IV	306
V	307

The victorious campaign against the Sarmatians in which the *Origo Constantini Imperatoris* alleges that Galerius attempted to get Constantine killed must be the third of these Sarmatian victories: he took the title *Sarmaticus maximus* for the first time for a victory won by Diocletian while he himself was in Egypt (Barnes 1976a: 187; 1982: 62), for the second time for a victory which he won while Constantine was with Diocletian shortly after the Persian War (Chapter 3), and for the fourth and fifth times when Constantine was already in Britain (Chapter 4).

APPENDIX C

THE *PANEGYRICI LATINI* AND CONSTANTINE

The collection of twelve Latin Panegyrics (*XII Panegyrici Latini*) was put together in its present form by Latinius Pacatus Drepanius, who delivered a panegyric of Theodosius before the Roman Senate in the presence of the emperor in 389 (*Pan. Lat.* 2[12]). In what has aptly been styled 'a clever stroke of ostensible modesty' (Syme 1968: 113), Pacatus placed his own speech in second place after Pliny's panegyric of Trajan, which he accorded primacy of place as the classic of the genre (Pichon 1906: 285–289). Pliny delivered what was technically a vote of thanks (*gratiarum actio*) for his suffect consulate in August 100, but his letters make clear that he spent several years polishing and expanding the original speech so that it could serve as a model and exemplar of imperial oratory. The third speech in Pacatus' corpus was another consular *gratiarum actio*, this one delivered by the praetorian prefect Claudius Mamertinus before the emperor Julian in Constantinople on 1 January 362, when he entered office as one of the ordinary consuls who gave their names to the year (*Pan. Lat.* 3[11]). The fourth speech is a panegyric delivered in Rome on 1 March 321 by the Gallic orator Nazarius to mark the *quinquennalia* of Crispus and Constantinus, the sons of Constantine, whose official *dies imperii* was exactly four years earlier (*Pan. Lat.* 4[10]).[1] Nazarius' speech together with the eight which follow and range in date between 289 and 313, appear to represent two earlier collections.

The manuscripts preserve the following note before the fifth speech in Pacatus' collection:

> Incipiunt Panegyrici diversorum vii
> Here begin seven panegyrics by different authors.

At the end of the fifth speech in the manuscript order an *explicit* states 'Finit primus' and before the sixth an *incipit* states 'Incipit secundus.' Similarly, after the sixth to

Constantine: Dynasty, Religion and Power in the Later Roman Empire, First Edition. Timothy Barnes.
© 2011 Timothy Barnes. Published 2011 by Blackwell Publishing Ltd.

ninth speeches and before the seventh to tenth, the manuscripts have the successive *explicits* and *incipits*:'Finit secundus / Incipit tercius';'Finit tercius / Incipit quartus'; 'Finit quartus / Incipit quintus';'Finitus quintus / Incipit sextus.'The tenth speech has no such *explicit*, nor has the twelfth, whose heading states that it was spoken before 'Constantine, the son of Constantius.' The eleventh has the subscription 'Finit Genethliacus Maximiani Augusti,' while its heading, despite some manuscript confusion, attributes it to one Mamertinus, who is stated also to be the author of the preceding speech.[2] In modern editions of the *Panegyrici Laini* each speech has two numbers, of which one is its numbered place in the manuscripts and the other what early editors believed to be its chronological place in the series of twelve speeches. Unfortunately, the early editors made an obvious blunder and mistakenly dated Eumenius' speech *Pro instaurandis scholis*, which seems in fact to have been delivered in 298, earlier than the speech delivered to celebrate the *quinquennalia* of the Caesar Constantius on 1 March 297. Accordingly, in his Budé edition, which was for some years the standard edition of the *Panegyrici Latini* in scholarly use, Édouard Galletier not only printed the speeches in the chronological order of their delivery, but changed the traditional renumbering to reflect their correct chrono-logical order. Since this has caused unnecessary confusion, I list here all three numerations which have been employed for the last eight speeches in the corpus and the date on which each of them was delivered:

Mss. order	Alternative number in the following standard editions: E. Baehrens (Leipzig, 1874) W. Baehrens (Leipzig, 1911) R. A. B. Mynors (Oxford, 1964) V. Paladini and P. Fedeli (Rome, 1976) D. Lassandro (Turin, 1992)	Number assigned by E. Galletier (Budé)	Year in which the speech was delivered[3]
5	8	8	311[4]
6	7	7	310
7	6	6	307
8	5	4	297
9	4	5	298
10	2	2	289
11	3	3	291
12	9	9	313

Important conclusions follow from the notations in the manuscripts and from the order of the speeches in the collection.They imply the existence of two collec-tions of Gallic panegyrics early in the fourth century, decades before Pacatus formed the surviving corpus of twelve *Panegyrici Latini* c. 390. The earlier of the two comprised the seven speeches delivered between 289 and 310 (viz., *Pan. Lat.* 5–11 in the manuscript order), which are arranged in reverse chronological order with two exceptions, of which one is obvious (*Pan. Lat.* 11[3] of 291 being clearly later than 10[2] of 289), the other less so (the speeches of 297 and 298 (*Pan. Lat.* 5 and 4 in the manuscript order). But this original collection was soon enlarged by the addition of two more speeches which framed it. The first speech in this second collection was the panegyric which Nazarius delivered in Rome in 321 (*Pan. Lat.* 4[10]). It was Nazarius himself, so it may reasonably be conjectured, who incorporated the earlier collection of seven speeches delivered in Gaul to form a corpus of speeches beginning with his own, which he placed first, perhaps to bring to the attention of readers in Rome the literary achievements of his fellow Gauls during the last generation. In the second most significant position in his collection, the last, Nazarius placed the speech of 313 (*Pan. Lat.* 12[9]), which was a panegyric of Constantine delivered in Gaul only a few months after the emperor's very public conversion to Christianity. The placing must have been deliberate.

Nazarius was a famous teacher of rhetoric. Jerome's continuation of Eusebius' *Chronicle* has entries for both Nazarius and his daughter Eunomia, under the eighteenth and thirtieth year of Constantine (324, 336) respectively:

> Nazarius rhetor insignis habetur (231[c] Helm)
> Nazarii rhetoris filia in eloquentia patri coaequatur (233[l] Helm).

Ausonius also records Nazarius as a famous rhetor of a generation earlier than his own when he names him in the poem in his cycle the *Commemoratio Professorum Burdigalensium* which he addressed to the recently deceased rhetor Censorius Atticus Agricius:

> tam generis tibi celsus apex quam gloria fandi,
>   gloria Athenaei cognita sede loci;
> Nazario et claro quondam delata Paterae
>   egregie multos excoluit iuvenes

> The nobility of your birth was not less lofty than the glory of your eloquence, glory acknowledged by a chair in the Athenaeum, a glory once bestowed on Nazarius and famous Patera which gave many young men an excellent training (*Professores* [XI Green] 14.7–10)

Ausonius and his original readers, probably in the 360s, knew which chair of rhetoric Nazarius had occupied in the 320s. But we do not. It has sometimes been deduced or assumed that Nazarius was one of the professors of Bordeaux (Étienne 1962: 240; *PLRE* 1.618–619, Nazarius) and Evelyn White in the Loeb edition translates *gloria Athenaei cognita sede loci* as 'renown, no stranger to your chair here in this second Athens' (1919: 121). But Patera, whom Ausonius names together with him, taught in Rome (Jerome, *Chronicle* 233[k] Helm) and there was an Athenaeum in Rome (Coarelli 1993: 131). It was probably in Rome therefore that Nazarius taught and delivered his panegyric (Booth 1978: 243–244).[5] The speech is a rather florid, bombastic and essentially vacuous composition, 'remarkable most of all for its lack of contemporaneous information' (Rodgers in Nixon & Rodgers 1994: 336–342). Nazarius was speaking at a time when Constantine and Licinius had very recently ceased to treat each other as colleagues, a breach symbolized by their proclamation of different pairs of consuls: in 321 Constantine nominated his sons Crispus and Constantinus, each for the third time, while the consuls in the East were Licinius for the sixth time and his son, born c. 315, for the second. It would have been completely inappropriate, therefore, for anyone praising Crispus and Constantinus to mention that 1 March 321 also marked the *quinquennalia* of the Caesar Licinianus. Nazarius' silence about recent and current events was deliberate, calculated and total. He concentrated instead on generalized praise of Constantine, filled the obligatory narrative section of his speech with an account of the defeat of Maxentius more than eight years earlier – and revealed himself as a cautious time-server at heart rather than a genuinely enthusiastic supporter of the emperors whom he lauded.[6]

APPENDIX D

EUSEBIUS, ON EASTER
(DE SOLLEMNITATE PASCHALI)

Cardinal Angelo Mai published the text translated here from Vaticanus graecus 1611, fols. 277a–278b in *Patrum Nova Bibliotheca / Novae Patrum Bibliothecae* 4 (Rome, 1847), 209–216. It forms part of the catena on Luke compiled by Nicetas of Heraclea (*CPG* 4. 140–141 no. C 135), most of which Mai had already published in his *Scriptorum Veterum Nova Collectio* 9 (Rome, 1837), 626–724. The work has the heading Εὐσεβίου περὶ τοῦ πάσχα, but the nature of its preservation does not make it clear whether the text is complete or not, although there is no obvious sign that anything has been lost at either the beginning or the end.

Eusebius composed what he calls 'a mystical explanation of the festival' of Easter, had it translated into Latin and sent it to Constantine, who thanked him in a letter which he quotes (*VC* 4.34–35). The work to which Eusebius refers cannot be the extant work (Cameron & Hall 1999: 326): its contents hardly correspond to a discussion of the 'mystical explanation' of Easter, and it is certainly not addressed to Constantine, whose presence at the Council of Nicaea it registers in the third person (8). Its purpose seems rather to be to justify Eusebius' acceptance of the Nicene decisions concerning the date of Easter. Its historical value lies in the fact that it attests the observance of a forty-day or six-week fast before Easter (4), so that it probably constitutes the earliest evidence for the observance of Lent in the East (Chapter 6).

Mai's text was reprinted together with the Latin translation which he provided *en face* by the Abbé Migne in *Patrologia Graeca* 24 (Paris, 1857), 693–706. Although there are translations into French and German of selected chapters (Salaville 1929: 258–260; Ortiz di Urbina 1963: 259–260 by G. Dumeige; Strobel 1997: 24–25), and incomplete doctored translations into Italian and English (Cantalamessa 1978: 93–101 no. 56 [chapters 1–5,7–9]; 1993: 65–70 no. 56 [with lacunae and the omission of chapters 6 and 12]), the whole work has never been translated into English.

Constantine: Dynasty, Religion and Power in the Later Roman Empire, First Edition. Timothy Barnes.
© 2011 Timothy Barnes. Published 2011 by Blackwell Publishing Ltd.

Moreover, modern discussions of the Nicene decisions relating to Easter (Burn 1925: 44–46; Leclercq 1938: 1542; Ortiz di Urbina 1963: 49–52, 93–95) make little or no use of Eusebius' tract, significant details in the text have sometimes been overlooked even by the most critical (e.g., Barnes 1981: 215–217, cf. di Berardino 1992: 374; Girardet 1992: 455; 1993: 347–348). I therefore offer an English translation of Mai's text with some minor corrections, which are noted together with Migne's deviations from Mai. I have checked on microfilm all the variant reports of what the manuscript (which I designate V) reads: they are mostly due to the fact that it is very difficult to distinguish between epsilon and eta (ε / η) and between omicron and upsilon (o / υ).

(1) Perhaps it would not be inopportune once more to talk about Easter (πάσχα),[1] which was long ago symbolically (ε'ικονικῶς) entrusted to the children of the Hebrews (Exodus 12.3).[2] When the Hebrews, the first to perform mere shadows of what was to be in the future, celebrated the festival of Phasek, a young animal was selected for them from the flock (this was a lamb or baby goat); they then sacrificed it themselves with their own hands; next first each of them anointed the lintels and doorposts of their own houses with the blood, by this means bloodying their thresholds and halls to avert wholesale slaughter; <then>, using the flesh of the young animal as food, surrounding their loins with belts, sharing the food of unleavened bread and adding herbs of the soil, they travelled from place to place, from the land of the Egyptians into the desert. For it had been laid down for them by law to do this together with killing and eating the lamb. Accordingly, the departure from Egypt fulfilled the name that they gave it of 'the passing over.'[3] However, this happened symbolically (τυπικῶς) to them, but it was for our sake that it was written down. Paul reveals and interprets the truth behind the ancient symbols through his words: 'For our Passover was sacrificed as Christ' (1 Corinthians 5.7). And the Baptist provides the reason for his being sacrificed by saying: 'Behold, the Lamb of God that taketh away the sin of the world' (John 1.29). For the body of the Savior was handed over to death as a sacrificial victim to avert all evils, which[4] atoned for the sin of the whole world like a purifying agent. Isaiah proclaimed loud and clear: 'He bears our sins and suffers on our behalf' (53.4).

(2) Nourished by the logical flesh of this sacrifice of our Savior which rescued the entire human race with his own blood, that is, <nourished> by his teachings and words which announce the kingdom of heaven, we justifiably enjoy the divine food.[5] But through faith in his blood, which he gave as a ransom for our salvation, by designating our bodies as homes of the soul, we also drive out of ourselves the whole race of demons who plot against us; and in celebrating the festival of Passover we prepare to pass over to the divine, just as long ago they passed from Egypt into the desert. In this way, therefore, we too are making a journey along a route that is untrodden and deserted for the vast majority, exiling from our very souls the ancient leaven of godless error and adding the true <though bitter> herbs through a bitter and painful way of life.[6]

The season of the festival is most timely. It was not introduced in the time of midwinter since this would have been ugly. It would have been alien in midsummer too, when the solstice[7] burns and takes away their beauty from those who spend time in the fields and when the hours are too long, not being divided into equal parts. The sight of the autumnal equinox is not pleasant because the ground is bereaved and deprived of its own fruits as if of children. Spring remains, the joyful, which commands the whole year as its head as if it were a body, when the sun has just galloped through the first part <of the year> and the moon correspondingly with full light exchanges the course of night for bright day. This removes the terrors of the noises of winter, removes the long expanses <of night> and checks the floods of water. With the young clear daylight shining forth, it makes the seas calm for those who sail and the air clear for travellers on land. The fields at this time on the land are pregnant with seeds, and plants swelling with fruit and rejoicing in the gifts of God provide blessings to farmers for returns on their labours.

(3) This season of the festival ushered in destruction for the Egyptians who were friends of the demons and freedom from their woes for the Hebrews who were holding a festival for God. This was that very season observed even at the first creation of everything, when the earth began to produce, when the light-givers came into existence, when heaven and earth and everything in them were brought forth. At this season too the Savior of the whole world brought to completion the mystery of his own festival, the great light-giver illuminated the inhabited world with rays of piety and the season seemed to embrace the birthday of the universe. At this season also the type was performed, the ancient Easter, which is also called Passover: it bore the symbol of the slaughter of a lamb, it used the image of the sustenance of unleavened bread <as a hint of something else>. This was all fulfilled at the festival of our Savior, for he was the lamb when he put on a <human> body. He was also the sun of righteousness, since the equinox of the spring of God and the Savior transfers the life of human beings from worse to the better. Even now god-driven whips[8] are still sent against the demons of the Egyptians, while the peoples who dwell everywhere on earth celebrate their liberation from godlessness which wanders around in error. With the cessation of the spirits that led the people astray and of the woes of winter, the abundance of new fruits crowns the church of God with various gifts of grace from the Holy Spirit. In brief, the whole human race has been changed into ours: all farmlands, receiving spiritual farming from the Word their farmer, have grown the beautiful flowers of virtue, and we, liberated from the evils of darkness, have been deemed worthy of the light of day <which is> the knowledge of God.

(4) Such are the new teachings which were adumbrated long ago by means of symbols and have recently been <brought forth> into the light and revealed. Indeed we ourselves rekindle the beginning of the festival periodically every year, before the festival receiving for the sake of preparation the spiritual training of forty days in imitation of Moses and Elijah and renewing the festival itself for an unceasing age. Setting out on our journey to God, therefore, we gird our loins well and truly with the bond of moderation, and carefully guarding the footsteps of our souls as if wearing sandals[9] we set out on the course of our heavenly calling, and using the staff of the divine Word in the power of prayers to ward off our enemies we cross with all eagerness the Passover that leads to heaven, hastening from what is here <on earth> to the heavenly things and from mortal life to immortality.[10] In this way another greater

festival will welcome us when we have well and truly made the crossing of our Passover from here: the children of the Hebrews call it Pentecost by name and it displays the image of the kingdom of heaven. Hence Moses says: 'When you set the sickle to harvest, you shall count for yourself seven weeks and you shall set aside for God newly-baked loaves from the new harvest' (Deuteronomy 16.9). So by prophetic typology he indicated the calling of the gentiles by 'harvest' and by 'new loaves' the souls won over to God through Christ and the churches of the gentiles, in which the greatest festival is celebrated for God who loves the human race. For we, harvested by the logical sickles of the Apostles and gathering together into one as if on to threshing floors the churches everywhere on earth, made one body by the unified expression of a statement of faith, seasoned with the salt of the teachings from the divine words, born again through the water and fire of the Holy Spirit, are offered through Christ as sustaining loaves, suitable and pleasing to God.

(5) In this way then the prophetic symbols in Moses become real when their fulfillments are more solemn. We ourselves have received the tradition of celebrating the festival in a clearer fashion, as if we are assembled with our Savior and enjoying his kingdom. No longer, therefore, do we agree to be distressed during this festival, but we are taught to present the image of the rest which we hope for in heaven. Hence we do not bend the knee even during prayers or burden ourselves with fasting, since it is no longer possible for those who have been deemed worthy of the resurrection according to God to fall on the ground anew or for those who have been liberated from sufferings to suffer in equal measure with those who are still enslaved. Accordingly, after Easter we celebrate Pentecost in seven complete weeks, having made men of ourselves during the previous period of training the days before Easter in six weeks. The number six is active and full of energy, which is why God is said to have created everything in six days. And it is for good reason that the second festival in seven weeks succeeds the labours in those <six weeks>, as our rest, of which the number seven wishes to signify the symbol, is multiplied. Yet the number of Pentecost does not stop at these seven weeks, but, overshooting them and with a monad which is the last after them, it sets the seal upon the special festival day of the Ascension of Christ.[11] For good reason then, delineating the rest that is to come in the days of the holy Pentecost, we rejoice in our souls and give our bodies rest, as if we are already with the Bridegroom and incapable of fasting.

(6) That the holy evangelists record that the suffering of our Savior occurred during the days of the Jewish Passover of the unleavened bread, no-one would dispute, since this was the reason for the law concerning the Passover spoken by Moses. For since the Lamb of God was going to be like a sheep to slaughter precisely by the Jews and to suffer this on behalf of the common salvation of all men at no time other than the season indicated, God anticipated the future through symbols figuratively (διὰ συμβόλων ε'ικονικῶς), and ordered an ordinary lamb to be sacrificed by the Jews at that very season when it was going to happen on some occasion during the course of years. And this was performed by them annually until the fulfillment of the truth circumscribed[12] the ancient images. As a result, from that time onwards the true festival of the mysteries has prevailed among the gentiles, while among the Jews not even the memory of the symbols is preserved, since the place where it was laid down by the

law that the ceremonies of the festival should be performed has been taken away from them. For good reason then the divine scripture of the gospels says that the Savior suffered at the time of the Jewish <festival of> unleavened bread, since at that time he was led like a lamb to slaughter in accordance with the utterances of the prophets.

(7) While according to Moses <the Jews> used to sacrifice the Passover lamb once in the whole year on the fourteenth of the first month towards evening, we of the New Testament, celebrating our Passover every Lord's day, 'are always filled with the body of our Savior and always partake of the blood of the Lamb' (Romans 2.29), always gird the loins of our souls with holiness and sobriety, always have our feet prepared in readiness for the Gospel, always have staffs in our hands and rest upon the rod that came forth from the root of Jesse, are always departing from Egypt, are always seeking solitude in human life, are always journeying towards God – and are always celebrating Passover. For the word of the gospel wishes us to do all this not once a year, but always and every day. Hence we celebrate the festival of our Passover every week on the Lord's day, the day of our salvation, fulfilling the mysteries of the true Lamb through whom we have been redeemed. We do not circumcise the body with iron,[13] but remove every evil from our souls with the knife of the Word; we do not use material unleavened bread, but only <the unleavened bread> of verity and truth. For grace, which has liberated us from senile habits, has entrusted to us the new man established according to God, the new law, a new circumcision, a new Passover and him who is a secret Jew (Romans 2.29). Thus has he set us free from the ancient times.

(8) When the question of Easter was brought forward for discussion, the most God-loving emperor sat in the midst of the holy council presiding and a lively debate ensued.[14] But the party of three-quarters of the whole inhabited world prevailed by the large number of their bishops as they opposed the <bishops> of the East. For the nations of the north, of the south and of the setting sun together, gaining strength by agreeing with one another, brought forward a custom opposite to the ancient one which the bishops of the East defended. Finally, the easterners yielded the argument, and thus a single festival of Christ came about: they separated themselves from the murderers of our Lord and adhered to those who shared their beliefs, since nature draws like towards like. If anyone were to say that it is written: 'On the first day of <the festival of> unleavened bread, the disciples approached our Savior and said "Where do you wish us to prepare for you to eat the Passover?", and that he sent them to someone instructing them to say: "I shall eat[15] Passover in your house" (Matthew 26.17–18),' then we shall say: This is not an instruction, but the account of an event which happened at the time of our Savior's passion. It is one thing to narrate an action from long ago, another to legislate and to leave instructions for those who come after.

(9) But our Savior did not celebrate Passover with the Jews at the time of his own passion. For it was not when they sacrificed the lamb that he conducted his own Passover <meal> with his own disciples. For the Jews did this on the day of preparation (Friday), on which our Savior suffered, which is why they did not enter the *praetorium*, but Pilate came out to them (John 18.28–29). Christ, however, reclined with his disciples a full day before on the fifth day of the week, and eating with them said: 'I greatly desired to eat this Passover with you' (Luke 22.15). You see how our Savior

did not eat the Passover with the Jews. Since that <event> was new and alien to normal Jewish customs, it was necessary for him to institute <a new custom> by saying: 'I greatly desired to eat this Passover with you before I suffer' (Luke 22.15). For the ancient and out-of-date customs, which he had <previously> eaten with the Jews, were not desirable: it was the new mystery of his New Testament, which he shared with his disciples, which was desirable to him. Rightly so, since many prophets and just men before him had desired to see the mysteries of the New Testament, and the Word himself, continually thirsting for universal salvation, was transmitting the mystery by which all men in future would celebrate the festival <and> he confessed that this was desirable to him. The Passover of Moses was not suitable for all nations at any time. How could it be, when it was laid down by the law that it be performed in one place, in Jerusalem? That is why it was not desirable, whereas the Savior's mystery of the New Testament, which suits all men, was for good reason desirable to him.

(10) He ate the Passover and completed the festival with his disciples before his passion, not with the Jews; after he had celebrated it in the evening, the high priests together with his betrayer came after him and set their hands upon him, for they had not eaten the Passover on that evening (if they had, they would not have exerted themselves over him); they arrested him and took him to the house of Caiaphas, where they spent the night; when day came, they first met and condemned him. Then, after this, they rose and together with the mob brought him to Pilate. At that point, says scripture, they did not enter the *praetorium* so that they should not be polluted, as they thought (John 17.28), by entering under a pagan roof, but by remaining pure, though they were <in fact> utterly defiled, should eat Passover when evening came on. Straining at a gnat and swallowing a camel (Matthew 23.24), those who had polluted their souls together with their bodies by devising murder against our Savior, were afraid to enter under the roof <of Pilate>. Yet, on that very day of the Passion they ate a Passover which destroyed their own souls, requesting the blood of the Savior not for themselves, but against themselves. But our Savior conducted the festival which he found desirable reclining with his disciples not then, but a day earlier.

(11) You see that from that time he separated himself from the Jews and withdrew from the bloodthirstiness of the Jews, and joined himself to his disciples, celebrating the festival that he desired with them. We too must therefore eat Passover with Christ, cleansing our minds from all the yeast of evil and villainy, filling them with the unleavened bread of truth and verity, having within ourselves in our souls the hidden Jew (Romans 2.29) and the true circumcision, and anointing the doorposts of our minds with the blood of the lamb that was sacrificed for us in order to ward off the destruction that threatens us. And <we must do this> not for a single period during the whole year, but every week. Let Friday[16] be a day of fasting, the symbol of suffering, for the sake of our previous sins and for the memory of our Savior's passion.

(12) I say[17] that the Jews have missed the truth from the start, from the time when they plotted against truth itself, driving the Word of life out of themselves. And the scripture of the holy gospels sets this before our eyes. For it supports the testimony of our Lord that he ate Passover on the first day of <the festival of> unleavened bread, while, as Luke says, they did not eat the Passover customary for them on the day on which

the Passover ought to have been sacrificed, but on the day immediately following, which was the second day of <the festival of> unleavened bread, the fifteenth day of the lunar month, on which they did not enter inside the *praetorium* while our Savior was being tried by Pilate. So they did not eat <Passover> according to the law on the first day of <the festival of> unleavened bread, on which it ought to have been sacrificed. For <, if they had,> then they too would have made Passover with our Savior. But from that time together with the plot against our Savior, blinded by their own evil, they have missed all truth. We, however, perform the same mysteries throughout the year, commemorating our Savior's passion by fasting on every day that precedes a Sabbath − a fast which the apostles observed then for the first time when the Bridegroom was taken away from them. But on every Lord's day we are enlivened by the sanctified body of the same Passover of our Savior and have our souls sealed by his precious blood.

APPENDIX E

NICAGORAS IN EGYPT

A pair of inscriptions from Egyptian Thebes record the visit of an Athenian aristocrat and intellectual in the consular year 326 (Baillet 1926: 489–492, no. 1889; 294–295, no. 1265):[1]

> In the seventh consulate of Constantine Augustus and the first of Constantius Caesar, I, Nicagoras, the son of Minucianus and an Athenian, the torchbearer of the Eleusinian <mysteries>, examined the divine burial-vaults and admired them
>
> I, <Nicagoras>, the son of Minucianus and an Athenian, torchbearer of the most holy mysteries at Eleusis, examined the divine burial-vaults many years after the divine Plato from Athens, admired them and gave thanks to the gods and to the most pious emperor Constantine, who granted me this. (Translation by G. Fowden, slightly modified)

Nicagoras belonged to one of the two oldest and noblest families in Athens, the Kerykes, which supplied the torchbearer, the herald and the altar priest of the Eleusinian mysteries, while the Hierophant of the mysteries always came from the equally ancient family of the Eumolpidae (Dittenberger 1885: 10–26). Nicagoras' recent forbears were famous Athenian literary figures. His father Minucianus, who flourished in the reign of Gallienus (260–268), composed a rhetorical textbook, rhetorical exercises (*progymnasmata*) and speeches (M 1087 [2.398 Adler]). Minucianus in turn was the son of another Nicagoras who was active as a rhetor and sophist in Athens twenty years earlier: he composed lives of illustrious men, 'the Trojan Cleopatra' and a *presbeutikos logos* addressed to the emperor Philip, who ruled from 244 to 249 (N 373 [2.465 Adler]), which prima facie implies that he went on an embassy to this emperor, who was favorably disposed towards Christians.

Constantine: Dynasty, Religion and Power in the Later Roman Empire, First Edition. Timothy Barnes.
© 2011 Timothy Barnes. Published 2011 by Blackwell Publishing Ltd.

The two Egyptian inscriptions have inspired some scholars to pleasing fantasies. Jean Baillet, who believed that Constantine practiced a policy of conciliation in religious matters after 324, imagined that the emperor honored Nicagoras as a prominent pagan priest by sending him on an official mission to Egypt, probably one of inspection and inquiry either into the state of the ancient temples of Egypt or into disaffection among adherents of the old cults, and he lamented the loss of the official report which he presumed that Nicagoras submitted on his return from Egypt (Baillet 1922: 288–289; 1926: 490–492). Garth Fowden also saw Nicagoras as 'an imperial emissary,' but one with a more specific purpose: he supposed Constantine sent him to Thebes 'to negotiate the removal from the temple of Amun at Karnak of both the great obelisk eventually erected by his son Constantius in the Circus Maximus at Rome, and now standing in the Piazza S. Giovanni in Laterano, and the obelisk which still stands where it was erected by Theosodius I in the Hippodrome at Constantinople' in an attempt to fulfill a promise which he had rashly made in Rome where he was in the summer of 326 to have an obelisk erected there (Fowden 1987: 53–57; 1991: 123–125). In refutation Cyril Mango observed that the story that the column had been brought to Constantinople from Rome first surfaces in the ninth century (1993b: 4–6, adducing Georgius Monachus pp. 500–501 de Boor).

Robin Lane Fox postulated an even closer relationship with the emperor than either Baillet or Fowden: speculating on the basis of the attested fact that the people of Oxyrhynchus were making preparations for an imperial visit in January and May 325 (*P. Oxyrhynchus* X 1261, XIV 1626), he conjured up the intriguing possibility that Constantine intended to take Nicagoras with him to Egypt as part of his entourage in order to help him search for the phoenix (Lane Fox 1986: 640–641), although in the event, the imperial visit to Egypt never took place.

In fact, the inscriptions attest only the prosaic fact that Constantine allowed Nicagoras to visit Egypt, presumably assisted him by granting him free use of the imperial post, and perhaps also provided incidental traveling expenses. Although Nicagoras was the torchbearer of the Eleusinian mysteries, that was not the reason why Constantine assisted his journey to Egypt: he was rather honoring an intellectual and man of letters in an emperor's traditional role of a patron of literature, Greek as well as Latin (Graindor 1926: 209–214). Nicagoras had presumably petitioned Constantine for leave to visit Egypt, perhaps in person. But even if he did, it need not follow that 'the event must surely signify an attempt by Constantine to show favor to, and to win the favor of, the established pagan aristocracy of Athens in the period after his victory over Licinius' (Millar 1969: 17 = 2004: 275). It is rather evidence that Constantine continued the obligatory custom of conferring benefits on subjects who petitioned the emperor, which Fergus Millar has documented on a gigantic scale (Millar 1977: 133–139; 491–506).

This inherited pattern of imperial patronage and protection was continued by both Constantine and his sons. The most striking example of this continuity concerns Delphi. Constantine removed the serpent column which the Greek cities that had fought and defeated the invading Persian army at Plataea in 479 BC inscribed with their names and dedicated to Apollo (Meiggs & Lewis 1969: 57–60 no. 27), whose oracles at Delphi and elsewhere had encouraged the 'Great Persecution' (Chapter 6), and installed it in his the new city Constantinople, where it graced the *spina* of the hippodrome (Bassett 2004: 224–227 no. 141). In 341, however, the college of praetorian prefects wrote two letters to the former *comes* Fl(avius) Felicianus, which the local magistrates of Delphi deposited in the municipal archives and which was inscribed in public: the letters (whose continuous surviving passages are translated at the end of Chapter 6) compliment Felicianus on his discharge of the priesthood of Pythian Apollo and note that he had been personally honored by Constantine.

APPENDIX F

PRAXAGORAS OF ATHENS

Photius, who was patriarch of Constantinople in the second half of the ninth century, owned a copy of what he describes as a *History of Constantine the Great* in two books which the Athenian Praxagoras wrote at the age of twenty-two (*Library*, Codex 62, whence *FGrH* 219).[1] Praxagoras was a prominent pagan who gave political support to the first Christian emperor, as did Nicagoras (Appendix E), and his name implies that, like Nicagoras, he belonged to the ancient Athenian family of the Kerykes: he probably traced his descent from Aelius Praxagoras of Melite, who was archon of Athens in 154/155 and an enemy of Herodes Atticus (Wilamowitz-Moellendorf 1925; Follet 1976: 278).

If Photius' summary is accurate, Praxagoras' work, which repeats many inventions of Constantinian propaganda, was more a panegyric than a dispassionate history – which reflects the fact that all serious historians who lived under the Roman Empire, from Livy to Ammianus Marcellinus, knew that it was impossible to write an honest and impartial history of the reigning emperor, who could only be the subject of praise and panegyric: thus Livy brought his history *Ab urbe condita* to a close with the death of Drusus in 9 BC and thus avoided writing about the embarrassing episode of Tiberius' withdrawal to Rhodes, while Ammianus ended his continuation of Tacitus with the defeat of Adrianople (9 August 378) and its aftermath (Barnes 1998a: 209–212, 183–184). When Praxagoras undertook to write the history of Constantine during his lifetime, he committed himself to a panegyrical account of the emperor. Photius' summary reads as follows:[2]

> Constantius, the father of Constantine reigned over Britain, Maximianus over Rome, the rest of Italy and Sicily, and the other Maximianus [i.e., Galerius] over Greece, Macedonia, Lower Asia and Thrace, while Diocletian, who was senior to the others, ruled Bithynia, Arabia, Libya and as much of Egypt as the Nile flows through and waters.

Constantine: Dynasty, Religion and Power in the Later Roman Empire, First Edition. Timothy Barnes.
© 2011 Timothy Barnes. Published 2011 by Blackwell Publishing Ltd.

His father sent Constantine to Diocletian in Nicomedia to be educated. Maximianus [i.e., Galerius], the ruler of Lower Asia, was present there and plotted against the young man and put the youth into battle against a fierce lion. But he overcame and killed the beast and detecting the plot fled to his father. When he died, his son succeeded him as emperor. Having gained this position, he defeated the neighboring tribes of Celts and Germans. Learning that Maxentius, who had established himself in power in Rome after Maximianus, was ruling his subjects with harshness and violence, he launched a campaign against him to make him pay the penalty for his injustice towards those ruled by him, and having defeated him in battle he forced him to flee. In his flight he was himself fatally destroyed by the contrivance that he craftily designed for his enemies and fell into the ditch which he had prepared. Some of the Romans cut off his head, fixed it on a pole and carried it round the city. This realm too eagerly and with joy went over to Constantine. But when he learned that Licinius, who, after the death of the Maximianus who had devised and set the plot against Constantine [i.e., Galerius], reigned over his portion <of the Empire>, was treating his subjects cruelly and inhumanely, he did not tolerate the unbearable outrages inflicted on his fellow-citizens, but marched against him in order to make him change from tyranny to ruling as a <proper> emperor.

Licinius, however, hearing of the emperor's expedition against him, became fearful and concealed his savagery with a pretence of generosity and offered oaths that he would show himself a good <ruler> to those under his control and would keep inviolate the treaties which he had made. The emperor therefore desisted from fighting on that occasion. But, since evil cannot remain inactive, when he had later broken his oaths and lapsed into every sort of wickedness, <Constantine> defeated him in hard-fought battles, forced him to retreat to Nicomedia and besieged him. From there he took refuge with the emperor dressed as a suppliant and lost his position as emperor.

It thus came about that, at a time when the great empire was seeking a worthy <leader>, Constantine the Great had gathered to himself the following territories. He was the heir of his father's territory, of that of the Romans by deposing Maxentius, and of Greece, Macedonia and Lower Asia by removing the said Licinius from rule <over them>. In addition, he acquired dominion over the remaining portion, which Diocletian used to rule, since Licinius had this too under his control after taking it by law of war from Maximinus, who had become the heir of Diocletian. Having thus acquired and united the whole empire, he founded Byzantium as a city named after himself.

Although Praxagoras was a pagan in religion, he says that the emperor Constantine put into the shade all those who had been emperors before him by his many virtues, by the excellence of his character and by all his successes. With this his two books end.

Photius adds that Praxagoras himself says that he was in his twenty-second year when he wrote this work, that he had already written two books on the ancient kings of Athens when he was eighteen, and that he composed four books on the Macedonian king in his thirtieth year. Photius then concludes by appraising the style of Praxagoras, who wrote in the Ionic dialect: it was 'clear and agreeable, though a little less vigorous than it should have been.'

The latest historical event which Photius mentions in his summary of Praxagoras' work is the foundation of Constantinople. It is a reasonable conjecture, therefore, that Praxagoras went to Constantinople to present his panegyrical history to the emperor in person at the time of the ceremonial dedication of the new city (Jacoby 1930: 662). However, even if he presented his history to Constantine in 330, Praxagoras presumably brought his main narrative to a close with the emperor's victory over Licinius in 324 so that he could remain silent about embarrassing later events, such as the deaths of Licinius, Crispus and Fausta (Winkelmann 2003: 14–15).[3] That 330 must be the approximate date for the completion of Praxagoras' history of Constantine is confirmed by the fact that he published a history of Alexander the Great nine years later. The appropriate historical and intellectual context for this later work is the early years of the reign of Constantius, which also saw the composition of the so-called *Itinerarium Alexandri*, which can be dated precisely to the spring of 340, after the death of Constantinus, but before the writer knew that his memory had been abolished (2.4, cf. Callu 1992: 438–439; Tabacco 2000: viii–x), when Constantius was the same age as Alexander was when he crossed into Asia (4.8). In a work to which he gave the title *itinerarium* rather than *breviarium* (2.3), the writer, who has plausibly been identified as the Polemius who was one of the ordinary consuls of 338 (Lane Fox 1997: 240–247), described the routes taken by Alexander the Great and the Roman emperor Trajan when they invaded Persia. (Unfortunately the second half of the work, which dealt with Trajan's campaigns against the Parthians in 115–117, has been completely lost.). He set out to encourage Constantius to prosecute vigorously the task that his father has bequeathed him, to follow up his initial success (1.1), to liberate the Persians from slavery by making them free men with Roman citizenship living in Roman provinces (2.5).

APPENDIX G

AN ANONYMOUS PANEGYRIC OF CONSTANTINE

Two groups of papyrus fragments in London and Vienna were published separately by Joseph Bidez in 1906 and Hans Oellacher in 1932 under the titles 'fragments of an unknown Greek philosopher or rhetor' (*P. Lit. Lond* 163, ed. Bidez 1906) and 'panegyric on an emperor (probably Julian)' (*P. Rainer* I 14, ed. Oellacher 1932: 105–123).[1] In 1990 Augusto Guida edited the two sets of fragments together, showing that they both form part of the same work preserved in a single papyrus which was divided after its discovery c. 1900. Guida edited the work as 'an anonymous panegyric on the emperor Julian' (Guida 1990: 31–68). In 1995, at the international papyrological congress in Berlin, I argued that, while the fragments do indeed belong to an imperial panegyric, the emperor praised was not Julian, but Constantine (Barnes 1997b). The proposal has been completely ignored in several subsequent books about the religious policies of Constantine. It will be apposite, therefore, to reiterate and expand the arguments for identifying the emperor praised as Constantine rather than Julian.

Unfortunately, the damage to the papyrus is so extensive that only a few passages of connected prose are preserved. I offer here a translation of all the fragments where some continuous sense can be discerned:[2]

> First, then, whereas all others considered the reward of monarchy to be luxury as if [3] some law had bestowed <on them> the <right> to indulge in the pleasures of these things by every sort of device, he alone, after abolishing the law and in small matters and large ... (III.17–24)

> ... fighting thus against [...] itself which had become customary by nature, so that this was almost forgotten. Moreover, he also of course neglects adornments for the body, [considering unworthy of himself][4] the wearing of many womanish circles of <precious> stones around his head. (IV.17–24)

Constantine: Dynasty, Religion and Power in the Later Roman Empire, First Edition. Timothy Barnes.
© 2011 Timothy Barnes. Published 2011 by Blackwell Publishing Ltd.

... either the toils of generals or the endurance of soldiers or ... to the smallest number (V.20–21, 24)

... to [practice] equal restraint, and considering this the greatest [power] of enjoyment (VI.24–26)[5]

and ...charges to (or by) acts of laziness of [earlier][6] emperors, but opposing his own resolution and good fortune to their misfortunes or weaknesses ...

flinching from neither ... nor enormous expenses, but being able to ... greater than any epoch ... (VII.20–24, 27–29)

In what way it was (or is) necessary to complete the construction of buildings ... Byzantium alone ... (VIII.2–4)

But whenever they are once sent out, instructions are similarly given to avoid the spoliation of shrines and ill-gotten gains from the administration of their offices, so that from a single intention flow three results – subjects are governed by magistrates who cannot be bribed ... of the imperial treasuries ... with justice ... in addition ... (IX.13–22)

... and he has adopted the same practice for nights as for days. Although nature has decided to give the one in succession to the other, he alone is equally active in both periods of time, allowing himself in his labors no alternation or rest, but manifestly proving that it has not been truly said that 'sleep is the king of both all the gods and all men' (Iliad 15.233) (X.12–22)

... entrusting to their foresight, he released ... on them, appointing one as treasurer of the imperial finances, setting up another as judge in charge of cases of murder, and ordering one to deal with embassies and another to receive and in turn to reply to letters ...

of the emperor's foresight that to each of these[7] is assigned the administration to which each seems suited by nature. Since nature has taken care that through one emperor ... I can show [you][8] by way of supplement also that ... and ... the others. There is no matter great or small which receives a decision according to another's judgment, but every treasurer, prefect, judge in cases of murder, arbiter in disputes over contracts, commander of fighting men, answerer of letters, [dispenser] of outgoings,[9] appraiser[10] of embassies, evaluator of ... and whomsoever else in addition to these you might name takes a single leader as if for some journey, whom they follow, while they themselves ... of their business (XI.9–17, 19–40)

He does not order everyone to obey his decisions without reflection, allowing the discoverer, if anyone believes that he will find something better, to propound his speculations. But if all have already been convinced by his proposal, either being unable to find anything better or abandoning their own original ideas as inferior, then he names them as sharers in the good fortune of the imperial position and the wisdom of his decision. Thus in all matters what is decided upon comes into effect, so that if anyone were to say that there is a single opinion that [moves through] the whole inhabited world like a soul and by it preserves it, he could not be convicted of speaking falsely. Moreover, [if anyone] ... were to lighten the labors of his soul, he is conspicuous in his bodily <labors>, continually being snowed upon while he exchanges one wintry location for another as if in fine weather, continually spending time under the blazing sun in the suffocating harsh heat of midday as if resisting the heat in some places of his soul (XII.8–35)

The central and decisive argument against identifying the emperor praised as Julian is the statement that those sent out by him are given instructions not merely not to derive 'ill-gotten gains from the administration of their offices,' for which any emperor could be praised, whether justifiably or to encourage better behavior in future, but 'to avoid the spoliation of shrines' (IX.13–17). Under Julian such instructions were totally unnecessary, since his policy was to restore shrines and temples despoiled under Christian emperors (Bidez 1930: 219–235, 261–276, 281–315; Barnes 1998a: 155–162). Under Constantine, however, such instructions were indeed given: the commissioners who toured every province in Asia Minor confiscating temple treasures and any contents and fittings of value such as doors and gold statues had orders not to destroy places where the traditional gods were worshipped except for those very few temples whose the cult rituals were deemed criminal or whose priests had encouraged Diocletian to persecute the Christians (Chapter 6).

Most of the praise which the panegyric lavishes on the unnamed emperor is general and conventional. What praiseworthy ruler, for example, did not spend sleepless nights in a constant endeavor to better the lot of his subjects? Claudius Mamertinus emphasized that Julian did (*Pan. Lat.* 3[11].13.3, 20.2). But so too, according to their panegyrists, did both Trajan before him and Theodosius after him (*Pan. Lat.* 1.10.3; 2[12].8.3). And the same claim was made for Maximian (*Pan. Lat.* 7[6].11.6), whom Lactantius presents as an avaricious and lustful tyrant (*Mort. Pers.* 8.2–7). Moreover, this rhetorical commonplace of the ever-wakeful leader persisted into the modern world. It animates the masterly portrait of Napoleon in his study by the French painter David (now in Washington), in which the emperor stands, his sword put aside, in front of a desk next to a manuscript of pages of the Code Napoléon with a candle sputtering out on a side table and a grandfather clock against the wall showing the time as thirteen minutes past four o'clock in the morning.

NOTES

1 INTRODUCTION

1   Later writers give his age at death as between 60 and 65: Malalas 13.14 (p. 324.10–11 Bonn), citing the obscure late fifth-century chronographer Nestorianus (60 years and 3 months); Victor, *Caes.* 41.16 (62); *Epitome* 41.15 (63); Sozomenus, *HE* 2.34.3; Zonaras 13.4 (c. 64); Eutropius, *Breviarium* 10.8.2; Jerome, *Chronicle* 234ᵇ; Socrates, *HE* 1.39.1, 40.3; *Vita Metrophanis et Alexandri* (*BHG* 1279), as reported by Photius, *Bibliotheca* 234 (65).

2   The Greek presumably renders *admodum puer etiam tunc audiebam* or something closely similar in the original Latin.

3   On the conflation of the two wars by Eusebius, which some used as an argument that he could not have written the *Life of Constantine* or at least the section of the *Life* where it occurs, see Petit 1950: 568–569; Moreau 1955: 237–242; Winkelmann 1962b: 192–194, 226–230). Petit wrote before and Moreau in ignorance of the re-dating of the first war from 314 to 316/317 by Bruun 1953. 17–91; 1961 10–22; Habicht 1958. This re-dating removed the apparent anachronism in Eusebius' reference to Constantine's *decennalia* in 315 (*VC* 1.48).

4   On his first appearance, Orwell introduced Syme as 'a philologist, a specialist in Newspeak' (51). Surely, therefore, he named his *unperson* after the master prosopographer Ronald Syme whose devastating exposure of 'political catchwords' (Syme 1939: 149–161) he must have read, even though there is no entry for Ronald Syme in the 'Cumulative Index' to *The Complete Works of George Orwell*, ed. P. Davison, assisted by I. Angus & S. Davison 20: *Our Job is to Make Life Worth Living 1949–1950* (London, 1998), 351–538.

5   It is therefore surprising to find a recent writer asserting, in a misguided attempt to sound judicious, that he is 'accepting Eusebius as the author of most – if not necessarily all – of the *V(ita) C(onstantini)*' (Williams 2008: 31 n.23).

6   In this respect Lactantius' pamphlet resembles the British satirical magazine *Private Eye*, which has so often printed stories about politicians, judges, officials and others which more 'respectable' newspapers have not printed for fear of being sued for libel.

Constantine: Dynasty, Religion and Power in the Later Roman Empire, First Edition. Timothy Barnes.
© 2011 Timothy Barnes. Published 2011 by Blackwell Publishing Ltd.

7   Although my interpretation of Constantine has frequently been criticized and rejected in whole or in part since 1981, my demonstration that Eusebius was a provincial bishop in Palestine, not a habitué of the imperial court, has to the best of my knowledge never been challenged in any serious way, though Hal Drake makes a specious attempt to circumvent my conclusions by positing a fifth meeting and arguing that Eusebius' quotations of what Constantine said 'point in the direction of more extended contact' – whatever he may mean by that vague phrase (2000: 371).

8   The original German is even sharper: 'er ist in die Hände des widerlichsten aller Lobredner gefallen, der sein Bild durch unde durch verfälscht hat. … Eusebius ist nicht etwa ein Fanatiker;… er ist aber der erste durch und durch unredliche Geschichtschreiber des Altertums. … so sind dies im Munde eines Euseb, der die Wahrheit wusste, nichts als verächtliche Erfindungen' (J. Burckhardt, *Die Zeit Constantin's des Grossen*[2] [Leipzig, 1880], 307, 334–335, 355)

9   Jones had presented his discovery in Oxford in September 1951 at the first International Conference on Patristic Studies, whose proceedings were not published. The papyrus (*PLond*. 878) had received no more than a brief notice in the *Catalogue of Greek Papyri in the British Museum* 3 (London, 1907), xli, and Skeat failed to recognize that the verso preserves parts of *VC* 2.26-29 in his publication in 1950: 127–130. The letter is also preserved in some manuscripts of Eusebius' *Ecclesiastical History* with a text superior to that in the *Life* and closer to that of the papyrus (Winkelmann 1962a: 66–70, 121–131, 164), from which it may be deduced that Eusebius made a copy of the letter for future use c. 325 at a time when he was contemplating the composition of a continuation of his *Ecclesiastical History* beyond 324 (Barnes 1989b: 112–114).

10   Lest readers suspect that I am being unfair to a justly respected scholar, let me quote a few sentences from the long endnote in which Baynes couples together and argues against Pasquali 1910 and Maurice 1913: 'In this article Dr. Pasquali contended that the original text of the *Vita* had suffered very considerable additions and alterations. … Pasquali argues that the original version of the *V. C.* did not contain the text of Constantine's letter to the Provincials (i. e., 2.24–42). … I can see no trace of later interpolation … Thus, in my judgement, neither Dr. Pasquali nor M. Maurice has proved his contention' (Baynes 1931: 42–49). Despite declaring that in his opinion 'Dr. Pasquali has failed to prove his case,' Baynes then appropriated his conclusion: 'We may still regard the *V. C.* in the form that we possess it as the work of Eusebius, though we may readily admit that it never received final revision at its author's hands' (Baynes 1931: 45, 49).

11   Hence *PLRE* 1.889–894, Themistius 1: 'an epigram of Palladas *Anth. Gr.* XI 292 written during or after his prefecture mocks at him' (892).

12   The entries in the first volume of the *Prosopography of the Later Roman Empire*, published in 1971, to which Palladas is relevant are due to Alan Cameron (*PLRE* 1.vi): they all either state or assume that Palladas was writing in the reign of Theodosius (*PLRE* 1.657–658, Palladas, cf., e.g., 390, Gennadius 1; 394–395, Gessius 1).

13   Wilkinson's commentary explains why it is necessary to read οἷς (sheep) with the Yale papyrus rather than ὕς (pig.)

14   My translation, though based initially on Van Dam 2007: 366–367, differs significantly from it: in particular, his translation of *anniversaria vice* (line 31) as 'annual duty' and *per vices temporis* (line 51) as 'at the time of year' reflects a failure to understand that what the petitioners request is that the provincial games be held in Volsinii and Hispellum

in alternate years. The precise nature of the request was correctly understood by Millar 1977: 453.

15 That is, provincial high priests of the imperial cult.

16 With Dessau I delete *difficultates* (line 21). I have silently adopted all of Dessau's grammatical corrections.

17 In the West, Cirta in Numidia, which is attested as Colonia Constantina c. 343 (*ILS* 1235, 1236, cf. *PLRE* 1.466–467, Italicus 3) presumably acquired its new name for services rendered to Constantine in 312, while Arelate was renamed Constantina in 328 or 329 in honor of Constantinus (*RIC* 7.266–270, Arles: nos. 301–340, cf. Bruun 1966: 232–233). In the East several cities were renamed Constantia by Constantine or Constantius (Jones 1937: 222, 267, 280, 285–286, 288, 372): Antaradus received the status of a city and the name Constantia from Constantine because inhabitants were predominantly Christian (Sozomenus, *HE* 2.5 8; Hierocles, *Synecdemus*, p. 716.6–7, cf. *Collectio Sangermanensis* 25 [*ACO* 2.5.44.29]: *Atticus episcopus Aradi et Constantiae*) and Maiuma, the Christian port of pagan Gaza was similarly renamed for the same reason (Sozomenus, *HE* 2.5.7, 5.3 6), while Salamis, the metropolis of Cyprus was renamed Constantia when Constantius rebuilt it after a disastrous earthquake in 342 (Malalas 13.48 [313 Bonn = 240–241.26–32 Thurn]; Theophanes, a. 5834, p. 37.14–15 de Boor). In contrast, Maximianopolis, formerly Tella in Mesopotamia, was probably renamed Constantina by Constantius while still Caesar (Ammianus 18.7.9 [where the transmitted *Constantinam* is conventionally emended to *Constantiam*], 9.1; Malalas 13.12 [323 Bonn = 248.47–52 Thurn). A Constantia or Constantina appears to be attested on the northern fringes of the Trachonitis (Jones 1937: 545, Table XXXVIII, no. 17; Devreesse 1945: 237).

18 Millar 1977: 453 noted the geographical problem, observing that 'by what means this missive had been brought to Constantine … is not clear.'

19 The literary sources are conveniently collected in translation by Bassett 2004: 192–199: I shall therefore not provide individual documentation for uncontested facts about it. The column itself does not survive in its original form: stonework added in 1779 now sheathes the steps, the whole of the base and the lowest of its seven porphyry drums of the column, while a brick cylinder and a plain masonry capital had been added above the topmost porphyry drum before 1574 (Mango 1965: 306–313; Bassett 2004: 192–201 with Plates 20, 23). Against the strange theory, based on a joke in the *Historia Augusta* (*Heliogabalus* 24.7) that 'before settling for a column of drums, Constantine sent a mission to Thebes to see whether a suitable monolith could be found there' (Fowden 1991: 121–125), see Mango 1993b: 5–6, who argues that the seven drums, each weighing about 63 tons, were ordered directly from the quarries of the Mons Porphyrites, since a monolith of the size of the column would have weighed about 440 tons (Mango).

20 I take this to be the force of the prefix in δίκην ἡλίου προλάμποντα.

21 For what it is worth, Nicephorus Callistus reports that the right hand of the statue held an apple with part of the Holy Cross stuck in it (*HE* 7.49 [*PG* 145.1325]).

22 Bergmann 2006: 154–155 posits that Constantine was depicted with a radiate crown in the original, but that it has been removed from the medieval copy of the *Tabula Peutingeriana* that survives ('dass die Strahlen bei der mittelalterlichen Kopie einer winzigen spätantiken Darstellung weggefallen sind, scheint mir unproblematisch').

23 It is not clear what significance can or should be read into the base for an equestrian statue from Termessus in Pisidia which reads: Κωνσταντείνω Σεβ(αστῶ) / ‘Ηλίω / παντεπόπτη / ὁ δῆμος (*Tituli Asiae Minoris* 3.45).

2   THE SOLDIER AND THE STABLE-GIRL

1   G. Alačević, *Bullettino di Archeologia e Storia Dalmata* 5 (1882), 136, published the inscription 'di una memoria del defunto Stephano Petković di Knin.' Hirschfeld's critical apparatus to *CIL* 3.6980 refers to Alačević, then continues: 'ex schedis Stephani Petković Kninensis, quas post mortem eius frustra a se quaesitas esse idem litteris certiorem me fecit.'

2   O. Hirschfeld, *CIL* 3, Supp. 2 (Berlin, 1902), p. 43*; A. Stein, *PIR*² F 390.

3   P. Kos and M. Šašel Kos, *Barrington Atlas: Map-by-Map Directory* 1 (2000), 301, place Stridon among the 'unlocated toponyms' with appeal to Mayer 1957: 323.

4   My translation differs significantly from that of Deferrari 1953: 325–326.

5   In the present context it is unnecessary to attempt to decide whether Rufinus took the story from the shadowy Gelasius of Caesarea (Drijvers & Drijvers 1997: 13) or the ecclesiastical historians of the mid-fifth century took it from a Greek version of Rufinus used by Socrates, *HE* 1.17.1–9, 12; Theodoret, *HE* 1.18; Sozomenus, *HE* 2.1.2–10, 2.4.

6   I have emended the transmitted *stercora*, which can only be the plural of the neuter noun *stercus* (= dunghills) to the nominative feminine of the adjective *stercoreus* which means 'associated with manure.'

7   Ambrose alludes to Helena's construction of the Church of the Nativity in Bethlehem (Eusebius, *VC* 3.43.1–2)

8   For the former absence I rely on an electronic search, for the latter on R. Mayr, *Vocabularium Codicis Iustiniani* 1 (Prague, 1923), 2301.

9   Lammert 1929: 1926, took *stabulum* in Apuleius, *Met.* 10.1.3 to designate a special hostel where Roman soldiers could lodge overnight while traveling.

10 Thus the editions of E. Baehrens (Leipzig, 1874), W. Baehrens (Leipzig, 1911), E. Galletier (Paris, 1952), R. A. B. Mynors (Oxford, 1964), V. Paladini and P. Fedeli (Rome, 1976) and D. Lassandro (Turin, 1992). The conjecture *campi videre Vindonii* was made by Johann Arntzen, according to his son H. J. Arntzen, *Panegyrici veteres* (Utrecht, 1790), 358, although he himself printed *campi videre Vindonissae*.

11 Birth in 273 corresponds approximately to what all ancient authors except Constantine himself say about his age at the time of his death in 337 (Chapter 1 at nn.1–2).

12 Drinkwater specifically adduces the claim of the orator of 289 that 'whatever I gaze upon beyond the Rhine is Roman' (*Pan. Lat.* 10[2].7.7: *quidquid ultra Rhenum prospicio Romanum est*). But that must refer primarily to the area immediately across the Rhine from Cologne. Moreover, from his novel supposition Drinkwater deduces that Maximian took no military action against the Alamanni after 287 (2007: 181, 183).

13 Accepting that Hannibalianus was the biological father of Theodora, Nixon argued that he is not the man to whom the orator alludes because the phrase *vota pietatis* is better explained as referring to a son-in-law rather than to the former husband of the addressee's wife (Nixon & Rodgers 1994: 71 n.38).

14 Despite the date of publication of the whole volume, the section containing Enmann's long article was in fact published in June 1883 (Klussmann 1912: 70; Barnes 1970: 14).

15 A college of two praetorian prefects is attested again after the defeat of Maximinus in 313, both when Constantine and Licinius were the sole members of the imperial college (Optatus, App. 8: a travel pass issued on 28 April 315; *ILS* 8938 [Tropaeum Traiani,

314/316]) and even for some time after the joint proclamation of three Caesars on 1 March 317 (*AE* 1938.85 = *Inschriften von Ephesos* 312).

16 There is no basis in the ancient evidence for the speculative conjecture that Galerius may have been Diocletian's praetorian prefect (Barnes 1982: 38).

17 Chausson 2002; 2007: 117, 120–121 doubts whether Anastasia really was Theodora's daughter and suggests instead that she may be Constantius' daughter from his marriage to Helena and a younger sister of Constantine (born between 275 and 285).

18 Odahl 2006: 124 assumes that Helena was detained in the East as a hostage first by Galerius, then by Maximinus and was only reunited with her son in the summer of 313 when Licinius captured Nicomedia and arranged safe passage for her. That is purely fanciful (Barnes 2007a: 218–219).

19 On medieval legends connecting Helena to Trier, to other German cites and to Britain, see Pohlsander 1995: 31–72.

20 The palace was deliberately destroyed after Crispus was executed in 326 (Simon 1986: 7–8, cf. Drijvers 1992: 21–30).

21 The earliest surviving text to connect Helena with the discovery of the True Cross is the funeral oration for Theodosius, which Ambrose delivered in Milan on 25 February 395 (*De obitu Theodosii* 42 [*CSEL* 73 (1955), 393]).

22 The Greek word is γνώρισμα, which Cameron and Hall (1999: 134, 282–283) translate as 'pledge' in order to deny any reference to the True Cross. But the primary meaning of γνώρισμα is 'that by which a thing is made known, mark, token' (LSJ⁹ 355, cf. Lampe 318, s. v. 4: 'sign, proof'). It is therefore false to allege that the discovery of the True Cross is 'in fact first attested only in the 350s' (so Lenski 2008: 270).

23 For Rusguniae, see *Barrington Atlas*, Map 30F3. The find-spot of the other inscription is said to be the modern Kherbet Oum el Ahdam, identified as the ancient Tixter south-east of Sitifis by Duval 1982: 331; Matthews 1988: 535 n.123. But I cannot find either of those names in the index to the *Barrington Atlas* or in the *Map-by-Map Directory* to the map of Mauretania Sitifensis (1.475–482).

24 *PLRE* 1.633–634, 635–636, argues that the epigraphically attested Flavius Nuvel is not to be identified with the Nubel in Ammianus on the grounds that relics of the True Cross 'were not common until the late fourth century.'

25 I shall waste no time on the theory that Helena was Jewish (Vogt 1976), which perhaps owes its origin to its author's earlier acceptance of the Nazi concept of race (Vogt 1943b: 8: 'eine weitere Schwerung der Arbeit beruht in der Tatsache, daß die Antike den modernen Rassebegriff nicht gekannt hat'). The theory was thoroughly refuted by Drijvers 1992: 36–38.

3 CONSTANTINE, THE RUINS OF BABYLON AND THE COURT OF PHARAOH

1 The *dies imperii* of both Caesars was 1 March 293 (Barnes 1982: 7). The *Paschal Chronicle* states that Galerius was invested with the imperial purple on 21 May 293 (512 Bonn = p. 2 Whitby & Whitby), which was presumably the day on which the official announcement of his appointment reached Alexandria (Barnes 1982: 62 n.73).

2 The term 'tetrarchy' is a nineteenth- century invention and therefore, strictly speaking, anachronistic (Leppin 2006: 13–27). I use it as a convenient designation of a group of four emperors who mutually recognized one another as colleagues in the same imperial college.

3 Oenbrink 2006: 171 n.7 dates Maxentius' birth c. 279 and his marriage to 293/294: one of these dates could in theory be correct, but both cannot be – unless Maxentius married before he turned fifteen.

4 For the evidence relating to the famous achievements of these three men, see Broughton 1951: 95 (Camillus); 243, 254, 285 (Fabius Maximus); 183–184, 195 (Curius Dentatus).

5 Eunapius, who is echoed by the *Epitome de Caesaribus* 41.4 and Zosimus 2.20.2, the only two extant sources who name Minervina, describe her as a concubine, but this allegation is discredited by the fact that Eunapius denied that any of Constantine's sons was born in wedlock (Zosimus 2.29.1). Nevertheless, this ancient *canard* has been accepted as historical fact by modern historians such as Seeck 1921: 476–478; Ensslin 1932: 1807; Syme 1971: 207. As a result of his mistaken assessment of the relevant evidence for the age of Constantine, whose birth he placed in 288 (Chapter I at nn.1–2), Seeck dated the birth of Minervina's son Crispus to late 306 or early 307 (1895: 45–46, 442–443 = 1921: 47, 477). He also made the gratuitous assertion that Constantine must have had an unbroken string of mistresses all the time that he was married to Fausta (1895: 63 = 1921: 67: 'scheint er auch während seiner Ehe mit Fausta kaum je ohne Liebchen gewesen zu sein').

6 My carefully argued date of 301 or 302 has recently been misreported by Drake 2009: 221, who cites me as if I adopted the date of 297 or 298.

7 On 'Constantine as Moses' in Eusebius, see further Williams 2008: 36–42, though he has failed to realize that Eusebius avoided assimilating Constantine to Moses as a law-giver because he regarded the Mosaic dispensation as a purely temporary arrangement (Appendix D, cf. Barnes 1981: 93, 101, 123, 127).

8 There is no basis in the ancient evidence for putting Fausta's birth as late as 300 (Chastagnol 1982: 109) or describing her as a 'child bride' or 'still a child' in 307 (Stephenson 2009: 3, 163).

9 On the chronology of the Persian war, see Zuckerman 1994: 65–70, correcting Barnes 1981: 17–18; 1982: 54–55, 63.

10 Mackay 1999: 207–209 shows that Maximinus' original name was not *Daia*, which stands in the manuscript of Lactantius, *Mort. Pers.* 18.13, but *Daza*, which is a well-attested Illyrian name: the manuscripts of *Epitome* 40.18 have *ante imperium Daza dictus*, which Pichlmayr mistakenly emended to *Daca*. Lactantius' Diocletian protests that Severus is a drunkard who revels all night and whose only talent is as a dancer, to which Galerius replies that he has been a loyal commander of soldiers (*Mort. Pers.* 18.12). Nothing more is known about the career of Severus before 305 (*PLRE* 1.837–838, Severus 30). In Barnes 1999: 460 I hazarded the guess that he too could be a relative of Galerius.

11 On the abdication, see also the excellent brief analysis by Corcoran 2008: 249–250. In flat contradiction to the ancient evidence, Lenski makes the multiply false assertion that 'Galerius and Constantius immediately appointed *Caesares* of their own' after Diocletian and Maximian had already abdicated (2008: 257).

4 THE ROAD TO ROME

1 Lenski 2008: 257–258 transfers the joint campaign of father and son in Scotland from 305 to 306.

2 Frere 1975: iii–iv suggested that there might be archaeological evidence that the Roman fort at Cramond, originally constructed in the 140s and used during Septimius Severus'

expedition into Scotland, was reoccupied 'at the time of the Scottish campaign of the emperor Constantius.' But a recent assessment of the archaeological finds at Cramond (for the excavations, see Rae & Rae 1974; Holmes 2003: 3–144) excludes that possibility (Holmes 2003: 156).

3 It is inexcusable first to deny that Constantius proclaimed his son Augustus and then to claim that 'there was in any case no constitutionally established procedure whereby an emperor was made' (Averil Cameron 2006a: 20).

4 For careful discussion of the issue, see Corcoran 1995: 266–292, 340–341; 2006b: 36–37.

5 The Brigetio Table was found in the camp of the legion XI Claudia Pia Fidelis; a second copy of the same text with very slight differences in wording has recently been published (*AE* 2007.1224): it probably comes from the camp of the legion I Adiutrix at Durostorum; it is headed E(xemplum) S(acrarum) L(itterarum), but no addressee is named and there is no subscription.

6 When I attributed the right to legislate to Caesars as well as Augusti (Barnes 1982: 48–49, 62), the only example that I could produce of an edict issued by a Caesar was the edict against incestuous marriages preserved in the fourth-century Jewish collection *Lex dei* 6.4, whose subscription states that it was posted at Damascus either in late April or on 1 May 295 (also *CJ* 5.4.17). I attributed the edict to Galerius on the grounds that Galerius was active in the Syrian region and Egypt between 293 and 296, while Diocletian was in the Balkans (Barnes 1982: 52–54, 62–63). But the easy emendation of the place of issue from *Damasco* to *Demesso*, an obscure mining town or village in the Balkans between Singidunum and Viminacium, restores the law to Diocletian (Barnes 2005b).

7 Heck's dating is contested by Digeser 1994: 38–50, who argues that Lactantius wrote the passage in 313 – which would enhance its value as evidence for what Constantine did in 306.

8 The translation by A. Bowen in Bowen & Garnsey 2003: 59 seems to me to tone down Lactantius' claim that Constantine acted at once after his accession to power. For *iustitia* = Christianity and *iustus* = Christian in Lactantius, see the passages collected by S. Brandt in the index to his edition (*CSEL* 27 [1893], 320–321).

9 For example, a collection of ancient texts relating to the period 284–363 published in 1998 excludes Lactantius, *Mort. Pers.* 24.9 and dismisses attempts to lend credence to Lactantius as totally misconceived (Brandt 1998: 32 n.53); Constantine's action finds no mention in Charles Odahl's recent account of the proclamation of Constantine as emperor (Odahl: 2006: 78–81, with 309 n. 10), in the chronological table introducing the catalog of an exhibition held in York to mark the seventeenth anniversary of Constantine's proclamation in that city (Corcoran 2006a: 12–14) or in an essay on 'Constantine and Christianity' in that volume (Averil Cameron 2006b: 96–103).

10 Bleicken 1992: 10–11 dismissed Lactantius on the grounds that Christianity was never legally tolerated before 311 and that Constantine had no occasion or motive to change his father's religious policy. Both arguments are equally false: Christianity achieved full legal recognition in 260 (Barnes 2010a: 97–105), and in 306 Constantine had very strong political motives both for distancing himself from the other three emperors and for asserting his status as an Augustus by issuing an edict which expressly put an end to the persecution of the Christians which was still their official policy. Four more recent studies of Constantine assert that Lactantius proves nothing more than that the new emperor continued his father's policies (Bleckmann 1996: 70; Clauss 1996: 22; Girardet

1998b: 26; Marcone 2002: 55). In addition, one of these writers totally mistakes the nature and extent of our knowledge of the decade of persecution (303–313) by arguing that, if Constantine really had issued such a law, then it would have left some other trace in the historical evidence which survives, particularly in Eusebius' *Ecclesiastical History* or *Life of Constantine* (Girardet 1998b: 26). In refutation, see Barnes 2006: 4.

11 Mitchell 1988: 123 prefers to emend the date to 1 June 312, as proposed by Demandt 1971: 693. From that it would follow that Maximinus did not abolish the census in 311 as Lactantius reports.

12 On the order of the emperors' names in *CIL* 3.12133, where Licinius precedes Maximinus, see below, 221n1 (B).

13 Two coin hoards from Čentur, which is near the ancient Parentium in Istria (*Barrington Atlas* Map 20A4) are also relevant: Čentur A, whose latest coins belong to mid-310 (Jeločnik 1973: 163–167) and Čentur C, whose terminal date appears to be a year earlier (Jeločnik & Kos 1983: 39–40). I am tempted to infer that the hoards with their high incidence of recent Maxentian issues indicate that (i) Licinius' troops attacked and captured a fort in the area in 309, (ii) Maxentius' forces reoccupied it within a few weeks or months, and (iii) Licinius' troops retook it in 310 (cf. Jeločnik 1973: 167).

14 I now think that the single coin type advertising an imperial visit (*RIC* 6.129, Londinium: no. 82) is insufficient to support the hypothesis that Constantine went to Britain in 307 (Barnes 1982: 69).

15 Chausson inclines to accept the story that Constantine was a great-grandson of a sibling of Claudius as authentic because he considers that it has not definitively been proved to be fictitious (2007: 25–95). His arguments often appear to confuse the normal criteria used by historians with the standard of proof required in a modern court of law – a tactic all too frequently employed by scholars who wish to defend ancient inventions in the *Historia Augusta* and elsewhere.

16 Together with Maximian the same issues commemorate as *divi* Maxentius' *cognatus* Constantius, the father of Constantine, and his father-in-law Galerius: on the omission of Diocletian, who died on 3 December 311, see Barnes 2010c.

17 Heuss joined the Nazi party on 1 May 1937 as member no. 4,526,799 (Rebenich 2000a: 668–673). Instead of commenting on Weiss's revolutionary essay, Heuss attacked the modern German historian Fritz Fischer, who had proved beyond all rational contestation that the German government actively provoked the outbreak of a general European war in 1914 in his two books *Griff nach der Weltmacht: der Kriegszielpolitik des kaiserlichen Deutschland, 1914/18* (Düsseldorf, 1961; 3rd revised and expanded edition, 1967) and *Krieg der Illusionen: die deutsche Politik von 1911 bis 1914* (Düsseldorf, 1969): slightly abbreviated English versions are published as *Germany's Aims in the First World War* (London, 1967) and *War of Illusions: German Policies from 1911 to 1914*, trans. M. Jackson (London, 1975).

18 Note the entirely non-committal reference to it in Bringmann 1995: 21–22 n.2.

19 It is probably misleading to translate the German phrase into English as 'the Constantinian revolution:' the German noun *Wende* has a wide variety of meanings (Barnes 1999b: 289–290).

20 In the same volume Jacqueline Long also agrees that 'Weiss has made a persuasive case' (2009: 227).

21 Stephenson also commends 'scepticism on the need to find a rational or natural explanation for Constantine's vision' (2009: 332, citing Nicholson 2000: 309–323 and Averil Cameron 2006b: 96–103).

22 Girardet quoted with approval the verdict that 'Astronomische Spekulationen, wie sie immer wieder einmal eingestellt werden, sind amüsant, mehr nicht' (Clauss 1996: 35).

23 Thus, for example, Nicholson 2000: 309–310: Eusebius 'gives his description in the course of narrating Constantine's campaign of 312.' This mistaken dating gave rise to the theory that what Constantine and his army saw in the sky might have been the alignment of Jupiter, Saturn and Mars to form the horizontal cross-piece of a chrism with stars on evening of 21 October 312 (DiMaio, Zeuge & Zotov 1988: 342 fig. 1).

24 It should be remembered that Grégoire denied Eusebius' authorship of the *Life of Constantine*, which he falsely believed to have been revised and rewritten long after Eusebius' death (1930–31: 254, 270).

25 For photographs and diagrams of solar halos in addition to those provided by Weiss, see R. Greenler, *Rainbows, Halos, and Glories* (Cambridge, 1980), 105–124; W. Tape, *Atmospheric Halos. Antarctic Research Series* 64 (Washington, 1994), 3, 8–9, 19, 23, 30, 37, 44, 92.

26 It is hypercritical to doubt the good faith of both Constantine and Eusebius, as does Averil Cameron, who argues that 'it is only in the *Life* that we find the fully developed story of the vision' (1983a: 73) and that 'the elaborate account of Constantine's vision, *supposedly* communicated to the writer by the emperor himself' (1983a: 88: my italics).

27 For this interpretation, rather than the traditional 'a text attached to it,' Staats 2008: 355 n.46, quoting Peter Weiss.

28 In a passage which he added to his Latin translation of Eusebius' *Ecclesiastical History*, Rufinus not only put Constantine's vision immediately before the Battle of the Milvian Bridge, but also transformed it into a dream (p. 827. 33–34 Mommsen: *videt per soporem ad orientis partem in caelo signum crucis igneo fulgore rutilare*).

29 Rufinus incorporates Eusebius' account in the *Life of Constantine* into his translation of Book IX of the *Ecclesiastical History*, but changes it significantly: he places the vision during Constantine's expedition against Maxentius and the emperor sees a cross in the sky while asleep with angels intoning 'in this conquer' (*HE* 9.8.15, p. 827.26–p. 829.8 Mommsen).

30 The original German reads: 'Um die Stunde der Mittagszeit, da sich der tag schon neigte' (Weiss 1993: 155).

31 The word *labarum* is erroneously stated not to be attested before the Theodosian age by Grosse 1925: 241; Turcan 2006: 155–157 (who has clearly misread my endnote). Some manuscripts of the *Life* and some later Greek writers have the forms λάβορον, λάβωρον and λάβουρον (see Winkelmann's critical apparatus to p.4.18 and Mommsen's to *CTh* 6.25.1 = *CJ* 12.18.1).

32 It is possible that a corrupt and probably confused passage of Zosimus preserves a memory of this important fact when it alleges that Maxentius was contemplating an advance into Raetia (2.14.1).

33 In a later rewriting of this passage Lenski changes 'vaulted' to the less colorful 'charged,' and mistakenly postpones Constantine's invasion of Italy to the summer of 312 (2008: 259).

34 The authenticity of the letters was denied in his critical edition of the poet by Giovanni Polara, who dismissed them as a much later school exercise (Polara 1973: 1. xxxi–xxxii, 2.19–27). His arguments are a priori, aesthetic, unhistorical and completely unconvincing. The more recent argument that the letter represents only the general tenor of imperial

policy, not the emperor's personal views, since the text was prepared by the imperial chancery (Eigler 2006: 62), is pedantic hair-splitting: the same could be said of almost all of Constantine's legislative enactments. Two Christian Latin poems survive from the reign of Constantine (Green 2010: 71–76): the *Laudes domini cum miraculo quod accidit in Aeduico* was apparently written by an anonymous poet in Autun to celebrate a local miracle (*CPL* 1386), and the biblical paraphrase *Evangeliorum Libri Quattuor*, a hexameter epic along Virgilian lines in four books by the Spanish poet Juvencus (*CPL* 1385).

35 There is nevertheless still much of value in the discussion of 'Constantine's ecclesiastical building policy' in Rome by Krautheimer 1993: 519–546.

36 The list of the endowments of the *Titulus Equitii* has been transferred to the beginning of the entry for Silvester (34.3).

37 Before Champlin, the donor Gallicanus had erroneously been identified as Flavius Gallicanus, consul in 330 (*PLRE* 1.382–383, Gallicanus 1).

38 The first four lines of the inscription read as follows:

> *hic Petrus et Paulus mundi <duo> lumina praesunt*
> *quos coelum similes hos habet aula pares.*
> *coeperat hanc praesul* (i.e., Silvester, the bishop of Rome) *fundare terra[m].*
> *filius implevit quod voluit genitor.*

I deeply regret that I was unaware of this inscription when I discussed the cults of Peter and Paul in Barnes 2010a: 23–35.

5   BROTHERS-IN-LAW

1 For proof that this letter of Constantine must be 'the most perfect law on behalf of the Christians' issued by Constantine and Licinius to which Eusebius, *HE* 9.9.12, cf. 9a.12, refers, see Barnes 1982: 67–68.

2 Like John, Victor, *Caes.* 41.9; *Epitome* 41.6–7; Zosimus 2.25.5 all state that Licinius raised Martinianus to the rank of Caesar. The coins minted in his name, however, style him Augustus (*RIC* 7.608, Nicomedia: nos. 45–47; 645, Cyzicus: no. 16).

3 Zuckerman shows that none of the men whom I listed as *vicarii* of dioceses before 313 (Barnes 1982: 141, 145, cf. *PLRE* 1.1079–1085) was in fact the *vicarius* of a diocese, though Valerius Alexander in Africa foreshadowed the new type of *vicarius* (2002: 624–628). Zuckerman notes that, although Lactantius complains about the slicing of provinces into small pieces and Diocletian's appointment of *vicarii praefectorum* to condemn, proscribe and confiscate continuously (*Mort. Pers.* 7.4), he makes no mention of the creation of dioceses. Hence Zuckerman regards the following four *vicarii* as deputies of one or both praetorian prefects who were active elsewhere:

  (i)   Aemilianus Rusticianus, deputy of the praetorian prefects in 298 (P. Oxyrhynchus XII 1469, cf. Vandersleyen 1962: 62–63);

  (ii) Aurelius Agricolanus was *agens vicem praefectorum praetorio* at Tingi on 30 October 298 (Acts of Marcellus: Barnes 2010a, 357 no. XI);

  (iii) Sossianus Hierocles, whom Lactantius calls *ex vicario praesidem* in 303 (Mort. Pers. 16.4);

(iv) Valerius Alexander, who is epigraphically attested as *v(ir) p(erfectissimus) agens vic(em) praef(ectorum) praet(orio)* at Aqua Viva in 303 and at Lepcis under Maxentius (*AE* 1942–43.81; *Inscriptions of Roman Tripolitania* 464) and who, as L. Domitius Alexander, rebelled against Maxentius in 308, proclaimed himself an ally of Constantine and was suppressed in 309 (Victor, *Caes.* 40.17: *pro praefecto gerens*; Zosimus 2.12.2: τόπον ἐπέχειν τοῖς ὑπάρχοις τῆς αὐλῆς ἐν Λιβύῃ καθεσταμένος, cf. *PLRE* 1.43, Alexander 17; Barnes 1982: 14–15).

Hierocles requires further discussion. Lactantius is normally interpreted as referring to Hierocles as governor of Bithynia in 303 (*PLRE* 1.432, Hierocles; Barnes 1982: 155). But Lactantius' emphasis on his demotion ('a <mere > governor after being a <higher ranking> *vicarius*') could allude rather to Hierocles' subsequent prefecture of Egypt in 310–311 (Barnes 1982: 150), which was in fact the governorship of a province. The author of the *Contra Hieroclem*, who was in reality not Eusebius of Caesarea, but a sophist writing in north-western Asia Minor shortly before February 303 (Hägg 1992; Barnes 1996b: 550), calls Hierocles 'a man appointed to the highest courts with general powers' and 'a man entrusted with the highest courts with general powers' (4.4, 20, slightly modified from the translations of C. P. Jones 2006: 165, 195).

4 Barnes 1982: 201–203 provides a bibliography of earlier editions and a diplomatic transcript of the Verona List on the grounds that even to add modern punctuation constitutes an interpretation of the List rather than a simple reporting of its evidence.

5 My attempts to show that the Verona List is not a unitary document (Barnes 1975d; 1982: 203–205) were misguided, and I recanted long ago (Barnes 1996b: 548–550). Zuckermann 2002: 631 makes the attractive suggestion that the Verinus who waged war against the Armenians and became *praefectus urbi* at Rome from 13 September 323 to 4 January 325 (Symmachus, *Ep.* 1.2.7, cf. Barnes 1982: 118–119) was Maximinus' commander in Armenia in the winter of 312/313, but switched his allegiance to Licinius when Maximinus attacked his imperial colleague in the spring of 313. However, his assumption that *CTh* 12.11.1 shows that Verinus held office in the West under Constantine by 30 January 314 is vulnerable.

6 The Arabia Nova of the Verona List, which is also attested in a papyrus of 315/316 (*P. Oxyrhynchus* L 3574, cf. XIV 1722), cannot be a new province carved out of the Diocletianic province of Aegyptus (as argued in Barnes 1982: 151, 211): rather the plain Arabia, which precedes Arabia Nova in the List is Arabia Petraea, and the two Arabiae reflect a division of the Trajanic province of Arabia, which may have been made before November 303 (*AE* 1987.961, cf. Barnes 1996b: 550).

7 I relegate to an endnote the fact, surprising only to those unfamiliar with recent French scholarship, that the sole French contributor to the volume not only treats the letter of Licinius as issued by Constantine alone, but quotes as coming from the Edict of Milan (without quotation marks) several sentences which come from a later ecclesiastical historian's summary of a law which Constantine issued in 324 after the defeat of Licinius (Depeyrot 2006: 247, 252 n. 67, quoting Sozomenus, *HE* 1.8.2).

8 On the evidence which shows that Gregory the Illuminator was consecrated bishop of the Armenian kingdom at a council of bishops in Caesarea in Cappadocia in the autumn of 314, see Ananian 1961: 324–344.

9 The speech of 311, which is often misdated to 312 (see Barnes 1996b: 541), tells us little about Constantine, though much about Late Roman taxation and the imperial census.

The orator's main theme, from which he hardly deviates at all, is the emperor's generosity in alleviating the tax burden of his city Autun, whose assessment he has reduced from 32,000 capita to 25,000 (*Pan. Lat.*5[8]. 11–12, cf. Barnes 1982: 233–234).

10 Compare *Aeneid* 6.724–725: *totamque infusa per artus / mens agitat molem et magno se corpore miscet.*

11 Rodgers removes the allusion by omitting *sunt* and transferring *voluisti* to another clause to produce the mistranslation 'whose names you wished to be as many as the tongues of the nations' (Nixon & Rodgers 1994: 332).

12 I cannot find anything similar in any text independent of Genesis which Gera discusses. Unfortunately she does not mention this passage.

13 The fanciful reconstruction of the episode by MacMullen 1969: 96–97 assumes that the Battle of Cibalae occurred in October 314, not 316 as had been proved long before he wrote.

14 The name Constantius implies that the envoy was a relative of Constantine. Hence *PLRE* 1.224, Constantius 1, suggests that he is 'perhaps to be identified' with the Flavius Constantius who was praetorian prefect in the mid-320s and consul in 327 (*PLRE* 1.225, Constantius 5). I tentatively identify both the envoy and the praetorian prefect as Constantius, the brother of Constantia and Anastasia, who may have been born as early as c. 290 (Chapter 2). In order to sustain this identification I posit that when Constantius was given the revived title of *patricius* (which is only explicitly attested for him in papyri with the consular date of 335), his *nomen* was changed from Flavius to Julius. Chausson not only identifies these three Constantii, but also implausibly claims that the composite Constantius was born c. 280 – and hence a son of Helena and a full brother of Constantine (2007: 121).

15 The translation by J. Stevenson in Lieu & Montserrat 1998: 45 seems to suggest that Constantine requested Licinius to make Bassianus Caesar – which is quite impossible.

16 Degrassi 1954: 109–125 (who deduced from Herodian that Emona was transferred from Pannonia Superior to Italy between c. 150 and 238, probably in the military emergency of 169/170); Šašel 1968: 574–575; T. J. Cornell & J. F. Matthews, *Atlas of the Roman World* (Oxford, 1982), 140; R. J. A. Talbert, *Atlas of Classical History* (London/Sydney, 1985), 128, 143, 170, 176. Thomsen 1947: 141–142 had even argued, despite the evidence of Pliny and Ptolemy, that Augustus included Emona in the tenth region of Italy.

17 The text as printed by Cuntz reads: μεταξὺ δὲ Ἰταλίας ὑπὸ τὸ Νωρικὸν καὶ Παννονίας πάλιν Ἡμῶνα λϛ´ με´ γ″. That does not say that Emona was situated outside the territory of the Roman province of Pannonia, as Thomsen claimed (1947: 141).

18 Compare Christian reaction to the divorce and remarriage of Valentinian decades later (Barnes 1998a: 123–126).

19 The calendar of Polemius Silvius gives 7 August as the day on which Constantinus was born (*CIL* 1², p. 271), which I accepted on the grounds that it must be approximately correct (Barnes 1982: 44–45). But the abolition of Constantinus' memory in 340 makes it most unlikely that his date of birth was officially remembered in the fifth century. Accordingly, since Constantinus' younger brother Constantius was born on 7 August 317 (*CIL* 1², pp. 255, 270; *CTh* 6.4.10, cf. Barnes 1982: 43), *natalis Constantini* in Polemius Silvius must be an error of transcription: when Attilio Degrassi re-edited the calendar of Polemius Silvius, he duly printed the entry as *natalis Constanti[n]]i minoris* (Degrassi 1963: 271). On the other hand, there is no warrant for arguing that Constantinus was born as late as February 317 and deducing that he was therefore

'probably illegitimate since his brother Constantius was born to Fausta on 317 Aug. 7' (*PLRE* 1.223, Constantinus 3). Julian, *Orat.* 1, 9d, states explicitly that Constantinus was the son of Fausta (Barnes & Vanderspoel 1984).

20 *PLRE* 1.820, Senecio 1, suggests that he might be identical with either the Senecio who is attested as a *dux* at Viminacium in Moesia, probably in the early fourth century (*AE* 1903.310, whence PLRE 1.820, Senecio 2), or the Senecio who was *dux* of Noricum c. 311 (ILS 664, whence *PLRE* 1.821, Senecio 4). Such posts are highly improbable for a Roman aristocrat.

21 The manuscript has *in campo mardiense*, the emendation *in campum Ardiensem*, which Moreau prints, is due to Grégoire 1938a: 564–565 n.5; 1938b: 586.

22 In 1993 Corcoran also followed me in attributing to Licinius, albeit with some hesitation, the so-called *edictum de accusationibus*, which had traditionally been attributed to Constantine (Corcoran 1993: 115–117, cf. Barnes 1976d: 275–276; 1981: 69; 1982: 127–128). But Corcoran has now proved that it was in fact issued by Galerius in 305/306 (Chapter 4).

23 For speculation about possible relatives of this Helena later in the fourth century, see Barnes 1982: 44; Chausson 2007: 104–107, 108), the latter of whom holds that she was the granddaughter of Helena, the mother of Constantine, and hence Crispus' cousin (2007: 110, 121, 127, 151, 256). One of the messages which Publilius Optatianus Porfyrius wove into a poem praising Constantine (*Carmen* 10) may indicate that Crispus and Helena were expecting another child in 324 or 325 (p. 42 Polara: *pater imperas, avus imperes*, cf. Barnes 1975c: 181).

6   THE TRANSFORMATION OF THE EAST

1 Licinius was put to death in the spring of 325 on the alleged grounds that he was plotting insurrection: his death might be connected with the removal from office of one of the ordinary consuls of the year in May 325 (Barnes 1981: 214; 1982: 96, 102).

2 They are summarized by Eusebius in a passage which now stands before Constantine's letter (2.20–22), but which belongs to an alternative draft of this section of the *Life* (Pasquali 1910: 369–376; Barnes 1989b: 99–100, 105).

3 The practice continued in the Senate at Rome until 357 when Constantius removed the Altar of Victory during his visit to the city (Symmachus, *Relatio* 3.3–7).

4 My translation omits the words τὰς ἐκκλησίας τοῦ θεοῦ, which I believe to be a gloss on τῶν εὐκτηρίων οἴκων τὰς οἰκοδομάς earlier in the sentence.

5 Bishops in the West may well have received a similar letter before 325, even though the bishop of Rome did not begin the construction of the great basilica of Saint Peter's in Rome until well after 324 (Chapter 4).

6 Dörries gave his German translation of the document the less misleading title of 'Lehrbrief an die Provinzialen' (1954: 51–54).

7 Constantine is here both angry and allusive, and he may mingle or conflate references to the oracles of Apollo at Delphi, Didyma and Daphne (Cameron & Hall 1999: 245; Digeser 2004: 57–62). Digeser has argued that Diocletian consulted the oracle at Daphne when he was in Antioch after negotiating peace with Persia in 299, that this consultation is related to the episode in Lactantius, *Mort. Pers.* 10.1–6, and that the abortive sacrifice in Antioch, at which Constantine was probably present, since he was with

Diocletian and Galerius in Antioch in 299, led to the purge of the eastern armies in 300 (2004: 63–69, 73–77). For possible flaws in her argument, see J. Rist 2010: 58–60.

8 Contrast Barnes 1981: 212: in 324 Constantine founded 'a new city' which was to be 'a Christian city in which Christian emperors could hold court in an ambience untainted by the buildings, rites, and practices of other religions.'

9 Dagron 1974: 32 speaks of 'la cérémonie traditionelle de *limitatio* et de *consecratio*.' But neither *consecratio* nor *limitatio* seems quite right. The *Oxford Latin Dictionary* defines *consecratio* as the 'action of making sacred; deification; devoting as a criminal or scapegoat' (*OLD* 411), while *limitatio* is normally used of the marking out of agricultural land (Fabricius 1926).

10 On the repeated *hic* as meaning 'here in Nicomedia,' see Creed 1984: 89, even though he translates 'here …, there …, here …, there …' (13).

11 It should be noted that Baynes believed that the *Speech* lacked 'any reference to Licinius' (1931: 56).

12 There are two notable exceptions to the general consensus. (i) The authenticity of the *Speech* and as a corollary of the *Life of Constantine* has recently been doubted by Cataudella 2001: 171–181, who alleges that Chapters 14 and 22 of the *Speech* reflect an anti-Constantinian polemic which was first formulated by Julian the Apostate. (ii) Robin Lane Fox argued that Constantine composed the *Speech* in Greek rather than Latin, despite Eusebius' clear statement to the contrary (1986: 629–652). In an endnote he dismissed as 'unfounded' the widely accepted scholarly verdict that the *Speech* comments on Virgil's original Latin, while the Greek translations from the Fourth Eclogue have been adjusted to accord with the emperor's exegesis. Unfortunately, Lane Fox has not yet (to the best of my knowledge) deigned to provide the proof of this assertion which he promised when stating it (1986: 778 n.9).

13 Earlier articles by Kurfess on the same theme are listed by Barnes 1981: 425; Cristofoli 2005: 152.

14 Constantine was not in Rome at any Easter in any year during his reign (Barnes 1982: 69–80). Edwards therefore canvassed the possibility that 'the speech was delivered by a surrogate' at a time when 'we may imagine that there was discontent in Rome' (2003 xxix). The *status quaestionis* is grotesquely misreported by Williams 2008: 27 n.5, who holds that 'the date is still in question' because 'Edwards 2003 prefers an earlier date than Bleckmann 1997, who is followed in most details by Barnes 2001.' Let me repeat therefore: Bleckmann proved incontestably that Constantine was speaking in Nicomedia, while I showed that delivery in Nicomedia carries the inescapable corollary that the date must be 325, not 328 as Bleckmann had argued.

15 The manuscripts have πρός: I print and translate the emendation which Heikel proposed in his critical apparatus (on p. 188.2), but did not print.

16 This rules completely out of court the date of 12 April 328 argued by Bleckmann 1997 197–200, who makes no mention of John Rist's arguments, which were contested by Edwards 1995, partly on the basis of a translation which removed the telling phrase 'second god' from the passage. When challenged by Barnes 2002a: 34–35, Edwards improved his translation, but continued to deny that there is any 'Arian tendency' in the passage (Edwards 2003: 15).

    Davies 1991 claims to have detected 'another Arian notion' in addition to that identified by Rist: he argues that a later passage of the *Speech* assimilates the relationship between Father and Son to that of cause and effect (11.8, p. 168.15–18), that Constantine cannot have uttered such 'Arian notions' at any time after the controversy over Arius' views broke out c. 318, and hence that Eusebius has interpolated the passage in order to make the emperor express his own theological views. The argument both attributes to Eusebius a degree of conscious dishonesty which exceeds the bounds of credibility and relies on a dubious translation of the passage in question (Barnes 2002a: 36 n.47).

17 I have obelized ἠπιώτατος, which can only mean 'most gentle,' because whether Plato 'excelled all others in gentleness' (Edwards 2003: 14) is irrelevant to his standing as a philosopher. I supply the equivalent of σοφώτατος on the grounds that, if ἠπιώτατος stood in the copy of the *Speech* which Eusebius used, it must be a mistranslation or misunderstanding of the original Latin.

18 On the meaning of ὕπαρξις here, see Rist 1981: 158. Edwards 2003: 15 correctly translates as 'concrete existence,' but then glosses his translation with the footnote 'For *hypostasis* as the concrete expression of essence or *ousia*, see Porphyry, *Isagoge* 18.25' (15 n.2) – as if τὴν ὑπόστασιν, not τὴν ὕπαρξιν stood in the Greek text.

19 The *Speech* was correctly dated to Easter 325 by Mazzarino 1974: 114–116; Lane Fox 1986: 627–635. But Mazzarino proposed delivery in the newly founded Constantinople, Lane Fox delivery in Antioch, both of which are impossible. Maximinus never resided in Byzantium, which he passed quickly through twice in the spring of 313 (Barnes 1982: 65–67), while Constantine cannot have been in Antioch at Easter 325, even though it is possible that he might have set foot in the city between November 324 and February 325 (Barnes 1982: 76).

20 I read ἐκκλησία τε ἀώρου καὶ ἀδαοῦς ἡλικίας τιθήνη with mss. MAE; reading ἀώρου τε καὶ ἀδαοῦς with mss. VJ, Heikel proposed to delete ἀκκλησία. Edwards 2003: 3 n.6 follows Lane Fox 1986: 631 in alleging that 'the word *ekklêsia* is inserted by Heikel.': Both have clearly confused Heikel's sigla for add (+) and subtract (<).

21 In Book VII of his *Divine Institutes* Lactantius quotes lines 8 (19.9), 23 (16.11), 25–26 (20.3) of the acrostic as quoted by Constantine, of which *Oracula Sibyllina* 8.217–250 has a longer form.

22 For a brief overview of Virgil's status as an authority in antiquity, see den Boeft 1988; on modern exegeses of the Fourth Eclogue, Nisbet 1978. Many of the interpretative problems that puzzle modern scholars, who have written about the poem, especially those with a literary bent, arise from their failure to realize that Virgil originally composed most of the poem for the beginning of Pollio's consulate on 1 January 40 BC, then hastily adapted it to serve as an epithalamium for the marriage of Mark Antony to Octavia after the Treaty of Brundisium in early October 40 – as William Tarn demonstrated long ago (Tarn 1932: 159–160).

23 The Greek has which obviously renders *campus* in the Latin original.

24 Edwards 2003: 19 translates τῶν ὑπηκόων as 'those who hear us.'

25 I translate on the assumption that the Greek εἴ που (p. 166.8) renders *siquidem* in the original Latin (Barnes 1981: 325 n.148); Edwards' translation 'if indeed' implies that Constantine doubted whether one who had been a Christian from childhood was blessed (2003: 20).

26 For ample surveys of modern discussions of the theological aspects and the disputed chronology of the controversy over Arius' views before 325, see respectively Löhr 2005, 2006; Brennecke, Heil, von Stockhausen & Wintjes 2007: xix–xxxiv.

27 Woods 2002: 206–222 argues that Constantine addressed this letter not to Alexander and Arius at all, but to 'the bishops gathered at Antioch to elect a successor to Eulalius'

and that it was taken from the imperial court to Syria by Acacius, the former *comes Macedoniae* (*CTh* 11.3.2; 27 February 327), as *comes consistorianus* in late 327 (*VC* 3.53.2, 62.1, cf. *PLRE* 1.6, Acacius 3, 4). Woods attributes the erroneous identification of the recipients of the letter to a later editor of the *Life of Constantine*, whom he tentatively identifies as Euzoius, bishop of Caesarea from c. 366 to 379. That is all most improbable, and there is no basis in the ancient evidence for Woods' further claim that Acacius 'seems to have been Constantine's senior ecclesiastical adviser' in succession to Ossius (222–223, with appeal to Woods 2001).

28 See the recent survey, with ample bibliography, by Kany 2007: 95–124.

29 Before this the ecclesiastical historians of the fifth century interpose an episode in which bishops deposit in Constantine's lap petitions accusing one another: Rufinus, *HE* 10.2; Socrates, *HE* 1.8.18–19; Theodoret, *HE* 1.11.4–6; Sozomenus, *HE* 1.17.3–5 ; Anonymus, *HE* 2.8.1–4. Although I used to accept the story (Barnes 1981: 215), I am now inclined to reject it as an invention of Gelasius of Caesarea (frag. 11 Winkelmann).

30 On the debate and its wider context, see di Berardino 1992.

31 On the superiority of John's account of the arrest and crucifixion of Jesus, see Millar 1990, who showed that it is illegitimate to combine John with elements from the other three gospels in an attempt to produce a unified account of 'the trial of Jesus.'

32 On the obscurities in these chapters (and a novel exegesis of what the divergent practices were), see Dugmore 1961.

33 Thirty-five years later Athanasius, *De Synodis* 5.1–2, identified the areas in which the celebration of Easter diverged from the norm as Syria, Cilicia and Mesopotamia, and he repeated the statement in 369 in the *Letter to the Bishops of Africa*, which he composed in the name of a council that met in Alexandria (*Ep. ad Afros* 2.5). I am tempted to suppose that Cilicia is simply a mistake.

34 Funk, who believed that the observance of Lent had its origin in the East, since the earliest clear attestations in the West are in Ambrose, *De Noe* 13,44; *De Elia et ieiunio* 10,34 (*CSEL* 32.1 [1897], 442; 32.2 (*CSEL* [1897], 430) and are, therefore, later than the earliest clear attestations in the East, proposed to emend τεσσαρακοστῆς to πεντεκοστῆς (1897: 258–260). The emendation is unnecessary, but Funk correctly adduced the twentieth canon of the Council of Antioch, which confirms that τεσσαρακοστῆς in the fifth Nicene canon must refer to a period of forty days after Easter (*EOMIA* 2.290–293).

35 The canon assumes that the meaning of the Greek word τεσσερακοστή is well known (Cobb 1978: 412): it cannot therefore refer to something not known in the East until after 325.

36 This Gallic chronicle appears to have taken the date from an augmented epitome of Jerome's *Chronicle* (Burgess 2001: 86).

37 The Christian character of the new city was acknowledged by Jones 1964: 83; Krautheimer 1983: 41–67. It is still denied by Berger 2003: 71; Bassett 2004: 22–36; Stephenson 2009: 201–203. Investigations of the archaeological traces of Constantine's Constantinople are surveyed by Barsanti 1992.

38 An endnote states 'I owe this observation to Professor J. F. Matthews' (O'Donnell 2009: 402 n.1).

39 Not only this, but many other invented stories are accepted in the discussion of 'the foundation of Constantinople' by La Rocca 1993: 553–583.

40 *PLRE* 1.772–774, Praetextatus 1, opines that 'if he is identical with Praetextatus ὁίεροφάντης who took part ... in the ceremonies at the inauguration of Constantinople in 330, he must have been born by c. 310.'

41 O'Donnell has recently reasserted the traditional opinion that: 'in his (sc. Constantine's) not quite Christian way, the rituals mixed Christian and traditional elements' (2009: 181).

42 This is the generally accepted emendation of the transmitted and meaningless καινερεου.

43 Mango 1985 has shown that Eusebius describes a tall rotunda, to which Constantius added the basilical Church of the Holy Apostles. It has sometimes been claimed, quite implausibly, that the placing of Constantine's body between the two rows of empty sarcophagi of the Apostles equated him with Christ (Rebenich 2000b). That would have constituted blasphemy, as Constantine well knew.

44 On Constantine as a reformer, see recently Bleckmann 2007a; on his religious legislation as it is reflected in the Theodosian Code, see Gaudemet 1947; Hunt 1993.

45 See in general Jones 1964: 745–746, 912. I hope to discuss elsewhere all the laws of the period 313–383 in the relevant title of the Theodosian Code (CTh 16.2).

46 Seeck 1919: 61, 179 mistakenly emended the date to 18 July 329 since he believed that Bassus did not become praetorian prefect until 329. Bassus is now known to have been appointed in 317 or 318 (Chapter 7).

47 The exile of Athanasius in 335 is a unique and exceptional case: Constantine disallowed Athanasius' condemnation by the Council of Tyre as invalid, but sent him to Trier for insolence and disrespect while allowing him to retain his status as bishop of Alexandria (Barnes 1981: 239–240; 1993a: 23–25).

48 Seeck 1919: 88, 173 emended the transmitted date of *VI id(us) Iun(ias) Sabino et Rufino cons(ulibu)s* to 8 June 323 (*Severo et Rufino cons(ulibu)s*); in favor of the much easier emendation of *Iun(ias)* to *Ian(uarias)*, see Barnes 1981: 50–51; 1982: 73.

49 The subscription reads: *data viiii kal(endas) Iulias Constantinopoli A(ugusto) et Crispo Caes(are) cons(ulibu)s*: Seeck 1919: 7, 57, 166 emended *Constantinopoli* to *ipso* to give a date of 23 June 318, while Millar 1977: 591 n.7 argued that the extract included in the Theodosian Code comes from a law of Licinius issued at Byzantium. Millar's hypothesis was accepted by Barnes 1981: 312 n.80; 1982: 82, who suggested that Licinius was reiterating an enactment of Constantine for his own territories. Against ascription to Licinius, see Corcoran 1993: 108, 111–113; 1995: 284–285.

50 Eusebius states that Constantine wrote to bishops everywhere (*VC* 2.45.2), but also that he wrote to 'those who presided over the churches in each province' (2.24.6), which implies that he wrote only to metropolitan bishops, of whom Eusebius was one. Modern scholars have not opted consistently for either interpretation: see Pietri 1983: 71 n.33; Barnes 1993a: 178; Cameron & Hall 1999: 244.

51 See the essays edited by Holman 2008.

52 Seeck 1919: 44, 48, 55, 106, 115, 187–188 emended dates in the Theodosian Code to make Evagrius the recipient in 339 of laws issued by Constans, which produces a false antithesis between Constantine's allegedly milder attitude towards the Jews and the harsher policies of his sons (e.g., Blanchetière 1983).

53 PLRE 1.284–285, Evagrius 2, plausibly emends the transmitted consular date of 339 (*Constantio A. ii et Constante A. conss.*) to 329 (*Constantino A. viii et Constantino C. iv conss.*). But 13 August 326 (*Constantino A. vii et Constantio C. conss.*) also falls within Evagrius' prefecture.

54 The authenticity of this law is doubted by Edwards 2006: 143.

55 Dismissed as 'not a special favour to Christianity but merely a tidying-up operation' by Harries 2010: 92.

56   Seeck 1919: 61 remarked that this law is one of a group that 'enthalten keine chronologische Kennzeichen.'

57   The transmitted text is both grammatically defective and linguistically peculiar: a feminine noun such as *ecclesiae* is needed for the adjective *catholicae* to qualify, and it is anomalous for the positive *venerabilique* to follow the superlative *sanctissimo*. Both can be removed by the simple expedient of emending the transmitted *venerabilique* to *ecclesiae* (Barnes 2007a: 205 n.65).

58   It is misleading to assert, without any qualification, that 'Theodosius I (379–95) had ruled a unified Empire' (Millar 2007: 3).

59   For a full discussion of 'East and West' in the divided empire of Valentinian and Valens, see Errington 2006: 79–128.

60   Presumably including Manichaeism: although Diocletian had declared it to be a novel religion whose adherents were to be executed or, if *honorati,* sent to the mines of Phaeno or quarries of Proconnesus (*Lex Dei* 15.3 [*FIRA* 2.580–581], cf. Barnes 1976c: 246–250; 1982: 55, 169), after 324 Constantine seems to have treated Manichees as deviant Christians (Lieu 1992: 125–132).

61   Note, however, that while the association of iron-workers in Hermonthis in Upper Egypt sacrificed an ass in the temple of Hatshepsut at Deir el-Bahari on 27/28 December 324, the inscriptions which record acts of devotion by the same association to the same deity later in the fourth century imply that an animal was no longer slaughtered (*SEG* 41.1612–1615, cf. Bingen 1999: 615–618).

7   DYNASTIC POLITICS AFTER THE COUNCIL OF NICAEA

1   Staats dates the death of Crispus to the Ides of March 326 because he has misunderstood Seeck 1919: 176, who places Crispus' death between laws which he dates to 15 March and 1 April (*CTh* 12.1.1[Seeck]; 9.24.1).

2   The Budé text of Victor by P. Dufraigne (Paris, 1975) prints *indicio*, which is nothing more than a careless misprint (Tarrant 1978: 357).

3   Seeck emended the transmitted date of *CTh* 10.4.1 (5 March 313) to show Constantine in Heraclea on 5 March 326 and interpreted the subscription to *CTh* 2.10.4, which lacks a consular date, as showing that he was in Constantinople on 8 March (1919: 51, 176, accepted by Barnes 1982: 77). If Constantine was in Aquileia in early April 326, these emendations cannot be correct.

4   This brief article, which explains why the poet Ovid was sent to Tomi, has been totally ignored by Ovidian scholars for a whole generation.

5   Reinhart Staats advances the theory that Constantine condemned Crispus to death on the basis of a misunderstanding of Paul's first letter to the Christians of Corinth, in which the apostle comments on a sexual scandal in the young church of Corinth (1 Corinthians 5.1–5) arising from the adultery of a man with his father's wife, that is, his stepmother (Staats 2002; 2008: 363). Paul urged the Christian community of Corinth to deliver the offender to Satan for the destruction of his body so that his spirit might be saved at the Day of Judgment, which was normally interpreted in the early church as enjoining excommunication for sexual transgressors, but which Staats argued that Constantine took to recommend death as the appropriate penalty for such sexual transgression and on

the basis of this misinterpretation condemned his son to death. But Staats fails to discuss where Crispus and Fausta could have conducted a secret *amour* and his assertion that 'the attractive Fausta' told her husband of the affair after it finished has a strong whiff of anachronism. Moreover, the 'infidelity' of Constantine's wife with his son which he assumes probably never occurred.

6   I discount as unfounded gossip the allegation, presumably made by Eunapius, that Constantine killed Fausta for committing adultery with an *agens in rebus* (Philostorgius, *HE* 2.4, 4a [p. 16.1, 16–21 Bidez]).

7   Hermann-Otto 2007: 141, 238–240 posits a political plot, which Constantine tried to conceal through the story of adultery – as if he deliberately advertised himself as a cuckold!

8   Beck's discussion of Maternus' exegesis is unsatisfactory (2007: 97–100): he makes repeated and irritating use of baseball terminology and follows the incompetent English translation of Bram (1975) in transforming Maternus' *ad Asiae proconsulatum* into 'was made proconsul of Africa' – an error which he could easily have avoided by consulting Barnes 1975b.

9   I propose to supply the missing consulate in *Math.* 2.29.10 and read: *de exilio raptus in administrationem Campaniae primum destinatus est, deinde <ad> Achaiae proconsulatum, post vero ad Asiae proconsulatum, <ordinarium consulatum> et praefecturam urbis Romae* – on the assumption that the manuscripts have omitted it by haplography.

10 It may be relevant that Firmicus Maternus denies that an emperor's horoscope, unlike anyone else's, reveals when he will die because the fate of the emperor alone is not determined by the stars (*Mathesis* 2.30.4, cf. Cramer 1954: 280).

11 For a careful evaluation of Eusebius' reports of Constantinian churches in Palestine, see Walker 1990: 93–116, 171–281.

12 An adaptation of Oedipus' curse on his sons Eteocles and Polynices (Euripides, *Phoenissae* 68: θηκτῷ σιδήρῳ δῶμα διαλαχεῖν τόδε).

13 The *Origo* and Ammianus clearly mean that Constantina was the wife of Hannibalianus, not merely betrothed to him, as does Philostorgius when he calls her the widow of Hannibalianus (*HE* 3.22: Ἀνναβαλλιανοῦ δὲ ἦν κεχηρωμένη γυνή).

14 On the possible sources of Zonaras' knowledge of Constantine, see Bleckmann 1992: 151–161.

15 There is no other evidence that Constantina was an Augusta: the story that her father had created her an Augusta (in 335 according to Kienast 1996: 308) was presumably invented in 350 to give her a spurious seniority to her brother Constantius, and thus to legitimize her investment of Vetranio as an Augustus.

16 For two recent assessments, Vera 2005: 26–35; Bleckmann 2007a: 26–68.

17 That the end of 'the Severan Empire' in 260 marked a fundamental break in continuity between the Early and High Roman Empire and the Later Roman Empire was first clearly demonstrated by Potter 2004: esp. 217–262.

18 On editors' reports of the name as *Eroco*, see Festy 1999: 186. Skepticism about the status, role and even historicity of Crocus is expressed by Wood 2006: 82.

19 The name is transmitted only in *CJ* 12.35.9, 12.42.1, which are addressed to *Aelio p. p.* and *Aeliano* respectively: *PLRE* 1.17, Aelianus 3, rightly prefers the latter.

20 Demandt 1970: 562: 'der erste nachweisbare Germane im Oberkommando.'

21 The verses are inscribed in capital letters: hence the V of the name SEVSO can be either vocalic or consonantal. Moreover, if the hexameter is to contain six full metrical feet, then *Seuso* should be scanned as two long syllables followed by one short.

22 Some confusion has been caused by John the Lydian, who identifies the early imperial *quaestores Augusti* with *quaestores candidati Caesaris* and quotes Ulpian's *De officio quaestoris* in Greek to that effect (*De Magistratibus* 1.28, cf. Bonfils 1981: 51–53). The quotation can hardly be genuine and it is not included in among the fragments of Ulpian's *De officio quaestoris* in O. Lenel, *Palingenesia Iuris Civilis* 2 (Leipzig, 1889), 992 nos. 2252–2253.

23 Three successive praetorian prefects are attested for Maxentius: Rufius Volusianus, who suppressed the rebellion of Domitius Alexander in Africa in 309; Manilius Rusticianus after 309; and Ruricius Pompeianus in 312 (Barnes 1996b: 547–548). On other prefects besides Bassus who have been alleged for the period 317–324, see Barnes 1982: 128–131.

24 Acindynus had been *corrector Tusciae et Umbriae* and was both a *pontifex maior* and a *quindecimvir sacris faciundis* (Carlos Saquete 2000): despite Barnes 1992a: 253 n.18; 1994b: 3, 7; 1995: 141, therefore, Acindynus was both a pagan and an aristocrat of Rome.

25 Earlier discussions of the praetorian prefects of Constantine have assumed that the Maximus to whom *CTh* 13.4.2 is addressed was Valerius Maximus, the consul of 327 and have hence deduced that he was the praetorian prefect of Dalmatius on 2 August 337 (so *PLRE* 1.590–591, Maximus 49; Barnes 1982: 103, 132, 134–135, 138, 139). But Dalmatius was killed many weeks before the law of 2 August 337 was issued (Burgess 2008: 29–35), and the office held by the addressee of *CTh* 13.4.2 is unknown. According to Mommsen's critical apparatus, the only manuscript of the Theodosian Code and all manuscripts except one of *CJ* 11.66.1, which derives from it, head the law *Idem A(ugustus) ad Maximum*, without giving Maximus any title: there is, therefore, no valid evidence that Valerius Maximus was praetorian prefect in the summer of 337.

26 The date at which Ablabius encompassed the death of the philosopher Sopater (Eunapius, *Lives of the Philosophers* 6.2.1, 7–8, pp. 462, 463–464; Zosimus 2.40.3, cf. *PLRE* 1.846, Sopater 1) is unclear: Sopater had been a habitué of the court of Licinius several years before 324 ([Julian], *Epp.* 185, 439bc; 184, 417d, cf. Barnes 1978b: 102–106).

27 In accordance with the official truth of 337–340, Eusebius speaks only of the three sons of Constantine and projects their division of the empire between them on 9 September 337 on to Constantine's different division of 335 (*VC* 4.51.1, cf. Barnes 1982: 198–200).

28 Salway 2007: 1283–1286 accepts Feissel's date of 1 March 336 uncritically and without argument.

29 *PLRE* 1.3–4, Ablabius 4, which dates the inscription to 337 (as was reasonable in 1971), gratuitously postulates that Ablabius is 'erroneously placed second instead of first.'

30 The partly forged letter of Eusebius to Constantia permits no inferences (*CPG* 3503, cf. Barnes 2010c), and the story that Constantia's dying wishes persuaded Constantine to recall Arius from exile (Rufinus, *HE* 10.12; Socrates, *HE* 1.25; Theodoret, *HE* .2.3.1–3; Sozomenus, *HE* 2.27.1–4, both apparently deriving from Gelasius of Caesarea, frag. 22 Winkelmann) deserves little credence.

31 On the evolution of the title *patricius* in the fourth and fifth centuries, see Barnes 1975e.

32 I cannot understand why Chausson 2007: 113 dates the betrothal a decade later, to the late 340s.

33 A more skeptical assessment is implicit in a recent archaeological survey of the Roman Danube (Wilkes 2005).

34 Trajan died without adopting Hadrian, who was his nearest male relative, his presumed and his actual successor: on the political context and the subsequent execution of four senior generals, see Syme 1958: 242–248.

35 Constantine's regnal years continued to be used in Egypt even after the death of Dalmatius became known (*P. Oxyrhynchus* XLVIII 3386 [28 March 338]); indeed, they were still in use in 354/355 (*P. Oxyrhynchus* LX 4092.10).

36 Burgess has, in my opinion, proved that 'there can be no serious doubt that Constantius was behind the assassinations and that it was he who rejected his father's succession and dynastic plans, not the soldiers' and that the assassinations probably occurred 'in Constantinople or its environs in early June of 337' (2008: 42).

37 The mss. read and editors print *divi Constantini filius*, which must be emended to *Constantii*: see F. Boll, *RE* 6 (1909), 2366.

38 My translation often diverges from that of Bram 1975: 29–30.

39 Viz., Flavius Ursus and Flavius Polemius. The earlier careers of both men appear to be otherwise completely unattested (*PLRE* 1.989, Ursus 4; 710, Polemius 4). The latter, however, was at the court of Constantius in 345 (Athanasius, *Historia Arianorum* 22.1) and should be identified with the Julius Valerius Polemius, *vir clarissimus*, who translated the Alexander Romance of Pseudo-Callisthenes into Latin and probably composed the *Itinerarium Alexandri* (*PLRE* 1.709–710, Polemius 3, cf. Appendix F).

APPENDIX A: THE CAREER OF LACTANTIUS

1 'Caelius' has better attestation in the manuscripts of most of Lactantius' works (*CSEL* 19.1), but the sole manuscript of *On the Deaths of the Persecutors* has *Lucii C(a)ecilii*, that is, the antiquated Roman Republican style of *praenomen* and *gentilicium* alone without either *cognomen* or *signum*: the attestation of a L(ucius) Caecilius Firmianus at Cirta (*CIL* 8.7241), who could be a relative or ancestor (*PLRE* 1.338, Firmianus 2), confirms that his *gentilicium* was indeed Caecilius.

2 Nicomedia appears to have been Diocletian's main residence only in the very early years of his reign, then between late 294 and early 296 and from 302 to 305 (Barnes 1982: 49–56).

3 This inference is logically independent of the argument that Lactantius was preparing a second edition of his *Divine Institutes* in 324 (Chapter 4 at n.7).

4 Digeser 1994: 50–52 argues on different grounds that Lactantius became Crispus' tutor in 310 and instructed Constantine in Christianity between 310 and 313.

APPENDIX B: GALERIUS' SARMATIAN VICTORIES

1 The name of the third emperor, which has been erased, must be that of Maximinus. The order of names, therefore, does not reflect seniority within the imperial college as reckoned by each emperor's *dies imperii*, but the order of their appointment as Augustus as recognized by Galerius.

2 Corcoran also notes that the new inscription entails that the victory of 27 June 310 (*ILS* 664) was the occasion of Galerius' assumption of the title *Carpicus maximus VI*

(not *Sarmaticus maximus V*, as argued by Barnes 1982: 81, 257) and removes the victory over the Carpi in 308 or 309 postulated by Barnes 1982: 64, 257.

APPENDIX C: THE *PANEGYRICI LATINI* AND CONSTANTINE

1   It should be noted that at this period the main celebrations of imperial anniversaries were held at both the beginning and the end of the anniversary year: hence the main celebrations of Constantine's *quinquennalia* occurred on both 25 July 310 and 25 July 311 *Pan. Lat.* 5[8], cf. (Barnes 1982: 70 n.107), of his *vicennalia* on both 25 July 325 and 25 July 326 (*CIL* 1², p.268; Jerome, *Chronicle* 231ᵉ; *Descriptio consulum* 326) and of his *tricennalia* on both 25 July 335 and 23 July 336 (*Descriptio consulum* 335; Eusebius, *Panegyric of Constantine*, cf. Drake 1975).

2   The title of the speech is clear, but its authorship is not. Mynors prints what stood in the lost archetype of the surviving fifteenth-century manuscripts: *eiusdem magistri* †*memet* † *Genethliacus Maximiani Augusti* (256), while Lassandro replaced *memet* with *Mamertini*, which stands in one of the surviving manuscripts (1992: 331). Otto Seeck offered two conjectural supplements for the obviously corrupt *memet*. In his entry for Eumenius in Pauly-Wissowa, he supplemented the ascription *Item eiusdem <...Mamertini v(iri) p(erfectissimi)> magistri mem<oriae> et <rhetoris latini>*, leaving a space for the *gentilicium* of Mamertinus, which is unknown (1907: 1106). This conjecture is recorded with minor inaccuracies in their critical apparatus by Mynors and by Palladini & Fedeli 1976: 227, and it is accepted by Nixon & Rodgers 1994: 10, 81. Earlier, however, Seeck had suggested the following reconstruction of the heading to the speech, which he argued to reproduce authentic information (1888: 714):

> *Item eiusdem <Mamertini>*
> *magistri mem(oriae) et < com(itis) ord(inis) primi>*
> *genethliacus Maximiani Augusti.*

If Seeck's first thoughts of 1888, which seem preferable to his second, were correct, then Mamertinus' title would provide a parallel for Jacques Moreau's emendation of Constantine's title in 305 according to Lactantius, *Mort. Pers.* 18.10: *tribunus <et comes> ordinis primi*, cf. Chapter 3).

Seeck, it should be noted, attributed all the eight speeches delivered between 289 and 313 (*Pan. Lat.* 5–12 [2–9]) to Eumenius (1888 713–726; 1907: 1105–1108). That cannot be: the only one of the eight speeches of which Eumenius is the undisputed author is *Pan. Lat.* 9[4 = 5 Galletier], and it differs from all the other eleven speeches in the whole collection in not being either a panegyric or delivered before an emperor. For a careful discussion of whether the speech of 291 is in fact by the same author as the anonymously transmitted speech of 289, as the heading implies, see Rees 2002: 193–204.

3   From Barnes 1996b: 539–542.

4   The speech was delivered on 25 July 311 (*Pan. Lat.* 5[8].13.1–2: *o lustrum quod merito hanc imperii tui aequavit aetatem! ... quinquennalia tua nobis, sed iam perfecta, celebranda sunt*). Despite Baglivi 1977; Chastagnol 1980; 1983, the evidence clearly indicates that Constantine celebrated both the beginning and the end of his anniversary years – not

only his *quinquennalia* on 25 July 310 and 311, but his *vicennalia* both on 25 July 325 in Nicomedia and on 25 July 336 in Constantinople and his *tricennalia* on 25 July in both 335 and 336.

5 What Ausonius means by *Athenaei …loci* is unclear: see Green 1991: 349–350, who rejects Evelyn White's translation and construes the phrase as a reference to Athens itself. Green also holds that Nazarius may have taught in Bordeaux when Ausonius was young (Green 1985: 504).

6 Nazarius was claimed as a covert Christian by Liebeschuetz 1979: 289–290, while Bowersock construed his speech as 'the pagan response to Constantine's espousal of Christianity,' citing the array of traditional deities invoked in *Pan. Lat.* 4[10].14.1–3 (1986: 302).

APPENDIX D: EUSEBIUS, *ON EASTER*
(*DE SOLLEMNITATE PASCHALI*)

1 Eusebius throughout assumes the equivalence, even identity of the Jewish Passover and the Christian Easter.

2 This view of the relationship between the Mosaic dispensation and Christianity, which recurs later in this and in Chapter 4, permeates Eusebius' thinking (Barnes 1981: 127, 171, 285). For the wording used here, compare *General Elementary Introduction* 1.9 (*PG* 22.1052B): τυπικῶς τε αὐτοῖς καὶ εἰκονικῶς τὰ θεῖα διὰ συμβόλων ἠνίχθαι; 3.23 (*PG* 22.1148B): τούτων δὲ καὶ κατὰ τὴν ἱστορίαν περὶ τ... τότε Ἰησοῦν τυπικῶς ὡς εἰκὸς γεγενημένων; *Commentary on Psalm 80.4* (*PG* 23.973D): οὗτος (sc. God) ἦν ὁ ταῦτα καὶ διὰ Μωϋσέως εἰκονικῶς τῷ λαῷ πράττειν διαταξάμενος; *Commentary on Psalm 79* (*PG* 23.956D): ταῦτα δὲ τυπικῶς παρὰ Μωϋσέι διὰ χρυσοῦ πεποιημένα.

3 The original and etymological meaning of διαβατήρια was 'offerings before crossing a border or river,' but Philo used the word to mean Passover (LSJ 390) and Origen stated that πάσχα means διαβατήρια (*Contra Celsum* 8.22, p. 239.22 Koetschau). Eusebius has a word-play on the two meanings.

4 ὃ δὴ Migne] ὃ δὲ Mai.

5 I read τροφήν in V; Mai, followed by Migne, reads τρυφήν and translates *deliciis merito divinis deliciamur*.

6 I have tried to reproduce Eusebius' pun on the noun πικρίδες (= herbs) and the adjective πικρός (= bitter).

7 V has τροφή, which Mai corrected to τροπή.

8 μάστιγες Mai, Migne] V seems to have μάστυγες.

9 ὥσπερ ἐν ὑποδήμασι δή V Migne] δέ Mai.

10 The whole sentence is an expansion and rewriting of Exodus 12.11:

οὕτως δὲ φάγεσθε αὐτό· αἱ ὀσφύες ὑμῶν περιεζωσμέναι, καὶ τὰ ὑποδήματα ἐν τοῖς ποσὶν ὑμῶν, καὶ αἱ βακτηρίαι ἐν ταῖς χερσὶν ὑμῶν· καὶ ἔδεσθε αὐτὸ μετὰ σπουδῆς· πασχα ἐστὶν κυρίῳ (LXX).

And thus shall ye eat it; with your loins girded, your shoes on your feet, and your staff in your hand; and ye shall eat it in haste: it is the Lord's passover (Authorized version).

11   On this passage, see Salaville 1929: 260–271, who documents the joint celebration in the fourth century of both the bodily ascension of Christ into heaven and the descent of the Holy Spirit on the Apostles (the later Pentecost). Eusebius makes the same equation when stating the day of Constantine's death: 'the utterly sacred and holy Pentecost, honoured with seven weeks and sealed with a single day, on which divine words describe the ascension into heaven of the common Savior <of all> and the descent of the Holy Spirit among men' (*VC* 4.64.1).

12   Or 'limited': on the meaning of the verb περιγράφω in Christian texts, where it is often applied to the Incarnation, see Lampe 1063.

13   That the circumcision of male infants on the eighth day after their birth, as prescribed in the Torah (Genesis 17.9–14, 21.4; Leviticus 12.3), was performed with an iron knife is also asserted by Gregory of Elvira, *Tractatus Origenis* 4.2 (*CCSL* 69.27) and Zeno of Verona, *Tractatus* 1.3[13].1.2, 11.21 (*PL* 11.345, 353 = *CCSL* 22.24, 29).

14   The Greek of the whole sentence reads:

πλὴν τοῦ θεοφιλεστάτου βασιλέως, μέσου τῆς ἁγίας συνόδου προκαθεζομένου, ὡς ἤχθη εἰς μέσον τὸ περὶ τοῦ Πάσχα ζήτημα, ἐλέγετο μὲν ὅσα καὶ ἐλέγετο.

Girardet 1993: 347–348 translates the main clause of the Greek very differently, so that his German version of the whole sentence reads: 'Doch als das Problem des Osterfestes zur Sprache kam, hat der von Gott in höchstem Maße geliebte Kaiser – (inmitten der heilige Synode als der Vorsitzende) – gesagt, was er gesagt hat.' But the verbs in ἐλέγετο μὲν ὅσα καὶ ἐλέγετο are grammatically in either the middle or passive voice, not in the active, and hence cannot mean 'he said what he said.' On the other hand, Girardet is right to insist that the verb προκαθέζομαι must mean 'preside over:' Eusebius' usage is clear and consistent (*HE* 3.23.13, quoting Clement of Alexandria, *Quis dives salvetur?* 42.8; *Commentary on Psalms* 57.7–8, 90.1 [*PG* 23.525.46; 984.23]; *VC* 2.59.1, 3.58.4, 3.62.1).

15   The Greek has the colorless ποιῶ = do.

16   Literally 'the day of Preparation' (παρασκευή).

17   Ἰουδαίους γε μήν … φημί V] μέν Mai, Migne.

APPENDIX E: NICAGORAS IN EGYPT

1   Baillet's edition supersedes that of Wilhelm Dittenberger *OGIS* 720, 721: although Dittenberger provides valuable notes, he was unaware of the consular date, which was first published by Baillet 1922: 283, and he included the extra line '<May> Plato <be> gracious to us here also,' which need not belong with the inscriptions of Nicagoras (Baillet 1926: 294 no. 1263).

APPENDIX F: PRAXAGORAS OF ATHENS

1   Praxagoras' name is given as 'Protagoras' by Amerise 2008: 29. The erroneous name is duly repeated in the index to the volume.

2   I offer a new English translation because I do not consider the translation by S. Lieu in Lieu & Montserrat 1998: 7–8 sufficiently accurate.

3   Jacoby stated the terminus of Praxagoras' work as '326?' (1930: 662) – apparently because he believed that the construction of Constantinople began in that year.

APPENDIX G: AN ANONYMOUS PANEGYRIC OF CONSTANTINE

1   Registered in R. A. Pack, *The Greek and Latin Texts from Greco-Roman Egypt* (Ann Arbor, 1965) as nos. 2573, 2531.

2   The Roman and Arabic numerals denote the pages and lines of the papyrus in Guida's numeration.

3   I omit the otiose καί before ὥσπερ.

4   I accept Paul Maas' supplement ἐξαπτομέ- [νας ἀναξίους νομίζων (or δοκῶν)] ἑαυτοῦ σε- [in lines 23–24 (reported by Oellacher 1932: 118–119).

5   The supplements ἀσκεῖν and ἐξουσίαν are due to Bidez 1906: 166, who commented perceptively 'est-ce d'un roi qu'on parle?'

6   Supplementing π[ροπέρω]ν βα- σιλέων in lines 20–21.

7   Reading ἑ[καστῷ] before τούτων in line 20.

8   Guida marks a gap of about four letters in line 25: ὑμῖν fills it perfectly.

9   The noun governing ἀναλωμά-τ[ων] in lines 34–35 is irretrievably lost.

10 Guida prints ἐπιγ[ν]ώ-[μων] in lines 35–36, but with dots indicating uncertainty under the epsilon, gamma and omega: for ἐπιγνώμων as a noun meaning 'arbiter, umpire, judge,' see LSJ⁹ 627.

BIBLIOGRAPHY

Listed below under (A) are (i) the editions of ancient authors and sources which I have used and quoted in the present work, and (ii) the best available published translation into English, incuding some of dubious accuracy. I have alerted readers wherever I print or translate a text different from that in the edition listed here. Other editions of these authors and texts and editions of some other authors and texts are entered below under the name(s) of their author(s) in (B), which registers modern works to which I have referred, but is in no way intended as a complete or even a selective bibliography of scholarly writing about Constantine.

A. ANCIENT SOURCES

Anonymous Greek panegyric of Constantine
Guida, A. 1990. *Un anonimo panegirico per l'imperatore Giuliano. (Anon.* Paneg. Iul. Imp.). *Studi e Testi per il Corpus dei papiri filosofici greci e latini* 4. *Accademia Toscana di Scienze e Lettere "La Columbaria": Studi* 107 (Florence).
Translated in Appendix F.

Chronicon Paschale
L. Dindorf, *Chronicon Paschale. Corpus Scriptorum Historiae Byzantinae* 16, 17 (Bonn, 1832).
Michael Whitby & Mary Whitby, *Translated Texts for Historians* 7 (Liverpool, 1989).

Codex Theodosianus
T. Mommsen, *Theodosiani Libri XVI cum Constitutionibus Sirmondianis* 1.2 (Berlin, 1904; reprinted 1954, 1962).

C. Pharr, *The Theodosian Code and Novels and the Sirmondian Constitutions. A Translation with Commentary, Glossary, and Bibliography* (Princeton, 1952, reprinted 2001).

Constantine, *Speech to the Assembly of the Saints*
I. A. Heikel, *Eusebius Werke* 1. GCS 7 (Leipzig, 1902), 151–192, whose reports of manuscript readings in more than forty passages are corrected by Winkelmann 1984: 6–7. References to the *Speech* are given by chapter and section and/or by page(s) and line(s) in Heikel's edition.
M. J. Edwards, *Constantine and Christendom. The Oration to the Saints; The Greek and Latin Accounts of the Discovery of the Cross. The Edict of Constantine to Pope Silvester. TTL* 39 (Liverpool: 2003), 1–62.

Descriptio consulum (otherwise known as *Consularia Constantinopolitana*)
R. W. Burgess, *The Chronicle of Hydatius and the* Consularia Constantinopolitana. *Two Contemporary Accounts of the Final Years of the Roman Empire* (Oxford, 1993), 215–245. (References are given by the Julian equivalents of the consular years.)

Epitome (de Caesaribus)
F. Pichlmayr, *Sexti Aurelii Victoris liber de Caesaribus* (Leipzig, 1911; reprinted with addenda and corrections by R. Gründel, 1961), 131–176.

Eusebius, *Ecclesiastical History*
E. Schwartz, *Eusebius Werke* 2. GCS 9.1 (Leipzig, 1902), 9.2 (1908).
P. L. Maier, *Eusebius: The Church History* (Grand Rapids, MI, 1989).

Eusebius, *Life of Constantine*
F. Winkelman, *Eusebius, Über das Leben des Kaisers Konstantin. Eusebius, Werke* I.1. GCS 57 (Berlin, 1975; revised edition 1991, reprinted 2008).
Averil Cameron & S. G. Hall, *Eusebius: Life of Constantine* (Oxford, 1999).

Eusebius, *Panegyric of Constantine* and *Speech on the Church of the Holy Sepulchre*
I. A. Heikel, *Eusebius Werke* 1. GCS 7 (Leipzig, 1902), 193–259, with revisions to the apparatus criticus by Winkelmann 1984: 4–6.
H. A. Drake, *In Praise of Constantine. A Historical Study and New Translation of Eusebius' Tricennial Orations. University of California Publications: Classical Studies* 15 (Berkeley, 1976).

Eusebius, *On Easter*
For editions and a complete English translation, see Appendix C.

Eutropius, *Breviarium*
C. Santini, *Eutropii Breviarium ab urbe condita* (Leipzig, 1979; reprinted Stuttgart & Leipzig, 1992).
H. W. Bird, *The Breviarium ab Urbe condita of Eutropius. Translated Texts for Historians* 14 (Liverpool, 1993).
Gelasius of Caesarea (*CPG* 3521)
Fragments as reconstructed by Winkelmann 1966: 348–356.

Jerome, *Chronicle*
R. Helm, *Eusebius Werke 7: Die Chronik des Hieronymus*[2]. *GCS* 47 (Berlin, 1956) (All references are given by page and the letter which Helm attaches to the relevant entry or entries).

Lactantius, *Divine Institutes*
S. Brandt, *L. Caeli Lactanti opera omnia* 1. *CSEL* 19 (Vienna, 1890).
E. Heck & A. Wlosok, *Lactantius: Divinarum Institutionum libri septem* 1: *Libri I et II* (Munich & Leipzig, 2005).
A. (J.) Bowen & P. (D. A.) Garnsey, *Lactantius: Divine Institutes. Translated Texts for Historians* 40 (Liverpool, 2003).

Lactantius, *On the Deaths of the Persecutors*
J. L. Creed, *Lactantius: De Mortibus Persecutorum* (Oxford, 1984) (text and translation).

Lex Dei
Lex dei quam praecepit dominus ad Moysen (conventionally known as the *Mosaicarum et Romanarum legum collatio*)
FIRA 2.543–589
M. Hyamson, *Mosaicarum et romanarum legum collatio* (London & New York, 1913; reprinted Buffalo, 1997), 57–149.

Optatus
K. Ziwsa, *S. Optati Milevetani libri vii. CSEL* 26 (Vienna, 1893).
M. J. Edwards, *Optatus: Against the Donatists. Translated Texts for Historians* 27 (Liverpool, 1997).

Origo Constantini Imperatoris (Anonymi Valesiani Pars Prior)
J. Moreau, *Excerpta Valesiana* (Leipzig, 1961; reprinted with addenda and corrections by V. Velkov, 1968), 1–10.
J. Stevenson, 'The Origin of Constantine,' in Lieu & Montserrat 1996: 43–48.

Palladas: in
H. Beckby, *Anthologia Graeca: griechisch-deutsch* (Munich, 1957–1958; revised edition, Munich, 1965).
W. R. Paton, *The Greek Anthology. Loeb Classical Library* 67–68, 82–84 (London & New York, 1916–1918).

Panegyrici Latini
R. A. B. Mynors, *Panegyrici Latini* (Oxford, 1964).
C. E. V. Nixon & B. S. Rogers, *In Praise of Later Roman Emperors: The Panegyrici Latini. Transformation of the Classical Heritage* 21 (Berkeley, Los Angeles & London, 1994).

Philostorgius, *Ecclesiastical History*
J. Bidez, *Philostorgius Kirchengeschichte. GCS* 21 (Leipzig, 1913; 2nd and 3rd editions revised by F. Winkelmann, Berlin, 1972 & 1981).

P. Amidon, *Philostorgius: Church History. Writings from the Greco-Roman World* 23 (Leiden & Boston, 2007).

Praxagoras

F. Jacoby, *Die Fragmente der griechischen Historiker* 2: *Zeitgeschichte* B (Berlin, 1929), 948–949 no. 219.
Appendix F.

Publilius Optatianus Porfyrius

G. Polara, *Publilii Optatiani Porfyrii Carmina. Corpus Scriptorum Latinorum Paravianum* (Turin, 1973).

Rufinus, *Ecclesiastical History*

T. Mommsen, in E. Schwartz, *Eusebius Werke* 2. *GCS* 9.1 (Leipzig, 1902), 9.2 (1908).
P. Amidon, *The Church History of Rufinus, Books 10 and 11* (New York, 1997).

(Aurelius) Victor, *Caesares / De Caesaribus*

F. Pichlmayr, *Sexti Aurelii Voctoris liber de Caesaribus* (Leipzig, 1911; reprinted with addenda and corrections by R. Gründel, 1961), 75–129.
H. W. Bird, *Aurelius Victor: De Caesaribus. Translated Texts for Historians* 17 (Liverpool, 1994).

Zosimus

F. Paschoud, *Zosime: Histoire Nouvelle* 1² (Paris, 2000); 2.1–2 (1979); 3.1 (1986); 3.2 (1989).
R. T. Ridley, *Zosimus: New History. Byzantina Australiensia* 2 (Canberra, 1982; reprinted 1984).

B. MODERN WORKS OTHER THAN EDITIONS, TRANSLATIONS AND COMMENTARIES LISTED UNDER A

Abramowski, L., 1975. 'Die Synode von Antiochien 324/25 und ihr Symbol,' *Zeitschrift für Kirchengeschichte* 86: 356–366.
Alföldi, A., 1926. 'Die Donaubrücke Konstantins des Grossen und verwandte historische Darstellungen auf spätrömischen Münzen,' *Zeitschrift für Numismatik* 36: 161–174.
—, 1948. *The Conversion of Constantine and Pagan Rome*, trans. H. Mattingly (Oxford; reprinted with an added prefatory note in 1969).
—, 1959. 'Cornuti. A Teutonic Contingent in the Service of Constantine the Great and its Decisive Role in the Battle of the Milvian Bridge,' *Dumbarton Oaks Papers* 13: 171–179.
Alföldi, M.-R., 1964. 'Die Sol-Comes- Münze vom Jahre 325: Neues zur Bekehrung Constantins,' *Mullus: Festschrift für Theodor Klauser. Jahrbuch für Antike und Christentum,* Ergänzungsband 1 (Münster), 10–16.
Amelotti, M., 1966. *Il Testamento romano attraverso le prassi documentali. Studi e testi di papirologia* 1 (Florence).
Amerise, M. 2008. 'Das Bild Konstantins des Großen in der *Bibliothéke* des Photius,' in Goltz & Schlange-Schöningen 2008: 23–38.

Ananian, P., 1961. 'La data e le circostanze della consecrazione de S. Gregorio Illuminatore,' *Le Muséon* 74: 43–73, 319–360.

Anderson, W. B., 1965. *Sidonius: Poems and Letters* 2 (London & Cambridge, MA).

Andreotti, R., 1964. 'Contributo alla discussion del rescritto costantiniano di Hispellum,' *Atti del I° Convegno di Studi Umbri* (Perugia), 249–290.

Arjava, A., 1988. 'Divorce in Later Roman Law,' *Arctos* 22: 6–21.

—, 1996. *Women and Law in Late Antiquity* (London).

Athanassiadi, P., 1991. 'The Fate of Oracles in Late Antiquity: Didyma and Delphi,' *Δελτίον Χριστιανικῆς Ἀρχαιολογικῆς Ἐτερείας* / *Deltion Christianikês Archaiologikês Etereias*[4] 15 (1989/90, pub. 1991), 271–278.

Baehrens, E., 1874. *XII Panegyrici Latini* (Leipzig).

Baehrens, W., 1911. *XII Panegyrici Latini* (Leipzig).

Baglivi, N., 1977. 'Ricerche sul dies imperii e sulla celebrazione dei quinquennalia di Costantino I,' *Koinonia* 1: 53–138.

—, 1984. 'Paneg. IX(12), 26,5: attualità ideologica e problem interpretative,' *Orpheus*, N. S. 5: 32–67.

Baillet, J. 1922. 'Constantin et le dadouque d'Éleusis,' *Comptes Rendus de l'Académie des Inscriptions et Belles Lettres* 1922: 282–296.

—, 1926. *Inscriptions grecques et latines des tombeaux des rois ou syringes. Mémoires publiés par les membres de l'Institut français d'archéologie orientale du Caire* 42 (Cairo).

Barceló, P. A., 1988. 'Die Religionspolitik Kaiser Constantins des Grossen vor der Schlacht an der Milvischen Brücke (312),' *Hermes* 116: 76–94.

—, 2001. 'Constantins Visionen: Zwischen Apollo und Christus,' *Humanitas – Beiträge zur antiken Kulturgeschichte. Festschrift für Gunther Gottlieb zum 65. Geburtstag*, ed. P. Barceló & V. Rosenberger (Munich), 45–61. Reprinted in Schlange-Schöningen 2007: 133–149.

Barnes, T. D., 1970. 'The Lost Kaisergeschichte and the Latin Historical Tradition,' *Bonner Historia-Augusta-Colloquium 1968/1969* (Bonn), 13–43. Reprinted as Barnes 1984a, no. IV.

—, 1971. *Tertullian. A Historical and Literary Study* (Oxford; 2nd edition with postscript, 1985).

—, 1973. 'Lactantius and Constantine,' *Journal of Roman Studies* 63: 29–46. Reprinted as Barnes 1984a, no. VI.

—, 1975a. 'The Beginnings of Donatism,' *Journal of Theological Studies*, N. S. 26: 13–22. Reprinted as Barnes 1984a, no. VIII.

—, 1975b. 'Two Senators under Constantine,' *Journal of Roman Studies* 65: 40–49. Reprinted as Barnes 1984a, no. IX.

—, 1975c. 'Publilius Optatianus Porfyrius,' *American Journal of Philology* 96: 173–186. Reprinted as Barnes 1984a, no. X.

—, 1975d. 'The Unity of the Verona List,' *Zeitschrift für Papyrologie und Epigraphik* 16: 275–278.

—, 1975e. '*Patricii* under Valentinian III,' *Phoenix* 29: 155–170.

—, 1976a. 'Imperial Campaigns, A. D. 285–311,' *Phoenix* 30: 174–193. Reprinted as Barnes 1984a, no. XII.

—, 1976b. 'The Emperor Constantine's Good Friday Sermon,' *Journal of Theological Studies*, N. S. 27: 414–423

—, 1976c. 'Sossianus Hierocles and the Antecedents of the Great Persecution,' *Harvard Studies in Classical Philology* 80: 239–252.

—, 1976d. 'Three Imperial Edicts,' *Zeitschrift für Papyrologie und Epigraphik* 21: 275–281.

—, 1977. 'Two Speeches by Eusebius,' *Greek, Roman and Byzantine Studies* 18: 341–345. Reprinted as Barnes 1984a, no. XVI.

—, 1978a. 'Emperor and Bishops, A.D. 324–344: Some Problems,' *American Journal of Ancient History* 3: 53–75. Reprinted as Barnes 1984a, no. XVIII.

—, 1978b. 'A Correspondent of Iamblichus,' *Greek, Roman and Byzantine Studies* 19: 99–106. Reprinted as Barnes 1984a, no. XVII.

—, 1980. 'The Editions of Eusebius' *Ecclesiastical History*,' *Greek, Roman and Byzantine Studies* 21: 191–201. Reprinted as Barnes 1984, no. XX.

—, 1981. *Constantine and Eusebius* (Cambridge, MA).

—, 1982. *The New Empire of Diocletian and Constantine* (Cambridge, MA).

—, 1983. 'Between Theodosius and Justinian: Late Roman Prosopography,' *Phoenix* 37: 248–270.

—, 1984a. *Early Christianity and the Roman Empire* (London: Variorum Reprints).

—, 1984b. Constantine's Prohibition of Pagan Sacrifice,' *American Journal of Philology* 105: 69–72.

—, 1985a. 'Constantine and the Christians of Persia,' *Journal of Roman Studies* 75: 126–136.

—, 1985b. 'The Conversion of Constantine,' *Classical Views* 29: 371–393.

—, 1985c. 'Proconsuls of Africa, 337–392,' *Phoenix* 39: 144–153, 273–274.

—, 1986. 'The Constantinian Reformation,' *Ernest Crake Memorial Lectures 1984* (Sackville, New Brunswick), 39–57.

—, 1987a. 'Regional Prefectures,' *Bonner Historia-Augusta-Colloquium 1984/1985* (Bonn), 13–23. Reprinted as Barnes 1994a.

—, 1987b. 'Himerius and the Fourth Century,' *Classical Philology* 82: 206–225. Reprinted as Barnes 1994a.

—, 1989a. 'Pagans and Christians in the Reign of Constantius,' in Dihle 1989: 301–337. Pages 322–337 are reprinted as Barnes 1994a, no. VIII.

—, 1989b. 'Panegyric, History and Hagiography in Eusebius' *Life of Constantine*,' *The Making of Orthodoxy. Essays in Honour of Henry Chadwick*, ed. R. Williams (Cambridge), 94–123. Reprinted as Barnes 1994a.

—, 1989c. 'Jerome and the *Origo Constantini Imperatoris*,' *Phoenix* 43: 158–161.

—, 1990. Review of A. Camplani, *Le lettere festali di Atanasio di Alessandria. Studio Storicocritico* (Rome, 1989). *Journal of Theological Studies*, N. S. 41: 258–264.

—, 1992a. 'Praetorian Prefects, 337–361,' *Zeitschrift für Papyrologie und Epigraphik* 94: 249–260. Reprinted as Barnes 1994a, no. 94

—, 1992b. 'The Constantinian Settlement,' *Eusebius, Judaism and Christianity*, ed. Gohei Hata & H. W. Attridge (Detroit), 635–657. Reprinted as Barnes 1994a.

—, 1993a. *Athanasius and Constantius. Theology and Politics in the Constantinian Empire* (Cambridge, MA).

—, 1993b. Review of Scheid 1991. *Phoenix* 47: 81–87.

—, 1994a. *From Eusebius to Augustine. Selected Papers 1982–1993* (Aldershot).

—, 1994b. 'The Religious Affiliation of Consuls and Prefects, 317–361,' Barnes 1994a, no. VII.

—, 1994c. 'The Two Drafts of Eusebius' *Life of Constantine*,' Barnes 1994a, no. XII.

—, 1994d. 'Scholarship or Propaganda? Porphyry *Against the Christians* and its Historical Setting,' *Bulletin of the Institute of Classical Studies* 38: 55–70.

—, 1995. 'Statistics and the Conversion of the Roman Aristocracy,' *Journal of Roman Studies* 85: 135–147.

—, 1996a. 'Oppressor, Persecutor, Usurper: The Meaning of "Tyrannus" in the Fourth Century,' *Historiae Augustae Colloquia*, N. S. IV: *Colloquium Barcinonense MCMXCIII* (Bari), 53–63.

—, 1996b. 'Emperors, Panegyrics, Prefects, Provinces and Palaces,' *Journal of Roman Archaeology* 9: 532–552.

—, 1997a. 'Christentum und dynastische Politik (300–325),' *Usurpationen in der Spätantike*, ed. F. Paschoud & J. Szidat. *Historia Einzelschriften* 111 (Stuttgart), 99–109.

—, 1997b. 'Julian or Constantine? Observations on a Fragmentary Imperial Panegyric,' *Akten des 21. Internationalen Papyrologen-congresses in Berlin 1995*, ed. B. Kramer, W. Luppe, H. Maehler & G. Poethke. *Archiv für Papyrusforschung*, Beiheft 3 (Leipzig), 1: 57–60.

—, 1998a. *Ammianus Marcellinus and the Representation of Historical Reality* (Ithaca)

—, 1998b. 'Constantine and Christianity: Ancient Evidence and Modern Interpretations,' *Zeitschrift für Antikes Christentum* 2: 274–294.

—, 1999a. 'The Wife of Maximinus,' *Classical Philology* 94: 459–460.

—, 1999b. Review of Mühlenberg 1998. *Zeitschrift für Antikes Christentum* 3: 289–291.

—, 2001. 'Constantine's *Speech to the Assembly of the Saints*: Place and Date of Delivery,' *Journal of Theological Studies*, N. S. 52: 26–36.

—, 2002. 'From Toleration to Repression: The Evolution of Constantine's Religious Policies,' *Scripta Classica Israelica* 21: 189–207.

—, 2004. Review of Edwards 2003. *Journal of Theological Studies*, N. S. 55: 351–354.

—, 2005a. 'The Sack of the Temple in Josephus and Tacitus,' *Flavius Josephus and Flavian Rome*, ed. J. Edmondson, S. Mason and J. Rives (Oxford), 129–144.

—, 2005b. 'Demessus, not Damascus,' *Zeitschrift für Papyrologie und Epigraphik* 151: 266–268.

—, 2005c. 'The Date of the Martyrdom of Lucian of Antioch,' *Zeitschrift für Antikes Christentum* 9: 350–353.

—, 2006. 'The Young Constantine as Judged by his Contemporaries,' in Demandt & Englemann 2006: 13–20.

—, 2007a. 'Constantine after Seventeen Hundred Years: The Cambridge Companion, the York Exhibition and a Recent Biography,' *International Journal of the Classical Tradition* 14: 185–220.

—, 2007b. 'The New Critical Edition of Athanasius' *Defence before Constantius*,' *Zeitschrift für Antikes Christentum* 11: 378–401.

—, 2008. 'Aspects of the Severan Empire I: Severus as a New Augustus,' *New England Classical Journal* 35: 251–267.

—, 2009a. 'Aspects of the Severan Empire II: Christians in Roman Provincial Society,' *New England Classical Journal* 36: 3–19.

—, 2009b. 'The Exile and Returns of Arius,' *Journal of Theological Studies*, N. S 60: 109–129.

—, 2010a. *Early Christian Hagiography and Roman History. Tria Corda. Jena Lectures on Judaism, Antiquity and Christianity*, ed. W. Ameling, K.-W. Niebuhr & M. Vielberg (Tübingen).

—, 2010b. 'Eusebius of Caesarea,' *Early Christian Thinkers. The Lives and Legacies of Twelve Key Figures*, ed. P. Foster (London), 236–264. Reprinted from *Expository Times* 121 (2009), 1–14.

—, 2010c. 'The Letter of Eusebius to Constantia (*CPG* 3503),' *Studia Patristica* 46: 313–317.

—, 2010d. 'Maxentius and Diocletian,' *Classical Philology* 105: 318–322.

Barnes, T. D. & J. Vanderspoel, 1984. 'Julian on the Sons of Fausta,' *Phoenix* 38: 175–176.

Barrett, A. A., 2008. *Lives of the Caesars*, ed. A. A. Barrett (Malden, MA, Oxford & Carlton, Victoria).

Barsanti, C., 1992. 'Costantinopoli: testimonianze archeologiche di età costantiniana,' in Bonamente & Fusco 1992: 115–150.

Bassett, S., 2004. *The Urban Image of Late Antique Constantinople* (Cambridge).

Baynes, N. H., 1931. *Constantine the Great and the Christian Church* (London). Also published in the *Proceedings of the British Academy* 15 (1929, pub. 1931), 341–442 (a Raleigh Lecture on History read to the British Academy on 12 March 1930 with the addition of more than seventy pages of notes). 2nd ed. with a preface by H. Chadwick (Oxford, 1972).

—, 1939. 'Constantine,' *Cambridge Ancient History* 12. *The Imperial Crisis and Recovery A.D. 193–324*, ed. S. A. Cook, F. E. Adcock, M. P. Charlesworth & N. H. Baynes (Cambridge), 678–699.

Beck, R., 2007. *A Brief History of Ancient Astrology* (Malden, MA & Oxford).

Berchem, D. van, 1952. *L'armée de Dioclétien er la réforme constantinienne. Institut Français d'Archéologie de Béyrouth: Bibliothèque Archéologique et Historique* (Paris).

Berger, A. 2003. 'Konstantinopel, die erste christliche Metropol?,' *Die spätantike Stadt und ihre Christianisierung. Symposion vom 14. bis 16. Februar 2000 in Halle/Saale*, ed. G. Brands & H.-G. Severin (Wiesbaden), 63–71. Reprinted in Schlange-Schöningen 2007: 204–215.

Bergmann, M., 2006. 'Konstantin und der Sonnengott. Die Aussagen der Bildzeugnisse,' in Demandt & Engeman 2006: 143–162.

Berrens, S., 2004, *Sonnenkult und Kaisertum von den Severen bis zu Constantin I. (193–337 n. Chr.). Historia Einzelschriften* 185 (Stuttgart).

Bidez, J. 1906. 'Fragments d'un philosophe ou d'un rhéteur grec inconnu,' *Revue de philologie* 30: 161–172.

—, 1925. 'Amiens, ville natale de l'empereur Magnence,' *Revue des études anciennes* 27: 312–318.

—, 1930. *La vie de l'empereur Julien* (Paris).

Bingen, J., 1999. 'L'épigraphie grecque de l'Égypte post-constantinienne,' *XI Congresso Internazionale di Epigrafia greca e latine, Roma 18–24 settembre 1997: Atti* (Rome) 2. 613–624.

Biondi, B., 1945. 'Leges populi Romani,' *Acta Divi Augusti* 1, ed. S. Riccobono (Rome), 101–223.

Birley, A. R., 1988. *The African Emperor: Septimius Severus* (London).

Blackburn, B. & Holford Strevens, L., 1999. *Oxford Companion to the Year*, ed. B. Blackburn & L. Holford Strevens (Oxford).

Blanchetière, F. 1983. 'L'évolution du statut des Juifs sous la dynastie constantinienne,' in Frézouls 1983: 127–141.

Bleckmann, B., 1992. 'Pagane Visionen Konstantins in der Chronik des Johannes Zonaras,' in Bonamente & Fusco 1992: 151–170.

—, 1996. *Konstantin der Große* (Reinbek bei Hamburg).

—, 1997. 'Der Kaiser als Prediger,' *Hermes* 125: 183–202.

—, 2006. 'Sources for the History of Constantine,' in Lenski 2006a: 14–31.

—, 2007a. 'Konstantin der Große: Reformer der römischen Welt,' in Schuller & Wolff 2007: 26–68.

—, 2007b. 'Einleitung' in *Eusebius von Caesarea, De Vita Constantini / Über das Leben Konstantins*, trans. H. Schneider. *Fontes Christiani* 83 (Turnhout).

Bleicken, J., 1992. *Konstantin der Große und die Christen. Überlegungen zur konstantinischen Wende. Historische Zeitschrift*, Beiheft, N. F. 15 (Munich). Pages 1–23, 34–43 and 48–66 are reprinted in Schlange-Schöningen 2007: 64–108.

—, 1993. *Colloquium aus Anlass des 80. Geburtstages von Alfred Heuss*, ed. J. Bleicken. *Frankfurter Althistorische Studien* 13 (Kallmünz).

Boatwright, M. T., D. J. Gargola & R. J. A. Talbert, 2006. *A Brief History of the Romans* (New York and Oxford: Oxford University Press).

Bolhuis, A., 1950. *Vergilius' Vierde Ecloga in de Oratio Constantini ad sanctorum coetum* (diss. Amsterdam, publ. Ermelo, 1950).

Bonamente, G., 1992. 'Sulla confisca dei beni mobili dei templi in epoca costantiniana,' in Bonamente & Fusco 1992: 171–201.

—, 2003. 'Minor Latin Historians of the Fourth Century A. D.,' in Marasco 2003: 85–125.

Bonamente, G. & F. Fusco, 1992, 1993. *Costantino il Grande dall'antichità all'umanesimo. Colloquio sul Cristianesimo nel mondo antico Macerata 18–20 Dicembre 1990* (Macerata), 1, 2.

Bonfils, G. de, 1981. *Il comes et quaestor nell'età della dinastia costantiniana. Pubblicazioni della Facoltà Giuridica dell'Università di Bari* (Naples).

Booth, A. D., 1978. 'Notes on Ausonius' *Professores*,' *Phoenix* 32: 235–249.

Boschung, D., & W. Eck, 2006. *Die Tetrarchie. Ein neues Regierungssystem und seine mediale Präsentation*, ed. D. Boschung & W. Eck (Wiesbaden).

Bowersock, G. W., 1986.' From Emperor to Bishop: The Self-Conscious Transformation of Political Power in the Fourth Century A.D.,' *Classical Philology* 81: 298–307.

—, 2005. 'Peter and Constantine,' *St. Peter's in the Vatican*, ed. W. Tronzo (Cambridge, 2005), 5–15. This chapter is a more fully documented version of the essat published under the same title in Carrié & Lizzi Testa 2002: 209–217.

Bowman, A. K., P. Garnsey & Averil Cameron (eds.), 2005. *Cambridge Ancient History*[2] 12: *The Crisis of Empire A.D. 193–337* (Cambridge).

Bowra, C. M., 1959. 'Palladas and Christianity,' *Proceedings of the British Academy* 45: 255–267.

—, 1960. 'Palladas and the Converted Olympians,' *Byzantinische Zeitschrift* 53: 1–7.

Bram, J. R., 1975. *Ancient Astrology. Theory and Practice* (Park Ridge, NJ).

Brandt, H. 1998. *Geschichte der römischen Kaiserzeit. Von Diokletian und Konstantin bis zum Ende der konstantinischen Dynastie (284–363)* (Berlin).

—, 2006. *Konstantin der Grosse. Der erste christliche Kaiser. Eine Biographie* (Munich).

Brennecke, Heil, von Stockhausen & Wintjes, 2007. See Abbreviations, s. v. *Dokument(e)*.

Bringmann, K., 1995. 'Die konstantinische Wende: Zum Verhältnis von politischer und religiöser Motivation,' *Historische Zeitschrift* 260: 21–47.

Broise, H., & J. Scheid, 1987. *Recherches archéologiques à La Magliana. Le Balneum des frères arvales. Roma antica* 1 (Rome).

Brosch, P., 2006. 'Zur Präsentation der Tetrarchie in den Panegyrici Latini,' in Boschung & Eck 2006: 83–101.

Broughton, T. R. S., 1951. *The Magistrates of the Roman Republic* 1: 509 B.C.–100 B.C. *Philological Monographs published by the American Philological Association* 15.1 (Lancaster, PA & Oxford).

Brown, P. (R. L.), 1971. *The World of Late Antiquity* (London).

Bruun, P., 1953. *The Constantinian Coinage of Arelate. Finska Fornminnesföreningens Tijdskrift* 52.2 (Helsinki).

—, 1958. 'The Disapperance of Sol from the Coins of Constantine,' *Arctos*, N. S. 2: 15–37. Reprinted in his *Studies in Constantinian Numismatics. Papers from 1945 to 1988*, ed. A. Tammisto. *Acta Instituti Romani Finlandiae* 12 (1991), 37–48.

—, 1961. *Studies in Constantinian Chronology. Numismatic Notes and Monographs* 146 (New York).

—, 1966. *The Roman Imperial Coinage 7: Constantine and Licinius A.D. 313–337* (London).

Bulić, F. 1920. 'Stridone luogo natale di S. Girolamo,' *Miscellanea Geronimiana. Scritti varii pubblicati nel XV centenario dalla morte di San Girolamo* (Rome), 253–330.

Burckhardt, J. 1853. J. Burckhardt, *Die Zeit Constantin's des Grossen* (Basle; second edition Leipzig, 1880, often reprinted).

—, 1949. *The Age of Constantine the Great*, trans. M. Hadas (London).

Burgess, R. W., 1996. 'The Date of the Persecution of Christians in the Army,' *Journal of Theological Studies*, N. S. 47: 157–158.

—, 1997. 'The Dates and Editions of Eusebius' *Chronici Canones* and *Historia Ecclesiastica*,' *Journal of Theological Studies*, N. S. 48: 471–504.

—, 1999a. *Studies in Eusebian and Post-Eusebian Chronography 1: The* Chronici Canones *of Eusebius of Caesarea: Structure, Content and Chronology, AD 282–325 Historia Einzelschriften* 135 (Stuttgart).

—, 1999b. 'The Dates of the Martyrdom of Simeon bar Sabba'e and the "Great Massacre",' *Analecta Bollandiana* 117: 9–66 (Appendix II: 'The Dates in Syriac Martyr Acts' [47–63] is by R. Mercier).

—, 2000. 'The Date of the Deposition of Eustathius of Antioch,' *Journal of Theological Studies*, N. S. 51: 150–160.

—, 2001. 'The Gallic Chronicle of 511: A New Critical Edition with a Brief Introduction,' *Society and Culture in Late Antique Gaul. Revisiting the Sources*, ed. R. W. Mathisen & D. Shanzer (Aldershot & Burlington, VT), 85–100.

—, 2008. 'The Summer of Blood. The "Great Massacre" of 337 and the Promotion of the Sons of Constantine,' *Dumbarton Oaks Papers* 62: 5–51.

Burn, A. E., 1925. *The Council of Nicaea. A Memorial for its Sixteenth Century* (London).

Cain, A., & N. Lenski, 2009. *The Power of Religion in Late Antiquity*, ed. A. Cain & N. Lenski (Farnham & Burlington, VT).

Callu, J.-P., 1992. 'La préface à l'Itineraire d'Alexandre,' in *De Tertullien aux Mozarabes. Mélanges offerts à Jacques Fontaine 1. Antiquité tardive et Christianisme ancien (III-IV siècles)* (Paris), 429–444.

Cameron, Alan, 1964. 'Palladas and the Nikai, *Journal of Hellenic Studies* 84: 54–62.

—, 1965a. 'Palladas and Christian Polemic,' *Journal of Roman Studies* 55: 17–30.

—, 1965b. 'Notes on Palladas,' *Classical Quarterly*, N.S. 15: 215–229.

—, 1993. *The Greek Anthology from Meleager to Planudes* (Oxford).

—, 2007. 'The Imperial Pontifex,' *Harvard Studies in Classical Philology* 103: 341–384.

—, 2011. *The Last Pagans of Rome* (New York).

Cameron, Averil, 1983a. 'Eusebius of Caesarea and the Rethinking of History,' *Tria Corda. Scritti in onore di Arnaldo Momigliano*, ed. E. Gabba. *Bibliotheca di Athenaeum* 1 (Como), 71–88.

—, 1983b. 'Constantinus Christianus', *Journal of Roman Studies* 73: 184–191.

—, 1997. 'Eusebius' *Vita Constantini* and the Construction of Constantine,' *Portraits. Biographical Representation in the Greek and Latin Literature of the Roman Empire*, ed. M. J. Edwards & S. (C. R.) Swain (Oxford), 145–174.

—, 2006a. 'Constantius and Constantine: An Exercise in Publicity,' in Hartley, Hawkes & Henig 2006: 18–30.

—, 2006b. 'Constantine and Christianity,' in Hartley, Hawkes & Henig 2006: 96–103.

Cameron, Averil & S. G. Hall. See (A) above, Eusebius.

Camplani, A., 1989. *Le lettere festali di Atanasio di Alessandria. Studio Storicocritico* (Rome).

—, 2003. *Le lettere festali.*

Campbell, B., 1984. *The Emperor and the Roman Army 31 B C.–A.D. 235* (Oxford).

Cantalamessa, R., 1978. *La Pasqua nella Chiesa antica. Tradito Christiana* 3 (Turin).

—, 1993. *Easter in the Early Church. An Anthology of Jewish and Early Christian Texts. Newly Translated from the Sources and Edited with Further Annotations*, J. M. Quigley & J. T. Lienhard (Collegeville, MI).

Carlos Saquete, J. 2000. 'Septimius Acindynus, corrector Tusciae et Umbriae. Notes on a new inscription from Augusta Emerita (Mérida, Spain),' *Zeitschrift für Papyrologie und Epigraphik* 129: 281–286.

Carrié, J.-M., & R. Lizzi Testa, 2003. '*Humana sapit.*' *Études d'Antiquité tardive offertes à Lellia Cracco Ruggini*, ed. J.-M. Carrié and R. Lizzi Testa, *Bibliothèque de l'Antiquité tardive* 3 (Turnhout).

Castritius, H., 1969. *Studien zu Maximinus Daia. Frankfurter Althistorische Studien* 2 (Kallmünz).

Cataudella, M. R., 2001. 'Costantino, Giuliano e l' *Oratio ad Sanctorum Coetum*,' *Klio* 83: 167–181.

Cecchelli, M., 1992. 'S. Marco a Piazza Venezia: una basilica romana del periodo costantiniano,' in Bonamente & Fusco 1992: 299–310.

Chadwick, H., 1966. *Early Christian Thought and the Classical Tradition. Studies in Justin, Clement and Origen* (1966) (Oxford).

—, 1972. See Baynes 1931.

—, 2000. *The Church in Ancient Society: From Galilee to Gregory the Great* (Oxford).

Champlin, E. J., 1982. 'Saint Gallicanus (Consul 317),' *Phoenix* 36: 71–76.

—, 1991. *Final Judgments. Duty and Emotion in Roman Wills 200 B.C.–A.D. 200* (Berkeley).

Chantraine, H., 1992. *Die Nachfolgeordnung Constantins des Grossen. Abhandlungen der Akademie der Wissenschaften zu Mainz*, Geistes- und sozialwissenschaftliche Klasse 1992, Nr. 7 (Stuttgart).

Chastagnol, A., 1968. 'Les préfets du prétoire de Constantin,' *Revue des études anciennes* 70: 321–352. Reprinted in his *L'Italie et l'Afrique au Bas-Empire. Études administrative et prosopographiques. Scripta varia* (Lille, 1987), 179–210.

—, 1980. 'À propos des quinquennalia de Constantin,' *Revue Numismatique*[6] 22: 106–119.

—, 1980–1981. 'Maximien Hercule à Rome,' *Bulletin de la Société nationale des Antiquaires de France* 1980–1981: 187–191. Reprinted in his *Aspects de l'Antiquité tardive*, ed. I. Tantillo. *Saggi di Storia Antica* 6 (Rome, 1994), 303–307.

—, 1981. 'L'inscription constantinienne d'Orcistus,' *Mélanges de l'École Française de Rome, Antiquité* 93: 381–416. Reprinted in *Aspects de l'Antiquité tardive* (1994), 105–142.

—, 1982. *L'évolution politique, sociale et économique du monde romain de Dioclétien à Julien. La mise en place du régime du Bas-Empire* (Paris).

—, 1983. 'Les jubilés impériaux de 260 à 337,' in Frézouls 1983: 11–25.

—, 1986. 'Les inscriptions africaines des préfets du prétoire de Constantin,' *L'Africa romana, Atti del III convegno di Sassari, 13–15 dicembre 1985*, ed. A. Mastino (Sassari, 1986), 263–273. Reprinted with addendum in *Aspects de l'Antiquité tardive* (1994), 81–92.

—, 1989. 'Un nouveau préfet du prétoire de Dioclétien: Aurelius Hemogenianus,' *Zeitschrift für papyrologie und Epigraphik* 78: 165–168. Reprinted in *Aspects de l'Antiquité tardive* (1994), 171–176.

Chausson, F., 2002. 'Une sœur de Constantin,' in Carrié & Lizzi Testa 2003: 131–135.

—, 2007. *Stemmata Aurea: Constantin, Justine, Théodose. Revendications généalogiques et idéologie imperiale au IVe siècle ap. J.-C.* Centro ricerche e documentazione sull'antichità classica: *Monografie* 26 (Rome).

Chiusi, T. J., 2007. 'Der Einfluß des Christentums auf die Gesetzgebung Konstantins,' in Girardet 2007a: 55–64.

Clauss, M., 1980. *Der magister officiorum in der Spätantike (4.-6. Jahrhundert). Das Amt und sein Einfluß auf die kaiserliche Politik. Vestigia* 32 (Munich).

— 1996. *Konstantin der Grosse und seine Zeit* (Munich).

Christol, M., & T. Drew-Bear, 1999. 'L'intitulatio de la constitution de Galère et ses collègues affichée à Sinope (CIL III 6769),' *Tyche* 14: 43–55.

Christodoulou, D. N., 2002. 'Galerius, Gamzigrad, and the Fifth Macedonian Legion,' *Journal of Roman Archaeology* 15: 275–281.

Clover, F. M., 1982. 'Emperor Worship in Vandal Africa,' *Romanitas-Christianitas. Untersuchungen zur Geschichte und Literatur der römischen Kaiserzeit*, ed. G. Wirth (Berlin), 661–674, reprinted as *The Late Roman West and the Vandals. Collected Studies* 401 (Aldershot, 1993), no. VII (No. VIII in the same volume is a French version of the same article, published in 1984 without any reference to its previous publication in English.)

Coarelli, F., 1993. 'Athenaeum,' in Steinby 1993: 131–132.

Cobb, P. G., 1978. 'The History of the Christian Year,' *The Study of Liturgy*, ed. C. Jones, G. Wainwright & E. Yarnold (London), 403–419.

Corcoran, S., 1993. 'Hidden from History: The Legislation of Licinius,' in Harries & Wood 1993: 97–119.

—, 1995, 2000. *The Empire of the Tetrarchs: Imperial Pronouncements and Government AD 284–324* (Oxford; 2nd edition with postscript, 2000).

—, 2002. 'A Tetrarchic Inscription from Corcyra and the *Edictum de Accusationibus*,' *Zeitschrift für Papyroligie und Epigraphik* 141: 221–230.

—, 2006a. 'Chronology,' in Hartley, Hawkes & Henig 2006: 12–14.

—, 2006b. 'The Tetrarchy: Policy and Image as Reflected in Imperial Pronouncements,' in Boschung & Eck 2006: 31–61.

—, 2006c. 'Galerius, Maximinus and the Titulature of the Third Tetrarchy,' *Bulletin of the Institute of Classical Studies* 49: 231–240.

—, 2007. 'Galerius' Jigsaw Puzzle: The Caesariani Dossier,' *Antiquité Tardive* 15: 221–250.

—, 2008. 'Diocletian,' in Barrett 2008: 228–254.

Coustant, P., 1721. *Epistolae Romanorum Pontificum* 1 (Paris).

Couzard, R., 1911. *Sainte Hélène d'après l'Histoire et la Tradition* (Paris).

Cracco Ruggini, 1978. 'Vettio Agorio Pretestato e la fondazione sacra di Constantinopoli,' φιλίας χάριν. *Miscellanea di studi classici in onore di Eugenio Manni* 2(Rome), 593–610.

Cramer, F. H., 1954. *Astrology in Roman Law and Politics. Memoirs of the American Philosophical Society* 37 (Philadelphia).

Cristofoli, R. 2005. *Costantino e l'Oratio ad Sanctorum Coetum. Studi e Testi di KOINΩNIA* (Naples, 2005).

Crivellucci, A., 1888. *Della fede storica di Eusebio nella Vita di Costantino. Appendice al vol(umine) primo della Storia delle relazione tra lo stato e la chiesa (Bologna, 1886)* (Livorno).

Dagron, G., 1974. *Naissance d'une capitale. Constantinople et ses institutions de 330 à 451* (Paris; second edition 1984).

—, 1984. *Constantinople imaginaire. Études sur le reueil des Patria* (Paris).

Davies, P. S., 1991. 'Constantine's Editor,' *Journal of Theological Studies*, N. S. 42: 610–618.

Davis, R., 1989. *The Book of Pontiffs (Liber Pontificalis). The Ancient Biographies of the First Ninety Roman Bishops to AD 715. Translated texts for Historians* 6 = Latin Series 5 (Liverpool).

De Giovanni, L., 2003. Revised and enlarged edition of *L'imperatore Costantino e il mondo pagano. Studi di politica e legislazione. KOINΩNIA* 2 (Naples, 1977, reprinted 1983).

Deferrari, R. J., 1953. *Funeral Orations by Saint Gregory Nazianzen and Saint Ambrose. Fathers of the Church* 22 (Washington).

Degrassi, A., 1954. *Il confine nord-orientale dell'Italia romana. Ricerche storico-topografiche. Dissertationes Bernenses*, ed. A. Alföldi 1.6 (Bern).

—, 1963. *Inscriptiones Italiae* 13.2 (Rome).

Delehaye, H., 1902. *Synaxarium Ecclesiae Constantinopolitanae*, ed. H. Delehaye. *Acta Sanctorum*, Propylaeum ad Novembrem (Brussels).

Demandt, A., 1970. 'Magister Militum,' *RE*, Supp. 12: 553–790.

—, 1971. Review of Castritius 1969. *Gnomon* 43: 692–697.

Demandt, A. & Engeman, J. 2006. *Konstantin der Grosse. Geschichte – Archäologie – Rezeption. Internationales Kolloquium vom 10.-15. October 2005 an der Universität Trier zur Landesausstellung Rheinland-Pfalz 2007 'Konstantin der Grosse'*, ed. A. Demandt & J. Engelmann. *Schriftenreihe des rheinischen Landesmuseums Trier* Nr. 32.

Demougeot, É. 1983. 'Constantin et la Dacie,' in Frézouls 1983: 91–112.

den Boeft, J., 1998. '*Nullis disciplinae expers*: Virgil's Authority in (Late) Antiquity,' in *The Use of Sacred Books in the Ancient World*, ed. L. V. Rutgers, P. W. van der Horst, H. W. Havelaar & L. Teugels. *Contributions to Biblical Exegesis and Theology* 22 (Leiden), 175–186.

Depeyrot, G., 2006. 'Economy and Society,' in Lenski 2006a: 226–252.

Devreesse, R., 1945. *Le patriarchat d'Antioche depuis la paix de l'église jusqu'à la conquête arabe* (Paris).

Di Berardino, A., 1992. 'L'imperatore Costantino e la celebrazione della Pasqua,' in Bonamente & Fusco 1992: 363–384.

Digeser, E. DeP., 1994. 'Lactantius and Constantine's Letter to Arles: Dating the *Divine Institutes*.' *Journal of Early Christian Studies* 2: 33–52.

—, 2000. *The Making of a Christian Empire, Lactantius and Rome* (Ithaca & London).

—, 2004. 'An Oracle of Apollo at Daphne and the Great Persecution,' *Classical Philology* 99: 57–77.

Dihle, A., 1989. *L'Église et l'empire au IV siècle*, ed. A. Dhile. *Entretiens sir l'Antiquité Classique* 34 (Vandœuvres-Geneva).

—, 2000. *The Making of a Christian Empire. Lactantius and Rome* (Ithaca & London).

DiMaio, M., J. Zeuge & N. Zotov, 1988. '*Ambiguitas Constantiniana*. The *Caeleste Signum Dei* of Constantine the Great,' *Byzantion* 58: 333–360.

Dittenberger, W. 1885. 'Die eleusinischen Keryken,' *Hermes* 20: 1–40.

Dörries, H., 1954, *Das Selbstzeugnis Kaiser Konstantins. Abhandlungen der Akademie der Wissenschaften in Göttingen*, Philologisch-historische Klasse[3] 34 (Göttingen).

—, 1960. *Constantine and Religious Liberty*, trans. R. H. Bainton (New Haven).

Donati, A. & G. Gentili, 2005. *Costantino il grande: la civiltà antica al bivio tra Occidente e Oriente*, ed. A. Donati & G. Gentili (Milan).

Drake, H. A., 1975. 'When was the *De Laudibus Constantini* delivered?' *Historia* 24: 345–356.

—, 1976. See (A) above, Eusebius.

—, 1982. Review of Barnes 1981, *American Journal of Philology* 103: 462–466.

—, 1999. 'Constantine,' in *Late Antiquity: A Guide to the Postclassical World*, ed. G. W. Bowersock, P. Brown & O. Grabar (Cambridge, MA & London), 389–391.

—, 2000. *Constantine and the Bishops* (Baltimore).

—, 2006. 'The Impact of Constantine on Christianity,' in Lenski 2006a: 111–136.

—, 2009. 'Solar Power in Late Antiquity,' in Cain & Lenski 2009: 215–226.

Dresken-Weiland, J., 2003. *Sarkophagbestattungen des 4.-6. Jahrhunderts im Westen des römischen Reiches. Römische Quartalschrift*, Supplementband 55 (Rome).

Drijvers, H. J. W., & H. W. Drijvers, 1997. *The Finding of the True Cross. The Judas Kyriakos Legend in Syriac. Introduction, text and translation. Corpus Scriptorum Christianorum Orientalium* 565 = Subsidia 93 (Leuven/Louvain).

Drijvers, J. W. 1992. *Helena Augusta. The Mother of Constantine the Great and the Legend of Her Finding of the True Cross. Brill's Studies in Intellectual History* 27 (Leiden).

—, 2009. 'The Power of the Cross: Celestial Cross Appearances in the Fourth Century,' in Cain & Lenski 2009: 237–248.

Drinkwater, J. F., 2005. 'Maximinus to Diocletian and the "crisis",' in Bowman, Cameron & Garnsey 2005: 28–66.

—, 2007. *The Alamanni and Rome 213–496 (Caracalla to Clovis)* (Oxford).

Duchesne, L., 1886. *Le Liber Pontificalis* 1 (Paris).

—, 1920. *Les origins du culte chrétien*[5] (Paris).

Dugmore, C. W., 1961. 'A Note on the Quartodecimans,' *Studia Patristica* 4. *Texte und Untersuchungen* 79 (Berlin), 411–421.

Duval, Y., 1982. *Loca Sanctorum Africae. Le culte des martyrs en Afrique du IVe au VIIe siècle. Collection de l'École française de Rome* 58 (Rome).

Eck, W., 2007. 'Eine historische Zeitenwende: Kaiser Constantins Hinwendung zum Christenetum und die gallischen Bischöfe,' in Schuller & Wolff 2007: 69–94.

Edwards, M. J., 1995. 'The Arian Heresy and the Oration to the Saints,' *Vigiliae Christianae* 49: 379–387.

—, 1999. 'The Constantinian Circle and the *Oration to the Saints,' Apologetics in the Roman Empire: Pagans, Jews and Christians*, ed. M. Edwards, M. Goodman & S. Price, with C. Rowland (Oxford), 251–275.

—, 2003. See (A) above, Constantine.

—, 2006. 'The Beginnings of Christianization,' in Lenski 2006a: 137–158.

Elm, S., 1989. 'An Alleged Book-Theft in Fourth-Century Egypt: P. Lips. 43,' *Studia Patristica* 18.2: 209–217.

Elton, H., 2006. 'Warfare and the Military,' in Lenski 2006a: 325–346.

Enmann, A., 1883. *Eine verlorene Geschichte der römischen Kaiser und das Buch de viris illustribus urbis Romae. Quellenstudien. Philologus*, Supplementband 4.3 (Göttingen) = 4: 335–501.

Ensslin, W., 1932. 'Minervina,' *RE* 15.2/30: 1807.

—, 1943. *Gottkaiser und Kaiser von Gottes Gnaden. Sitzungsberichte der Bayerischen Akademie der Wissenschaften*, Philosophisch-historische Klasse 1943. 6 (Munich).

Errington, R. M., 2006. *Roman Imperial Policy from Julian to Theodosius* (Chapel Hill).

Étienne, R., 1962. *Bordeaux antique* (Paris).

Evans Grubbs, E., 1993. 'Constantine and Imperial Legislation on the Family,' in Harries & Wood 1993: 120–142.

—, 1995. *Law and Family in Late Antiquity: The Emperor Constantine's Marriage Legislation* (Oxford).

—, 2002. *Women and the Law in the Roman Empire. A Sourcebook on Marriage, Divorce and Widowhood* (London & New York).

—, 2009. 'Church, State and Children: Christian and Imperial Attitudes Towards Infant Exposure in Late Antiquity,' in Cain & Lenski 2009: 119–132.

Evelyn White, H. G., 1919. *Ausonius* 1 (London & Cambridge, MA).

Fabbrini, F., 1965. *La manumissio in ecclesia. Pubblicazioni dell'Istituto di Diritto Romano dell' Uiniversità diRoma* 40 (Rome).

Fabricius, E., 1926. 'Limitatio,' *RE* 25/13.1 (Stuttgart), 672–701.

Feissel, D., 1985. 'Une dédicace en honneur de Constantin II César et les préfets du prétoire de 336,' *Travaux et Mémoires* 9: 422–434.

Festy, M., 1999. *Pseudo-Aurélius Victor: Abrégé des Césars* (Paris).

Fiocchi Nicolai, V., 1995–1996. 'La nuova basilica cruciforme della via Ardeatina,' *Rendiconti della Pontificia Accademia di Archeologia* 68: 69–233.

Fischer, T., 2006. 'Das römische Heer in der Zeit der Tetrarchie. Eine Armee zwischen Innovation und Kontinuität,' in Boschung & Eck 2006: 103–132.

Follet, S., 1976. *Athènes au IIe et au IIIe siècle. Études chronologiques et prosopographiques* (Paris).

Fowden, G. M., 1987. 'Nicagoras of Athens and the Lateran Obelisk,' *Journal of Hellenic Studies* 107: 51–57.

—, 1991. 'Constantine's Porphyry Column: The Earliest Literary Allusion,' *Journal of Roman Studies* 81: 119–131.

Franchi de' Cavalieri, P., 1928. *Note agiografiche7. Studi e Testi* 49 (Rome).

Frere, S. S., 1975. See Rae & Rae 1974.

Frézouls, E., 1983. *Crise et redressement dans les province européennes de l'Empire (milieu du IIIe – milieu du IVe siècle ap. J.-C.). Actes du colloque de Strasbourg (décembre 1981)*, ed. E. Frézouls (Strasbourg).

Frolow, A., 1944. 'La dédicace de Constantinople dans la tradition byzantine,' *Revue de l'histoire des religions* 127: 61–127.

Funk, F. X., 1897. 'Die Entwickelung des Osterfastens,' *Kirchengeschichtliche Abhandlungen und Untersuchungen* 1 (Paderborn), 241–278. (This is a revised and an expanded version of 'Die Entwicklung des Osterfastens,' *Theologische Quartalschrift* 75 [1893], 179–225.)

Galletier, É., 1949, 1952 *Panégyriques Latines* 1, 2 (Paris).

Garnsey, P., 2003. 'Introduction,' in Bowen & Garnsey 2003: 1–54.

Gascou, J., 1967. 'Le rescrit d'Hispellum,' *Mélanges d'archéologie et d'histoire* 79: 609–659.

Gaudemet, J., 1947. 'La législation religieuse de Constantin,' *Revue d'histoire de l'église de France* 33: 25–61.

—, 1990. 'La legislation anti-païenne de Constantin à Justinien,' *Cristianesimo nella storia* 11: 449–468.

Gera, D. H., 2003. *Ancient Greek Ideas on Speech, Language, and Civilization* (Oxford).

Girardet, K. M., 1974. 'Trier 385. Der Prozess gegen die Priszillianer,' *Chiron* 4: 577–608.

—, 1992. 'Kaiser Konstantin der Grosse als Vorsitzender von Konzilien. Die historische Tatsachen und ihre Bedeutung,' in Bonamente & Fusco 1992: 445–459.

—, 1993. 'Der Vorsitzende des Konzils von Nicaea (325) – Kaiser Konstantin d. Gr.,' *Klassisches Altertum, Spätantike und frühes Christentum. Adolf Lippold zum 65. Geburtstag gewidmet*, ed. K. Dietz, D. Hennig & H. Kaletsch (Würzburg), 331–360. Reprinted in Schlange-Schöningen 2007: 171–203.

—, 1998a. 'Die konstantinische Wende und ihre Bedeutung für das Reich. Althistorische Überlegungen zu den geistigen Grundlagen der Religionspolitik Konstantins d. Gr.,' in Mühlenberg 1998: 9–122. Republished in Girardet 2006a: 39–155.

—, 1998b. 'Christliche Kaiser vor Konstantin d. Gr.?' *Imperium Romanum: Studien zur Geschichte und Rezeption. Festschrift für Karl Christ zum 75. Geburtstag*, ed. P. Kneissl & V. Losemann (Stuttgart), 288–310. Republished in Girardet 2006a: 13–38.

—, 2004. 'Die Erhebung Kaiser Valentinians II. Politische Umstände und Folgen (375/76),' *Chiron*: 109–144.

—, 2006a. *Die konstantinische Wende. Voraussetzungen und geistige Grundlagen der Religionspolitik Konstantins des Großen* (Darmstadt).

—, 2006b. 'Konstantin und das Christentum: Die Jahre der Entscheidung 310 bis 314,' in Demandt & Engeman 2006: 69–81.

—, 2007a, *Kaiser Konstantin der Grosse. Historische Leistung und Rezeption in Europa*, ed. K. M. Girardet (Bonn).

—, 2007b. 'Das Christentum im Denken und in der Politik Kaiser Konstantins d. Gr.,' in Girardet 2007a: 29–53.

—, 2007c. 'Vom Sonnen-Tag zum Sonntag. Der *dies solis* in Gesetzgebung und Politik Konstantins d. Gr., *Zeitschrift für Antikes Christentum* 10: 279–310. Also published in French as 'L'invention du dimanche: du jour du soleil au dimanche. Le *dies solis* dans la législation et la politique de Constantin le Grand,' in *Empire chrétien et Église aux IVe et Ve siècles. Intégration ou "concorda"? Le témoignage du Code Théodosien. Actes du Colloque international (Lyon, 6, 7 et 8 Octobre 2005)*, ed. J.-N. Guinot & F. Richard (Paris, 2008), 341–380.

Goltz, A. & H. Schlange-Schöningen, 2008. *Konstantin der Grosse. Das Bild des Kaisers im Wandel der Zeiten*. Beihefte zum *Archiv für Kulturgeschiche* 66, ed. A. Goltz & H. Schlange-Schöningen (Cologne, Weimar & Vienna).

Gow, A. S. F., 1958. *The Greek Anthology. Sources and Ascriptions*. Society for the Promotion of Hellenic Studies, Supplementary Paper no. 9 (London).

Graindor, P., 1926. 'Constantin le Grand et le dadouque Nicagoras,' *Byzantion* 3: 209–214.

Grant, M., 1998. *Emperor Constantine*, 2nd edition (London: first edition 1993).

Green, R. P. H. 1985. 'Still Waters Run Deep: A New Study of the *Professores* of Bordeaux,' *Classical Quarterly* N.S. 35: 491–506.

—, 1991. *The Works of Ausonius. Edited with Introduction and Commentary* (Oxford).

—, 2010. 'Constantine as Patron of Christian Latin Poetry,' *Studia Patristica* 46: 65–76.

Grégoire, H., 1930–31. 'La "conversion" de Constantin,' *Revue de l'Université de Bruxelles* 36: 231–272. Reprinted as 'Die "Bekehrung" Constantins des Großen,' in Kraft 1974: 175–223.

—, 1932. 'La statue de Constantin et le signe de la croix,' *L'Antiquité classique* 1: 135–148.

—, 1938a. 'Eusèbe n'est pas l'auteur de la "Vita Constantini" dans sa forme actuelle et Constantin ne s'est pas "converti" en 312,' *Byzantion* 13: 561–583.

—, 1938b. 'Deux champs de bataille: "Campus Ergenus" et "Campus Ardiensis",' *Byzantion* 13: 585–586.

—, 1939. 'La Vision de Constantin "liquidée",' *Byzantion* 14: 341–351.

—, 1953. 'L'authenticité et l'historicité de la *Vita Constantini* attribuée à Eusèbe de Césarée,' *Bulletin de l'Académie Royale de Belgique*, Classe des Lettres 39: 462–479.

Grosse, R., 1925. 'Labarum,' *RE* 12: 240–242.

Grünewald, T., 1990. *Constantinus Maximus Augustus. Herrschaftspropaganda in der zeitgenössischen Überlieferung*. Historia Einzelschriften 64 (Stuttgart).

Gudeman, A., 1914. *P. Cornelii Taciti Dialogus de Oratoribus²* (Leipzig & Berlin).

Gurval, R. A., 1995. *Actium and Augustus. The Politics and Emotions of Civil War* (Ann Arbor).

Guthrie, P., 1966. 'The Execution of Crispus,' *Phoenix* 20: 325–331.

Guyon, J., 1987. *Le cimitière au deux lauriers. Recherches sur les catacombes romaines*. Bibliothèque des Écoles françaises d'Athènes et de Rome 264 (Rome).

Habicht, C., 1958. 'Zur Geschichte des Kaisers Konstantin,' *Hermes* 86: 360–378.

Hägg, T., 1992. 'Hierocles the Lover of Truth and Eusebius the Sophist,' *Symbolae Osloenses* 67: 138–150.

Halfmann, H., 1986. *Itinera Principum. Geschichte und Typologie der Kaierreisen im römischen Reich. Heidelberger Althistorische Beiträge und Epigraphische Studien* 2 (Stuttgart).

Hall, S. G., 1998. 'Some Constantinian Documents in the Vita Constantini,' in Lieu & Montserrat 1998: 86–103.

Hall, L. J., 1998. 'Cicero's *instinctu divino* and Constantine's *instrinctu divinitatis*: The Evidence of the Arch for the Senatorial View of the "Vision" of Constantine,' *Jopurnal of Early Christian Studies* 6; 647–671.

Hanson, R. P. C., 1973. 'The *Oratio ad Sanctos* attributed to the Emperor Constantine and the Oracle at Daphne,' *Journal of Theological Studies*, N. S. 24: 505–511.

—, 1988. *The Search for the Christian Doctrine of God: The Arian Controversy, 318–381* (Edinburgh).

Harries, J., 1988. 'The Roman Imperial Quaestor from Constantine to Theodosius II,' *Journal of Roman Studies* 78: 148–172.

—, 2010. 'Constantine the Lawgiver,' in *From the Tetrarchs to the Theodosians. Later Roman History and Culture, 284–450 CE*, ed. S. McGill, C. Sogno & E. Watts. *Yale Classical Studies* 34: 73–92.

Harries, J., & I. Wood, 1993. *The Theodosian Code. Studies in the Imperial Law of Late Antiquity*, ed. J. Harries & I. Wood (Duckworth).

Harris, W. V., 2005. 'Constantine's Dream,' *Klio* 87: 488–494.

Hartley, E. 2006. 'Introduction,' in Hartley, Hawkes & Henig 2006: 15–16.

Hartley, E., J. Hawkes & M. Henig, with F. Mee, 2006. *Constantine the Great: York's Roman Emperor* (York).

Hassall, M. W. C., 1976. 'Britain in the Notitia,' *Aspects of the Notitia Dignitatum. British Archaeological Reports*, Supplementary Series 15 (Oxford), 103–117.

Heck, E., 1972. *Die dualistischen Zusätze und die Kaiseranreden bei Lactantius. Untersuchungen zur Textgeschichte der Divinae institutiones unde der Schrift De opificio dei. Abhandlungen der Heidelberger Akademie der Wissenschaften*, Philosophisch-historische Klasse 1972, Abhandlung 2.

—, 2005. '*Defendere – instituere*. Zum Selbstverständnis des Apologeten Lactanz,' *L'apologétique chrétienne gréco-latine à l'époque prénicéenne*, ed. F. Paschoud & A. Wlosok. *Entretiens sur l'Antiquité classique* 51 (Geneva – Vandœuvres), 205–248.

—, 2009. 'Constantin und Lactanz in Trier – Chronologisches,' *Historia* 58: 118–130.

Heitsch, E., 1963. *Die griechischen Dichterfragmente der römischen Kaiserzeit* 1². *Abhandlungen der Akademie der Wissenschaften zu Göttingen*, Philosophisch-historische Klasse³ 49 (Göttingen).

Helm, R. 1923. *Eusebius' "Chronik" und ihre Tabellenform. Abhandlungen der preussischen Akademie der Wissenschaften*, Philosophisch-historische Klasse 1923 Nr. 4 (Berlin).

Hermann-Otto, E., 2007. *Konstantin der Grosse. Gestalten der Antike* (Darmstadt).

Heuss, A., 1993. 'De se ipse,' in Bleicken 1993: 171–221.

Holl, K., 1916. 'Die Schriften des Epiphanius gegen die Bilderverehrung,' *Sitzungsberichte der königlichen preussischen Akademie der Wissenschaften zu Berlin* 1916: 828–868. Reprinted in his *Gesammelte Aufsätze zur Kirchengeschichte* 2: *Der Osten* (Tübingen, 1928), 351–387.

—, 1923. *Die Entstehung der vier Fastenzeiten in der griechischen Kirche. Abhandlungen der preussischen Akademie der Wissenschaften*, Philosophisch-historische Klasse 1923, Nr. 5. Reprinted in his *Gesammelte Aufsätze* 2 (1928), 155–203.

Holman, S. R., 2008. *Wealth and Poverty in Early Church and Society*, ed. S. R. Holman (Grand Rapids, MI).

Holloway, R. R., 2004. *Constantine and Rome* (New Haven & London).

Holmes, N., 2003. *Excavation of Roman Sites at Cramond, Edinburgh*, ed. M. Collard & J. A. Lawson. Society of Antiquaries of Scotland, *Monograph* 23 (Edinburgh).

Honoré, A. M. (T.), 1998. *Law in the Crisis of Empire 379–455 AD. The Theodosian Dynasty and its Quaestors* (Oxford).

Humfress, C., 2006. 'Civil Law and Social Life,' in Lenski 2006a: 205–225.

—, 2007. *Orthodoxy and the Courts in Late Antiquity* (Oxford).

Humphries, M., 2008. 'From Usurper to Emperor: The Politics of Legitimation in the Age of Constantine,' *Journal of Late Antiquity* 1: 82–100.

Hunt, D., 1993. 'Christianising the Roman Empire: the Evidence of the Code,' in Harries & Wood 1993: 143–158.

Jacoby, F., 1930. *Die Fragmente der griechischen Historiker 2: Zeitgeschichte D. Kommentar zu Nr. 106–262* (Berlin).

Jeločnik, A., 1973. *čenturska Zakladna Najdba: Folisov Maksencija in Tetrarhije / The čentur Hoard: Folles of Maxentius and of the Tetrarchy. Situla* 12 (Ljubljana).

Jeločnik, A., & P. Kos, 1983. *Zakladna Najdba Čentur-C: Folisi Maksencija in Tetrarhije / The Čentur-C Hoard: Folles of Maxentius and of the Tetrarchy. Situla* 23 (Ljubljana).

Jones, A. H. M., 1937. *Cities of the Eastern Roman Provinces* (Oxford; reprinted with the esxtensive correction of minor inaccuracies, 1970).

—, 1949. *Constantine and the Conversion of Europe* (London).

—, 1964. *The Later Roman Empire. A Social, Economic and Administrative Survey* (Oxford).

Jones, A. H. M. with T. C. Skeat, 1954. 'Notes on the Genuineness of the Constantinian Documents in Eusebius's Life of Constantine,' *Journal of Ecclesiastical History* 5: 196–200.

Jones, C. P., 2006. *Philostratus: Apollonius of Tyana* 3 (Cambridge, MA & London).

Jullian, C., 1926. *Histoire de la Gaule* 7 (Paris).

Kähler, H., 1964. *Das Fünfsäulendenkmal für die Tetrarchen auf dem Forum Romanum. Monumenta Artis Romanae* 3

Kantorowitz, E. H., 1961. 'Gods in Uniform,' *Proceedings of the American Philosophical Society* 105: 368–393.

Kany, R., 2007. 'Kaiser Konstantin und das erste Konzil von Nizäa,' in Schuller & Wolff 2007: 95–124.

Kay, N. M., 2001. *Ausonius: Epigrams* (London).

Kelly, C., 2006. 'Bureaucracy and Government,' in Lenski 2006a: 183–204.

Kelly, G. (A. J.), 2003. 'The New Rome and the Old: Ammianus Marcellinus' Silences on Constantinople,' *Classical Quarterly*, N. S. 53: 588–607.

Kerboul, C. Y. M., 1993. *Constantin et la fin du monde antique* (Mayenne).

Kienast, D., 1996. *Römische Kaisertabelle: Grundzüge einer römischen Kaiserchronologie*[2] (Darmstadt).

Klussmann, R., 1912. *Bibliotheca Scriptorum Classicorum et Graecorum et Latinorum. Die Literatur von 1878 bis 1896 einschliesslich umfassend* 2.1. *Jahresbericht über die Fortschritte der klassischen Altertumswissenschaft begründet von Conrad Bursian* 156: Supplementband (Leipzig).

Koch, G., 2000. *Frühchristliche Sarkophage* (Munich).

Kmosko, M., 1907. *S. Simeon barr Sabba'e. Patrologia Syriaca* 1.2 (Paris), 659–1055.

Kolb, A., 2000. *Transport und Nachrichtentransfer im Römischen Reich. Klio, Beiträge zur Alten Geschichte*, Beihefte N. F. Band 2 (Berlin).

Kolb, F., 1987. *Diocletian und die erste Tetrarchie. Improvisation oder Experiment in der Organisation monarchischer Herrschaft? Untersuchungen zur antiken Literatur und Geschichte* 27 (Berlin & New York).

Kolbe, H.-G., 1962. *Die StatthalterNumidiens von Gallien bis Constantin (268–320). Vestigia* 4 (Munich).

Kotter, B., 1988. *Die Schriften des Johannes von Damaskos* 5: *Opera homiletica et hagiographica. Patristische Texte und Studien* 29 (Berlin & New York).

Kraft, H., 1974. *Konstantin der Große. Wege der Forschung* 131 (Darmstadt).

Krautheimer, R., 1937, 1959. *Corpus Basilicarum Christianarum Romae* 1, 2.

—, 1983. *Three Christian Capitals: Topography and Politics* (Berkeley).

—, 1993. 'The ecclesiastival building policy of Constantine,' in Bonamente & Fusco 1993: 509–552.

Kriegbaum, B., 1992. 'Die religionspolitik des Kaisers Maxentius,' *Annuarium Historiae Pontificiae* 30: 7–54.

Kubitschek, W., 1919. 'Karten,' *RE* 10.2/20: 2022–2149.

Kurfess, A., 1950. 'Zu Kaiser Konstantins Rede an die Versammlung der Heiligen,' *Theologische Quartalschrift* 130: 145–165.

La Rocca, E., 1993. 'La fondazione di Costantinopoli,' in Bonamente & Fusco 1993: 553–583.

Lammert, W., 1929. 'Stabulum 1,' *RE* 3A.2/6: 1926.

Lamoreaux, J. C., 1995. 'Episcopal Courts in Late Antquity,' *Journal of Early Christian Studies* 3: 143–167.

Lane Fox, R. J., 1986. *Pagans and Christians* (Harmondsworth; published also in New York, 1987).

—, 1997. 'The "Itinerary of Alexander:" Constantius to Julian,' *Classical Quarterly*, N. S. 47: 239–252.

Lassandro, D., 1992. *XII Panegyrici Latini. Corpus Scriptorum Latinorum Paravianum* (Turin).

Lauffer, S., 1971. *Diokletians Preisedikt. Texte und Kommentare* 5 (Berlin).

Leadbetter, B. (W.), 1998. 'The illegitimacy of Constantine and the birth of the tetrarchy,' in Lieu & Montserrat 1998: 74–85.

—, 2009. *Galerius and the Will of Diocletian* (London & New York).

Leclerq, H., 1938. 'Pâques,' *Dictionnaire d'archéologie chrétienne et de liturgie* 13: 1521–1574.

Leeb, R., 1992. *Konstantin und Christus: die Verchristlichung der imperialen Repräsentation unter Konstantin dem Großen als Spiegel seiner Kirchenpolitik und seines Selbstverständnis als christlicher Kaiser. Arbeiten zur Kirchengeschichte* 58 (Berlin & New York).

Lenski, N., 2006a. *The Cambridge Companion to the Age of Constantine*, ed. N. Lenski (Cambridge).

—, 2006b. 'Introduction,' in Lenski 2006a: 1–13.

—, 2006c. 'The reign of Constantine' in Lenski 2006a: 59–90.

—, 2007. Introduction to Reprint of Burckhardt 1949 (London: Folio Society): xi–xix.

—, 2008. 'Constantine,' in Barrett 2008: 255–279.

Lepelley, C., 2004. 'Une inscription d'*Heraclea Sintica* (Macédoine) récemment découverte, rélévant un rescrit de l'empereur Galère restituant ses droits à la cité,' *Zeitschrift für Papyrologie und Epigraphik* 146: 223–231.

Leppin, H. 2006. 'Zur Geschichte der Ersforschung der Tetrarchie,' in Boschung & Eck 2006: 11–30.

—, 2008. 'Konstantin der Große und das Christentum bei Jacob Burckhardt,' in Goltz & Schlange-Schöningen 2008: 263–276.

Liebeschuetz, J. H. W. G., 1979. *Continuity and Change in Roman Religion* (Oxford).

Lietzmann, H., 1937. 'Der Glaube Konstantins des Grossen,' *Sitzungsberichte der preussischen Akademie der Wissenschaften*, Philosophisch-historische Klasse 1937: 263–275. Reprinted in his *Kleine Schriften* 1. *Texte und Untersuchungen* 67 (Berlin, 1958), 186–201.

Lieu, S. N. C., 1992. *Manichaeism in the Later Roman Empire and Medieval China.*[2] *Wissenschaftliche Untersuchungen zum Neuen Testament* 63 (Tübingen).

—, 2006. 'Constantine in Legendary Literature,' in Lenski 2006a: 298–311.

Lieu, S. N. C., & D. Montserrat, 1996. *From Constantine to Julian: Pagan and Byzantine Views. A Source History,* ed. S. N. C. Lieu & D. Montserrat (London & New York).

—, 1998. *Constantine: History, Historiography and Legend. A Source History,* ed. S. N. C. Lieu & D. Montserrat (London & New York).

Linder, A., 1987. *The Jews in Roman Imperial Legislation* (Detroit & Jerusalem).

Löhr, W., 2005, 2006. 'Arius Reconsidered,' *Zeitschrift für Antikes Christentum* 9: 524–560; 10: 121–157.

Logan, A. H. L., 2010. 'Constantine, the *Liber Pontificalis* and the Christian basilicas of Rome,' *Studia Patristica* 50: 31–53.

Lohse, B., 1953. *Das Passafest der Quartadecimaner. Beiträge zur Förderung christlicher Theologie* 2. Reihe 54 (Gütersloh).

Long, J., 2009. 'How to Read a Halo: Three (or More) Versions of Constantine's Vision,' in Cain & Lenski 2009: 227–235.

Lorenz, R., 1986. *Der zehnte Osterfestbrief des Athanasius von Alexandrien. Beiheft zur Zeitschrift für die neutestamentliche Wissenschaft* 49 (Berlin & New York).

Luck, G., 1958. 'Palladas – Christian or Pagan?' *Harvard Studies in Classical Philology* 63 (1958), 455–471.

Mackay, C. S., 1999. 'Lactantius and the Succession to Diocletian,' *Classical Philology* 94: 198–209.

MacMullen, R., 1969. *Constantine. Crosscurrents in World History,* ed. N. F. Cantor (New York).

Magnou-Nortier, É., 2003. 'Codes et Codification – Sur l'origines des Constitutions sirmondiennes' *Revue de droit canonique* 51 (2001, published 2003), 279–304.

Mango, C., 1959. *The Brazen House. Study of the Vestibule of the Imperial Palace of Constantinople. With an Appendix by Ernest Mamboury. Arkæologisk-kunsthistoriske Meddelelser udguivet af det Danske Videnskabernes Selskab,* Bind. 4.4 (Copenhagen).

—, 1963. 'Antique Statuary and the Byzantine Beholder,' *Dumbarton Oaks Papers* 17: 55–75. Reprinted as *Byzantium and its Image. Variorum Reprints. Collected Studies* 191 (London, 1984), no. V.

—, 1965. 'Constantinopolitana,' *Jahrbuch des deutschen Archäologischen Instituts* 80: 305–336. Reprinted as Mango 1993a: no. II.

—, 1981. 'Constantine's Porphyry Column and the Chapel of St Constantine,' Χελτίον τῆς Χριστιανικῆς 'Αρχαιολογικῆς 'Ετερείας[4] 10: 103–110. Reprinted as Mango 1993a: no. IV.

—, 1985. *Le développement urbain de Constantinople (IVe – VIIe siècles). Travaux et Mémoires,* Monographies 2 (Paris).

—, 1993a. *Studies on Constantinople. Variorum Reprints. Collected Studies* 394 (Aldershot).

—, 1993b. 'Constantine's Column,' Mango 1993a: no. III.

Marasco, G., 2003. *Greek and Roman Historiography in Late Antiquity: Fourth to Sixth Century A. D.*, ed. G. Marasco (Leiden & Boston).

Marcone, 2002. *Costantino il Grande* (Rome & Bari).

Marucchi, O., 1921. 'Di una iscrizione storica che può attribuirsi alla *Basilica Apostolorum* sulla Via Appia,' *Nuovo Bullettino di Archeologia Cristiana* 27: 61–69.

Matthews, J. F., 1970. 'Olympiodorus of Thebes and the History of the West (A.D. 407–425),' *Journal of Roman Studies* 60 (1970), 79–97.

—, 1988. *The Roman World of Ammianus* (London).

—, 2000. *Laying down the Law: A Study of the Theodosian Code* (New Haven).

Maurice, J., 1913. 'Sur la vie de Constantine d'Eusèbe,' *Bulletin de la Société Nationale des Antiquaires de France* 1913: 387–396.

Mayer, A., 1957. *Die Sprache der alten Illyrier. Österreichische Akademie der Wissenschaften, Schriften der Balkankommission* 15.1 (Vienna).

Mazzarino, S., 1974. *Antico, tardoantico ed èra costantiniana* 1 (Bari).

McCormick, M., 1986. *Eternal Victory: Triumphal Rulership in Late Antiquity, Byzantium and the Early Medieval West* (Cambridge).

Meiggs, R., & D. M. Lewis, 1999. *A Selection of Greek Historical Inscriptions to the End of the Fifth Century B. C.* (Oxford).

Millar, F., 1969. 'P. Herennius Dexippus: The Greek World and the Third-Century Invasions,' *Journal of Roman Studies* 59: 13–29. Reprinted in his *Rome, The Greek World and the East* 2. *Government, Society, and Culture in the Roman Empire*, ed. H. M. Cotton & G. M. Rogers (Chapel Hill & London, 2004), 265–297.

—, 1977. *The Emperor in the Roman World 31 BC – AD 337* (London; 2nd edition with Afterword: Ithaca, 1992).

—, 1990. 'Reflections on the Trials of Jesus,' *A Tribute to Geza Vermes. Essays on Jewish and Christian Literature and History*, ed. P. R. Davies & R. T. White. *Journal for the Study of the Old Testament*, Supplementary Series 100 (Sheffield), 355–381.

—, 2007. *A Greek Roman Empire. Power and Belief under Theodosius II 408–450. Sather Classical Lectures* 64 (Berkeley, Los Angeles & London).

Mitchell, S., 1988. 'Maximinus and the Christians in AD 312: A New Latin Inscription,' *Journal of Roman Studies* 78: 105–124.

—, 1999. 'The Cult of Theos Hypsistos between Pagans, Jews, and Christians,' *Pagan Monotheism in Late Antiquity*, ed. P. Athanassiadi & M. Frede (Oxford), 81–148.

Mommsen, T., 1862, 1908. 'Verzeichniss der römischen Provinzen aufgesetzt um 297,' *Abhandlungen der königlichen preussischen Akademie der Wissenschaften* 1860: 489–518. Reprinted in his *Gesammelte Schriften* 5 (1908), 561–588.

Moreau, J., 1954. *Lactance, De la Mort des Persécuteurs. Sources chrétiennes* 39 (Paris).

—, 1955. 'Zum Problem der Vita Constantini,' *Historia* 4: 234–245 reprinted in his *Scripta Minora*, ed. W. Schmitthenner. *Annales Universitatis Saraviensis* 1 (Heidelberg, 1964), 124–134.

Morin, G., 1924. 'A-t-on retrouvé Stridon, le lieu natal de Saint Jérôme?,' *Bulićev Zbornik / Strena Buliciana* / Zagreb & Split), 421–432.

—, 1926. 'La patrie de Saint Jérôme; le missorium d'Exupérius: deux retractations nécessaires,' *Revue Bénédictine* 38: 217–220.

Mosshammer, A. A., 2008. *The Easter Computus and the Origins of the Christian Era* (Oxford).

Mühlenberg, E., 1998. *Die konstantinische Wende*, ed. E. Mühlenberg (Gütersloh).

Müller-Rettig, B., 1990. *Der Panegyricus des Jahres 310 auf Konstantin den Grossen. Übersetzung und historisch-philologischer Kommentar. Palingenesia* 31 (Stuttgart).

Mundell Mango, M. & A. Bennett, 1994. 'The Sevso Treasure.' *Journal of Roman Archaeology*, Supplementary Series 12 (Ann Arbor).

Nautin, P., 1961. *Lettres et écrivains chrétiens des IIe et IIIe siècles. Patristica* 2 (Paris).

—, 1977. *Origène. Sa vie et son œuvre. Christianisme antique* 1 (Paris).

Nicholson, O., 2000. 'Constantine's Vision of the Cross,' *Vigiliae Christianae* 54: 309–323.

Nieddu, A. M., 2009. *La Basilica Apostolorum sulla via Appia e l'area cimiteriale circostante. Monumenti di antichità cristiana*, Serie II.19 (Vatican City).

Nisbet, R. G. M., 1978. 'Virgil's Fourth Eclogue: Easterners and Westerners,' *Bulletin of the Institute of Classical Studies* 25: 59–78.

O'Connor, D. W., 1969. *Peter in Rome. The Literary, Liturgical and Archaeological Evidence* (New York & London).

O'Donnell, J. J., 2009. *The Ruin of the Roman Empire* (London).

Odahl, C. M., 2006. *Constantine and the Christian Empire*, 2nd edition (London & New York).

Oellacher, H., 1932. 'Prunkrede auf einem Kaiser (wahrscheinlich Julian), *Mitteilungen aus der Papyrussammlung der Nationalbibliothek in Wien (Papyrus Erzherzog Rainer)*, N. S. 1: *Griechische Literarische Papyri* 1, ed. H. Gerstinger, H. Oellacher & K. Vogel (Vienna), 105–123: no. XIV.

Oenbrink, W., 2006. 'Maxentius als *conservator urbis suae*. Ein antitetrarchisches Herrschafts konzept tetrarchischer Zeit,' in Boschung & Eck 2006: 169–204.

Ortiz di Urbina, I., 1963. *Nicée et Constantinople. Histoire des Conciles Œuméniques* 1 (Paris).

Orwell, G., 1949. *Nineteen Eighty-Four* (London).

Page, D. L., 1941. *Select Papyri* 3. *Literary Papyri: Poetry* (Cambridge, MA & London).

Palanque, J.-R., 1966. 'La préfecture du prétoie de Junius Bassus,' *Mélanges d'archéologie et d'histoire offerts à André Piganiol* 2 (Paris), 837–842.

Palladini, V. & P. Fedeli, 1976. *Panegyrici Latini. Scriptores graeci et latini consilio Academiae Lynceorum editi* (Rome).

Panella, C., 2009. 'Imperial Insignia from the Palatine Hill,' in *Rome and the Barbarians. The Birth of a New World*, ed. J.-J. Aillagon (Milan, 2008), 86–91, 611–613.

Parvis, S., 2006. *Marcellus of Ancyra and the Lost Years of the Arian Controversy 325–345* (Oxford).

Paschoud, F., 1993. 'Ancora sul rifiuto di Costantino di salire al Campidoglio,' in Bonamente & Fusco 1993: 737–748.

Pasquali, G., 1910. 'Die Composition der *Vita Constantini* des Eusebius,' *Hermes* 45: 369–386.

Patlagean, É., 1977. *Pauvreté économique et pauvreté sociale à Byzance 4e – 7e siècles* (Paris).

Peeters, P., 1932. 'Les débuts du Christianisme en Géorgie d'après les sources hagiographiques,' *Analecta Bollandiana* 50: 5–58.

Penella, R. J., 2007. *Man and the Word. The Orations of Himerius. Transformation of the Classical Heritage* 43 (Berkeley, Los Angeles & London).

Petit, P., 1950. 'Libanius et la "Vita Constantini",' *Historia* 1: 562–582.

Pfättisch, J. M., 1908. *Die Rede Konstantins des Grossen an die Versammlung der Heiligen auf ihre Echtheit untersucht. Strassburger Theologische Studien* 9.4 (Freiburg im Breisgau).

—, 1910. 'Platos Einfluss auf die Rede Konstantins an die Versammlung der Heiligen,' *Theologische Quartalschrift* 92: 392–417.

—, 1913. 'Die Rede Konstantins an die Versammlung der Heiligen,' *Konstantin der Grosse und seine Zeit*, ed. F. J. Dölger. *Römische Quartalschrift*, Supplementband 19 (Freiburg im Breisgau), 96–121.

Pichon, R., 1901. *Lactance. Étude sur le mouvement philosophique et religieuse sous le règne de Constantin* (Paris).

—, 1906. 'L'origine du recueil des *Panegyrici Latini*,' *Les derniers écrivains profanes. Études sur l'histoire de la littérature latine dans les Gaules* 1 (Paris), 270–291. Also published in *Revue des études anciennes* 8 (1906), 229–249.

Pietri, C. 1983. 'Constantin en 324. Propagande et théologie impériales d' après les documents de la *Vita Constantini*,' in Frézouls 1983: 63–90. Reprinted in his *Christiana Respublica. Éléments d'une enquête sur le christianisme antique* 1. Collection de l'École française de Rome (Rome, 1997), 253–280.

Piganiol, A., 1932. 'Dates constantiniennes,' *Revue d'histoire et de philosophie religieuse* 13: 360–372. Reprinted in his *Scripta Varia* 3. Collection Latomus 133 (Brussels, 1973), 229–239.

Pizzani, U., 1993. 'Costantino e l'*Oratio ad sanctorum coetum*,' in Bonamente & Fusco 1993: 791–822.

Pohlsander, H. A., 1995. *Helena: Empress and Saint* (Chicago).

—, 1996. *The Emperor Constantine* (London & New York).

Porena, P., 2003. *Le origini della prefettura del pretorio tardoantica. Saggi di stori antica* 20 (Rome).

Potter, D. S., 2004. *The Roman Empire at Bay AD 180–395* (London & New York).

Preger, T., 1901a. 'Konstantinos-Helios,' *Hermes* 36: 457–469.

—, 1901b, 1907. *Scriptores Originum Constantinopolitanarum* 1, 2 (Leipzig).

Rae, A. & Rae, V., 1974. 'The Roman Fort at Cramond,' *Britannia* 5: 163–224. Reprinted as *The Roman Fort at Cramond* (Edinburgh, 1975), with an introduction by S. S. Frere.

Rapp, C., 2005. *Holy Bishops in Late Antiquity. The Nature of Christian Leadership in an Age of Transition. Transformation of the Classical Heritage* 37 (Berkeley, Los Angeles & London).

Rebenich, S., 2000a. 'Alfred Heuß: Ansichten seines Lebenswerken. Mit einem Anhang: Alfred Heuß im Dritten Reich,' *Historische Zeitschrift* 271: 661–673.

—, 2000b. 'Vom dreizehnten Gott zum dreizehnten Apostel? Der tote Kaiser in der christlichen Spätantike,' *Zeitschrift für Antikes Christentum* 4: 300–324. Reprinted in Schlange-Schöningen 2007: 216–244.

Rees, R., 2002. *Layers of Loyalty in Latin Panegyric AD 289–307* (Oxford).

Rehm, A., 1939. 'Kaiser Diokletian und das Heiligtum von Didyma,' *Philologus* 93: 74–84.

Rist, John M., 1981. 'Basil's "Neoplatonsim": Its Background and Nature,' *Basil of Caesarea: Christian, Humanist, Ascetic. A Sixteenth-Hundredth Anniversary Symposium*, ed. P. J. Fedwick (Toronto).

Rist, Josef, 2010. 'Das Orakel des Apollon in Daphne und das Christentum,' *Studia Patristica* 44: 57–62.

Rodgers, B. S. 1980. 'Constantine's Pagan Vision,' *Byzantion* 50: 259–278.

Rosen, K., 1993. 'Constantins Weg zum Christentum und die *Panegyrici Latini*,' in Bonamente & Fusco 1993: 853–863.

Roueché, C., 1981. 'Rome, Asia and Aphrodisias in the Third Century,' *Journal of Roman Studies* 71: 103–120.

—, 1989. 'Aprodisias in Late Antiquity,' *Journal of Roman Studies Monographs* 5 (London).

Rummel, P. von, 2007. *Habitus barbarus. Kleidung und Repräsentation spätantiker Eliten im 4. und 5. Jahrhundert. Ergänzungsbände zum Teallexikon der Germanischen Altertumskunde*, ed. H. Beck, D. Geuenich & H. Steuer 55 (Berlin & New York).

Salaville, S., 1910. 'La τεσσαρακοστή au Ve canon de Nicée (325),' *Echos d'Orient* 13: 65–72.

—, 1911. 'Tessaracoste: Carême ou Ascension?' *Echos d'Orient* 14: 355–357.

—, 1929. 'Τεσσαρακοστή, Ascension et Pentecôte au IVe siècle,' *Echos d'Orient* 32. 257–271.

Salway, R. W. B., 2007. 'The Praetorian Prefecture of Africa under Constantine: A Phantom?' *Acta XII Congressus Internationalis Epigraphiae Graecae et Latinae. Provinciae Imperii Romani Inscriptionibu descriptae, 3–8 Septembris 2002*, ed. M. Mayer i Olivé, G. Baratta & A. Guzmán Almagro (Barcelona), 1281–1284.

Sapelli, M., 2005. 'La produzione dei sarcophagi in età costantiniana (312–313–circa 340),' in Donati & Gentili 2005: 166–175.

Sargenti, M., 1975. 'Il diritto private nella legislazione di Costantino. Problemi e prospettive nella letteratura dell'ultimo trentennio,' *Accademia Romanistica Costantiniana. Atti. I°Convegno Internazionale* (Perugia), 229–332.

Šašel, J., 1968. 'Emona,' *RE*, Supp. 11: 540–578.

Scheid, J., 1990. *Romulus et ses frères. Le college des frères arvales, modèle du culte public dans la Rome des empereurs. BEFAR* 275 (Rome).

—, 1992. 'Le dernier arvale,' *Institutions, société et vie politique dans l'Empire romain au IVe siècle ap. J.-C. Actes de la table ronde autour de l'œuvre d'André Chastagnol (Paris, 20–21 janvier 1989)*, ed. M. Christol, S. Demougin, Y. Duval, C. Lepelley and L. Pietri. *Collection de l'École française de Rome* 159 (Rome, 1992), 219–223.

Schlange-Schöningen, H., 2007. *Konstantin und das Christentum. Neue Wege der Forschung*, ed. H. Schlange-Schöningen (Darmstadt).

Schöll, R. & W. Kroll, 1895. *Corpus Iuris Civilis* 3. *Novellae* (Berlin: ninth edition photographically reprinted 1959).

Schmid, J. 1905. *Die Osterfestfrage auf dem ersten allgemeinen Konzil von Nicäa. Theologische Studien der Leo-Gesellschaft* 13 (Vienna).

Schuller, F., & H. Wolff, 2007. *Konstantin der Große. Kaiser einer Epochenwende*, ed. F. Schuller & H. Wolff (Lindenberg).

Schwartz, E., 1935. 'Zur Kirchengeschichte des vierten Jahrhunderts,' *Zeitschrift für die neutestamentliche Wissenschaft* 34: 129–213. Reprinted in his *Gesammelte Schriften* 4 (Berlin, 1960), 1–110.

Seeck, O., 1888. 'Studien zur Geschichte Diocletians und Constantins, I. Die Reden des Eumenius,' *Jahrbücher für classische Philologie* 34 = (*Neue*) *Jahrbücher für Philologie und Paedagogik* 137: 713–726.

—, 1891. 'Das sogenannte Edikt von Mailand,' *Zeitschrift für Kirchengeschichte* 10: 381–386.

—, 1907. 'Eumenius,' *RE* 6.1/11: 1105–1114.

—, 1895, 1921, 1922. *Geschichte des Untergangs der antiken Welt* 1 (Berlin); 4th edition (Stuttgart, 1921, with *Anhang* 1922).

—, 1919. *Regesten der Kaiser und Päpste für die Jahre 311 bis 476 n. Chr. Vorarbeit zu einer Prosopographie der christlichen Kaiserzeit* (Stuttgart).

Selb, W., 1967. 'Episcopalis audientia von der Zeit Konstantins bis zur Nov. XXXV Valentinas III,' *Zeitschrift der Savigny-Stiftung*, Romanistische Abteilung 84: 162–217.

Seston, W., 1946. *Dioclétien et la Tétrarchie* 1. *Guerres et réformes. BEFAR* 162 (Paris).

Simmons, M. B., 1995. *Arnobius of Sicca. Religious Conflict and Competition in the Age of Diocletian* (Oxford).

Simon, E., 1986. *Die konstantinischen Deckengemälde in Trier. Kulturgeschichte der antiken Welt* 34. *Trierer Beiträge zur Altertumskunde* 3 (Mainz). Revised edition published with the title *Das Program der frühkonstantinischen Decke in Trier* (Ruhpolding, 2007).

Skeat, T. C., 1950. 'Britain and the Papyri *(P. Lond. 878),' Aus Antike und Orient. Festschrift Wilhelm Schubart zum 75. Geburtstag* (Leipzig), 126–132.

Smith, R. R. R., 1988. *Hellenistic Royal Portraits* (Oxford).

Speidel, M. P., 1984. *Die Denkmäler der Kaiserreiter: Equites Singulares Augusti. Beihefte der Bonner Jahrbücher* 50 (Cologne).

—, 1994. *Riding for Caesar. The Roman Emperors' Horse Guards* (Cambridge, MA).

Staats, R., 2001. 'Kaiser Konstantin, Apostel Paulus und die deutsche Verfassung,' *Deutsches Pfarrerblatt* 101: 118–122.

—, 2008. 'Kaiser Konstantin der Große und der Apostel Paulus,' *Vigiliae Chrsitianae* 62: 334–370.

Steinby, M., 1993, *Lexicon Topographicum Urbis Romae*, ed. M. Steinby 1 (Rome).

Stephenson, P., 2009. *Constantine. Unconquered Emperor, Christian Victor* (London).

Stepper, R., *Augustus et sacerdos. Untersuchungen zum römischen Kaiser als Priester. Potsdamer altertumswissensch aftliche Beiträge* 9 (Wiesbaden).

Stevenson, J., 1957. 'The Life and Literary Activity of Lactantius,' *Studia Patristica* 1. *Texte und Untersuchungen* 63: 661–677.

Straub, J., 1942. 'Konstantins christliche Sendungsbewusstsein,' *Das Neue Bild der Antike*, ed. H. Berve (Leipzig, 1942), 374–394. Reprinted in Straub 1972: 70–88.

—, 1955. 'Konstantins Verzicht auf den Gang zum Kapitol,' *Historia* 4: 297–313. Reprinted in Straub 1972: 100–118.

—, 1957. 'Kaiser Konstantin als ἐπίσκοπος τῶν ἐκτός' *Studia Patristica* 1. *Texte und Untersuchungen* 63 (Berlin), 678–688. Reprinted in Straub 1972: 119–133.

—, 1972. *Regeneratio Imperii. Aufsätze über Roms Kaisertum und reich im Spiegel der heidnischen und christlichen Publizistik* (Darmstadt, 1972).

Strobel, A., 1977. *Ursprung und Geschichte des frühchristlichen Osterkalenders. Texte unde Untersuchungen zur Geschichte der altchristlichen Literatur* 121 (Berlin).

Sulzberger, M., 1925. 'Le Symbole de la Croix et les Monogrammes de Jésus chez les premiers chrétiens,' *Byzantion* 2: 337–448.

Sutherland, C. H.V., 1967. *The Roman Imperial Coinage 6: Diocletian to Maximinus A.D. 294–313* (London).

Syme, R., 1939. *Roman Revolution* (Oxford).

—, 1958. *Tacitus* (Oxford).

—, 1968. *Ammianus and the Historia Augusta* (Oxford).

—, 1971. *Emperors and Biography. Studies in the Historia Augusta* (Oxford).

—, 1983. 'The Ancestry of Constantine,' *Historia Augusta Papers* (Oxford), 63–79. Reprinted from *Bonner Historia-Augusta-Colloquium 1971* (Bonn, 1974), 237–253.

Tabacco, R., 2000. *Itinerarium Alexandri. Fondo Parini-Chirio* N. S.: Filologia 1 (Turin).

Tarn, W. W., 1932. 'Alexander Helios and the Golden Age,' *Journal of Roman Studies* 22: 135–160.

Tarrant, R. J., 1978. Review of P. Dufraigne, *Aurélius Victor, Livre des Césars* (Paris, 1975). *Gnomon* 50: 355–362.

Telfer, W., 1955. 'Constantine's Holy Land Plan,' *Studia Patristica* 1. *Texte und Untersuchungen* 63: 696–700.

Thomas, J. D., 1971. 'On Dating by Regnal Years of Diocletian, Maximian and the Caesars,' *Chronique d'Égypte* 46: 173–179.

Thomasson, B. E., 1984. *Laterculi Praesidum* 1 (Gothenburg).

Thomsen, R., 1947. *The Italic Regions from Augustus to the Lombard Invasion* (Copenhagen).

Tomlin, R. S. O., 1987. 'The Army of the Late Empire,' *The Roman World*, ed. J. Wacher (London & New York) 1: 107–133.

Torp, H., 1953. 'The Vatican Excavations and the Cult of Saint Peter,' *Acta Archaeologica* 24: 27–66.

Treggiari, S., 1991. *Roman Marriage. Iusti Coniuges from the Time of Cicero to the Time of Ulpian* (Oxford).

Tsontchev, D., 1959. 'La voie romaine Philippopolis – Sub Radice,' *Latomus* 19: 154–170.

Tudor, D., 1941–1942. 'Constantin cel Mare si recucerirea Daciei traiane,' *Revista istorică romană* 11–12: 134–148.

Turcan, R., 2006. *Constantin en son Temps. Le baptême ou le Pourpre?* (Dijon).

Usener, H., 1911. *Das Weihnachtsfest². Religionsgeschichtliche Untersuchungen* 1 (Bonn).

Van Dam, R., 2003. 'The Many Conversions of the Emperor Constantine,' *Conversion in Late Antiquity and the Early Middle Ages. Seeing and Believing*, ed. K. Mills and A. Grafton (Rochester, NY), 127–151.

—, 2007. *The Roman Revolution of Constantine* (Cambridge).

Van Deun, P., 2003. 'The Church Historians after Eusebius,' in Marasco 2003: 151–176.

Vandersleyen, C., 1962. *Chronologie des préfets d'Égypte de 284 à 395. Collection Latomus* 55 (Brussels).

Vatin, C., 1962. *Delphes à l'époque imperiale* (diss. Paris: unpublished).

Vera, D., 2005. 'Costantino riformatore,' in Donati & Gentili 2005: 26–35.

Veyne, P., 2007. *Quand notre monde est devenu chrétien (312–394)* (Paris).

Vittinghoff, F., 1989. 'Staat, Kirche und Dynastie beim Tode Konstantins,' in Dihle 1989: 1–28.

Vogt, J., 1943a. 'Streitfragen um Konstantin den Grossen,' *Mitteilunden des deutschen archäologischen Instituts*, Römische Abteilung 58: 190–203.

—, 1943b. 'Unsere Fragestellung,' in *Rom und Karthago. Ein Gemeinschaftswerk*, ed. J. Vogt (Leipzig), 5–8.

—, 1976. 'Helena Augusta, das Kreuz und die Juden. Fragen um die Mutter Costantins des Grossen,' *Saeculum. Jahrbuch für Universalgeschichte* 27: 211–222.

Volterra, E., 1958. 'Intorno a alcune costituzioni di Costantino,' *Rendiconti dell'Accademia Nazionale dei Lincei*, Classe di scienze morali, storiche e fililogiche[8] 13: 61–89.

Waas, M., 1965. *Germanen im römischen Dienst im 4. Jahrhundert nach Christus* (diss. Bonn).

Walker, P. W. L., 1990. *Holy City, Holy Places? Christian Attitudes to Jerusalem and the Holy Land in the Fourth Century* (Oxford).

Wallraff, M., 2001, 'Constantine's Devotion to the Sun after 324,' *Studia Patristica* 34: 256–269.

Watson, P. & C. Todeschini, 2006. *The Medici Conspiracy. The Illicit Journey of Antiquities from Italy's Tomb Raiders to the World's Greatest Museums* (New York).

Waugh, E. 1950, 1963. *Helena. A Novel* (London: Chapman & Hall; Harmondsworth: Penguin, often reprinted).

Weber, G., 2000. *Kaiser, Träume und Visionen in Prinzipat und Spätantike. Historia Einzelschriften* 143 (Stuttgart).

Weber, W., 1990. *Constantinische Deckengemälde aus dem römischen Palast unter dem Trierer Dom³* (Trier).

Weiss, P., 1993, 2003. 'Die Vision Constantins,' in Bleicken 1993: 143–169, translated into English by A. R. Birley with revisions and additions by the author as 'The Vision of Constantine,' *Journal of Roman Archaeology* 16: 237–259.

Wigtil, D. N., 1981. 'Towards a Date for the Greek Fourth Eclogue,' *Classical Journal* 76: 336–341.

Wilamowitz-Moellendorf, U. von, 1925. 'Lesefrüchte. CXCVIII,' *Hermes* 60: 313–314.

Wilkes, J. J., 2005. 'The Roman Danube: An Archaeological Survey,' *Journal of Roman Studies* 95: 124–225.

Wilkinson, K. W., (2009). 'Palladas and the Age of Constantine,' *Journal of Roman Studies* 99: 36–60.

—, 2010a. 'Palladas and the Foundation of Constantinople,' *Journal of Roman Studies* 100: 1–16.

—, 2010b. 'Some Neologisms in the Epigrams of Palladas,' *Greek, Roman and Byzantine Studies* 50: 295–308.

Williams, M. S., 2008. *Authorised Lives in Early Christian Biography: Between Eusebius and Augustine* (Cambridge).

Winkelmann, F., 1962a. *Die Textbezeugung der Vita Constantini des Eusebius von Caesarea. Texte und Untersuchungen* 84 (Berlin).

—, 1962b. 'Zur Geschichte des Authentizitätsproblems der Vita Constantini,' *Klio* 40: 187–243. Reprinted in his *Studien zu Konstantin dem Grossen und zur byzantinischen Kirschengeschichte, Ausgewählte Aufsätze*, ed. W. Brandes & J. F. Haldon (Birmingham, 1993), no. I.

—, 1966. 'Charakter und Bedeutung der Kirchengeschichte des Gelasius von Kaisareia,' *Polychordia. Festschrift Franz Dölger zum 75. Geburtstag*, ed. P Wirth. *Byzantinische Forschungen* 1 (Amsterdam), 348–385.

—, 1975. See (A) above, Eusebius.

—, 1984. 'Annotationes zu einer neuen Edition der Tricennatsreden Eusebs und der *Oratio ad sanctum coetum* in *GCS* (*CPG* 3498. 3497),' *ANTIΔΩPON. Hulde aan Dr. Maurits Geerard bij de voltooiing van de* Clavis Patrum Graecorum / *Hommages à Maurits Geerard pour célébrer l'achèvement de la* Clavis Patrum Graecorum 1 (Wetteren), 1–7.

—, 2003. 'Historiography in the Age of Constantine,' in Marasco 2003: 3–41.

Wissowa, G., 1912. *Religion und Kultus der Römer* (Munich; reprinted unchanged in 1971).

Wlosok, A., 1960. *Laktanz und die philosophische Gnosis. Untersuchungen zu Geschichte und Terminologie der gnostischen Erlösungsvorstellung. Abhandlungen der Heidelberger Akademie der Wissenschaften*, Philosophisch-historische Klasse 1960, Abhandlung 2 (Heidelberg).

—, 1961. 'Zur Bedeutung der nichtcyprianischen Bibelzitate bei Laktanz,' *Studia Patristica* 4. *Texte und Untersuchungen* 79: 234–250.

—, 1989. 'L. Caecilius Firmianus Lactantius,' *Handbuch der lateinischen Literatur* 5. *Restauration und Erneuerung. Die lateinische Literatur von 284 bis 374 n. Chr.*, ed. R. Herzog (Munich), 375–404 § 570.

Wood, I., 2006. 'The Crocus Conundrum,' Hartley, Hawkes & Henig 2006: 77–84.

Woods, D., 1998. 'On the Death of the Empress Fausta,' *Greece and Rome*[2] 45: 70–86.

—, 2001. 'The Church of "St." Acacius in Constantinople,' *Vigiliae Christianae* 55: 201–207.

—, 2002. 'Eusebius on some Constantinian Officials,' *Irish Theological Quarterly* 67: 195–223.

Woolf, G., 2003. 'Seeing Apollo in Roman Gaul and Italy,' *Roman Imperialism and Provincial Art*, ed. S. Scott & J. Webster (Cambridge), 139–153.

Ziegler, J., 1970. *Zur religiösen Haltung der Gegenkaiser im 4. Jh. N. Chr. Frankfurter Althistorische Studien* 4 (Kallmünz).

Zuckermann, C., 1994. 'Les campagnes des tétrarques. Notes de chronologie,' *Antiquité Tardive* 2: 65–70.

—, 2002. 'Sur la Liste de Vérone et la province de Grande Arménie, la division de l'Empire et la date de la création des diocèses,' *Mélanges Gilbert Dagron. Travaux et Mémoires* 14 (Paris), 617–637.

INDEX

This index is primarily a selective index of proper names of persons and places, modern as well as ancient. It also includes a small number of especially important concepts, terms and words, but it does not cover the dynastic relationships set out schematically in Tables 7.1 and 7.2 (pp. 170–171) or the translation of Photius' summary of Praxagoras' history of Constantine (pp. 195–196).